TAKING SIDES

Clashing Views in

Educational Psychology

TAKING SIDES

Clashing Views in
Educational Psychology

SIXTH EDITION

Selected, Edited, and with Introductions and Postscripts by

Leonard Abbeduto
University of Wisconsin–Madison

and

Frank Symons
University of Minnesota, Twin Cities

The McGraw-Hill Companies

Connect
Learn
Succeed™

TAKING SIDES: CLASHING VIEWS IN EDUCATIONAL PSYCHOLOGY, SIXTH EDITION

Published by McGraw-Hill, a business unit of The McGraw-Hill Companies, Inc., 1221 Avenue of the Americas, New York, NY 10020. Copyright © 2010 by The McGraw-Hill Companies, Inc. All rights reserved. Previous edition(s) 2008, 2006, 2004. No part of this publication may be reproduced or distributed in any form or by any means, or stored in a database or retrieval system, without the prior written consent of The McGraw-Hill Companies, Inc., including, but not limited to, in any network or other electronic storage or transmission, or broadcast for distance learning.

Some ancillaries, including electronic and print components, may not be available to customers outside the United States.

Taking Sides® is a registered trademark of the McGraw-Hill Companies, Inc.
Taking Sides is published by the **Contemporary Learning Series** group within the McGraw-Hill Higher Education division.

1 2 3 4 5 6 7 8 9 DOCDOC 9

MHID: 0-07-812754-8
ISBN: 978-0-07-812754-0
ISSN: 1091-8787

Managing Editor: *Larry Loeppke*
Senior Managing Editor: *Faye Schilling*
Senior Developmental Editor: *Jill Meloy*
Editorial Coordinator: *Mary Foust*
Production Service Assistant: *Rita Hingtgen*
Permissions Coordinator: *Shirley Lanners*
Editorial Assistant: *Cindy Hedley*
Senior Marketing Manager: *Julie Keck*
Marketing Communications Specialist: *Mary Klein*
Marketing Coordinator: *Alice Link*
Project Manager: *Erin Melloy*
Design Specialist: *Tara McDermott*
Cover Graphics: *Rick D. Noel*

Compositor: MPS Limited
Cover Image: © Corbis/RF

Library of Congress Cataloging-in-Publication Data

Main entry under title:
    Taking sides: clashing views on controversial issues in educational psychology/selected, edited, and with introductions by Leonard Abbeduto and Frank Symons.—6th ed.

    Includes bibliographical references.
    1. Multicultural education. I. Abbeduto, Leonard, and Symons, Frank *comp.*
                                                            370.19

www.mhhe.com

Editors/Academic Advisory Board

Members of the Academic Advisory Board are instrumental in the final selection of articles for each edition of TAKING SIDES. Their review of articles for content, level, and appropriateness provides critical direction to the editors and staff. We think that you will find their careful consideration well reflected in this volume.

TAKING SIDES: Clashing Views in EDUCATIONAL PSYCHOLOGY

Sixth Edition

EDITORS

Leonard Abbeduto
University of Wisconsin–Madison
        and
Frank Symons
University of Minnesota, Twin Cities

ACADEMIC ADVISORY BOARD MEMBERS

Preface

The field of educational psychology seems to be constantly enmeshed in controversy. Some of the controversies are ongoing; occasionally, the debate may die down a bit only to return in full force again, perhaps in a slightly different form. Other controversies are more short-lived; either they are resolved or they are abandoned as intractable. From the outside it may seem that these controversies reflect inefficiency and a lack of progress in the field of educational psychology. But are these controversies really as counterproductive as they appear?

In fact, controversies provide the foundation for deeper understanding of the educational issues involved, thereby leading to progress. This is not merely our personal belief. There is considerable empirical evidence from research in educational psychology and cognitive science to support the contention. It is not too difficult to see why this is the case. When we engage in discussion of a controversy, we are forced to muster evidence to support our position and to fully develop in a systematic fashion all of its implications. This can lead us to see gaps in our evidence and fallacies in our reasoning, or to recognize previously unrealized implications. As a result, we may decide to gather additional evidence, modify our position, or even abandon it entirely. It is this spirit of controversy and argumentation that is the basis of this textbook.

This book contains 17 issues in educational psychology, each of which has elicited sharply divergent responses from scholars and practitioners. We have organized these issues into three parts. In the first part, are issues that concern the impact of the diverse needs and characteristics of the students found in most classrooms in U.S. schools today: gender equity, student failure, inclusion of students with special educational needs, the achievement gap between ethnic and racial majority and minority students, the role of student self-esteem in education, and values or moral education. In the second part, are issues that concern the theoretical foundations of teaching and learning in the classroom: the value of constructivism, the effectiveness of rewards for enhancing student learning, the educational implications of Howard Gardner's theory of multiple intelligences, the impact of standards on student motivation, and the pedagogical implications of recent work on brain development. The final part of the book features issues surrounding the effectiveness of teaching and assessment in the classroom: the whole language approach to teaching reading, the impact of parental involvement on student outcomes, the role of new technologies in education, the impact of class size on student outcomes, methods for dealing with violent and disruptive students, and the amount of time students should spend in school.

Each issue is stated as a question and is represented by two previously published articles, the first supporting a yes answer to the question and the second arguing a no response. Each issue is accompanied by an introduction, which provides background and a context for evaluating the articles. Each issue ends with a postscript, which points out additional dimensions on which the issue might be analyzed as well as suggesting some further reading. We have also provided a brief introduction to each part of the book as well as relevant Internet site addresses (URLs) on the Internet References page accompanying the introduction to each part.

Changes to this edition   To bring this edition of *Taking Sides: Clashing Views in Educational Psychology* up to date, a new issue has been added: "Should Student Time in School be Changed?" (Issue 17). In addition, we have replaced five other articles from issues retained from the fifth addition to bring a fresh perspective to the debate. In all, there are seven new selections. Also, many of the postscripts have been revised to include more recent suggestions for further reading.

A word to the instructor   An Instructor's Resource Guide with Test Questions (multiple choice and essay) is available for use with Taking Sides. Also available is a general guidebook, *Using Taking Sides in the Classroom,* which includes a discussion of techniques for integrating the pro–con format into an existing course. Instructors adopting this text also have access to an online version of *Using Taking Sides in the Classroom* as well as a correspondence service at http://www.mhcls.com/usingts/.

   Taking Sides: Clashing Views in Educational Psychology is only one of many titles in the Taking Sides series. Users of this text may find *Taking Sides: Clashing Views on Controversial Educational Issues* and *Taking Sides: Clashing Views on Controversial Psychological Issues* to be particularly relevant to some of the issues considered in the present text. For a complete table of contents for these or any other title in the Taking Sides series, visit the Taking Sides Web site at http://www.mhcls.com/takingsides/.

Acknowledgments   I am indebted to Terry McMenamin for her many hours of painstaking library work and for her thoughtful comments on many of the introductions and postscripts in this volume. Thanks also to my colleagues at the University of Wisconsin–Madison for their support and for teaching me so much about educational psychology. Finally, this book would not have been possible without the encouragement, boundless understanding, and good humor of my wife, Terry, my sons, Jackson and Mack, my mother, Dorothy, and my friend and mentor, Sheldon Rosenberg—I am forever in their debt.

Leonard Abbeduto
University of Wisconsin–Madison

Dedicated to the early enriched environment created for me by Red. I am thankful to Alicia Vegell for her assistance on this volume and her enduring patience with me. Thanks to my friends and colleagues in the Special Education

Program and the Department of Educational Psychology at the University of Minnesota for an intellectually inspiring academic environment. Gratitude goes to my family—Stacy, Stewart, and Elisabeth—from whom I learned about clashing views and for whom I continue to appreciate this.

Frank Symons
University of Minnesota, Twin Cities

Contents In Brief

Contents

UNIT 1   MEETING THE DIVERSE NEEDS OF A DIVERSE CLASSROOM   1

Frances R. Spielhagen, a postdoctoral research fellow at the Center for Gifted Education at the College of William and Mary, argues that single-gender classes are viewed as more conducive to learning than are coeducational classes by students, especially younger students. Jo Sanders and Sara Cotton Nelson argue that gender differences in achievement in physics, chemistry, and computer sciences are caused by inequities in classroom practices that deny young girls full participation in the activities required for success in these academic domains. They also describe a program initiated in the Dallas school system in which the classroom behavior of teachers and students in coeducational classrooms is targeted for change so as to provide more gender-equitable pedagogical experiences.

Jon Lorence, an associate professor of sociology, and Anthony G. Dworkin, a professor of sociology, both cofounders of the Sociology of Education Research Group at the University of Houston, argue that although the majority of educational researchers contend that making low-performing students repeat a grade is ineffective, careful analysis of primary-grades data from school districts in Texas shows persistent positive effects of retention on academic performance over time. Nancy Frey, an associate professor of literacy in the School of Teacher Education at San Diego State University, argues that the policy of retention and associated procedures such as social promotion and academic "redshirting," in which there is purposeful delayed entry into kindergarten, are largely flawed, with little compelling evidence to support their practice.

Michael F. Giangreco, who is a professor of education at the University of Vermont, argues that even students with severe disabilities are best served within the "regular" education classroom along with their typically developing peers. He also outlines strategies for achieving inclusion and shows how it creates a classroom that benefits all students, regardless of ability level. James M. Kauffman, who is a professor at the University of Virginia at Charlottesville, and Kathleen McGee and Michele Brigham, who are both special education teachers, argue that the goal of education for students with disabilities should be to increase their level of competence and independence. They conclude that full inclusion involves "excessive" accommodations that actually become barriers to achieving this goal.

Carol Corbett Burris and Kevin G. Welner argue that the achievement gap between white students and African American and Hispanic students is a consequence of the overrepresentation of students from ethnic and racial minorities in low achieving-track classes. They argue that the watered-down curriculum and low expectations associated with low achieving-track classes prevent ethnic and racial minority students from achieving the same levels of academic success as white students. William J. Mathis argues that the achievement gap between white and African American and Hispanic students has been created by discriminatory social and political pressures that pervade all facets of life. He argues that it is, therefore, unreasonable to expect to eliminate the gap through curricular or other innovations in the schools. Mathis cites school vouchers as an example of a failed attempt to use schooling as a means of undoing the achievement gap.

Robert Sylwester, an emeritus professor of education at the University of
Oregon, argues that self-esteem is rooted in brain biology and that low
self-esteem can result in impulsive and violent actions. He sees schools
as a particularly important mechanism for delivering the positive feedback
and successes that are required for the development of high self-esteem.
Maureen A. Manning, a school psychologist in the Maryland public
schools, argues that self-esteem should not be targeted independent of
academic skills. In particular, she believes that the best method to
increase self-esteem is to improve student academic skills.

Merle J. Schwartz, Alexandra Beatty, and Ellen Dachnowicz, who are all
affiliated with Character Education Partnership in Washington, DC, argue
that identifying and teaching core values such as civic engagement and
virtue can improve academic performance, school climate, and individual
character. Pamela Bolotin Joseph, a faculty member at Antioch University,
and Sara Efron, a faculty member at National-Louis University, argue for
a broader moral curriculum, one that goes beyond character education to
include cultural competence and a commitment to peace, justice, and
social action.

Mark Windschitl, a member of the faculty in the department of curriculum
and instruction at the University of Washington, argues in favor of
constructivism, a child-centered approach to education that is defined by
student participation in hands-on activities and extended projects that are
allowed to "evolve" in accordance with the students' interests and initial
beliefs. E. D. Hirsch, Jr., a professor in the School of Education at the
University of Virginia, Charlottesville, argues that child-centered approaches
have failed and points to research demonstrating the superiority of fact-
based, teacher-centered approaches.

Tashawna K. Duncan, Kristen M. Kemple, and Tina M. Smith, from the School of Teaching and Learning at the University of Florida, argue that reinforcement has a long history of successful application in the classroom. They dismiss concerns that it lowers intrinsic motivation or that it is ethically equivalent to paying children to learn. They do acknowledge, however, that reinforcement must be integrated with a consideration of the developmental and unique needs of each child. Charles H. Wolfgang, a professor of early childhood education, admits that reinforcement and other techniques derived from behaviorist theory do control children's behavior in the short term. He asserts, however, that such techniques do little to encourage internalization of the types of standards that will ultimately lead children to behave effectively and appropriately in a range of situations in the future.

Seana Moran, a graduate student at Harvard University, Mindy Kornhaber, an associate professor of education at the Pennsylvania State University, and Howard Gardner, the long-time Harvard University faculty member who originally proposed the theory of multiple intelligences, argue that the theory can transform the ways in which teachers teach and students view themselves. Perry D. Klein, a member of the Faculty of Education at the University of Western Ontario, argues that although a number of diverse pedagogical practices have been inspired by Gardner's theory, the theory is really too broad to be particularly informative about education.

Lauren B. Resnick, a professor of psychology at the University of Pittsburgh, presents a plan for reforming American schools. One critical feature of the plan is clear achievement standards set for all students, not just those who are assumed to have the highest academic aptitude. Such standards, Resnick argues, will motivate students to work harder and, thus, increase achievement by all students. Kennon M. Sheldon and Bruce J. Biddle, both members of the faculty in the department of psychology at the University of Missouri, argue that the mission of schooling must be to create "lifelong, self-directed learners"— adults who enjoy learning for its own sake. They argue that an emphasis on standards is inconsistent with this mission because it rewards (and punishes) students and teachers for achieving a narrowly defined set of outcomes.

Eric P. Jensen, from the University of California, San Diego and co-founder of the Brain Store and the Learning Brain Expo, argues that recent findings from neuroscience research have important and immediate implications for classroom practices. Gerald Coles, an educational psychologist who writes regularly on a range of educational issues, considers current claims about the neural bases of reading problems. He concludes that the research is often ambiguous about whether learning problems arise from differences in brain structure or function or from limitations in experience or skill, which in turn affect brain development.

Stephen Krashen, a professor emeritus from the University of Southern California, argues that flawed studies and misinterpretations plague research on this topic and that the evidence to date suggests whole language is effective. G. Reid Lyon, chief of the Child Development and Behavior Branch of the National Institute of Child Health and Human Development (NICHD), at the time of this article, argues that becoming a skilled reader requires explicit, systematic, and direct instruction and practice.

Laura Van Zandt Allen and Eleanor T. Migliore point to evidence that parental involvement in children's schooling is associated with improvements in children's academic performance and social-emotional development. Van Zandt Allen and Migliore also describe a program to help teachers solicit and use parental input, something the authors argue few teachers are normally prepared to do. Although Rodney T. Ogawa acknowledges that there is evidence that parental involvement has a positive impact on student outcomes, he questions the assumption that if some parental involvement is good, more must be even better. Ogawa argues, instead, that schools must build "buffers" as well as bridges between themselves and parents.

Marcia C. Linn, a professor of cognition and development, and James D. Slotta, director of the Web-based Integrated Science Environment (WISE) project library at the University of California, Berkeley, present an overview of the WISE project, which is designed to teach science and technological literacy through Web-based activities. They contend that this project will make teachers more effective and increase their flexibility in the classroom. Lowell W. Monke, an assistant professor at Wittenberg University, argues that schools have been too uncritical in their adoption of computers and related technologies. Moreover, he suggests that younger students might not be "ready" for such technology and that the premature introduction of the technology might interfere with their ability to acquire important academic, social, and ethical foundation.

Bruce J. Biddle, a professor emeritus of psychology and sociology at the University of Missouri, Columbia, and David C. Berliner, a regent's professor of psychology in education at Arizona State University, argue that the gains from smaller classes in the primary grades benefit all types of students, and, importantly, that the gains are greatest for students traditionally disadvantaged in educational access and opportunity. Kirk A. Johnson, a senior policy analyst in the Center for Data Analysis, Heritage Foundation, argues that although the notion of reducing class size is popular among politicians, it is a costly initiative. He argues that the research suggests that in terms of raising achievement, reducing class size does not guarantee success.

The late Albert Shanker, long-time president of the American Federation of Teachers (AFT), advocates a policy of zero tolerance for violence and other disruptive behavior in school. He argues that such a policy is necessary because disruptive and violent behavior denies equal access to educational opportunities for the nonoffending students in a class or school. Alfie Kohn, a writer and commentator on issues related to children, parenting, and schools, argues that not only are zero-tolerance polices ineffective, they are also harmful—creating fear rather than a sense of security and trust and replacing programs that are effective in treating the root causes of youth violence.

Elena Rocha, a scholar at the Center for American Progress and education consultant, uses multiple case examples and argues that the expansion of school learning time is necessary for meaningful school reform and improving student outcomes. Larry Cuban, a professor emeritus of education at Stanford University, provides a brief history of school reform efforts related to school time and argues that the call for expanding learning time in the form of lengthening the school day or year is not new and has little evidence supporting its effectiveness.

Correlation Guide

The *Taking Sides* series presents current issues in a debate-style format designed to stimulate student interest and develop critical thinking skills. Each issue is thoughtfully framed with an issue summary, an issue introduction, and a postscript. The pro and con essays—selected for their liveliness and substance—represent the arguments of leading scholars and commentators in their fields.

Taking Sides: Clashing Views in Educational Psychology, 6/e is an easy-to-use reader that presents issues on important topics such as *autism, student time in school,* and *effective teaching.* For more information on *Taking Sides* and other *McGraw-Hill Contemporary Learning Series* titles, visit www.mhhe.com/cls.

This convenient guide matches the issues in **Taking Sides: Clashing Views in Educational Psychology,** 6/e with the corresponding chapters in one of our best-selling McGraw-Hill Educational Psychology textbooks by Santrock.

Taking Sides: Educational Psychology, 6/e	Educational Psychology, 4/e by Santrock
Issue 1: Are Single-Gender Classes Necessary to Ensure Equal Educational Opportunities for Boys and Girls?	**Chapter 3:** Social Contexts and Socioemotional Development **Chapter 16:** Classroom Assessment and Grading
Issue 2: Should Struggling Students Be Retained?	**Chapter 4:** Individual Variations **Chapter 13:** Motivation, Teaching, and Learning **Chapter 16:** Classroom Assessment and Grading
Issue 3: Is Full Inclusion Always the Best Option for Students with Disabilities?	**Chapter 4:** Individual Variations **Chapter 11:** Learning and Cognition in the Content Areas
Issue 4: Can Schools Close the Achievement Gap Between Students from Different Ethnic and Racial Backgrounds?	**Chapter 4:** Individual Variations **Chapter 5:** Sociocultural Diversity
Issue 5: Should Schools Try to Increase Students' Self-Esteem?	**Chapter 13:** Motivation, Teaching, and Learning **Chapter 16:** Classroom Assessment and Grading
Issue 6: Should Character Education Define the Values We Teach Students?	**Chapter 3:** Social Contexts and Socioemotional Development
Issue 7: Should Schools Adopt a Constructivist Approach to Education?	**Chapter 10:** Social Constructivist Approaches
Issue 8: Does Reinforcement Facilitate Learning?	**Chapter 13:** Motivation, Teaching, and Learning **Chapter 8:** The Information-Processing Approach

(Continued)

Taking Sides: Educational Psychology, 6/e	Educational Psychology, 4/e by Santrock
Issue 9: Can Howard Gardner's Theory of Multiple Intelligences Transform Educational Practice?	**Chapter 4:** Individual Variations
Issue 10: Will a Push for Standards and Accountability Lead to More Motivated Students?	**Chapter 13:** Motivation, Teaching, and Learning **Chapter 15:** Standardized Tests and Teaching
Issue 11: Do Recent Discoveries about the Brain and Its Development Have Implications for Classroom Practice?	**Chapter 2:** Cognitive and Language Development
Issue 12: Is the Whole Language Approach to Reading Effective?	**Chapter 2:** Cognitive and Language Development
Issue 13: Is Greater Parental Involvement at School Always Beneficial?	**Chapter 14:** Managing the Classroom
Issue 14: Should Schools Embrace Computers and Technology?	**Chapter 12:** Planning, Instruction, and Technology
Issue 15: Should Schools Decrease Class Size to Improve Student Outcomes?	**Chapter 14:** Managing the Classroom
Issue 16: Can a Zero-Tolerance Policy Lead to Safe Schools?	**Chapter 14:** Managing the Classroom
Issue 17: Should Student Time in School Be Changed?	**Chapter 14:** Managing the Classroom

Introduction

Leonard Abbeduto and Frank Symons

What Is Educational Psychology?

Educational psychology has traditionally been defined as the application of psychological theories, methods, and findings to the study of learning and teaching. This has led educational psychologists to study such topics as the development of particular academic skills (e.g., reading); the ways in which children acquire and represent knowledge in particular substantive domains (e.g., mathematics), and how those representations can be supported by classroom instruction; individual differences in intelligence and achievement, and their relation to classroom instruction; how student motivation is related to learning and to different pedagogical practices; the relations between different domains of ability and functioning in students, including the relation between the cognitive and social domains; how best to assess ability, achievement, and teaching effectiveness; and how to effect change in the beliefs and practices of teachers.

Such a diverse range of interests has always required an eclectic approach. Thus, educational psychologists have traditionally drawn on the concepts and tools of many of the subdisciplines of psychology: developmental psychology, psychometrics, cognitive psychology, clinical psychology, learning science, and social psychology, to name but a few. In recent years, moreover, educational psychologists have begun to more fully understand the complexity of the factors and systems at play in teaching and learning. This has led them to cross disciplinary boundaries and draw on the theories, methods, and findings from other disciplines, including cultural anthropology, linguistics, philosophy, educational administration, political science, sociology, social work, and even neuroscience. In turn, they have begun to ask questions and examine variables that have not previously been seen as within their purview, such as the relation between family variables and academic performance, the role of cultural identity in student achievement, the relation between economic conditions and pedagogical practices, the impact of changing societal conceptions of juvenile crime on the educational process, the role of the school in the life of a community, and the interaction between experience and the biological processes underlying brain structure, function, and development.

Educational psychologists have also begun to see the need to more fully understand the domains that form the subject matter of schools, which has led them to questions about the nature of expertise in domains such as mathematics and science. And finally, educational psychologists have come to view themselves as the agents of educational reform. In short, traditional boundaries between educational psychology and other disciplines concerned with children, families, learning, education, and social change have begun to blur.

This expansion of scope and crossing of disciplinary boundaries, however, have meant that educational psychologists have become enmeshed in an increasing number of controversies.

Controversies in Educational Psychology: Where They Come from and How They Can Be Resolved

In this text, each of 17 controversies has been framed as a question, such as *Is full inclusion always the best option for children with disabilities?* This approach is useful because, at its most basic level, educational psychology is the science of providing answers to questions about teaching and learning. Sometimes these questions arise from outside the field of educational psychology or even from outside the field of education, as when business leaders turn to educators with questions about how to prepare children for the technological workplace they will face as adults, or when political leaders ask educational psychologists whether or not the inclusion of students with disabilities within the regular classroom is "working." At other times, the questions come from within the field of educational psychology itself, as in the case of questions about the best way to measure student achievement. Whatever the sources of these questions, it often happens that educational psychologists and other stakeholders in the educational process end up holding sharply different views about the answers. What creates these controversies? Why do experts in the field hold contrasting theories and beliefs? Analyzing some of the causes of controversies in educational psychology may allow us to understand the paths that must be taken to resolve them.

Empirical Data

Many questions become controversial because the empirical data needed to supply the answer are lacking. In some cases, the lack of data simply reflects the fact that the question has been asked only recently and, thus, there has not been sufficient time to conduct the necessary research. In other cases, however, the question has become controversial *because* of the data that have been collected. That is, the data generated have been inconsistent across studies or can be interpreted as providing support for conflicting theories. Such ambiguity often occurs when the question has been addressed through a *correlational* approach rather than through an *experimental* approach.

In a correlational study, an investigator examines the relationship that exists naturally between two or more variables. In this approach, the scientist does not control or manipulate nature but, rather, measures it, or at least parts of it. Consider, for example, the controversy surrounding the implementation of explicit and uniform educational standards and procedures for ensuring the accountability of students, teachers, and schools for failing to achieve those standards (Issue 10). One way to address this "standards" question would be to find schools that have adopted the approach for some length of time and compare the achievement of the students in those schools to the achievement of students from schools that have not adopted such an approach. The interpretive problems for such a study, as for any correlational study, are that there may be other differences between the two types of schools—differences that have nothing to do with standards—and these unmeasured differences may really be responsible for any differences in student achievement that are observed. These differences might include differences in family demographics (e.g., socioeconomic status, race, and ethnicity), resources available to the schools, level of parental commitment, and so on.

Such alternative interpretations could be ruled out by adopting an experimental approach. In an experiment, the researcher exerts control over the variables. In a true experiment, participants (e.g., students, classes, or schools) are assigned at random to the various *conditions* of interest (e.g., the standards and nonstandards approaches in our example). The value of such random assignment is that—given a large enough sample of participants—it ensures that the conditions being compared are similar on all variables except those being studied. So, for example, if we have a large number of schools in our sample and we assign them randomly to the standards and the nonstandards conditions, we will end up, on average, with about the same number of affluent and economically disadvantaged schools in each condition, the same number of ethnically diverse and ethnically homogeneous schools in each condition, the same number of initially high-achieving and low-achieving schools in each condition, and so on. Such similarity across conditions makes for unambiguous results. In this example, an experimental approach would entitle us to conclude unambiguously that any differences in student achievement observed between the two types of schools had been caused by the difference in their adoption of the standards approach.

If the experimental approach allows for unambiguous interpretation and the correlational approach does not, it would seem sensible to always opt for the experimental approach and thereby avoid any controversy about what the data say. Unfortunately, it is not that simple. For many questions about teaching and learning, it is not possible to do an experiment. Either the situation does not allow the researcher to control the relevant variables or control can be achieved only by creating such an artificial version of the phenomenon to be studied that the possibility of generalizing from the results of the experiment to the "real world" seems remote. Examining the relative effectiveness of gender-segregated and coeducational classes (Issue 1) provides an example of a question that does not easily lend itself to an experimental approach. In particular, it is likely that many students, parents, teachers, and school administrators will feel strongly about whether gender segregation is a good idea or not. This means that it is highly unlikely that they will submit to being randomly assigned to a gender-segregated or coeducational class. And if random assignment is not possible, neither is the experimental approach. In this case, we might need to be content with comparisons among naturally formed classes (i.e., the correlational approach), trying to rule out some of the alternative interpretations by recourse to other statistical or logical means.

In the postscripts to many of the 17 issues in this volume, we have briefly summarized the empirical data that are available and discussed whether or not these data have helped to fuel the controversy. Much of what we have had to say in this regard hinges on the distinction between the correlational and experimental approaches. We also have made suggestions, when possible, about the studies needed to resolve the controversies, as well as pointing out the difficulties that might be encountered in such studies.

Theoretical Perspectives

Questions can also become controversial because different theories can lead to different answers. The role of theory in advancing scientific understanding is frequently misunderstood. This misunderstanding most often takes the form of a statement (or an attitude) such as "It's only a theory" (meaning "as opposed to a fact or objective truth"). But it would be impossible for any science—including the science of educational psychology—to advance very far without theories. Theories serve three purposes:

1. Theories specify which observations are relevant and which are irrelevant to understanding the phenomena of interest. By way of illustration, consider the task of understanding children's cognitive development. Think of all the things that a child does in his or her very busy day. Although the child engages in many behaviors, not all will be relevant to understanding how his or her cognitive skills develop. We might easily dismiss behaviors such as sneezing, blinking, coughing, giggling, and a host of other seemingly irrelevant behaviors. But what about cases in which the child talks to himself or herself while trying to figure out how a toy works? Or how about the length of time he or she stares at a math problem before beginning to work on it with pencil and paper? For these and a host of other behaviors, theories tell us whether these behaviors are relevant or irrelevant to understanding cognitive development.

2. Theories help to explain the observations that have been collected about the phenomena of interest. They tell us why the observations are relevant. In the theory of Jean Piaget, for example, children's self-talk (i.e., talking aloud to the self) is relevant to understanding cognitive development because it reflects the child's egocentrism, or self-centeredness—a characteristic that prevents the child from recognizing flaws in his or her reasoning about other people and about problems in the physical world. In Piaget's theory, self-talk is a behavior to be overcome by development.

3. Theories generate predictions that can then be tested by collecting new observations. If the predictions are supported, then we can have more confidence in the theory. If the predictions are not supported, then we must either revise the theory or abandon it. Consider, for example, the explanation of the infant's formation of an attachment to its parent. Behaviorist theories traditionally proposed that the infant "learns" to become attached to its mother not because of any quality of the mother or infant but because the mother typically provides food and, thus, comes to have reinforcing properties. One of the predictions of such a theory is that the failure of a mother to provide food should preclude the infant's attachment to her. In fact, this prediction was not supported either by experimental work with

nonhuman primates or by correlational studies involving humans. Hence, behaviorist theories have been largely abandoned by researchers seeking to understand attachment.

Although theories serve valuable roles, typically the process of theory testing is a protracted one. Seldom do the results of a single empirical study lead to the rise of one theory and the downfall of another. In part, this is because theories often can be revised to accommodate inconsistent results—although at some point the revisions may become so extensive as to render the theory useless. In addition, different theories often lead their proponents to examine very different sorts of observations (i.e., those depicted as relevant by the theory), which means that direct comparison of the predictions of contrasting theories is sometimes difficult or impossible. Whatever the reasons, the fact is that different theories, each of which attempts to explain the same phenomena (e.g., classroom learning), can coexist and enjoy support, which, of course, ensures controversy. Eventually, however, these controversies will be resolved as evidence accumulates in favor of one theory and against the others.

The role of theory in generating (and resolving) controversy is an important theme throughout this book. In fact, the controversies in Unit 2 of this book are motivated almost entirely by theoretical disputes. The reader will see that often the controversies emerge from the clash of formal theories—theories built within, and explicitly recognized by, a particular academic discipline, such as educational psychology. In some instances, however, the reader will see that the controversy is fueled by informal theories that are held tacitly by the people involved and that are the product of the contexts in which they themselves have lived and grown.

Contextual Influences on the Stakeholders in the Educational Process

Many of the controversies that arise in educational psychology are not the product of vagaries in empirical data or of the existence of competing theories. Instead, many controversies result from contextual influences on the various stakeholders in the educational process—students, teachers, administrators, parents, civic leaders, and politicians. The late William Kessen, a professor at Yale University, was among the first to draw attention to the influence of context on children and on those who care for and study children. He outlined these influences in the provocatively entitled article "The American Child and Other Cultural Inventions," *American Psychologist* (October 1979). Three of Kessen's points are particularly important for understanding the source (and the potential resolution) of many of the 17 controversies considered in this text.

1. Children's lives and development are shaped by the contexts in which they live. These contexts are multidimensional and can be defined by, among other things, physical variables (e.g., whether or not children are exposed to lead paint through living in an older home), family variables (e.g., whether they live in a two-parent or single-parent home), economic variables (e.g., whether their families are economically disadvantaged or affluent), social variables (e.g., whether they live in a safe or high-crime neighborhood), institutional variables (e.g., whether they are required to attend school or to hold down a job), cultural variables (e.g., parental beliefs and practices related to disciplining children), and historical variables (e.g., whether they happen to live during a time of war or peace). When we think about children attending schools in the United States today, for example, we need to remember that those children are living in very different contexts than were children living during, for example, the early part of the twentieth century. We should also remember—especially as we compare today's students in the United States to those attending schools in other countries—that the contexts for children in the United States may differ in important respects from those of children in Japan or in South Africa. And finally, we should remember that not all children attending U.S. schools today are growing up in precisely the same contexts. Unfortunately, far too many children come to school carrying the scars of homelessness, abuse, and racial discrimination—scars that may interfere with their ability to derive maximum benefit from the educational opportunities afforded them. In other words, Kessen argued that the diverse circumstances of children's lives—diversity across historical time, across cultures or nations, and even within a culture or nation—can lead to a diversity of outcomes.

Many of the questions considered in this text have arisen in part because of such contextually determined diversity. Concerns about the decline in student achievement in the United States in recent years have led to the question of whether or not schools should return to a curriculum that emphasizes "basic" academic skills and drill-and-practice (Issue 7). Concerns about the diversity within any classroom with regard to student background, preparation, and needs have led to a host of questions about whether and how to accommodate such diversity in the classroom. In fact, it is questions of the latter sort that form Unit 1 of this book. Questions about contextually determined diversity have become controversial in part because of empirical data. They also have become controversial, however, because of two other types of contextual influences identified by Kessen.

2. The views and behaviors of those who care for children are also shaped by the contexts in which they have lived. By this, Kessen meant that the parents, teachers, community leaders, politicians, and other adults who directly or indirectly influence children's lives are themselves the product of the contexts in which they have lived. As a result, the attitudes they have about the nature of children (e.g., whether children are born inherently willful or inherently loving), about appropriate child-rearing practices (e.g., whether or not children should be spanked), about the developmental outcomes that are optimal (e.g., whether it is better for children to grow into compliant and conforming adults or into autonomous and critical adults), and, of course, about education will differ depending on the contexts of their own lives. In short, the answers that teachers, administrators, civic leaders, and politicians arrive at when faced with questions about education—and, thus, the controversies surrounding these questions—are sometimes determined more by the contexts of their lives than by any formal theory or the results of any empirical investigations.

Many of the questions considered in this text have become controversial precisely because of this type of contextual influence. Consider, for example, controversy surrounding the inclusion of students with disabilities in classrooms alongside their peers without disabilities (as opposed to being in separate classrooms). For many advocates of inclusion, the issue is rooted in questions about the civil rights of students with disabilities. In fact, these advocates see the issue as the same as that faced in the 1950s and 1960s when racial segregation was battled on the grounds that "separate" social institutions and systems precludes "equal" opportunities.

3. The views and behaviors of scholars who study children, development, and education are also shaped by the contexts in which they have lived. Kessen was among the first to chastise education researchers and theorists for their rather "superior attitude"—the assumption that somehow they were immune from the same influences that affect parents, teachers, and the rest of the public, and the assumption that somehow their scientific objectivity transcended historical time and place. Kessen was not simply arguing that scholars have incomplete knowledge and that somehow, as they learn more, they get closer to the truth and less susceptible to contextual influence. Instead, he argued that scholars are people too and that they can never escape the influence of the contexts in which they have lived. Some of the controversies considered in this text have arisen from these types of contextual influence. We see this, for example, in a tendency of researchers to have an almost blind devotion to a particular investigative approach or method of measurement, one in which they see only the advantages and none of the disadvantages.

Throughout this book, we have endeavored to point out various contextual influences on the controversies considered. It is our hope that by doing so, we take a step toward clarifying these influences and thereby move closer to resolving the controversies. Identifying these contextual influences, however, is a difficult and ad hoc process. It is also, of course, a subjective process, shaped by our own contexts. We urge the reader to look critically at the ways in which context shapes the views of the writers of these selections. We urge the reader also to examine how his or her own context may be affecting how he or she regards the data and theories presented in these selections.

Internet References . . .

American Association of University Women

The AAUM addresses issues of gender equity through research, education, and advocacy. The organization is a resource for research on gender and education on all levels, including K–12.

http://www.aauw.org

Association for Supervision and Curriculum Development

The Association for Supervision and Curriculum Development (ASCD) is an international, nonprofit educational association that promotes professional development in curriculum and supervision through a variety of activities, including conferences and publications. In recent years, the organization has considered a variety of controversial issues, including grade retention.

http://www.ascd.org

Wisconsin Education Association Council

WEAC is the organization for nearly 100,000 professional educators in Wisconsin. The Web site includes useful resources for educators, including an array of definitions, guidelines, and links on inclusion laws, policies, and practices.

http://www.weac.org/issues_advocacy.aspx

Schools of Hope Literacy Project

This site describes a project conducted in the public schools of Madison, WI. The goal of the project is to reduce the achievement gap, especially in literacy, between majority and minority ethnic and racial groups.

http://www.mmsd.org/soh

National Association for Self-Esteem

The National Association for Self-Esteem (NASE) is devoted to promoting the wide-scale adoption of self-esteem concepts in educational and other contexts in the lives of children and adults. This site includes bibliographies and "think pieces" by scholars and laypeople alike.

http://www.self-esteem-nase.org

Center for the Fourth and Fifth Rs

The Center for the Fourth and Fifth Rs, which is designed to serve as the source on character education, is directed by developmental psychologist Thomas Lickona. The center disseminates articles on character education, publishes a newsletter, and works with schools that are interested in implementing curricula that focus on teaching respect, responsibility, and other ethical values that are considered the bases of good character.

http://www.cortland.edu/character/

Meeting the Diverse Needs of a Diverse Classroom

*T*oday, *it seems that schools in the United States are being asked to do more and more. On the one hand, the scope of education for any individual student is more inclusive than ever before. Schools must now meet not only the needs of students in traditional academic domains, such as mathematics and science, but also the needs they have (or are perceived to have) in the social and emotional domains. So, for example, educators now pledge to educate the "whole" child. On the other hand, there has been an increased recognition of the diversity that characterizes the student population and an increased effort to tailor the curriculum to the unique needs of various subgroups. This has led, for example, to separate science and math classes for male and female students, separate tracks for higher- and lower-achieving students, and calls for greater attention to the disparate academic outcomes often seen for students of different ethnicities and races. Some of these attempts to expand the educational agenda have been legislated, as in the case of the inclusion of students with disabilities in regular classrooms. Other attempts have emerged from particular ideological positions, as in the case of the self-esteem and moral education "movements." These changes in the educational agenda, however, have not gone unchallenged. In this section, we consider the controversies that have arisen as schools have tried to meet the diverse needs of a diverse classroom.*

- Are Single-Gender Classes Necessary to Ensure Equal Educational Opportunities for Boys and Girls?
- Should Struggling Students Be Retained?
- Is Full Inclusion Always the Best Option for Children with Disabilities?
- Can Schools Close the Achievement Gap between Students from Different Ethnic and Racial Backgounds?
- Should Schools Try to Increase Students' Self-Esteem?
- Should Character Education Define the Values We Teach Students?

ISSUE 1

Are Single-Gender Classes Necessary to Ensure Equal Educational Opportunities for Boys and Girls?

YES: Frances R. Spielhagen, from "How Tweens View Single-Sex Classes," *Educational Leadership* (April 2006)

NO: Jo Sanders and Sarah Cotton Nelson, from "Closing Gender Gaps in Science" *Educational Leadership* (November 2004)

ISSUE SUMMARY

YES: Frances R. Spielhagen, a postdoctoral research fellow at the Center for Gifted Education at the College of William and Mary, argues that single-gender classes are viewed as more conducive to learning than are coeducational classes by students, especially younger students.

NO: Jo Sanders and Sarah Cotton Nelson argue that gender differences in achievement in physics, chemisty, and computer sciences are caused by inequities in classroom practices that deny young girls full participation in the activities required for success in these academic domains. They also describe a program initiated in the Dallas school system in which the classroom behavior of teachers and students in coeducational classrooms is targeted for change so as to provide more gender-equitable pedagogical experiences.

Despite changing attitudes and the enactment of laws designed to ensure that males and females are afforded equal educational opportunities, gender-related differences in academic achievement still exist. In reading and language arts, girls score higher on achievement tests and are less likely to be referred for remedial programs than are boys. In math and science, boys maintain an advantage. Although gender differences in academic achievement are relatively small, and certainly less than the differences observed among males or among females, they are important because of their influence on the career paths available to men and women.

Gender-related differences in academic achievement are due, in part, to the beliefs that children bring to school and to their behavior in the classroom.

Importantly, there is considerable evidence that differences in academic preparation and behavior are largely the result of the environment rather than of direct biological influences on development.

Parents are an important part of the environment that serves to push boys and girls down different academic paths. The role of the media has also been much debated. Unfortunately, teachers and the culture of most U.S. schools are at fault as well. Consider the following:

1. In preschool and early elementary school years, the physical arrangement of the classroom often segregates boys and girls and reinforces the differences between them. For example, a pretend kitchen and associated role-playing materials are typically housed in a different location than are blocks and other building materials.
2. Teachers attend more to boys than to girls, are more likely to ask boys questions (especially open-ended, thought-provoking questions), and give boys more constructive criticism. Such behaviors are especially evident in traditionally male domains, such as science.
3. Teachers are more tolerant of interruptions from boys than from girls and encourage the latter to wait their turn.
4. Teachers are more likely to provide help to girls during difficult academic tasks, including during experiments and other hands-on science activities, while encouraging boys to resolve difficulties on their own.
5. Teachers spend more time with girls during reading and language arts classes but more time with boys during math classes.
6. Teachers are less likely to assign girls than similarly achieving boys to high-math-ability groups. In general, girls are less likely than boys to be identified for inclusion in programs for gifted students.

How can schools be reformed to ensure that they help children to break free of gender stereotypes rather than maintain and even exacerbate achievement differences between boys and girls? Much of the debate surrounding the question of reform has focused on the achievement gaps in math and science, which appear to have the greatest potential for limiting career options. Two approaches to reform have been advocated. In the first, and certainly more popular approach, scholars and policymakers, assuming that coeducational classrooms are a fact of life, have made suggestions for changing the culture and practices of these classrooms. Proponents of the second, more controversial, approach argue that gender-segregated classes are necessary to allow girls the opportunity to learn in a climate that is suited to their characteristics and needs.

The following two selections weigh in on this issue of gender-segregated classes. In the first, Frances R. Spielhagen presents excerpts from interviews with middle-school students. In general, the students support single-gender classes, seeing them as containing fewer distractions and more supports for learning, although an interest in romantic relationships leads older students to "overlook" the shortcomings of coeducational classrooms. In the second selection, Jo Sanders and Sarah Cotton Nelson maintain that gender equity is possible within the context of the coeducational classroom provided that teachers and student behavior are the focus of change.

YES

Frances R. Spielhagen

How Tweens View Single-Sex Classes

Have you ever heard that saying, 'Time flies when you're having fun?' All-boy classes are fun! James, a 6th grader, cheerfully offered this opinion of the single-sex academic classes at Hudson Valley Middle School.[1] He quickly added, "I will probably want to be with girls when I am in high school."

Melissa, 13, expressed an older adolescent's point of view: "You can say what you want in all-girl classes and not be afraid of being teased, but sometimes we just want to be with the guys."

James and Melissa are part of the majority of students at this middle school in the rural Hudson Valley of upstate New York who have chosen to attend single-sex classes in language arts, math, science, and social studies. Hudson Valley Middle School, a public school whose 600 students come mostly from low-income backgrounds, has offered voluntary single-sex academic classes to its 6th, 7th, and 8th grade students for the last three years. Students remain in mixed groups for nonacademic classes and at lunchtime so they are not isolated from opposite-gender peers. In the first year of this reform, approximately 75 percent of the school's students chose to take single-sex classes; during the last two years, the majority of those students continued with that choice.

As part of my research into single-sex education (Spielhagen, 2005), I interviewed 24 Hudson Valley students a combination of 6th, 7th, and 8th graders who had attended single-sex classes for at least one academic year. Their comments offer insights into the minds of tweens who have sampled single-sex learning. Their perspectives indicate that voluntary single-sex classes can be a viable option for middle school students, but that such arrangements are most effective when classes are designed to address students' developmental needs. The younger students were more likely to find being in a single-sex class a positive experience; as students got older, they expressed more desire to be in mixed classes, even when that choice entailed potential problems.

Why Try Single-Sex Learning?

Concern over state standardized test scores prompted Hudson Valley Middle School to create voluntary single-sex classes. The school hoped that providing an environment free of the distraction caused by mixed-gender social interaction would lead to higher scores.

In the 19th century, single-sex schools were common, especially in grades 7 through 12. However, because classes for girls did not include academic subjects that would lead to higher education, early feminists urged that schools give *all* students access to the entire academic curriculum. Coeducational schools soon became the preferred model of public education, opening the doors to college enrollment for substantial numbers of girls.

Even then, secondary schools continued to maintain single-sex physical education classes until 1975. In that year, the provisions of Title IX (Tyack & Hansot, 2002) specifically forbade separate-gender physical education classes. According to Salomone (2003), many school districts misunderstood Title IX as a ban on all single-sex classes. Either way, emphasis on coeducational physical education classes quickly led to coeducation as the norm for public schools.

Meanwhile, over the last 20 years, education policymakers have noted the need to reverse declines in achievement among both boys and girls. Researchers agree that the middle school years are crucial to forming sound study habits (Clewell, 2002), but they have mixed opinions as to whether a return to single-sex classes would enhance the achievement of young adolescents.

For example, in 1995, Sadker and Sadker claimed that coeducational schools shortchange girls. At the same time, the American Association of University Women (AAUW) endorsed single-sex arrangements as a means of promoting female achievement, particularly in mathematics and science. Within a few years, however, the AAUW (1998) reversed its stance and concluded that single-sex classes could lead to programming decisions that discriminated against girls. In terms of boys, Sommers (2002) believes that single-sex arrangements are advantageous for boys who lag in academic areas, particularly reading and writing.

Listening to Student Voices

From ages 9 through 13, young adolescents experience tremendous physical, emotional, and cognitive development, so it is not surprising that the responses of students with whom I talked varied according to their ages. I asked students about their classroom choices, their perceptions of the classroom environment in single-sex as compared with mixed-gender groups, and their satisfaction level. The majority of the students had positive feelings about single-sex classes, with 62 percent stating that they could focus better without the opposite sex present. In general, the younger the student, the more enthusiastic the praise of the single-sex arrangement.

The 6th Grade Perspective

Sixth grade students' comments revealed a pre-adolescent viewpoint that the behavior of the other sex was a problem. Both boys and girls in 6th grade referred to their opposite-gender peers as "noisy" and "annoying."

James, a slightly built 11-year-old, responded energetically to questions about being in all-boy classes. He admitted that his favorite class was gym "because you get to play games using your skills," but noted that he didn't pay much attention to the girls in the mixed gym classes because he and his friends (all boys) liked to be on teams together. James also said that he felt "more challenged" in his all-boy classes because he enjoyed the competition with other boys:

> I want to try to beat them. I didn't try to beat the girls [when I was in mixed classes] because I didn't think I could beat the top girls, so why bother?

The comments of 6th grade girls reinforced the conventional wisdom that girls experience more freedom in single-sex academic classes, particularly math and science. Alison, 11, said she "loves all-girl classes," especially math classes, because she's "good at math." She emphasized that in all-girl classes, "you don't have to worry about boys making fun of you." Twelve-year-old Becky echoed Alison's concerns about intellectual safety in mixed classes. When asked why she chose all-girl classes, she replied,

> The boys always picked on me because I am smarter than they are. In all-girl classes, the teachers word things better and say them differently. In mixed classes, they say things more simply for the boys.

She added that all-girl classes are fun and the students get more accomplished, even though the girls "get loud and ask too many questions."

7th and 8th Grade Perspectives

Although by 7th grade many students' attitudes had begun to shift toward typically adolescent emotional and social concerns, 7th graders consistently remarked on their ability to focus better in their single-sex classes. Mary, a 13-year-old 7th grader, reported that she had meant to try all-girl classes for just a year but had decided to stay with the arrangement. She reported a definite improvement in her grades, noting that "I can concentrate better. I am not afraid to raise my hand."

Another 7th grader, Nancy, reported that

> In mixed classes, you are too nervous to ask a question and be wrong and the boys might laugh at you. We get higher grades because we pay attention more and don't get distracted.

On the other hand, Heather, 13, complained that she was in an all-girl class because "my mom decided to torture me." Heather went along with her mother's choice because she was curious. She conceded that she liked the all-girl classes because they made it easier to relate to her girlfriends but added that the situation allowed girls to "help each other with guy problems." Heather was clearly becoming more interested in mixed-gender social pairing. She offered another adolescent insight, noting,

> In some ways it's really nice to be with your friends, but sometimes the girls get catty, and it is hard to get space away from them.

The 7th and 8th grade boys were less enthusiastic than the girls about single-sex classes. Bullying seemed to become more of a problem with only boys present. Danny, 13, noted that he had been curious about all-boy classes, but that after two years in such classes, he planned to choose mixed-gender classes for 8th grade. In the all-boy classes, Danny reported, he could talk more about sports with his friends and "just hang out," but that "boys try to act tougher" in that environment. Eighth grader Jim, also 13, admitted that he had been picked on by other boys in mixed classes in 7th grade, but that mistreatment was worse in the all-boy classes. He explained, "The guys who pick on us would be more interested in impressing the girls" in a mixed-gender group. Jim added that he missed being with his female friends.

What Are the Students Telling Us?

From these tweens' perspective, single-sex classes can clearly contribute to a comfortable yet intellectually challenging middle school experience. Such arrangements work as long as students can choose whether or not to participate.

Students in all grades reinforced the importance of emotional, intellectual, and physical safety perennial concerns in the middle grades. The problem of bullying reared its head among the 7th and 8th grade boys, but the students did not agree on which arrangement might be less bully-prone. However, caution dictates that schools take measures to ensure that a *Lord of the Flies* scenario does not emerge from a policy that keeps boys in the same single-sex grouping during all three years of middle school. Sorting students into different all-male configurations for different years might address this problem.

The overwhelmingly positive responses from the girls in this study suggest that single-sex classes are particularly beneficial to middle school girls. Even 8th grade girls supported the notion that greater concentration is possible in all-girl classes. As the girls grew older, they became more assertive about their interest in boys. Unlike the boys, however, they expressed a feeling of bonding with their female classmates and enjoyed discussing issues about boys together.

Students experienced the distraction presented by the opposite gender in different ways as they grew older. Younger kids complained about the noisiness of their opposite-sex peers, whereas older students simply referred to the social distractions of having the opposite sex in their classrooms. However, older students loudly and clearly stated their preference for facing those distractions.

Offering Multiple Options

Turning Points 2000 (Jackson & Davis, 2000), a landmark document on middle school reform, recommended that middle schools organize learning climates that promote intellectual development and shared academic purpose. According to the students in my study, single-sex classes in public middle schools support these goals. *Turning Points 2000* also called for middle schools to offer

multiple options to students. Hudson Valley Middle School displays innovative programming by restricting single-sex classes to the academic core courses
so that students can experience the benefits of both single-sex classes and day-
to-day interaction with students of the other sex. Offering subject-specific
single-sex classes in each grade might provide even more flexibility, as long as
the curriculum remains identical for both genders.

Providing optional single-sex environments for young adolescents with
the existing public middle school framework would offer cost-effective school
choice for parents, involving them as stakeholders in the education of their
children. For many tweens, single-sex classes provide an enviable situation in
which learning time flies because students are having fun.

Note

1. All names in this article are pseudonyms.

References

American Association of University Women. (1998). *Separated by sex: A critical look at single-sex education for girls.* Washington, DC: Author.

Clewell, B. (2002). Breaking the barriers: The critical middle school years. In E. Rassen, L. Iura, & P. Berkman (Eds.), *Gender in education* (pp. 301–313). San Francisco: Jossey-Bass.

Jackson, A., & Davis, G. (2000). *Turning points 2000: Educating adolescents in the 21st century.* New York: Carnegie Corporation.

Sadker, M., & Sadker, D. (1995). *Failing at fairness: How our schools cheat girls.* New York: Simon & Schuster.

Salomone, R. (2003). *Same, different, equal: Rethinking single-sex schooling.* New Haven, CT: Yale University Press.

Sommers, C. (2002). Why Johnny can't, like, read and write. In E. Rassen, L. Iura, & P. Berkman (Eds.), *Gender in education* (pp. 700–721). San Francisco: Jossey-Bass.

Spielhagen, F. (2005). *Separate by choice: Single-sex classes in a public middle school.* Unpublished manuscript.

Tyack, D., & Hansot, E. (2002). Feminists discover the hidden injuries of coeducation. In E. Rassen, L. Iura, & P. Berkman (Eds.), *Gender in education* (pp. 12–50). San Francisco: Jossey-Bass.

**Jo Sanders and
Sarah Cotton Nelson**

 **NO**

Closing Gender Gaps in Science

High school students across the United States, hoping to get a head start on their college credits, took 1,700,000 advanced placement (AP) exams in 34 subjects in 2003. Students who take these exams tend to be the more ambitious ones. The presence of AP exams in a school's curriculum is a good indication of where tomorrow's academic high achievers will be coming from and what fields these students might enter.

An interesting aspect of the AP exams is how lopsided many of them are by gender. Girls constitute the majority of test takers of many of the exams—66 percent in art history, for example, and 64 percent in English literature and composition. These female-dominant imbalances can create serious gender issues for boys: It's not healthy for us as a society, or for boys individually, to think that excellence in reading and writing is "feminine."

As for the male-dominant imbalances, girls used to be a minority in AP exams on mathematics, biology, and chemistry, but these numbers have equalized in recent years to the point where girls make up roughly half the test takers in these subjects.

The AP exams of continuing concern for girls since the 1970s are the three physics exams (the AP Physics B exam, the AP Physics C exam on electricity and magnetism, and the AP Physics C exam on mechanics) and the two computer science exams (CS-A and the more advanced CS-AB). . . .

In computer science, girls' track record has actually worsened. In 1992, girls represented 21 percent of the CS-A test takers and 13 percent of the CS-AB test takers, compared with 16 percent and 10 percent respectively in 2003. The 2003 numbers show an average of only 44 girls in each state taking the CS-A exam and a mere 14 girls in each state taking the CS-AB exam.

When many *Educational Leadership* readers went to high school, students were exhorted to take as much mathematics as possible because math, we were told, was the key to a whole raft of high-paying, high-status careers in technical areas. For the new generation, however, science and technology have replaced math as the gateways to a wide variety of technical careers in the sciences and in engineering. When high school girls represent only one-fourth to one-third of students enrolled in AP physics—and when they represent an even smaller portion of those enrolled in computer science—they are deprived of an important leg up to technology-related majors in college. Girls'

From *Educational Leadership*, November 2004, pp. 74–77. Copyright © 2004 by ASCD. Reprinted by permission. The Association for Supervision and Curriculum Development is a worldwide community of educators advocating sound policies and sharing best practices to achieve the success of each learner. To learn more, visit ASCD at www.ascd.org.

under-representation in these fields must be taken seriously because society simply cannot afford to waste this much talent.

Data on Gender Disparity

In Dallas, Texas, enrollments in the AP mathematics and the AP biology courses are fairly equally balanced in terms of gender, but enrollments in AP physics and computer science remain primarily male. These patterns mirror the national situation. Further, the pass rates in Dallas on AP exams in physics and computer science were found to be substantially lower for girls than for boys.

We discovered that the problem went far beyond gender imbalances in AP course enrollment and test taking. To test a frequently heard argument that boys are simply better suited to higher-level math and science we correlated girls' and boys' PSAT math scores in the Dallas Independent School District with their pass rates on the AP exams in science and technology. It was a revelation: Girls who scored in the 70s in PSAT math (a score equivalent to a 700 in the SAT) scored considerably lower in the AP exams than equally qualified boys did.

For instance, all the boys who scored 70 or above in the PSAT math exam passed the AP chemistry exam; the same was true for only 50 percent of the high-scoring girls. In the Physics C exam on mechanics, the pass rate for boys who scored 70 or above in the PSAT math exam was 94 percent; for girls in the same category, the pass rate was 71 percent. Six of the nine boys who scored 70 or above in the math exam passed Physics B, but none of the four girls who took Physics B passed it. In Computer Science AB, the pass rates for boys and girls who scored 70 or above in the PSAT math exam were 44 percent and 25 percent respectively.

Therefore, not only do fewer girls in Dallas take the science and technology exams to begin with, but girls with high ability as measured by their PSAT math exams also score lower in their AP exams than comparably qualified boys do. What's going on that would lead to such gender disparities among students who sit in the same classrooms and learn from the same teachers?

Four interested parties decided to find out: the Dallas Independent School District; several women employees from Texas Instruments; the Dallas Women's Foundation; and AP Strategies, a not-for-profit agency in Texas that works to improve student pass rates in the state on AP exams. Together, these four parties created a program to advance girls' participation and performance in AP science and technology in Dallas high schools: the Dallas Gender Equity Project.

The Dallas Gender Equity Project

The Dallas Gender Equity Project began in October 2003 with a full-day workshop for 14 teachers of AP chemistry, physics, and technology courses in Dallas high schools. The workshop instructor presented the data on girls' underachievement in Dallas AP exams. Despite some initial skepticism about gender equity, the data-oriented science and technology teachers were curious about the causes of the imbalance. The teachers talked at length about the gender issues they were seeing in their classes and about the efforts they had made to deal with the disparity. Some pointed out their unsuccessful efforts to recruit girls for their classes; others noted the girls' reticence to speak up in class despite invitations to do so.

Every few months for the rest of the school year, participants met in half-day follow-up workshops held after school. Before each workshop, teachers completed mini-assignments that focused on gender issues surfacing in such venues as toy stores, Saturday morning television shows, or magazines and Web sites familiar to high school students. Other mini-assignments dealt more directly with school, requiring participants to look for gender bias in textbooks, in teacher-student interactions, and even in classroom wall displays.

Each workshop focused on a specific topic, such as teacher expectations and stereotype threat, interpersonal dynamics among minority and nonminority groups, and curriculum bias. The instructor also introduced interesting research studies on gender in science or technology. In fact, one of the program's strengths was that it addressed the gender issue with solid data. Physics teacher and workshop participant Rebecca McGowan Jensen explained,

> We were given real data from education journals, the context in which to understand [this information], and concrete methods to change our classroom instruction and get quantifiable results. We were treated as collaborators rather than people to be lectured at.

Reality versus Perception

Teachers brought fascinating stories back to the group from classroom experimentation. Daniel Brown, an AP physics teacher, reported that he had initially been skeptical of any gender inequity in his classroom. "Maybe in other teachers' classrooms," he insisted, "but certainly not in mine." He set out to prove the statistics wrong for his classroom by conducting an experiment.

He asked a teacher to observe his class and time his responses to both his male and female students. This was a gender issue that one of the earlier workshops had tackled. Just knowing that someone was clocking him during that period made him extra aware; he was all the more certain that his time allocation would be fair. At the end of the class, his colleague showed him the results: Taking into account the class's gender representation, the teacher had spent 80 percent of his time responding to boys and 20 percent to girls. "It absolutely bowled me over," Brown said.

He worked hard the next month on implementing strategies presented in the workshops to make the classroom environment more gender-equitable. Making changes in his teaching practice meant becoming aware of a number of gender-based patterns that are below most teachers' level of conscious awareness. He paid attention to which students he called on, how much time he spent waiting for their responses, how much eye contact he maintained, which types of questions he asked specific students, and whether he accepted or refused called-out answers.

Once again, he asked his colleague to observe him in class. During that period of observation, he felt that he had gone overboard in his attention to the girls. He was sure that the observing teacher would tell him that he had swung the pendulum completely back the other way—that he was now spending 80 percent of his time responding to girls and 20 percent to boys. At the end of the period, the observing teacher told him the results: "Fifty-fifty, dead on."

Changes in the Classroom

Science teacher Chris Bruhn, a former aerospace engineer, appreciated the need for getting more girls into technical fields and had experienced similar gender imbalances in science classrooms. Said Bruhn,

> When I was in college, there were at least five boys for every girl in the engineering classes. My graduating class of 30 aerospace engineers included only one female, and I soon learned that the workforce was not much different. One of my missions when I became a physics teacher was to convince more girls to become engineers.

Bruhn experimented with two gender-related activities in his high school physics classes. The results were eye-opening. In the first experiment, he asked students to determine the tension in a string suspended from the ceiling. At the end of the string was a toy eagle that could "fly" around in a circle. He gave no instructions for getting the eagle to fly or suggestions about equipment to use, measurements to make, or equations to apply. Although there were several ways to determine the string's tension, solving the problem really only required a stopwatch, a meter stick, and a balance. He asked the girls to set up the equipment and the boys to record the data. This resulted, in his words, "in a meltdown in the classroom." According to Bruhn,

> The girls did not want to do it! "We don't know how to do it," they said. "Can the boys set it up?" Of course, the boys were all too eager to do it for them. This was an appalling surprise to me. Needless to say, I had a lot of work to do, but by the end of the year the girls were just as possessive of the lab equipment as the boys were.

In the second experiment, Bruhn videotaped a class period. When he watched the tape, he discovered that he was allowing boys to interrupt the girls. "This had the effect of rewarding the boys for being outspoken and rewarding the girls for being quiet," he said. "This was the exact opposite of what I wanted." Bruhn then explained to the students why he had videotaped the class and what he had found. The students were intrigued and a discussion followed of what the teacher had been learning in the Gender Equity Project. In subsequent classes, the boys began to apologize when they interrupted the girls or when they tried to take over; they eventually learned to wait their turn. Just as important, the girls learned to stand their ground during discussions in class, and they took on positions of leadership.

Daniel Brown noticed similar changes when he began to focus on the girls in his class. The girls became more confident that they could do physics, they participated more in class, and they learned to deal more effectively with some of the disruptive male behaviors. Brown revised his teaching style in all six of his classes; in three of them, he specifically announced the changes he was making and his reasons for making them because the subject happened to come up in class. The girls pointed out that they had not even noticed anything wrong with his teaching style because they were so used to it.

Changes entailed making sure to ask both girls and boys deeper follow-up questions, calling on girls as often as on boys, and refusing to permit the boys to interrupt the girls. In the classes in which he made the announcement, the girls became even bolder and more confident than the girls in the other three classes. According to Brown, making this conscious effort every period of every day prevented him from "slipping back into his old ways."

Changes in Brown's teaching practices have resulted in enrollments in AP physics jumping from four girls out of 13 students in the 2003–2004 school year to 10 out of 20 for the 2004–2005 school year, or from 31 percent to 50 percent female. He has seen a dramatic increase in minority enrollment as well.

What's Next?

Gender-equitable teaching practices have started flowing into mainstream Dallas schools. The Gender Equity Institute, supported by the Women of TI Fund, was initiated this year at the University of Texas at Arlington to serve both teacher education students and classroom teachers seeking continuing education credits. A gender equity component will be included in a math training program for teachers. In addition, other local school districts are becoming interested in adopting the Gender Equity Project approach.

Gender equity activities continue to thrive in Dallas high schools. Several "booster shot" workshops will take place during the 2004–2005 school year, with a whole new round of workshops scheduled for teachers who teach pre-AP classes. High school principals and counselors have already attended an evening workshop on gender equity. Female students of science, technology, and engineering from Southern Methodist University in Dallas and women from Texas Instruments who are involved in technical careers have volunteered to attend the sessions.

Commenting on the program, one physics teacher said,

> The most important lesson I took away for my female students was this: Each student needs to feel that she is competent, important, and talented. The number one thing we can do for a student is to sit her down, look her in the eye, and tell her that she's good at this subject.

And this is what we did. No one can change the world entirely, but we found that focusing on gender equity in our classrooms helped us change a bit of it.

POSTSCRIPT

Are Single-Gender Classes Necessary to Ensure Equal Educational Opportunities for Boys and Girls?

Can we rely on empirical research to decide whether or not single-gender classes ensure that boys and girls have equal chances to succeed in all academic fields? In principle, the answer is yes. It should be possible, for example, to compare the math or science achievement of girls enrolled in girls-only classes to that of girls enrolled in coeducational classes. Do the former have higher achievement than the latter? Does their achievement equal that of boys? In fact, several studies suggest that achievement is higher for girls in single-gender classes than in coeducational classes. See "The Effects of Sex-Grouped Schooling on Achievement: The Role of National Context," by David P. Baker, Cornelius Riordan, and Maryellen Schaub, *Comparative Education Review* (November 1995). Unfortunately, interpreting such comparisons is often not a straightforward matter because researchers have been content largely with comparisons of "naturally occurring" classes, that is, classes over which they had little or no control in terms of the assignment of students and teachers to classes or the curriculum. As a result, the classes that were compared may have differed in many ways, including in parental beliefs about innate differences between boys and girls, the motivation of the students to master the subject in question, the intensity and content of the instruction, and the extent to which single-gender classes are perceived to have high status or prestige by the community. This makes it difficult to determine whether differences in achievement between girls in girls-only classes and girls in coeducational classes are due to the gender composition of the classes (and the associated differences in climate) or to one or more of these "confounding" factors. Controlled experiments are needed to show the full impact of single-gender classes on the achievement of girls.

Few would deny that schools are a powerful source of change in our society and that we must do all we can to ensure that they are settings in which all children can reach their fullest potential. Valuable insights about schooling and gender-related differences in academic achievement can be found in Deborah A. Garrahy, "Three Third-Grade Teachers' Gender-Related Beliefs and Behavior," *The Elementary School Journal* (vol. 102, 2001), pp. 81–94, Michael Gurian and Kathy Stevens, "With Boys and Girls in Mind," *Educational Leadership* (November 2004), Christy Belcher, Andy Frey, and Pamela Yankeelov, "The Effects of Single-Sex Classrooms on Classroom Environment, Self-Esteem, and Standardized Test Scores," *School Social Work Journal* (Fall 2006), and David M. Sadker and Myra P. Sadker, *Failing at*

Fairness: How America's Schools Cheat Girls (Simon & Schuster, 1994). And finally, Kelley King and Michael Gurian consider the possibilities that class-rooms are biased against boys in "Teaching to the Minds of Boys," *Educational Leadership* (September 2006).

ISSUE 2

Should Struggling Students Be Retained?

YES: Jon Lorence and Anthony Gary Dworkin, from "Elementary Grade Retention in Texas and Reading Achievement among Racial Groups: 1994–2002," *Review of Policy Research* (September 2006)

NO: Nancy Frey, from "Retention, Social Promotion, and Academic Redshirting: What Do We Know and Need to Know?" *Remedial and Special Education* (November/December 2005)

ISSUE SUMMARY

YES: Jon Lorence, an associate professor of sociology, and Anthony G. Dworkin, a professor of sociology, both cofounders of the Sociology of Education Research Group at the University of Houston, argue that although the majority of educational researchers contend that making low-performing students repeat a grade is ineffective, careful analysis of primary-grades data from school districts in Texas shows persistent positive effects of retention on academic performance over time.

NO: Nancy Frey, an associate professor of literacy in the School of Teacher Education at San Diego State University, argues that the policy of retention and associated procedures such as social promotion and academic "redshirting," in which there is purposeful delayed entry into kindergarten, are largely flawed with little compelling evidence to support their practice.

"Do no harm" is part of the oath taken by practitioners of medicine. Increasingly, the majority of educational researchers and leaders are concluding that the requirement to have academically low-performing students repeat a grade is not only inappropriate, but may, in fact, be a harmful educational practice. When students fail to achieve by the end of a school year, the question is a very basic one to all educators—what should be done? Historically and continuing through the present the main options have been to either retain or promote the student. From a professional perspective, organizations such as the National Association of School Psychologists (NASP) view the practice of grade retention as seriously deficient, urging "schools and parents to seek alternatives to retention" (NASP, 2003). From a research perspective, educational researchers such as Mantzicopoulos and Morrison writing in the *American Educational Research Journal* (vol. 29, 1992) contend that "Unlike mixed empirical evidence on other educational issues, research on elementary school nonpromotion [i.e., retention] is unequivocal. . . . [R]etention is not an effective policy" (p. 183).

However, there is disagreement among educational researchers and policymakers regarding how compelling the evidence is concerning the deleterious effects of retention for low-achieving students. There is also no firm agreement on alternatives, which range from extending the school day to extending the school year to summer school and individualized tutoring. The lack of agreement is based, in part, on little firm evidence one way or the other about effective practice in the face of persistent underachievement, and as suggested by Nancy Frey, the field needs a new generation of studies focusing on the effectiveness of these practices and effective alternatives.

The practice of retention has it roots, at least in part, in the expansive nature of American public education as it progressed from local to mandatory with consequent massive increases in numbers and abilities. One structural adaptation to diversity, predicated on a philosophy of innate individual differences, was ability tracking and homogenous grouping of students. Along with tracking and grouping, retention emerged as a logical outcome for the remediation of students failing to achieve the curricular goals for their chronological age and academic level. Partly as a result of tracking and ability grouping, but also because of the practice of social promotion (passing to the next grade level with one's peers despite failing grade-level academic requirements), retention rates dropped slowly but steadily over much of the course of the twentieth century. Near the end of the century, however, rates appeared to be on the rise; most likely tied to emergent policies of no or low tolerance for low achievement brought about by the current accountability movement.

Within the context of accountability, the practice of promoting students a grade level in the absence of academic mastery of grade-level material runs counter to the expectations of many, including parents, educators, and policymakers. The movement relies on the implementation of so-called "high stakes" year-end testing determining student achievement of the expected standards. With this movement, the issue has once again become dichotomized with the pendulum swinging back to retention applied rigidly in practice despite the lack of widespread support for its use among the educational research community.

The following selections examine the issue of whether struggling students should be retained. In the first selection, Jon Lorence and Anthony Gary Dworkin reach a different conclusion, suggesting that the findings from the research literature have serious shortcomings and that under some circumstances repeating a grade can benefit academically struggling students. In the second selection, Nancy Frey, after reviewing the available evidence in relation to aims of teachers and the needs of students, concludes that retention is academically ineffective and possibly detrimental.

17

YES

**Jon Lorence and
Anthony Gary Dworkin**

Elementary Grade Retention in Texas and Reading Achievement among Racial Groups: 1994–2002

Background

For over two decades public officials, the business community, and other interested individuals have subjected public schools to greater standards of accountability. Beginning with the publication of *A Nation at Risk* (National Commission on Excellence in Education, 1983) and culminating in passage of the No Child Left Behind Act of 2001 (2002), school administrators and teachers have been increasingly forced to address the needs of academically challenged students who struggle to learn an increasing amount of required material. Although there is overwhelming agreement that students failing their courses should be helped, there is little consensus as to which remediation strategies are best for enabling low-performing children to meet new accountability standards. A commonly used practice is to require students who fail a grade to repeat the grade in the next school year. Many educators believe that giving these children an additional year to learn the material they have failed will provide them an adequate foundation to proceed successfully through the remainder of their education. It is often assumed that students will be unable to learn the more advanced material in the next grade if they do not understand the subject matter of the current grade. Therefore, the long-run effect of grade retention should be to improve student academic outcomes. Conversely, researchers in colleges of education contend that making low-performing students repeat a grade is detrimental to their academic achievement. Retention is viewed as ineffective because gains in academic achievement during the repeated year are presumed to be either negligible or quickly fade if they do occur. Instead of requiring a failing student to repeat a grade, most educational researchers contend that it is better to place the child in the next grade, even if the student has not learned all the material required for promotion. Appropriate supplemental instruction during the year of promotion should enable low-performing students to catch up with their classmates who were not experiencing academic difficulty. This practice of "social promotion" is presumed to be more beneficial than grade retention because the child can remain with

From *Review of Policy Research*, vol. 23, no. 5, 2006, pp. 999–1005, 1010, 1011, 1014, 1016, 1021, 1026–1033 (tables omitted). Copyright © 2006 by Policy Studies Organization and American Political Science Association. Reprinted by permission of Wiley-Blackwell.

the same classmates and the student is not perceived as a failure. Proponents of social promotion argue that grade retention only damages the child's self esteem; the child becomes alienated and psychologically withdraws from school. In short, opponents of grade retention contend that making low-performing students repeat a grade is detrimental to their long-term educational progress and will eventually lead to dropping out of school (e.g., Jimerson, Anderson, & Whipple, 2002).

In spite of these warnings about the potential negative consequences of grade retention, given the demand for greater accountability, more state and local school districts have mandated that students in certain grades be held back if they do not meet mandated promotion criteria. For example, the Chicago Public Schools in 1996 ended the practice of social promotion by requiring all students in the third, sixth, and eighth grades to obtain a specified minimum score on the Iowa Test of Basic Skills before moving to the next grade (Roderick & Nagaoka, 2005). Beginning in 2003, Texas required that third graders receive a minimum score on the state's mandated reading test before promotion to grade four. Starting in 2005, Texas fifth graders were required to meet predetermined scores in reading and mathematics before being allowed to proceed to the sixth grade. Because the implementation of high-stakes testing promotional standards has been relatively recent, few educational systems have sufficient data to evaluate the impact of grade retention on academic performance. With few exceptions, almost all of the research assessing the impact of grade retention on academic achievement has pertained to teacher-initiated retention. That is, teachers and principals use their own judgmental criteria to make the decision to retain a pupil, rather than being forced to make students repeat a grade largely on the basis of a standardized test score. The current article focuses on the patterns of academic achievement among academically challenged students who were either retained or socially promoted at the discretion of their teachers and principals. We examine whether the effects of teacher-initiated grade retention vary across racial/ethnic groups. An investigation of the variables predicting grade retention is also presented. We first briefly summarize the literature on the academic impact of making students repeat a grade. A description of the data and analytical strategy to be used then follows. After presenting the findings we speculate on their implications for educational policy.

Prior Findings Regarding the Effect of Grade Retention

Conflicting Conclusions

The overwhelming consensus among researchers in colleges of education is that requiring low-achieving students to repeat a grade is an inappropriate educational practice. To illustrate, Mantzicopoulos and Morrison (1992, p. 183) contend that "Unlike mixed empirical evidence on other educational issues, research on elementary school nonpromotion is unequivocal. It supports the conclusion that retention is not an effective policy." Some opponents of grade retention argue that "retention worsens rather than improves the level of student achievement in years following the repeat year" (Shepard & Smith, 1990, p. 88). These strong beliefs about the ineffectiveness of grade retention are primarily derived from two reviews examining the impact of making students repeat a grade. Two meta-analyses are frequently cited as definitive studies that demonstrate that requiring low-performing students to repeat a grade is a futile educational practice. Holmes (1989) aggregated findings from 63 separate retention studies from 1960 to 1987. More recently, Jimerson (2001) reviewed 22 research articles published largely during the 1990s. Both authors concluded their summaries demonstrated that requiring students to repeat a grade is an ineffective strategy to improve student learning. However, Alexander, Entwisle, and Dauber (2003) questioned the conclusions from both the Holmes and Jimerson meta-analyses and argued that a large number of the retention studies were flawed, resulting in erroneous interpretations based on "bad science."

Whereas Alexander et al. (2003) pointed out general shortcomings of the literature examining the effect of grade retention, Lorence (2006) systematically examined the individual published studies pertaining to educational achievement that compose the two major meta-analyses on the retention literature. His reexamination of the retention literature utilized multiple criteria to assess the quality of the listed studies. Published studies were assumed to be of higher quality than unpublished convention papers, master's theses, or dissertations. The extent to which research designs controlled for rival hypotheses was also assessed by examining the comparability of matched students or the use of statistical controls. The basis of comparisons (usually age or grade) between retained and nonretained students was also investigated. Comparability in the measurement scales of tests given to promoted and retained pupils was assessed when evaluating the impact of making students repeat a grade. The size of samples and their effect on statistical power were also considered in the evaluation of the meta-analysis papers. On the basis of these criteria, Lorence (2005) found the methodological adequacy of the vast majority of studies cited in the Holmes (1989) to be highly suspect. Only 10 of the 63 retention studies Holmes cited had been subjected to a peer review process. Of these, six studies lacked appropriate controls for initial differences between retained and promoted students prior to retention. These studies did not have initial measures of student outcomes or did not statistically adjust for earlier indicators of student ability when students were retained. Results from the four studies that had more adequate controls for initial differences in abilities between students prior to retention were mixed. Two studies (Dobbs & Neville, 1967; Niklason, 1987) concluded against making low-performing students repeat a grade, but the extent of initial similarity between promoted and retained students was uncertain. Further, same-age comparisons were made that likely biased the results in favor of the promoted students who had covered an additional year of more advanced material. Conversely, two studies which controlled for student differences existing prior to retention found that the academically challenged students who repeated a grade outperformed their socially promoted peers (Chansky, 1964; Peterson, DeGracie, & Ayabe, 1987). The sample sizes were so small in the ten studies Holmes cited that statistical significance could not be reached even if the retained students obtained higher achievement scores than the promoted students. In only one of the ten studies was there more than 100 retained or promoted pupils. Contrary to the assertions of those who cite the Holmes meta-analysis to support their criticism of making students repeat a grade (e.g., Heubert & Hauser, 1999, p. 129; Shepard, 2000), there is no overwhelming body of evidence in the Holmes review showing that grade retention is an ineffective strategy to assist academically struggling students.

Many of the shortcomings observed in the Holmes review also pervade Jimerson's (2001) meta-analysis. Although Jimerson summarized 18 published studies examining academic achievement, few studies adequately adjusted for initial differences between retained and nonretained students. In addition, the sample sizes were so small in several studies that insufficient statistical power did not allow authors to reject a null hypothesis of no difference between retained and socially promoted students when retained pupils surpassed the academic performance of the promoted students. Even if low-performing retained students caught up with promoted students, most researchers concluded that making students repeat a grade was ineffective because the authors assumed that the retained pupils should outperform their nonretained classmates. Like the Holmes meta-analysis, Jimerson's review of grade retention studies does not conclusively demonstrate that retention is an ineffective remediation practice. However, one panel study meeting acceptable research standards analyzed academically challenged economically disadvantaged minority children in the Chicago Public Schools during the 1980s. Reynolds (1992) found that low-performing students who repeated a grade did no better than socially promoted students who were also struggling with school. Alternately, several studies indicated that making students repeat a grade seemed to boost their test scores or grades, at least temporarily (e.g., Alexander, Entwisle, & Dauber, 1994; Pierson & Connell, 1992). More recent retention studies of comparable research quality also indicate that retained students obtained higher test scores than low-performing socially promoted students (Jacobs & Lefgren, 2004; Karweit, 1999; Lorence, Dworkin, Toenjes, & Hill, 2002; Pomplun, 1988).

That researchers disagree on the impact of making low-performing students repeat a grade can also be illustrated by comparing the findings from two studies based on almost identical data from the Chicago Public Schools. Analyses by Jacobs and Lefgren (2004) suggest that making academically challenged Chicago elementary school students repeat third grade increased their academic achievement, but children repeating sixth grade obtained no benefit from retention. Conversely, Roderick and Nagoaka (2005) use the same set of test scores, but conclude that making students repeat third grade had no effect on test scores. Moreover, students who failed the required standardized sixth grade test and repeated the grade experienced less academic growth than their promoted counterparts. The different conclusions are unexpected because both analyses utilized a regression discontinuity design by examining students just below and above the preset cutoff criteria for promotion to the next grade. A partial explanation for the divergent conclusions may be that the two studies used somewhat different subsets of Chicago elementary children. Jacobs and Lefgren excluded students who were placed in special education whereas Roderick and Nagaoka kept special education students in their analyses. Another possible reason for the dissimilar findings is that the two studies used different procedures to gauge academic achievement. Jacob and Lefgren incorporated the initial third grade test scores during the base year prior to retention as a control variable. Roderick and Nagaoka, however, compared observed test scores after grade retention with predicted test scores derived from growth curve models of academic achievement beginning in first grade. The latter two authors believe their method better controls for regression to the mean artifacts; that is, the low-performing third graders who were retained had likely fallen below their true level of academic ability. Roderick and Nagaoka suggested that the positive effect of retention Jacobs and Lefgren reported was not attributable to repeating a grade, but instead occurred as a result of the retained children naturally rising back to their true levels of ability.

Contrary to the conventional wisdom among educational researchers, there is no overwhelming body of scientifically sound evidence demonstrating that making academically challenged students repeat a grade is ineffective or harmful to academic achievement. With only a few exceptions, the vast majority of studies that conclude that retention is an ineffective educational practice contain so many limitations that inferences from them are highly questionable if not unwarranted. It appears that, among the more methodologically sound studies, some find that grade retention may improve academic achievement while others report repeating the same grade has little effect, or may even result in negative educational outcomes. It appears as though the research findings evaluating the impact of making students repeat a grade are as inconclusive as they were in Jackson's (1975) seminal review of grade retention studies over 30 years ago.

The Inequitable Nature of Grade Retention

A major criticism of making elementary school pupils repeat a grade is that factors not directly related to academic performance have been found to be related to the retention decision. Critics of retention argue that children with specific social and demographic characteristics are more likely to be held back regardless of their cognitive abilities. Specifically, race/ethnicity, family social status, and gender have been hypothesized to influence grade progression, independent of student ability. Several studies examining bivariate relationships between social characteristics and nonpromotion show that racial and ethnic minorities exhibit higher probabilities of being retained than white students. For example, Abidin, Golladay, and Howerton (1971) reported that over one-half of the retained first and second graders in a southeastern urban school district were black. Similarly, minority students were overrepresented among nonpromoted students in two Utah school districts (Niklason, 1984). An examination of the National Education Longitudinal Study of 1988 found that retention rates were significantly higher among African American and Hispanic students when compared to whites (Meisels & Liaw, 1993). Jacobs and Lefgren (2004) also noted large percentages of African American and Hispanic students in Chicago have been required to repeat third and sixth grade.

Several of these studies have also suggested that students from lower socioeconomic backgrounds are also more likely to be held back in grade (Abidin et al., 1971; Meisels & Liaw, 1993). Further, these same studies found gender was associated with retention; boys were much more likely to repeat a grade than girls. Many of the earlier studies investigating the impact of student social background characteristics on grade retention, however, did not control for cognitive abilities and levels of academic performance. Analyses of Baltimore and Chicago public school students indicated that neither race nor family economic background were related to the likelihood of being required to repeat an early elementary grade after controlling for student cognitive skill levels and course grades (Dauber, Alexander, & Entwisle, 1993; Reynolds, 1992). But Karweit's (1999) analyses of a large nationally representative sample of first graders revealed that boys were significantly more likely to be held back in first grade than girls. Results from this national data set also indicated that more economically disadvantaged children evidenced higher retention rates, even after adjusting for student reading performance and other possible predictors of nonpromotion.

Critics of grade retention argue that, regardless of the net predictors of retention, requiring minorities to repeat a grade disadvantages them in several ways. Given that grade retention is presumed to be an ineffective remediation strategy, low-performing minority students will continue to fall behind their promoted classmates. Holmes (1989, p. 25) noted that studies suggesting retention was effective were based on white children and did not include black students, thus implying that grade retention will not help minority students. Reynolds (1992) examined only African American students and specifically argued against making minority students repeat a grade because retention would further impede their academic progress. These studies suggest that the effect of grade retention will vary by racial/ethnic group. Insofar as few studies have simultaneously examined the impact of grade retention on racially diverse groups of low-performing children, it is worthwhile to investigate whether students of specific racial/ethnic backgrounds are adversely affected by this educational practice.

The major focus of this article is to assess whether making academically challenged students repeat a grade is an ineffective remediation practice. We present findings from a panel of Texas elementary school children. Previous research on the effects of grade school retention in Texas have been described in reports to the Texas Education Agency, unpublished convention papers, and a book chapter (Dworkin et al., 1999; Dworkin & Lorence, 2003; Lorence, Dworkin, & Toenjes, 2000; Lorence et al., 2002). The findings presented extend our previous published analyses in several ways. First we investigate those factors associated with initial grade retention, a topic not examined in our earlier papers. The new findings are also based on outcome measures of student performance over a greater number of school years, which better enable us to assess the long term effect of grade retention on academic performance. Further, we investigate whether grade retention results in differential effects on student performance across racial/ethnic categories. . . .

To help gauge the possible impact of a bill pending in the state legislature to eliminate social promotion among low-performing elementary school students, the Texas Education Agency (TEA) initially provided anonymous annual individual-level data of all students enrolled in Texas public schools from 1994 through 1998. TEA later supplemented the initial data to include test information from the 1999–2000, 2000–2001, and 2001–2002 school years. A major advantage of the current dataset is that it contains the entire population of Texas public school children over a 9-year period. Most studies of grade retention have been able to examine the academic effects of nonpromotion from only a limited number of students over a few years. The Texas state dataset is also large enough to enable comparisons of retention effects across broadly defined racial/ethnic segments of the school population. We focus on student reading performance because scores on the state's standardized reading examination became the basis for third grade retention beginning in 2003. During the academic years examined, the Texas Assessment of Academic Skills (TAAS) Test was required to be taken by all eligible students in the state public school system. We begin with 1994 reading scores because this was the year in which all Texas public school students in grades three through eight and grade ten began to be tested annually in the spring of the academic year.[1]

We analyze only those third grade students who failed the May, 1994 TAAS reading examination (i.e., they did not correctly answer 75% of the 44 questions asked). Following the progress of third graders in the 1993–1994 school year through tenth grade also maximizes the number of comparisons that can be made between retained and socially promoted low-performing students. The focal independent variable is grade retention. We compare the average reading scores of those failing students required to repeat third grade (the experimental group) with that of the socially promoted students who also did not have a passing third grade reading score (the control group). . . .

The percentages of children required to repeat the third grade were somewhat higher among Hispanic and African American students. Although about 50% of the children not exempted from taking the 1994 reading test were boys, boys were overrepresented among children failing to correctly answer 75% of the reading items, the designated passing cutoff. Hispanic and African American low-performing students were much more likely to be economically disadvantaged than non-Hispanic white children. More than three-quarters of the minority children qualified for the federal lunch program, compared to about 36% of the academically challenged non-Hispanic white students. Alternately, the proportion of students classified as being in special education among non-Hispanic whites was almost twice the magnitude of the minority children. Hardly any of the non-Hispanic white and African American students were listed as having difficulty with English, but over one-quarter of the Hispanic children were classified as having limited proficiency in English. . . .

Hispanic and African American boys were slightly more likely to be retained than girls; however, girls had somewhat higher retention rates among the non-Hispanic white students. Children who qualified for either a free or reduced-price lunch were somewhat more apt to be held back another year than children who did not participate in the federally subsidized program.

Special education status appeared to be unrelated to grade retention among non-Hispanic white and Hispanic children. But it is noteworthy that African American students classified with a disability were less likely to be held back in grade than black children with no disability. Hispanic children with limited proficiency in English were somewhat less likely to be retained. Their teachers may have believed that the English of the LEP students would improve sufficiently to enable them to pass fourth grade. . . .

Effect of Retention on Reading Performance

We assess the impact of grade retention on academic performance when students were in the same grade. In this comparison, the reading results for the retained students are for the same grade as the socially promoted students; but the reading scores were obtained one year after that of the nonretainees. The socially promoted children are one grade ahead of the third grade repeaters even though both groups of students are of a similar age. Karweit (1999, pp. 43–44) argues that same-grade instead of same-year comparisons (i.e., students are of comparable ages but in different grades) should be utilized to assess the effect of retention. Examining mean differences in academic achievement between students in different grades is inappropriate because the promoted students have covered an additional year of curriculum than the retained students. The socially promoted have had more instruction over newer material and should therefore score higher than the retained students who are one grade behind. Same-grade comparisons are preferred because they capture differences in academic achievement between retained and promoted students who have covered the same material. . . .

After the year of repeating third grade, however, the average 1995 third grade reading score of the retained students (76.6) significantly surpassed the initial 1994 third grade reading score (61.1) of the children placed into grade four. Given that the retained students likely covered the same material twice, it is not surprising that they correctly answered more items at the end of their repeated grade than did the socially promoted low-achieving children who experienced third grade only once. More important is that, in fourth grade the average same-grade reading scores of the retained non-Hispanic white students (68.1) was greater than the fourth grade score of the socially promoted pupils (62.5). With the exception of grades eight and ten, the average same-grade reading scores of the retained third graders were significantly larger than those of the promoted children. Moreover, those non-Hispanic white students who repeated grade three in 1994–1995, on average, began passing the TAAS reading test after being held back in grade; socially promoted third graders, however, did not exceed the required level of proficiency until sixth grade.

A similar pattern occurred for both the Hispanic and African American students. Low-performing third grade students who repeated the grade markedly improved their TAAS reading scores by the end of their retention year. Although reading scores of the retained minority children fell after the year of retention, Hispanic and African American retainees in general correctly answered more questions than the socially promoted students. One exception arose among Hispanic students when in grade six. The retained Hispanic students, on average, slightly missed passing the required reading sixth grade test while the nonretained Hispanic adolescents barely obtained the mean minimum number of correct answers necessary to pass. Even though African American third grade retainees did not obtain average passing reading scores until eighth grade, the students required to repeat third grade usually answered more questions than the socially promoted African American pupils. Although the mean reading scores of the socially promoted African American pupils in sixth and eighth grade were slightly higher than those of the retained third graders. Third grade African American retainees, however, obtained significantly higher scores on the tenth grade reading test than did the nonretainees. . . .

The positive effect of grade retention was replicated within each of the minority groups. Once again, differences in initial ability, gender, special education classification, limited English proficiency, and economic status between the retained and socially promoted third graders were statistically adjusted using an analysis of covariance model. . . . The effect sizes derived from the adjusted mean differences between the retained and socially promoted students reveal that making low-performing minority students repeat a grade is associated with higher reading scores. Third grade retention allows failing students the opportunity to learn material they missed. Not only do the nonpromoted students catch up with the socially promoted pupils, but the mean adjusted reading scores indicate that the retainees evidence higher levels of reading ability in the following grades. As anticipated, the greatest relative gain in reading scores between the nonpromoted and socially promoted pupils occurs during the year of retention. At the end of the second year of third grade, the average reading score of the retained students is over one and one-half standard deviation larger than that of the previous year's third grade mean of the socially promoted. The gap between the retained and promoted third graders decreases somewhat in fourth and eight grades among Hispanic children. However, the retained students obtain reading scores that are statistically larger than their socially promoted counterparts. Moreover, after controlling for initial differences between the two groups, the retained Hispanic students begin passing the state reading test every year after being held back. The socially promoted Hispanic children did not meet minimum passing expectations until the fifth grade.

Among the African American students, retained children pass the reading test sooner than the nonretainees, once initial differences in student performance and other social background characteristics are adjusted. It is only in grade eight that the black pupils held back in third grade do not obtain significantly higher reading scores. Unlike the case for the non-Hispanic whites, Hispanic and African American third grade retainees on average correctly answer 6% more questions than the socially promoted minorities when in grade ten. The average tenth grade reading score of the retained minority third graders is about four-tenths of a standard deviation greater than that of the nonretained students, indicating that the effects of retention persisted during the sophomore year of high school. . . .

Summary and Discussion

Unlike many previous studies on grade retention that conclude that making students repeat a grade results in no academic benefit, the current findings reveal that requiring low-performing students to retake third grade is associated with increased reading performance. After repeating third grade, the reading scores of the retainees surpassed the initial third grade scores and remained comparable to those of the socially promoted. But after controlling for initial differences between the nonpromoted and socially promoted students, the advantage in academic performance became even more pronounced among the retained children. Comparing adjusted same-grade reading scores through six grades after retention revealed that socially promoted pupils lagged behind the reading ability of the retainees. The mean adjusted scores of the retained students were from 0.13 to 0.64 standard deviations larger than those of the socially promoted. Socially promoted students also took an extra grade of school before passing the state reading test. The positive association between retention and reading performance was replicated across the three largest racial/ethnic groups in the state. Making low-performing African American and Hispanic children repeat third grade also helped increase their reading levels when contrasted to test scores of their socially promoted classmates. There is no evidence in the data that making academically challenged children repeat a grade harms their academic progress. Indeed, retention seems to boost the ability of the initially low-performing minority readers over that of the socially promoted African American and Hispanic students who failed the state reading test. . . .

One reason this study found a positive relationship between retention and greater reading performance is that we examined the impact of holding students back a year in only third grade. The impact of retention may vary by specific grade level. For example, Alexander et al. (2003) reported more beneficial effects of retention when students repeated third and higher elementary grades. Children required to repeat first grade did not experience the same levels of achievement growth observed among students retained in later grades. The degree of educational improvement experienced after retention is likely related to the reasons for the retention. Young children are retained in first or second grade because of learning disabilities, emotional immaturity, or behavioral problems (e.g., Abidin et al., 1971; Caplan, 1973; Mantzicopoulos, Morrison, Hinshaw, & Carte, 1989). If children have severe learning problems, making them repeat a grade will probably not help them. Students retained in later grades may not have extensive learning difficulties or behavioral problems because they should have been retained in earlier grades. Children retained in third grade may need only additional exposure to class material in order to meet promotion criteria. Such students may be more likely to benefit from spending an extra year on the curriculum before moving up to the next grade. However, critics of grade retention often cite studies in which middle school and high school students required to repeat a grade did not benefit from the extra year. Given the large number of low-performing third graders in the 1993–1994 Texas cohort, future analyses will allow us to ascertain the degree to which retention in later grades affects academic performance.

A major explanation for the positive effect of grade retention we observed pertains to the nature of instructional practices that occur during the repeated grade. Critics of grade retention argue that making low-performing students repeat a grade is ineffective because teachers do little to help students, except cover the same material from the previous year. For example, with respect to retention practices in Chicago, Reynolds, Temple, and McCoy (1997, p. 36) state that "Once students are retained, however, they usually get no special help with their schooling. They are often placed in low academic tracks only to repeat the previous year's instruction and ultimately disengage from school." Likewise, Roderick and Nagaoka (2005) report that children retained in the Chicago public schools probably received no additional educational assistance during the year of retention. If students are not given additional instruction to help them learn material missed in the previous year, there is little reason to expect simply repeating the curriculum will enhance student learning outcomes. However, a study based on the Mesa, Arizona, school district suggests that retention was successful when students received extra educational support during the retention year. Teachers prepared individual educational plans to address the academic shortcomings of students who repeated a grade (Peterson et al., 1987). Grade retention was associated with increased school performance under these circumstances.

Although we lack knowledge about the specific educational practices retained children experienced, individual and group interviews with teachers and administrators in the largest Texas metropolitan school districts indicate that children required to repeat a grade were often given considerable extra assistance, for example, more individualized attention and staff tutoring on specific areas of weakness (Hill et al., 1999). Third grade retainees received additional educational support to help them learn material they had failed in the previous school year. Texas students who repeated a grade may have outperformed the socially promoted because of greater access to supplemental educational resources. However, the aforementioned qualitative interviews further revealed that *students failing the TAAS reading test also received the same compensatory educational services provided to the retained children.* Remediation practices apparently did not differ between the low-performing retained and socially promoted students. The additional educational resources provided the socially promoted students may help explain why such a large number of the children failing the state's third grade reading test eventually began passing the TAAS without being retained. Had the learning needs of the socially promoted pupils been ignored, the positive effects of grade retention would likely have been even more pronounced. At a minimum, our findings contradict the negative view that "the effects of retention plus remediation approaches are likely to be disappointing" (McCoy & Reynolds, 1999, p. 295). One of the major limitations of retention research is that little information exists describing the nature of instruction retainees experience. Future studies should attempt to identify the specific curriculums and instructional practices both retained and socially promoted academically challenged students confront after not meeting promotional standards.

The current findings may be viewed as particularly relevant for policy-makers, educational administrators, and teachers who must contend with the No Child Left Behind Act of 2001. The federal government's greater emphasis on making all students meet minimum academic standards has forced school districts to consider various strategies to help low-performing students become successful in school. Many states have implemented stringent promotion standards that require failing students to repeat the grade until able to demonstrate proficiency in the required subjects. Our results should not be interpreted to support the position that making poor-performing students repeat a grade will always enable them to catch up with regular performing classmates. In fact, earlier findings (Lorence et al., 2002) indicate that both low-performing retained and socially promoted third graders do not achieve the levels of reading proficiency observed among regular students. Nonetheless, our earlier and present findings suggest that repeating the school year *with* supplemental educational support enabled the failing third grade students to meet promotion standards. Further, the average reading scores of retained third grade students exceeded those of the socially promoted students.

It must be acknowledged that many of the socially promoted children eventually met minimum passing standards. Critics of retention could reasonably argue that promoting students to the next grade and providing them extra instructional support is equally effective. Assuming that the cost of retaining a student is $5,000, the figure usually mentioned by Texas educational administrators, the sum required to retain all of the 38,445 failing 1994 third graders we analyzed would have been slightly over $192 million. The question arises as to whether the cost is worth the benefit, especially when one considers that many of the socially promoted pupils eventually passed the TAAS reading test in later grades. The fact that the reading level of the socially promoted third grade students was one-half of a standard deviation larger than that of the retained children implies that students who answered less than 75% on the third grade reading test can pass later mandatory reading tests. The current findings indicate that the mandatory score for test success leading to annual progression in later grades could be lowered, perhaps to 70 or 65%. The data suggest that using a reading score of 75% correct as a cutoff point for identifying potentially academic failures may be overly stringent. However, we do not conclude that the automatic social promotion of academically challenged students will result in continual academic success. Unreported analyses reveal that about 10% ($n = 3,692$) of the socially promoted third graders were eventually retained prior to ninth grade and another 12% ($n = 4,607$) were required to repeat ninth grade.

Educational researchers (e.g., Darling-Hammond, 1998; Morris, 2001; Shepard, 2002, p. 62) have assumed that grade retention would be unnecessary if teachers correctly addressed students' learning gaps and additional resources like individual reading interventions and supplemental tutoring were made available to low-performing pupils. An examination of recent educational practices in Texas suggests that it may be unrealistic to presume that schools can provide all the services and additional instruction required to prevent retention. Texas elementary school teachers, particularly during the last four years, have used the strategies suggested for helping academically challenged children meet promotion standards. Teachers test their students at the beginning and middle of the academic year to assess areas of weakness and gaps in knowledge. Most third graders who have fallen behind their classmates have access to extended day programs, one-on-one instruction, pull-out programs, supplemental tutoring, summer school programs, and other remediation activities. Even with all of the effort devoted toward helping students progress to the next grade, 2.8% ($n = 8,924$) of the 2002–2003 Texas third graders were not allowed to proceed to the fourth grade (Texas Education Agency, 2004, Table 2). Critics of retention could argue that more money and staff are necessary to prevent students from failing. Our sense is that, unless seriously low-performing students are placed in an instructional setting with a teacher who has only a very limited number of students for the entire year, a small percentage of pupils will likely need to be retained in spite of the Herculean efforts of teachers and support staff. Some students begin the year so far behind their classmates that it will not be possible to raise them to the level of proficiency required for promotion. Many of the interviewed Texas educational personnel mentioned that students who entered Texas public schools after attending schools in other states often lagged behind the knowledge levels of children consistently enrolled in Texas (Hill et al., 1999).

We are doubtful that the current findings pertaining to the academic effects of grade retention and social promotion can be generalized to other states or school districts. It is important to stress that our results occurred within the context of a rigorous state educational accountability system. Not only does TEA require that all eligible students be tested annually, but test results are disaggregated by major sociodemographic categories. Test passage rates of various racial/ethnic and economic groups within individual schools and districts are available to the public and published in local newspapers. Public officials, businessmen, and parents pay particular attention to the percentage of students passing the TAAS in local schools. Consequently, administrators and schoolteachers are under intense pressure to ensure that all students, even those who are struggling, meet minimal levels of competency. It is no longer possible in Texas to ignore the academic performance of minority children and those who are economically disadvantaged. Few of the previous retention studies occurred in a high-stakes educational environment where administrators and teachers were held accountable for the performance of their students. In previous investigations, educators experienced neither positive nor negative consequences for the academic achievement of their pupils. The absence of any incentives for helping academically challenged students may also partially explain why students who repeated a grade demonstrated minimal, if any, improvement in school performance. Teachers could largely overlook children having trouble learning because there were no consequences for the educators. However, implementation of the No Child Left Behind Act of 2001 has resulted in the greater prevalence of disaggregated test results by various demographic groups across all states. Thus, the Texas results on grade retention may become less of an exception. As other states implement more rigorous accountability practices, researchers will have the opportunity to investigate whether retention, when contrasted to social promotion, yields the same sustained academic benefits observed among retained third grade children in Texas.

Note

1. Test scores are identified by the spring of the academic year. For example, test results from the spring of 1994 occurred in the 1993–1994 academic year.

References

Abidin, R. P., Golladay, W. M., & Howerton, A. L. (1971). Elementary school retention: An unjustifiable, discriminatory, and noxious educational policy. *Journal of School Psychology, 9*(4), 410–417.

Alexander, K. L., Entwisle, D. R., & Dauber, S. L. (1994). *On the success of failure: A reassessment of the effects of retention in the primary grades.* New York: Cambridge University Press.

Alexander, K. L., Entwisle, D. R., & Dauber, S. L. (2003). *On the success of failure: A reassessment of the effects of retention in the primary grades* (2nd ed.). New York: Cambridge University Press.

Bali, V. A., Anagnostopoulos, D., & Roberts, R. (2005). Toward a political explanation of grade retention. *Educational Evaluation and Policy Analysis, 27*(2), 133–155.

Campbell, D. T., & Kenny, D. A. (1999). *A primer on regression artifacts.* New York: Guilford Press.

Campbell, D. T., & Stanley, J. C. (1966). *Experimental and quasi-experimental designs for research.* Chicago: Rand McNally.

Caplan, P. J. (1973). The role of classroom conduct in the promotion and retention of elementary school children. *Journal of Experimental Education, 41*(3), 8–11.

Chansky, N. M. (1964). Progress of promoted and repeating grade 1 failures. *Journal of Experimental Education, 32*(3), 225–237.

Cohen, J. (1988). *Statistical power analysis for the behavioral sciences* (2nd ed.). Hillsdale, NJ: Erlbaum.

Darling-Hammond, L. (1998). Alternatives to grade retention. *The School Administrator, 55*(7), 18–21.

Dauber, S., Alexander, K. L., & Entwisle, D. R. (1993). Characteristics of early retainees and early precursors of retention in grade. *Merrill-Palmer Quarterly, 39*(3), 326–343.

Demaris, A. (1992). *Logit modeling: Practical applications.* Sage University Paper Series on Quantitative Applications in the Social Sciences, No. 07–086. Newbury Park, CA: Sage.

Dobbs, V., & Neville, D. (1967). The effect of nonpromotion on the achievement of groups matched from retained first graders and promoted second graders. *Journal of Educational Research, 60*(10), 470–475.

Dworkin, A. G., & Lorence, J. (2003). *Eight year longitudinal analyses of elementary school retention and social promotion in Texas: A final report*, prepared for the Texas Education Agency. Houston, TX: University of Houston, Department of Sociology.

Dworkin, A. G., Lorence, J., Toenjes, L. A., Hill, A. N., Perez, N., & Thomas, M. (1999). *Elementary school retention and social promotion in Texas: An assessment of students who failed the reading section of the TAAS,* prepared for the Texas Education Agency. Houston, TX: University of Houston, Department of Sociology.

Eide, E. R., & Showalter, M. H. (2001). The effect of grade retention of educational and labor market outcomes. *Economics of Education Review, 20,* 63–76.

Hauser, R. M. (1997). Indicators of high school completion and dropout. In R. M. Hauser, B. V. Brown, & W. R. Posser (Eds.), *Indicators of children's well being* (pp. 152–184). New York: Russell Sage Foundation.

Hauser, R. M. (2001). Should we end social promotion? Truth and consequences. In G. Orfield & M. Kornhaber (Eds.), *Raising standards or raising barriers? Inequality and high stakes testing in public education* (pp. 151–178). New York: Century Foundation.

Heckman, J. J. (1978). Dummy endogenous variables in a simultaneous equation system. *Econometrica, 46*(4), 931–961.

Heckman, J. (1979). Sample selection bias as a specification error. *Econometrica, 47*(1), 153–161.

Heubert, J. P., & Hauser, R. M. (1999). *High stakes: Testing for tracking, promotion, and graduation.* Washington, DC: National Academies Press.

Hill, A. N., Lorence, J., Dworkin, A. G., & Toenjes, L. A., Perez, N., Thomas, M., & Segvig, D. (1999). *Educational practices applied to Texas elementary students retained in grade,* prepared for the Texas Education Agency. Houston, TX: University of Houston, Department of Sociology.

Holmes, C. T. (1989). Grade level retention effects: A meta-analysis of research studies. In L. A. Shepard & M. L. Smith (Eds.), *Flunking grades: Research and policies on retention* (pp. 16–33). London: Falmer Press.

Hong, G., & Raudenbush, S. W. (2005). Effects of kindergarten retention policy on children's cognitive growth in reading and mathematics. *Educational Evaluation and Policy Analysis, 27*(3), 205–224.

Jackson, G. B. (1975). Research evidence on the effects of grade retention. *Review of Educational Research, 45*(4), 613–635.

Jacobs, B. A., & Lefgren, L. (2004). Remedial education and student achievement: A regression-discontinuity analysis. *The Review of Economics and Statistics, 86*(1), 226–244.

Jimerson, S. (2001). Meta-analysis of grade retention research: Implications for practice in the 21st century. *School Psychology Review, 30*(3), 420–437.

Jimerson, S., Anderson, G. E., & Whipple, A. D. (2002). Winning the battle and losing the war: Examining the relationship between grade retention and dropping out of high school. *Psychology in the Schools, 39*(4), 441–457.

Karweit, N. L. (1999). *Grade retention: Prevalence, timing, and effects* (Report No. 33). Baltimore: Johns Hopkins University, Center for Research on the Education of Students Placed at Risk.

Lorence, J. (2006). Retention research revisited. *International Education Journal*, 7(4).

Lorence, J., Dworkin, A. G., & Toenjes, L. A. (2000). *Longitudinal analyses of elementary school retention and promotion in Texas: A second year report*, prepared for the Texas Education Agency. Houston, TX: University of Houston, Department of Sociology.

Lorence, J., Dworkin, A. G., Toenjes, L. A., & Hill, A. N. (2002). Grade retention and social promotion in Texas, 1994–1999: Academic achievement among elementary school students. In D. Ravitch (Ed.), *Brookings papers on education policy 2002* (pp. 13–52). Washington, DC: Brookings Institution.

Mantzicopoulos, P., & Morrison, D. (1992). Kindergarten retention: Academic and behavioral outcomes through the end of second grade. *American Educational Research Journal*, 29(1), 107–121.

Mantzicopoulos, P., Morrison, D, Hinshaw, S. P., & Carte, E. T. (1989). Nonpromotion in kindergarten: The role of cognitive, perceptual, visual-motor, and demographic characteristics. *American Educational Research Journal*, 26(1), 107–121.

McCoy, A. R., & Reynolds, A. J. (1999). Grade retention and school performance: An extended investigation. *Journal of School Psychology*, 37(3), 273–98.

Meisels, S. J., & Liaw, F. (1993). Failure in grade: Do retained children catch up? *Journal of Educational Research*, 87(2), 69–77.

Morris, D. R. (2001). Assessing the implementation of high-stakes reform: Aggregate relationships between retention rates and test results. *National Association of Secondary School Principals Bulletin*, 85(629), 18–34.

National Commission On Excellence in Education. (1983). *A nation at risk: The imperative for educational reform*. Washington, DC: U.S. Government Printing Office.

Niklason, L. B. (1984). Do certain groups of children profit from a grade retention? *Psychology in the Schools*, 21(4), 485–499.

Niklason, L. B. (1987). Nonpromotion: A pseudoscientific solution. *Psychology in the Schools*, 24(4), 339–345.

No Child Left Behind Act of 2001, 20 U.S.C. § 6301 (2002).

Peterson, S. E., DeGracie, J. S., & Ayabe, C. R. (1987). A longitudinal study of the effects of retention/promotion on academic achievement. *American Educational Research Journal*, 24(1), 107–118.

Pierson, L., & Connell, J. P. (1992). Effect of grade retention on self-system processes, social engagement, and academic performance. *Journal of Educational Psychology*, 84(3), 300–307.

Pomplun, M. (1988). Retention, the earlier the better? *Journal of Educational Research*, 81(5), 281–287.

Reynolds, A. J. (1992). Grade retention and school adjustment: An explanatory analysis. *Educational Evaluation and Policy Analysis*, 14(2), 101–121.

Reynolds, A. J., Temple, J., & McCoy, A. (1997, September 17). Grade retention doesn't work. *Education Week*, p. 36.

Roderick, M., & Nagaoka, J. (2005). Retention under Chicago's high-stakes testing program: Helpful, harmful, or harmless? *Educational Evaluation and Policy Analysis*, 27(4), 309–340.

Rosenbaum, P. R., & Rubin, D. B. (1984). Reducing bias in observational studies using subclassification on the propensity score. *Journal of the American Statistical Association, 79*(387), 516–524.

Rosenbaum, P. R. & Rubin, D. B. (1985). Constructing a control group using multivariate matched sampling methods that incorporate the propensity score. *American Statistician, 39*(1), 33–38.

Schwager, M. T., Mitchell, D. E., Mitchell, T. K., & Hecht, J. B. (1992). How school district policy influences grade level retention in elementary schools. *Educational Evaluation and Policy Analysis, 14*(4), 421–438.

Shepard, L. (2000). Cited in Ending social promotion by Debra Viadero. *Education Week on the Web.* (March 15, 2000). . . .

Shepard, L. (2002). Comment on grade retention and social promotion in Texas, 1994–1999: Academic achievement among elementary school students. In D. Ravitch (Ed.), *Brookings papers on education policy 2002* (pp. 56–63). Washington, DC: Brookings Institution.

Shepard, L. A., & Smith, M. L. (1990). Synthesis of research on grade retention. *Educational Leadership, 47*(8), 84–88.

StatCorp. (2001). *Stata statistical software: Release 7.0.* College Station, TX: Stata Corporation.

Texas Education Association. (2004). *Grade-level retention in Texas public schools, 2002–2003.* (Document No. GE05 601 01). Austin, TX: Author.

Vella, F. (1998). Estimating models with sample selection bias: A survey. *Journal of Human Resources, 33*(1), 127–169.

Winship, C., & Morgan, S. L. (1999). The estimation of causal effects from observational data. In K. S. Cook & J. Hagan (Eds.), *Annual Review of Sociology*, Vol. 25 (pp. 659–707). Palo Alto, CA: Annual Reviews.

Nancy Frey

Retention, Social Promotion, and Academic Redshirting: What Do We Know and Need to Know?

"Held Back." "Repeating." "Left Back." These euphemisms are used by adults to soften the blow to a child of being retained in grade. "Flunking" is the term used by children themselves to describe retention, an event so feared that they report they would rather "wet in class" than be retained (Byrnes & Yamamoto, 1985). Both the policy and the practice of retention of a child who is deemed to be faltering academically or socially are fraught with hopes for the best and fears of the worst.

The decision to retain a student has repercussions that extend well beyond the repeated year. However, educators, parents, and politicians have also criticized *social promotion* (i.e., the practice of sending a student to the next grade level despite his or her failing to achieve expectations) as anachronistic in an era of standards, school reform, and high accountability. Increasingly common among parents—especially more affluent ones—is the practice of delaying entry into kindergarten, referred to as *"academic redshirting."* This article provides a review of the history of retention and social promotion in the United States. Furthermore, longitudinal studies on the rates of retention, the characteristics of students who are most likely to repeat a year of schooling, and the academic and social effectiveness of retention are discussed. By extension, the association of retention and dropping out of high school is examined. The prevalence of delayed kindergarten enrollment is examined. Thus, the purpose of this article is to examine the aims of the teaching profession in the effort to determine what needs to occur next when a child fails to live up to expectations. Recommendations for future research are discussed.

The History of Retention

The history of retention as an educational practice for the remediation of students who fail to achieve has its roots in the schoolhouses of mid-19th-century America (Holmes & Matthews, 1984). Schools were first legislated in Massachusetts in 1647 to ensure that children learned to read the Bible as the

From *Remedial and Special Education*, vol. 26, no. 6, November/December 2005, pp. 332–346. Copyright © 2005 by Hammill Institute on Disabilities and Sage in association with American Rehabilitation Counseling Association (ARCA). Reprinted by permission via Rightslink.

way to thwart the devil (the "Ould Deluder" law), so that "learning may not be buried in the graves of our fathers in the church" (Monaghan & Barry, 1999, p. 4). Because settlements were small and likely to be distant from one another, children of all ages were taught as a single class in a one-room schoolhouse. Morality as a democratic ideal and religious mandate was emphasized over reading excellence; therefore, uncertain readers were merely absorbed into the classroom community. In fact, children were often taught to read and write at home, before they ever attended school—literacy acquisition per se was not regarded as a function of schooling (Pulliam & Van Patten, 1995).

As the population of the new nation increased in the 1800s, schools shed some—but not all—of their religious trappings in favor of education as a means of equalizing citizens and reorienting immigrants to the philosophy of democracy (Pulliam & Van Patten, 1995). Despite the shift away from religious training, schools changed little in their service delivery model, although the slightly larger schools could now afford to expand to two rooms—primary and secondary (Pulliam & Van Patten, 1995). Compulsory education was still a policy in only a few communities—never for African Americans, and rarely for girls or any children older than 10. Students who failed to achieve might simply withdraw from school to work on the family's behalf (Mondale & Patton, 2001).

The arrival of the Industrial Revolution and the influx of immigrants and freed slaves from the defeated South after the Civil War both fundamentally changed education and gave rise to the practice of retention. Compulsory education was founded to supply the educated workers needed to staff the factories and mills (Mondale & Patton, 2001). At the same time, the population in urban areas was growing rapidly, and schools became bigger. The increased enrollment allowed schools to specialize both in what was taught and in how it was taught. Thus, subjects like geography, history, and spelling were added to the curriculum, and children were placed in graded classrooms according to their chronological age (Pulliam & Van Patten, 1995). At the same time, the expansion of compulsory education laws and a new era of pluralism brought previously disenfranchised groups to the schoolhouse door—especially freed slaves, immigrants, and girls. For the first time, schools were organized in a physical and curricular layout that left some children behind.

The emergence of the philosophy of social Darwinism and the science of psychology in the latter half of the 19th century ushered in a new set of beliefs about how people learn. Herbert Spencer's theory of social Darwinism set the stage for beliefs about "survival of the fittest" as a sociocultural phenomenon, not merely a biological mechanism of evolution (Hofstadter, 1955). In the meantime, William James was expanding the new science of psychology and promoting the perspective that all human thought could be constructed as conscious behavior. His influential *Talks with Teachers* (James, 1899) brought psychology into the classroom and fueled the emerging discipline of teacher education. . . .

The coupling of a renewed philosophy of difference among humans, based on purported scientific logic, and a pedagogy of learning driven by teacher stimulus and student response set the stage for retention as a widespread practice. All that was missing for retention to emerge was a way to further quantify and rank students. At the turn of the century, intelligence testing provided a mechanism for this.

The influence of intelligence testing on education is seen particularly in the way that intelligence scores (Binet & Simon, 1916) were used. The scientific approach to standardized measurement and evaluation of perceived ability was further evidenced in curriculum and instruction of reading and language arts through the establishment of practices of homogeneous grouping of students based on these assessments (Wheat, 1923). For example, in the New York City public schools, "Binet classes" were created for "the educationally retarded"—those students with IQ scores between 75 and 95 (Gates & Pritchard, 1942). Binet's original intent with intelligence testing had been to identify those children in need of specialized educational supports, not to use it as a device for irreversibly segregating low-performing students (Binet, 1969). Furthermore, Binet viewed intelligence not as a fixed and permanent construct but, rather, as one that could be influenced by instruction (Binet & Simon, 1916). The use of an "intelligence quotient" (so named because the student's chronological age is the denominator to compute an IQ score) to segregate students and limit their school and vocation options is an American idea, promoted chiefly by H. H. Goddard and Lewis Terman (Gould, 1996). Indeed, Goddard, the director of the Vineland (NJ) Training School for Feebleminded Boys and Girls, saw the use of IQ testing and subsequent placement of low-achieving students in proper vocations suitable for their abilities as the highest form of democracy. . . .

Terman held similarly strong opinions about the necessity of segregating low-achieving students and appeared to see segregation as a means to preserve a democratic way of life. He stated that segregated school placements of low-achieving students were necessary, and that without such educational engineering, low achievers would "drift easily into the ranks of the anti-social or join the army of Bolshevik discontents" (Terman, 1919, p. 285).

By some estimates, retention rates in the early part of this century were nearly 50%, and 20% of all students left school by eighth grade (Holmes & Matthews, 1984; Johnson, Merrell, & Stover, 1990). Retention had clearly become the intervention of choice for those who did not achieve. Many educators were alarmed with the high rates of failure among schoolchildren. The Russell Sage Foundation commissioned a study on "backward children" (the terminology then used to describe students who were past the age for their grade level), and the resulting work, *Laggards in Our Schools* (Ayres, 1909), made a case for differentiating expectations among students in order to foster their success. Ayres, a statistician and former superintendent, exposed school success figures that were tainted by unreported high retention and dropout rates.

Studies over the next 2 decades advocated homogeneous grouping within and across classrooms as an instructional arrangement that allowed the presentation of different material for high- and low-achieving students, although not all educators saw this as an improvement (Dewey, 1998). This pattern of grouping is perhaps most familiar from the practice of forming three reading groups within a class—the so-called "bluebirds, redbirds, and buzzards" plan.

Although the overuse of homogeneous groups has also fallen into disfavor (e.g., Cunningham, Hall, & Defee, 1998), a positive outcome of homogeneous grouping in classrooms was a corresponding decline in retention rates from the 1930s through the 1960s (Johnson et al., 1990).

In the latter half of the twentieth century, interest in the efficacy and effects of retention has spurred research on policy and on the associated attitudes connected to the practice of nonpromotion. Determining the extent to which retention is used, and whether multiyear trends can be identified, has been a challenge.

Rates of Retention

The rate and number of students who are retained each year have been difficult to ascertain, in part because the method to collect these data has varied widely between districts and states. However, some reliable statistics can be projected from the various longitudinal studies conducted over the last decade. . . .

Retention Studies Focused on Primary Grades

A nationally representative sample of 9,240 students was tracked by the Center for Research on Students Placed At Risk at Johns Hopkins University from their entry in first grade in the fall of 1991 until the spring of 1994. During this span of 3.5 years, 18.4% of these students had been retained at least once (Karweit, 1999). Similar results were obtained in a smaller study of 190 children from the Minnesota Mother–Child Interaction Project, who have been studied for 21 years, since their mothers enrolled in a prenatal health clinic. By third grade, 16.8% of the cohort had been retained at least once (Jimerson, Carlson, Rotert, Egeland, & Sroufe, 1997). It is important to note that the cohort from this study differs from that of the first study, as the families enrolled in the program qualified due to low income levels.

Multiyear Retention Studies

Since 1994, 120,000 seventh- to twelfth-grade students from 132 high schools in 80 communities have been participating in the National Longitudinal Study of Adolescent Health. This comprehensive study is examining influences on adolescent health behavior, including those in the home, school, and community. A stratified sample of 12,118 students from this database participated in a survey concerning aspects of their school life. Resnick et al. (1997) reported that 21.3% of all students had been retained at least once in their school career.

When the focus of a longitudinal study is on low-income, minority children, the retention rate is even higher. The Chicago Longitudinal Project has followed 1,164 children enrolled in Chicago public schools since 1986. These students were selected based on their socioeconomic status (SES) and ethnicity; 95% of the cohort is African American and 5% Hispanic. By the spring of 1994, when their age cohort had reached the eighth grade, 28% of the sample had been retained at least once (McCoy & Reynolds, 1999). Although individual studies vary in terms of the percentage of children retained in grade, they have consistently reported that the overall rate of retention hovers around 20% (Holmes & Saturday, 2000).

Rising Retention Rates

The yearly rate of retention appears to be rising, perhaps spurred by higher levels of accountability and the proliferation of "zero tolerance" policies regarding achievement in schools. The Center for Policy Research in Education reported in 1990 that 6% of schoolchildren were retained each year. In 1992, the annual rate of retention in the United States had nearly doubled to 11.1% (McMillen & Kaufman, 1993); by 1995, it had risen to 13.3% (Bureau of the Census, 1995). The National Association of School Psychologists has reported that grade retention has increased by 40% in the last 20 years (Dawson, 1998).

The proliferation of state policies that mandate high-stakes testing in order to progress to the next grade appears to be shifting the patterns of retention. Historically, the majority of retention events have occurred in kindergarten through third grade (Meisels & Liaw, 1993). However, a recent survey of 16 southern states revealed that the most common grade for retention is now ninth grade (Southern Regional Education Board, 2001). It has been suggested that this growth in ninth-grade retention rates is linked to high-stakes testing in tenth grade in these same states (Haney, 2001). Given the growth in retention rates in the early 1990s and the unavoidable lag in reports of statistical information, it is possible that studies released over the next 5 years will push these numbers even higher.

Who Is Retained?

Rates of retention appear to be related to gender, ethnicity, SES, and parental characteristics.

Ethnicity

Ethnicity has been identified as a predictor of retention. A large-scale study, the National Education Longitudinal Study of 1988 (NELS '88), followed 24,599 eighth-grade students from 1,000 schools. At the time of the study, it was the most comprehensive federal longitudinal study of its kind. Meisels and Liaw (1993) used the data from NELS '88 to analyze the characteristics of the students retained. Whereas the overall retention rate was 19.3% for all students, 29.9% of African Americans and 25.2% of Hispanics were held back, compared to only 17.2% of their European American peers (Meisels & Liaw, 1993). When gender and ethnicity are analyzed together, the variance increases. For example, the unbalanced range of retention rates in one study ranged from a low of 24% for White girls to a high of 47% for Hispanic/Latino boys at the end of eighth grade (Alexander, Entwisle, & Dauber, 1994). Using census data, Roderick (1995) reported a similar disparity at the end of ninth grade, ranging from a low of 15.8% for Hispanic girls to a high of 52% for African American boys.

Gender

The role of gender has been recognized as a factor in retention for at least 30 years (Abidin, Golladay, & Howerton, 1971; McCoy & Reynolds, 1999). In the South, boys are twice as likely to be retained as girls (Southern Regional Education Board, 2001). Similar figures have been derived from national studies. For instance, in the NELS '88 study, 24% of boys were retained, whereas only 15.3% of girls repeated a grade (Meisels & Liaw, 1993). Although it is not clear why boys are retained at higher rates, Meisels and Liaw have speculated that there may be a mismatch between expectations of school behavior and the typical development of male children. Another study probed the attitudes and beliefs of retained first-, third-, and sixth-grade boys and girls in an ethnically diverse community in the Southwest. Byrnes (1989) found that these children believed that retention was a punishment and felt stigmatized by it; 43% of the girls and 19% of the boys would not disclose to the researcher that they had been retained, even when directly questioned. Meisels and Liaw's (1993) evaluation of the NELS '88 data also confirmed the unique vulnerability of girls to the negative emotional effects of retention, which they speculated might be due to the need for affiliation and the establishment of identity.

Socioeconomic Status

Poverty is also a powerful predictor of retention. By some estimates, children from poor households are two to three times more likely to be retained (Southern Regional Education Board, 2001). The socioeconomic status (SES) of the students from the NELS '88 study was significantly related to retention: 33.9% of the students were in the lowest SES quartile, whereas only 8.6% lived in households from the highest SES quartile (Meisels & Liaw, 1993). The relationship between low SES schools and high rates of retention was confirmed in a study of 33 districts from the Council of Great City Schools (Gastright, 1989) and in an evaluation of retention patterns in Miami–Dade County, Florida (Morris, 2001). Nevertheless, in a 5-year analysis of retention rates in a midwestern school district with high-, middle-, and low-SES elementary schools, Gurewitz and Kramer (1995) found that individual differences in student performance could not account for disparate retention rates, and that middle SES schools had the highest retention rate. They theorized that low-SES students in middle-SES schools may appear more conspicuous. Other studies have further affirmed the compounded risk for those students who possess multiple predictive factors—especially African American boys living in poverty (Dauber, Alexander, & Entwisle, 1993).

Parental Factors

Characteristics of parents were found to be a factor influencing retention in several studies. In the aforementioned Minnesota Mother–Child Interaction Project, parent IQ, as measured by the *Wechsler Adult Intelligence Scale* (WAIS; Wechsler, 1997), was found to be significant at the $p < .05$ level, with mothers of retainees scoring lower on measures of cognitive functioning than the mothers of the promoted group. The researchers also reported that parent involvement at school was "the best predictor of children's promotion or retention status" (Jimerson et al., 1997, p. 21). This finding is consistent with the Chicago Longitudinal Study (Miedel & Reynolds, 1998). It is often assumed that all parents are aware of the type of literacy involvement that is expected of them. However, Lapp, Fisher, Flood, and Moore (2002) found that many low-income parents are not aware of this necessity, nor do they view early literacy training as their job. They do not believe that they have the knowledge or skills to assume this responsibility and, in fact, are concerned that they "might teach it wrong" (p. 275).

Exogenous factors—that is, variables present before the start of school—appear to weigh heavily on who is retained. In particular, boys, African American and Hispanic students, and students living in poverty (especially in urban environments) are most likely to be required to spend an extra year in school. This has raised concerns from educators, families, and policymakers, who have asked whether retention is effective.

Is Retention Effective?

A discussion of the effectiveness of retention as a practice for assisting students who do not achieve either academically or socially in a manner similar to their peers requires an explanation of the methodological limitations that have plagued some studies. The methodologies used in many retention studies have been criticized as flawed. Several researchers have analyzed dozens of early retention studies and found that many were too short in duration or lacked comparison groups (Holmes & Matthews, 1984; Jackson, 1975). The meta-analysis of Holmes and Matthews (1984) calculated effect sizes for 18 studies that did use a comparison group and found that retained students were significantly negatively affected, both academically and emotionally. In another meta-analysis, Holmes (1989) looked at 63 studies that met nominal research standards and found that 54 of them reported negative effects of retention. However, the dearth of rigorous studies highlighted the need for the examination of long-term effects of retention. Several longitudinal studies mentioned earlier in this article have attempted to do this, although limitations persist. A closer look at two such studies, the Minnesota Mother–Child Interaction Project and the Chicago Longitudinal Study, illustrates the current approaches to retention research.

Minnesota Mother–Child Interaction Project

The 190 children participating in this project were identified as at risk because of family poverty. One of the many purposes of the study was to determine the long-term effects of student retention in kindergarten through third grade. The 104 participants identified for the retention studies attended 120 different elementary schools (due to family mobility), and the results were published when the cohort was 10, 12, 14, 16, and 21 (Jimerson et al., 1997). Each student in the cohort was placed into one of three groups—never retained, retained once during primary grades, or socially promoted. However, it is important to note that these were comparison groups but not matched groups. Yearly achievement assessment batteries; interviews with teachers, mothers, and children; and measures of social and emotional well-being were conducted.

The researchers found that there were no significant differences between retained children and their socially promoted peers on achievement and intelligence measures. However, the two groups differed on behavioral, peer relation, and emotional measures. The researchers speculated that "perhaps retained children are perceived as poor students in large part because of their behavior in the classroom, since their school achievement does not distinguish them, but their behavior is distinctive" (Jimerson et al., 1997, p. 20).

The children from the Minnesota Mother–Child Interaction Project were followed throughout their high school years. Initially, retained students seemed to benefit in mathematics achievement, but this effect had disappeared by middle school (Jimerson & Schuder, 1996). No difference was found for reading comprehension or overall achievement, although retainees did continue to compare negatively to the rest of the cohort in both behavior and emotional health (Jimerson et al., 1997). Significantly, 52% of the socially promoted students graduated from high school, whereas only 24% of the retained students did the same (Jimerson & Schuder, 1996).

Chicago Longitudinal Study

Another series of studies is related to the Chicago Longitudinal Study, which followed 1,164 low-income children who had attended a preschool program from their entrance in kindergarten through age 14. Of these children, 296 had been retained once and 19 had multiple retentions. Besides analyzing data for predictors and demographics as discussed earlier, the researchers focused on academic outcomes, especially reading and mathematics, as measured by the *Iowa Test of Basic Skills,* a norm-referenced test with internal consistency coefficients of .92 and .95, respectively (McCoy & Reynolds, 1999). Regression analysis and matched comparison samples were used to control for differences between the groups. . . .

[T]he difference in scores between retained and nonretained students was 9.5 points ($p < .001$). By extension, early retention (Grades 1–3) had a greater effect on reading achievement than later retention (Grades 4–7). Similar results were obtained for mathematics achievement, with a difference of 8.9 points after multiple regression ($p < .001$).

The results of the Minnesota and Chicago studies have contributed to the knowledge base first analyzed by Jackson (1975) and Holmes and colleagues (Holmes, 1989; Holmes & Matthews, 1984). The use of a longitudinal approach has provided insight into the effects of retention across the years. These outcomes are useful as a lens to discuss other, more limited studies that nonetheless have yielded similar results, especially as they apply to nonacademic effects, high school dropout data, and adult outcomes.

Nonacademic Effects

In addition to academic achievement, grade retention apparently can be damaging to the social and emotional development of children, especially as it relates to personal adjustment. For example, the perception of school self-concept, as measured by a survey of 12 items, was more positive among retained students in the 1992 Chicago study (Reynolds, 1992), although this effect had vanished by the time the students reached age 14 (McCoy & Reynolds, 1999). However, delinquency, as measured by school discipline reports, was not associated with retention (McCoy & Reynolds, 1999).

In contrast, the retained children in the Minnesota project demonstrated significantly more behavior problems and lower peer acceptance than nonretainees. Other studies have examined the opinions held by students, teachers, and peers. In a study of third- through sixth-grade students in an urban center in New York, retained students scored lower than their peers on cognitive competence, defined as "beliefs that they can control academic outcomes, . . . that they have what it takes to do well in school, . . . and what it takes to execute those strategies" (Pierson & Connell, 1992, p. 301). These beliefs may persist in high school as well. An inquiry of secondary students in a rural New York community found that those who had been retained showed lower educational expectations for themselves, more disruptive behavior, less impulse control, and an external locus of control when compared to a group of matched-ability peers who had not been retained (Hagborg, Masella, Palladino, & Shepardson, 1991). . . .

High School Dropout Rates

A frequently quoted finding about retention concerns its association with dropping out of school. Indeed, retention and high school dropout are correlated (Rumberger, 1987; Rush & Vitale, 1994). Much of the evidence for this relationship has been documented in longitudinal studies like the ones discussed earlier. Another notable study is the federal High School and Beyond (HS&B) study, a project that was conducted as part of the larger NELS '88 research. HS&B followed a nationally stratified cohort of 30,030 students from 1,015 schools who were sophomores in 1980 through the end of the study in 1992. One aspect of the study included the examination of dropout rates. Among the cohort, researchers found that whereas the overall rate of dropout was 12.4%, the dropout rate jumped to 27.2% for retainees—leading the researchers to assert that retainees were twice as likely to drop out as students who were never retained (Barro & Kolstad, 1987). They also evaluated age in grade level and its correlation to dropping out. The modal age for entering ninth graders is 14.5 years, and, in this study, students entering at age 15 to 15.25 were twice as likely to subsequently drop out of high school. The figures are even more striking for those students entering at age 15.5 or above—the expected age for those who have been retained once in their educational career. These students were found to be three times as likely to drop out before completing high school (Barro & Kolstad, 1987), and these calculations remained consistent across gender and ethnicity groups.

Adult Outcomes

The groups from the Minnesota Mother–Child Interaction Project were again examined at the age of 21 (Jimerson, 1999). In addition to the continuation of academic and adjustment paths identified in the 1997 study, education and employment outcomes were also studied. Retainees were most likely to drop out of school (69%) compared to the low-achieving, nonretained group (46%) and the control group (29%) and were the least likely of the three groups to pursue postsecondary schooling. Furthermore, their average hourly pay at the age of 20 was adversely affected: Retainees averaged $6.59, versus $8.42 and $8.57 for the low-achieving and control groups, respectively, and these differences were statistically significant. Indeed, the comparison (low-achieving nonretained) group was found to be statistically similar to the control group on measures of postsecondary enrollment and employment, including "employment competence (stability, quality, commitment, and status of employment)" (Jimerson, 1999, p. 262).

The postschool outcomes for the retained students should be considered cautionary. An older study of adults who had been retained in school revealed that they were more likely to be incarcerated, abuse drugs and alcohol, and receive welfare than those that were never retained (Royce, Darlington, & Murray, 1983). Jimerson (1999) suggested that when students are retained in the early grades, a trajectory of likely negative outcomes is triggered, and that "numerous factors conspire toward its continuation" (p. 248). Nevertheless, other factors, such as the behavioral and social adjustment differences noted early in the lives of the Minnesota children, could also contribute to this trajectory.

The evidence gathered in the last 30 years on the practice of retention suggests that it is academically ineffective and is potentially detrimental to children's social and emotional health. The seeds of failure may be sown early for students who are retained, as they are significantly more likely to drop out of high school. Furthermore, the trajectory of adverse outcomes appears to continue into young adulthood, when wages and postsecondary educational opportunities are depressed.

Is Social Promotion the Answer?

In 1983, the National Commission on Excellence in Education released its report, *A Nation at Risk,* which reported on the quality of teaching and learning in America's schools. The report described a "rising tide of mediocrity" (p. 2) and charged educators and legislators with improving America's schools through the establishment of standards of learning.

No other educational reform in the last decade has changed the face of education like the standards movement. Forty-nine of the nation's 50 states have adopted academic content and performance standards in an effort to articulate exactly what is expected of public school students (Iowa remains the only state without a standards document). The algorithm of establishing standards in education is so deeply ingrained that in recent years, standards have also emerged for teachers (National Board for Professional Teaching Standards), administrators (Principal Leadership Standards of Excellence), paraprofessionals (Paraprofessional and School-Related Personnel Standards), and parent involvement (National Parent–Teacher Association). Clearly, the use of standards as a vehicle to communicate expectations to educators has become a standard itself.

The practice of *social promotion*—advancing a student to the next grade level when she or he has not mastered all of the content for the previous grade—has come under attack as a practice that dilutes the excellence of learning available in the public school system. Social promotion had been a popular practice through the 1970s (Kelly, 1999) and was now reconstrued as a by-product of the "soft-headed, open education, child-centered curriculum" of the era (Shepard & Smith, 1989, p. 1). By the mid-1980s, public opinion polls indicated that the general public felt strongly (72%) that promotion to the next grade level should be contingent on mastery of grade-level requirements (Shepard & Smith, 1989).

States and districts quickly responded and began instituting strict retention policies to make social promotion much more unlikely. The widely touted Promotional Gates Program was created in New York City in the 1980s as a mandatory end to social promotion. Competency levels were established, and students who did not pass were sent to special classes with an enrollment cap of 20, specially trained teachers, and new materials (House, 1989). The program was disbanded after 2 years because the $40 million dollar cost yielded no appreciable achievement gains (House, 1989). Despite the failure of this program, modified versions of it have been recreated in Chicago (Chicago Panel on School Policy, 2001); Washington, DC; Milwaukee; Denver; Long Beach (Kelly, 1999); and San Diego (San Diego Unified School District, 2001). Programs such as these have been criticized as being more about public relations than about scholarship (House, 1989). Meanwhile, the political rhetoric surrounding social promotion increased in the 1990s, and social promotion was even mentioned in the 1998 State of the Union Address: "When we promote a child from grade to grade who hasn't mastered the work, we don't do that child any favors. It is time to end social promotion" (Clinton, 1998). This renewed attention to social promotion prompted 17 states to create specific policies banning social promotion as an option (Thomas, 2000).

Although the practice of social promotion has been the subject of debate in and out of educational circles, the research on low-achieving children who are socially promoted to the next grade level is sparse. No data on social promotion are kept by states, and the U.S. Department of Education (1999) has described social promotion as "a hidden problem" (p. 6). Social promotion is commonly viewed as half of a bimodal choice, with retention being the only other option. Therefore, much of the research on social promotion is indirect and confined to the comparison groups of large studies on retention. The results of achievement measures by the comparison groups can be extrapolated to provide some evidence of the effect of social promotion. For example, Holmes (1989) performed a meta-analysis of 63 studies that included a low-achieving, nonretained subgroup in the research design. He reported that retained students averaged 0.33 standard deviations below their socially promoted peers on measures of academic achievement and personal adjustment.

Furthermore, he asserted that these findings were limited because, in these studies, the socially promoted groups did not receive any remediation. Similarly, Reynolds (1992) found that at the end of fourth grade, a socially promoted subgroup had gains of 8 months in reading and 7 months in math over their similarly achieving but retained peers, despite receiving no additional intervention. Important to note, the retained students performed below the socially promoted group even though they had an extra year of schooling. These findings have not been supported by other, smaller studies that reported no achievement differences between retained and socially promoted students (Johnson et al., 1990; Westbury, 1994). It is important to note that the Johnson et al. study employed a research design that favored social promotion because it did not use a matched sample but, rather, compared retained and nonretained students. In a study of 74 third through sixth graders, Pierson and Connell (1992) found no differences between retained and socially promoted students in self-worth, cognitive competence, and effort, although they did find that retained students outperformed their promoted peers in academic performance. . . .

The research on the effectiveness of social promotion has been thin, and the extrapolated results show limited benefits to the practice. A phase of high accountability coupled with content and performance standards has made social promotion a thorn in the side of administrators and educators who are attempting to raise achievement through higher expectations for all learners. Therefore, the practice and policy of retaining low-performing children has been used as an alternative to promoting students who have not met competency standards.

Voluntary Retention— "Academic Redshirting"

Prevalence

Whereas social promotion and retention continue to occur at alarming levels nationally, late kindergarten enrollment has emerged among parents and educators seeking to mitigate the harmful effects of either practice. Over the last decade, many young children have been enrolled a year or more after their fifth birthday in the hope of giving them an opportunity to develop early literacy behaviors. In 1995, 9% of all first and second graders had experienced delayed entry into kindergarten, according to the National Household Education Survey (Zill, Loomis, & West, 1997). The parents of these children typically cite one of two reasons for doing so—either the child's birthday occurs late in the year (July through December), making him or her younger than peers, or the child has exhibited less mature behavior (academic or social) than others of the same age. In both cases, the parents hope that their child will benefit from another year of growth and development before entering school. In some instances, the parents may be reluctant to admit that there may be a competitive component to the decision—a hope that their child's physical, emotional, and academic growth may give him or her a comparative advantage over classmates who may be up to a year younger (Kagan, 1990). For this reason, the purposeful delay of entry into kindergarten to improve future performance is sometimes called "academic redshirting," after the practice of benching college athletes for a year to allow them additional time to refine their skills and build physical prowess. The use of delayed kindergarten entry is so popular that a survey of state education officials estimated that between 10% and 50% of children experience delayed kindergarten enrollment (Gnezda, Garduque, & Schultz, 1991). Although the 50% figure represents an extreme, it is notable as an example of the "groupthink" that can emerge in a community.

The prevalence of academic redshirting is often ascribed to predominantly middle-class, White, suburban communities. Indeed, there is some evidence that children from higher income households are more likely to experience delayed kindergarten entry (Cosden, Zimmer, & Tuss, 1993). Delaying enrollment in school can be burdensome for many families, for school attendance represents childcare as well as education. For some families, this means that the primary caregiver can return to paid employment. The economic impact of keeping a child and the caregiver home an additional year may be prohibitive, and, therefore, lower income families are less likely to delay enrollment (Gredler, 1992).

The socioeconomic status of the family can also play a subtle role in determining whether the child has had preschool experience. A study of a school readiness instrument in Georgia revealed that students who had attended a preschool had higher scores on the instrument, regardless of the type of preschool program (Taylor, Gibbs, & Slate, 2000). Studies over the past 3 decades have found that preschool experience is positively correlated to kindergarten readiness (Gullo & Burton, 1992; Osterlind, 1980–1981). Access to high-quality preschool education has been identified as critical for later school success among children from low-income households (Bruner, 1960; Snow, Burns, & Griffin, 1998). Despite nearly 40 years of research on the importance of affordable preschool education for children of low-income families, the availability of preschool education is variable. Dickinson and Sprague (2001) quoted a Children's Defense Fund study reporting that only 42% of children from households with incomes under $15,000 annually were enrolled in preschool, compared with 65% of children whose parents earned more than $50,000.

However, other studies have found a stronger correlation of delayed enrollment with gender and ethnicity than with wealth or parent educational levels. The National Household Education Survey in both 1993 and 1995 found no correlation with income or education level, although the 1991 survey did (Zill et al., 1997). They found a far stronger correlation to gender—11% of all boys experienced delayed enrollment, compared to 6% of girls, $\beta = .57$, $p < .01$. Furthermore, the child's ethnicity was also a predictor, with White, non-Hispanic children more likely to be academically redshirted than African American children, $\beta = .50$, $p < .05$. However, Graue and DiPerna's (2000) study of the enrollment data of 8,000 Wisconsin students found somewhat different results. As in Zill et al.'s study, boys constituted the majority of kindergarten redshirts; however, the likelihood of delaying entry for these students seemed more closely tied to summer birthdays that fell just before the cutoff date for enrollment (Graue & DiPerna, 2000).

The data yielded by these surveys are valuable for describing the characteristics of children who experience delayed entry into kindergarten across the nation. However, other researchers studying the impact of readiness tests for kindergarten enrollment have presented different results regarding ethnicity. In many communities, these developmental screenings are administered to all incoming kindergartners, and the parents of those children not scoring high enough are counseled into forgoing enrollment for a year (Meisels, 1999). Many of these "less ready" children come from low-income African American and Hispanic households (Bredekamp & Shepard, 1989; Kagan, 1990). . . .

Kindergarten Readiness Tests

Most of the instruments used for kindergarten readiness are developmental inventories that assess an array of academic, social, and motor behaviors. Skills that are frequently targeted for measurement include the ability to recite one's own name, point to shapes and colors, count, stand on one foot, and tell a story (Lamberty & Crnic, 1994). These developmental screenings are often administered during so-called "kindergarten round-ups"—large meetings where parents have their children tested and registered for the upcoming school year. The predictive validity of such instruments has been called into question (Dever & Barta, 2001; Ellwein, Walsh, & Eads, 1991). Despite position statements from the American Academy of Pediatrics (1995) and the National Association for the Education of Young Children (1990) against the practice of using screening tests to make decisions about kindergarten entrance, it is estimated that one third of all states require such screenings (Cannella & Reiff, 1989). One of the most widely used instruments, the *Gesell Preschool Test,* has been found to be unreliable (Meisels, 1987). A meta-analysis of 60 studies of preschool screening results and their correlation to later student performance found only a small effect size ($r = .27$, or 10% of the variance) on social and behavioral domains, and a moderate effect size ($r = .49$, or 25% of the variance) for academic outcomes (La Paro & Pianta, 2000). The authors noted that "factors other than the child's skills (even in the same domain) account for the majority of the variability in academic/cognitive and social/behavioral performance in the early grades" (p. 475). Despite evidence of questionable results from these screenings and their impact on enrollment for African American and Hispanic children, they remain in wide use across the country.

It does not appear that what the Gesell Institute has called "the gift of time"—delayed enrollment—has meaningful positive effects. A comparison study of 314 second graders who had either been retained or experienced delayed enrollment found no significant differences in academic performance (Kundert, May, & Brent, 1995). It is because of results such as these that some critics have described academic redshirting as another form of retention.

A disturbing trend in the growing prevalence of delayed enrollment is its impact on the classroom environment. Undeniably, kindergarten expectations have altered considerably from the days when this first school experience was built around socialization and play experiences. Today's kindergartner encounters a far more academically rigorous experience than his or her parents did (Bracey, 2000). But the presence of older students may be influencing this trend as well. Some educators have charged that the "graying of the kindergarten" has resulted in higher teacher expectations for *all* students, including those who enrolled when first eligible (Meisels, 1992; Shepard & Smith, 1988). Graue and DiPerna (2000) reported that one of the Wisconsin school districts they studied had a redshirt rate of 94%—admittedly an extreme example, but a telling example of how a community can shift expectations for kindergarten without ever enacting a policy. Another concern is the de facto elimination of the natural diversity of the classroom. A homogenization occurs when certain groups of children—predominantly boys, children with later birthdays, or children with low readiness scores—are held out of kindergarten. Savvy parents understand this trend toward increasingly higher academic demands. Evelyn Vuko, education columnist for the *Washington Post,* held an online chat in February 2002 with parents of young children. Nearly 45% of the questions concerned kindergarten enrollment age (Vuko, 2002). Puzzled parents have begun to describe these conversations as the "begindergarten dilemma."

Recommendations: A Call for New Research

The failure of children in the primary grades has caused widespread concern among parents, educators, and researchers, even as enormous financial resources are allocated each year to educating these children. Social promotion—the practice of advancing a low-achieving child to the next grade in the hope he or she will "catch up"—has grown less acceptable to policymakers, even as the few studies conducted have shown little harm resulting from the practice. The growing disdain for social promotion seems to be fueled by political rhetoric rather than by documented student outcomes. Although research on in-grade retention of students who have failed academically (and often socially) is more prevalent, unanswered questions remain. What is clear is that students who have been retained are more likely to be boys, African American, and poor. Retainees are more likely to drop out of school, work at lower paying jobs, suffer from substance abuse problems, and spend time in jail. Despite these dire outcomes, the rates of retention have continued to rise the past decade.

Given the elimination of social promotion policies in many states and the negative outcomes of retention, parents of young children are increasingly opting for a third choice—delayed entry into kindergarten. This practice is associated with more affluent parents, who are not dependent on public school enrollment for childcare. However, as with retention, boys are more likely to be academically redshirted, as are children with late birthdays. It appears that kindergarten screening tests may be a factor in delayed enrollment. These screening instruments, which have been criticized by some researchers as lacking in predictive validity, do not favor students from low-income families. The practice of voluntary retention has resulted in a demographic aging of the kindergarten classroom. In some communities, nearly 50% of entering kindergarten students may be 6 years old on the first day of school (Vuko, 2002), causing some researchers to speculate about the effect on teacher expectations for kindergarten students.

Given the rapid increase in mandatory retention policies and the rising incidence of voluntary retention by parents, the field is in need of a new generation of studies that focus on the effectiveness of these practices. Educators are asking the following questions about effective interventions:

- Which students are best served by retention? Are there students for whom retention should not be considered?
- What are the long-term effects of retention and social promotion over the course of a child's academic career?
- Is social promotion effective for students? Under what circumstances might it be effective?
- Is delayed kindergarten enrollment changing the composition of the kindergarten classroom? Is this resulting in a change in expectations?
- Do children benefit from voluntary retention to delay kindergarten enrollment?
- How do children with disabilities respond to retention, social promotion, and delayed enrollment?
- Which early and ongoing interventions must accompany any of these practices?

These questions are perhaps best answered by the use of some of the methods employed in the Chicago and Minnesota studies. Large-scale, well-matched studies of children possessing a variety of skills and challenges could answer these questions. The aforementioned studies have contributed greatly to our knowledge of these practices. However, children with disabilities and students from a variety of socioeconomic backgrounds have not been studied as closely.

A limitation of this review is that it has not discussed early reading achievement. The body of research on reading acquisition and intervention is sufficiently large to warrant a separate review. It would be useful to the knowledge base to examine factors related to reading and intervention for students who fail to achieve using the lens of retention and promotion. For example, the work of Vellutino and Scanlon (2001) is promising in its emphasis on early intervention to prevent retention.

Retention, social promotion, and academic redshirting have, at one time or another, been called "the gift of time." Perhaps it is time to redefine this cliché. Perhaps the true "gift of time" is in the work of the educational researchers who can answer the questions of teachers, administrators, and parents.

References

Abidin, R. R., Golladay, W. M., & Howerton, A. L. (1971). Elementary school retention: An unjustifiable, discriminatory, and noxious policy. *Journal of School Psychology, 9,* 410–414.

Alexander, K. L., Entwisle, D. R., & Dauber, S. L. (1994). *On the success of failure: A reassessment of the effects of retention in the primary grades.* New York: Cambridge University Press.

American Academy of Pediatrics. (1995). The inappropriate use of school "readiness" tests. *Pediatrics, 95,* 437–438.

Ayres, L. P. (1909). *Laggards in our schools: A study of retardation and elimination in city school systems.* Philadelphia: Russell Sage.

Barro, S. M., & Kolstad, A. J. (1987). *Who drops out of high school? Findings from high school and beyond* (Technical Report no. CS 87–397c). . . .

Binet, A. (1969). *The experimental psychology of Alfred Binet: Selected papers* (R. H. Pollack & M. J. Brenner, Trans.). New York: Springer.

Binet, A., & Simon, T. (1916). *The development of intelligence in children: The Binet-Simon scale.* Baltimore: Williams and Wilkins.

Bracey, G. W. (2000). A children's garden no more. *Phi Delta Kappan, 81,* 712–713.

Bredekamp, S., & Shepard, L. (1989). How best to protect children from inappropriate school expectations, practices, and policies. *Young Children, 44*(3), 14–24.

Bruner, J. (1960). *The process of education.* Cambridge, MA: Harvard University Press.

Bureau of the Census. (1995). *Current population survey.* Washington, DC: Author.

Byrnes, D. A. (1989). Attitudes of students, parents, and educators toward repeating a grade. In L. A. Shepard & M. L. Smith (Eds.), *Flunking grades: Research and policies on retention* (pp. 108–131). New York: Falmer Press.

Byrnes, D., & Yamamoto, K. (1985). Academic retention: A look inside. *Education, 106,* 208–214.

Cannella, G. S., & Reiff, J. C. (1989). Mandating early childhood entrance/retention assessment: Practices in the United States. *Child Study Journal, 19*(2), 83–99.

Chicago Panel on School Policy. (2001). *Initiatives status report: Transition centers.* . . .

Children's Defense Fund. (2003). *Prekindergarten initiatives: Efforts to help children enter school ready to succeed.* . . .

Clinton, W. (1998). *1998 State of the union address: Full text.* . . .

Cosden, M., Zimmer, J., & Tuss, P. (1993). The impact of age, sex, and ethnicity on kindergarten entry and retention decisions. *Educational Evaluation and Policy Analysis, 15,* 209–222.

Cunningham, P. M., Hall, D. P., & Defee, M. (1998). Nonability-grouped, multilevel instruction: Eight years later. *The Reading Teacher, 51,* 652–664.

Dauber, S. L., Alexander, K. L., & Entwisle, D. R. (1993). Characteristics of retainees and early precursors of retention in grade: Who is held back? *Merrill-Palmer Quarterly, 39,* 426–433.

Dawson, P. (1998). A primer on student retention: What the research says. *Communique (Milwaukee, WI), 26*(8), 28–30.

Dever, M. T., & Barta, J. (2001). Standardized entrance assessment in kindergarten: A qualitative analysis of the experiences of teachers, administrators, and parents. *Journal of Research in Childhood Education, 15,* 220–233.

Dewey, J. (1998). Experience, knowledge, and value: A rejoinder. In J. A. Boydston (Ed.), *John Dewey: The later works, 1925–1953* (Vol. 15, pp. 3–90). Carbondale: Southern Illinois University Press (Original work published 1939).

Dickinson, D. K., & Sprague, K. E. (2001). The nature and impact of early childhood care environments on the language and literacy development of children from low-income families. In S. B. Neuman & D. K. Dickinson (Eds.), *Handbook of early literacy research* (pp. 263–280). New York: Guilford.

Ellwein, M. C., Walsh, D. J., & Eads, G. M., II. (1991). Using readiness tests to rout kindergarten students: The snarled intersection of psychometrics, policy, and practice. *Educational Evaluation and Policy Analysis, 13,* 159–175.

Gates, A. I., & Pritchard, M. C. (1942). *Teaching reading to slow-learning pupils: A report on an experiment in New York City public school 500 (Speyer School).* New York: Columbia University.

Gastright, J. F. (1989, March). *The nation reacts: A survey of promotion/retention rates in 40 urban school districts.* Paper presented at the annual meeting of the American Educational Research Association, San Francisco, CA. (ERIC Document Reproduction Service No. ED307–714)

Gnezda, M. T., Garduque, L., & Schultz, T. (1991). *Improving instruction and assessment in early childhood education.* Washington, DC: National Academy Press.

Gould, S. J. (1996). *The mismeasure of man.* New York: Norton.

Graue, M. E., & DiPerna, J. (2000). Redshirting and early retention: Who gets the "gift of time" and what are its outcomes? *American Educational Research Journal, 37,* 509–534.

Gredler, G. (1992). *School readiness: Assessment and educational issues.* Brandon, VT: Clinical Psychology.

Gullo, D. F., & Burton, C. B. (1992). Age of entry, preschool experience, and sex as antecedents of academic readiness in kindergarten. *Early Childhood Research Quarterly, 7,* 175–186.

Gurewitz, S., & Kramer, J. (1995). Retention across elementary schools in a midwestern school district. *Research in the Schools, 2*(2), 15–21.

Hagborg, W. J., Masella, G., Palladino, P., & Shepardson, J. (1991). A follow-up study of high school students with a history of grade retention. *Psychology in the Schools, 28,* 310–317.

Haney, W. (2001, January). *Revisiting the myth of the Texas miracle in education: Lessons about dropout research and dropout prevention.* Paper presented at the Dropout Research Conference, Cambridge, MA.

Hofstadter, R. (1955). *Social Darwinism in American thought* (rev. ed.). Boston: Beacon Press.

Holmes, C. T. (1989). Grade level retention effects: A meta-analysis of research studies. In L. A. Shepard & M. L. Smith (Eds.), *Flunking grades: Research and policies on retention* (pp. 16–33). New York: Falmer Press.

Holmes, C. T., & Matthews, K. M. (1984). The effects of nonpromotion on elementary and junior high school pupils: A meta-analysis. *Review of Educational Research, 54,* 225–236.

Holmes, C. T., & Saturday, J. (2000). Promoting the end to retention. *Journal of Curriculum and Supervision, 15,* 300–314.

House, E. R. (1989). Policy implications of retention research. In L. A. Shepard & M. L. Smith (Eds.), *Flunking grades: Research and policies on retention* (pp. 202–213). New York: Falmer Press.

Jackson, G. B. (1975). The research evidence on the effect of grade retention. *Review of Educational Research, 45,* 438–460.

James, W. (1899). *Talks to teachers on psychology: And to students on some of life's ideals.* New York: Henry Holt.

Jimerson, S. R. (1999). On the failure of failure: Examining the association between early grade retention and education and employment outcomes during late adolescence. *Journal of School Psychology, 37,* 243–272.

Jimerson, S., Carlson, E., Rotert, M., Egeland, B., & Sroufe, L. A. (1997). A prospective, longitudinal study of the correlates and consequences of early grade retention. *Journal of School Psychology, 35,* 3–25.

Jimerson, S. R., & Schuder, M. R. (1996). *Is grade retention an appropriate academic intervention? Longitudinal data provide further insights.* Paper presented at the Head Start National Research Conference, Washington, DC.

Johnson, E. R., Merrell, K. W., & Stover, L. (1990). The effects of early grade retention on the academic achievement of fourth-grade students. *Psychology in the Schools, 27,* 333–338.

Kagan, S. L. (1990). Readiness 2000: Rethinking rhetoric and responsibility. *Phi Delta Kappan, 72,* 272–279.

Karweit, N. L. (1999). *Grade retention: Prevalence, timing, and effects.* Technical Report, Center for Research on the Education of Students Placed at Risk. Baltimore: Johns Hopkins University.

Kelly, K. (1999, January–February). Retention vs. promotion: Schools search for alternatives. *Harvard Education Letter Research Online.* . . .

Kundert, D. K., May, D. C., & Brent, R. (1995). A comparison of students who delay kindergarten entry and those who are retained in grades K–5. *Psychology in the Schools, 32,* 202–209.

Lamberty, G., & Crnic, K. (1994). School readiness conference: Recommendations. *Early Education and Development, 5,* 165–176.

La Paro, K. M., & Pianta, R. C. (2000). Predicting children's competence in the early school years: A meta-analytic review. *Review of Educational Research, 70,* 443–484.

Lapp, D., Fisher, D., Flood, J., & Moore, K. (2002). "I don't want to teach it wrong": An investigation of the role families believe they should play in the early literacy development of their children. In D. L. Schallert, C. M. Fairbanks, J. Worthy, & B. Maloch, & J. V. Hoffman, (Eds.), *National Reading Conference Yearbook, 51* (pp. 275–286). Oak Creek, WI: National Reading Conference.

McCoy, A. R., & Reynolds, A. J. (1999). Grade retention and performance: An extended investigation. *Journal of School Psychology, 37,* 273–298.

McMillen, M., & Kaufman, P. (1993). *Dropout rates in the United States: 1993* (NCES Rep. No. 90–659). Washington, DC: U.S. Department of Education, National Center for Education Statistics.

Meisels, S. J. (1987). Uses and abuses of developmental screening and school readiness testing. *Young Children, 42*(2), 4–6.

Meisels, S. J. (1992). Doing harm by doing good: Iatrogenic effects of early childhood enrollment and promotion policies. *Early Childhood Research Quarterly, 7,* 155–174.

Meisels, S. J. (1999). Assessing readiness. In R. C. Pianta & M. Cox (Eds.), *The transition to kindergarten: Research, policy, training, and practice* (pp. 39–66). Baltimore: Brookes.

Meisels, S. J., & Liaw, F. (1993). Failure in grade: Do retained students catch up? *The Journal of Educational Research, 87,* 69–77.

Miedel, W. T., & Reynolds, A. J. (1998). Parent involvement in early intervention for disadvantaged children: Does it matter? *Journal of School Psychology, 37,* 379–402.

Monaghan, E. J., & Barry, A. L. (1999). *Writing the past: Teaching reading in colonial America and the United States 1640–1940.* Newark, DE: International Reading Association.

Mondale, S., & Patton, S. B. (2001). *School: The story of American public education.* Boston: Beacon Press.

Morris, D. R. (2001). Assessing the implementation of high-stakes reform: Aggregate relationships between retention rates and test results. *NASSP Bulletin, 85,* 18–34.

National Association for the Education of Young Children. (1990). *Guidelines for appropriate curriculum content and assessment in programs serving children ages 3 through 8. . . .*

National Commission on Excellence in Education. (1983). *A nation at risk: The imperative for educational reform.* Washington, DC: Author.

Osterlind, S. J. (1980–1981). Preschool impact on children: Its sustaining effects into kindergarten. *Educational Research Quarterly, 5*(4), 21–30.

Pierson, L. H., & Connell, J. P. (1992). Effect of grade retention on self-system processes, school engagement, and academic performance. *Journal of Educational Psychology, 84,* 300–307.

Pulliam, J. D., & Van Patten, J. (1995). *History of education in America* (6th ed.). Englewood Cliffs, NJ: Merrill.

Resnick, M. D., Bearman, P. S., Blum, R. W., Bauman, K. E., Harris, K. M., Jones, J., et al. (1997). Protecting adolescents from harm: Findings from the national longitudinal study on adolescent health. *Journal of the American Medical Association, 278,* 823–832.

Reynolds, A. J. (1992). Mediated effects of preschool intervention. *Early Education and Development, 3,* 139–164.

Roderick, M. R. (1995). Grade retention and school dropouts: Investigating the association. *American Educational Research Journal, 31,* 729–759.

Royce, J., Darlington, R., & Murray, H. (1983). Pooled analyses: Findings across studies. In the Consortium for Longitudinal Studies (Eds.), *As the twig is bent: Lasting effects of preschool programs* (pp. 411–459). Hillsdale, NJ: Erlbaum.

Rumberger, R. W. (1987). High school dropouts: A review of issues and evidence. *American Educational Research Journal, 32,* 101–121.

Rumberger, R. (1995). Dropping out of middle school: A multilevel analysis of students and schools. *American Educational Research Journal, 32,* 583–625.

Rush, S., & Vitale, P. A. (1994). Analysis for determining factors that place elementary students at risk. *The Journal of Educational Research, 87,* 325–333.

San Diego Unified School District. (2001, March). *The blueprint for student success: Expanded strategies for prevention, intervention, and retention.* San Diego, CA: Author.

Shepard, L. A., & Smith, M. L. (1988). Escalating academic demand in kindergarten: Counterproductive policies. *Elementary School Journal, 89,* 135–145.

Shepard, L. A., & Smith, M. L. (1989). *Flunking grades: Research and policies on retention.* London: Falmer Press.

Snow, C. E., Burns, S. M., & Griffin, P. (1998). *Preventing reading difficulties in young children.* Washington, DC: National Academy Press.

Southern Regional Education Board. (2001). *Finding alternatives to failure: Can states end social promotion and reduce retention rates?* (SREB Rep. No. 00H03). Atlanta, GA: Author.

Taylor, K. K., Gibbs, A. S., & Slate, J. R. (2000). Preschool attendance and kindergarten readiness. *Early Childhood Education Journal, 27,* 191–195.

Thomas, V. G. (2000). Ending social promotion: Help or hindrance? *Kappa Delta Pi Record, 37*(1), 30–32.

U.S. Department of Education. (1999). *Taking responsibility for ending social promotion: A guide for educators and state and local leaders.* Washington, DC: Author.

Vellutino, F. R., & Scanlon, D. M. (2001). Emergent literacy skills, early instruction, and individual differences as determinants of difficulties in learning to read: The case for early intervention. In S. B. Neuman & D. K. Dickinson (Eds.), *Handbook of early literacy research* (pp. 295–321). New York: Guilford.

Vuko, E. (2002, February 12). *Teachers say. . . .*

Wechsler, D. (1997). *Wechsler adult intelligence scale* (3rd ed.). San Antonio, TX: Harcourt Assessment.

Westbury, M. (1994). The effect of elementary grade retention on subsequent school achievement and ability. *Canadian Journal of Education, 19,* 241–250.

Wheat, H. G. (1923). *The teaching of reading: A textbook of principles and methods.* Boston: Ginn.

Zill, N., Loomis, L. S., & West, J. (1997). *The elementary school performance and adjustment of children who enter kindergarten late or repeat kindergarten: Findings from the National Surveys.* Washington, DC: Office of Educational Research and Improvement.

POSTSCRIPT

Should Struggling Students Be Retained?

With the demand for increased accountability, state and local district policymakers are mandating retention if required promotion benchmarks are not met. At the same time, professional opinion informed by research studies warn that the consequences of retention are not benign but can be detrimental. Discerning who is "right" or what the most effective course of action should be from a policy perspective but also for an individual struggling student remains a challenge with no clear or definitive answer. What inferences can be reasonably made when summaries of the same research findings reach different conclusions?

For starters, there are critical voices of the research by educational researchers themselves pointing out some of the shortcomings. One important observation made by Lorence and Dworkin, for example, highlights that almost all of the retention research is based on teacher-initiated judgment but contemporary criteria are largely based on standardized test scores. How this difference in decision making will affect outcomes is not well understood. Another important caveat, often ignored, is that retention impact may be very grade specific. There likely are very real differences between primary and secondary retention policy outcomes. A third issue concerns the possible reasons for retention in the first place. Educational improvement (or lack thereof) during a retained year will likely vary in relation to the reason the student was retained (academic failure, learning disability, emotional immaturity, behavioral problems) and, in each case, these reasons are likely prognostic. Finally, the nature of the instructional experience that occurs in the repeated year is likely a major explanation for the effect of retention, positive or negative. Repeated exposure to ineffective instruction is unlikely to be beneficial. Or, if a student is in need of enhanced educational assistance but does not receive the necessary support during the repeated grade, there is little reason to expect reasonable gains.

It is especially worth noting that lost in much of the debate and discussion are the needs of children with disabilities. How children with learning and behavioral disabilities respond to retention or social promotion has not been studied extensively. Considering broad policies of accountability with respect to achievement based on standardized testing, there are myriad concerns related to retention and the unique learning needs of student with special education requirements.

Given the potential costs to the student (e.g., negative self-esteem) and society (e.g., dropping out) associated with retention, as reviewed by Lisa

Bowman "Grade Retention: Is it a Help or Hindrance to Student Academic Success" in *Preventing School Failure* (Spring 2005), there should be considerable effort made at the individual but also the policy level to consider the consequences. Not the least of which should focus on pre- and in-service teacher education and preparation with respect to retention policy and practices. There needs to be additional focus on high-quality instruction and the value of progress monitoring to regularly evaluate student progress to help identify early on students in need of additional academic support. For educational researchers the focus needs to shift away from the dichotomy (yes versus no), but, as suggested by Frey, to the range of possible factors that influence outcomes both positive and negative.

For further reading regarding grade failure and its consequences, K. L. Alexander, D. R. Entwhisle, and S. L. Dauber provide an accessible book *On the Success of Failure: A Reassessment of the Effects of Retention in the Primary Grades* (New York: Cambridge University Press, 2003). An early account of policy recommendation against retention can be found in "Elementary School Retention: An Unjustifiable, Discriminatory, and Noxious Educational Policy" by R. P. Abidin, W. M. Golladay, and A. L. Howerton in the *Journal of School Psychology* (vol. 9, 1971). For a very readable collection of research reports and essays on reviewing alternatives to retention and social promotion, see *Moving Beyond Retention and Social Promotion,* edited by E. McCay in Phi Delta Kappa Hot Topic Series (January 2001). Finally, S. Jimerson provides an insightful series of observations in his chapter "Is Grade Retention Educational Malpractice? Empirical Evidence from Meta-Analyses Examining the Efficacy of Grade Retention," found in *Can Unlike Students Learn Together,* edited by H. Walberg, A. J. Reynolds, and M. C. Wang (Information Age Publishing, Inc., 2004).

ISSUE 3

Is Full Inclusion Always the Best Option for Children with Disabilities?

YES: Michael F. Giangreco, from "Extending Inclusive Opportunities," *Educational Leadership* (February 2007)

NO: James M. Kauffman, Kathleen McGee, and Michele Brigham, from "Enabling or Disabling? Observation on Changes in Special Education," *Phi Delta Kappan* (April 2004)

ISSUE SUMMARY

YES: Michael F. Giangreco, who is a professor of education at the University of Vermont, argues that even students with severe disabilities are best served within the "regular" education classroom along with their typically developing peers. He also outlines strategies for achieving inclusion and shows how it creates a classroom that benefits all students, regardless of ability level.

NO: James M. Kauffman, who is a professor at the University of Virginia at Charlottesville, and Kathleen McGee and Michele Brigham, who are both special education teachers, argue that the goal of education for students with disabilities should be to increase their level of competence and independence. They conclude that full inclusion involves "excessive" accommodations that actually become barriers to achieving this goal.

Public Law (P.L.) 94-142, the Education for All Handicapped Children Act (1975), required that all children with disabilities, whatever the nature or severity of their disability, be provided a free and appropriate education within the least restrictive environment possible. Later laws—P.L. 99-457, the 1986 Education of the Handicapped Act, and P.L. 101-476, the 1990 Individuals with Disabilities Education Act (IDEA)—clarified, strengthened, and expanded the 1975 legislation. Before the enactment of these laws, many children with disabilities, especially those with more severe or challenging disabilities, were segregated from their more typically developing peers. Students with disabilities attended special classes in their neighborhood schools, or they attended special schools for the disabled. In either case, they had minimal contact with their typically developing peers. Advocates for people with disabilities argued that a separate education denies children with disabilities the same opportunities afforded everyone else.

Rather than being segregated, many children with disabilities are now placed ("mainstreamed") into the regular classroom on at least a part-time basis. Mainstreaming ensures that students with disabilities have contact with their typically developing peers and the regular education curriculum. In recent years, advocates for people with disabilities have successfully argued that simple physical presence in the regular classroom may not lead to full participation in the classroom's intellectual or social life. Advocates, therefore, have argued that schools must move beyond mainstreaming to full inclusion. Full inclusion refers to placement in the regular classroom with appropriate supports and services—such as an interpreter who signs the teacher's talk for a student with impaired hearing—and includes active efforts to ensure participation in the life of the class. Moreover, it is argued that these supports and services must be tailored to the unique needs of each individual as set forth in the Individual Educational Plan (IEP). The IEP is prepared annually by a multi-disciplinary team composed of, for example, the school psychologist, a special education teacher, the regular classroom teacher, and a speech-language clinician, all of whom assess the student's current level of functioning and set short- and long-term goals for his or her educational progress.

Although full inclusion may be the ideal, school districts have been granted considerable latitude by the courts to make educational placements. For example, the courts have allowed less than full inclusion if a student is unlikely to derive sufficient academic or nonacademic benefit from inclusion, if a student's placement in the regular classroom is likely to be disruptive, or if the cost of inclusion would be prohibitive for the district. As a result of these constraints, many students experience less than full inclusion—some may have "pull-out" classes, which segregate them from their more typically developing peers for part of the school day; others may be segregated for almost their entire school experience.

Often, the issue of inclusion is most heated in the case of students with severe disabilities, and both of the accompanying selections focus largely on such students. In the first selection, Michael F. Giangreco argues that inclusion of students with even severe disabilities is possible and desirable, and he outlines strategies for accomplishing this. These strategies, which he terms the *multilevel curriculum and curriculum overlapping,* entail adapting the content of the curriculum or level of support provided to the student, but doing so within the shared activities of the classroom. In the second selection, James M. Kauffman and his colleagues argue, first, that the goal of education for students with disabilities is to provide them with the skills needed to increase their independence and bring them as close as possible in terms of functioning to their "mainstream" peers. They then argue that inclusion, with its emphasis on accommodation, thwarts this goal by actually increasing dependence on special assistance, reinforcing maladaptive behaviors, and failing to "push" students to acquire new skills.

YES

Michael F. Giangreco

Extending Inclusive Opportunities

Ms. Santos,[1] a 5th grade teacher, had successfully included students with learning disabilities or physical limitations in her classroom for years. Even in years when none of her students had been identified as having disabilities, her students' abilities and needs had varied, sometimes substantially. She regularly taught students whose native languages were not English and students who displayed challenging behaviors or fragile emotional health. The range of her students' reading abilities typically spanned several years.

Ms. Santos had confidently made *instructional* accommodations for all her students, for example, by modifying materials and giving individualized cues— but she had rarely needed to modify her curriculum. Students with and without disabilities in her class worked on the same topics, although sometimes at differing levels and paces. But when a boy who worked far below 5th grade level was assigned to her class, Ms. Santos faced a question that looms large for teachers trying to make inclusion work: How can we achieve true curricular inclusion for students who function substantially below grade level?

Facing a New Challenge

Last school year, Ms. Santos welcomed Chris into her 5th grade class. A boy new to the school, Chris had a good sense of humor, liked many kinds of music, and had a history of making friends and liking school. Unfortunately, in the eyes of most people, these qualities were overshadowed by the severity of his intellectual, behavioral, sensory, and physical disabilities. Because Chris came to her class functioning at a kindergarten or prekindergarten level in all academic areas, Ms. Santos had trouble conceiving of how he could learn well in a 5th grade class, and she worried about what Chris's parents and her colleagues would expect. By suggesting how a teacher might handle this kind of situation, I hope to assist teachers and other professionals who are attempting to successfully include students with significant disabilities within mainstream classrooms.

Extending Student Participation

The Individuals with Disabilities Education Improvement Act of 2004 presumes that the first placement option a school system must consider for each student with a disability, regardless of disability category or severity, is the regular classroom. Students with disabilities are entitled to supplemental supports that enable them to meaningfully pursue individually determined learning outcomes—including those from the general education curriculum. The question to be asked is not whether a student is able to pursue the same learning outcomes as his or her age-level peers, but whether that student's needs can be appropriately addressed in the general education setting.

The participation of students with disabilities within general education classes can be broadly characterized along two dimensions: each student's *program* (such as the goals of the student's individualized education program) and each student's *supports*. Supports are anything that the school provides to help the student pursue education goals—for example materials, adaptations, or a classroom aide (Giangreco, 2006).

Within a school day, or even within a single activity, an individual student will sometimes require modifications to the general education program and at other times be able to work within the standard program. Likewise, the number of supports teachers will need to provide for students will fluctuate greatly. In some scenarios, a student with a disability can do the same academic work his or her classmates are doing. These kinds of opportunities help teachers and students interact in a natural way, show classmates that students with learning needs don't always need special help, and allow students to avoid unnecessary supports.

Setting the Stage for Curricular Modifications

Chris was fortunate that he was assigned a teacher who already had good practices in place for including students with IEPs. Ms. Santos created opportunities for many types of instructional interactions through a busy classroom schedule of inquiry-based activities. Her ability to teach students with disabilities grew out of her belief that the core of teaching and learning was the same, regardless of whether a student had a disability label.

Although Ms. Santos was not sure how to meet the challenge of including Chris in her classroom, she asked important questions to clarify her own role as a team member, understand the curricular expectations for Chris, and get a vision for how to teach a class with a wider mix of abilities than she had encountered before. As part of that vision, she drew on the power of relationships, both in drawing Chris into her plans for students and in building a collaborative team of special educators, parents, and others. In her classroom community, she expected students to help one another learn and be responsible for helping the classroom run smoothly. As much as possible, she also planned for Chris to have an active voice in telling his teachers which supports helped him and which did not.

For Chris to be a viable social member of the classroom, he would have to participate in the academic work, not just be physically present or socially accepted. Ms. Santos knew how frustrating and embarrassing it can be for students when curriculum content is over their heads, and she also knew the hazards of underestimating students. She sought ways to adjust the curriculum to an appropriate level of difficulty for Chris, while leaving opportunities for him to surprise her with his capabilities.

When Curriculum Modifications Are Essential

In many inclusion scenarios, such as the one Ms. Santos faced, modifications to the general education program will be essential. Sometimes the student will need individualized content but will not require specialized supports to work with that content. For example, the teacher might assign a student five new vocabulary words instead of 10, or assign that learner single-digit computation instead of decimals.

In some situations, the classroom teacher will need to both modify the general education program and provide individualized supports. Although students with more severe disabilities may often need both program and support accommodation to succeed in a mainstream class, teachers may not need to alter both the curriculum and the types of support available for all classroom work a student with a disability undertakes. Even a student with significant disabilities, like Chris, rarely needs both an individualized education program and individualized supports all the time.

Multilevel Curriculum and Curriculum Overlapping

Multilevel curriculum and *curriculum overlapping* are two approaches to adapting curriculum that facilitate participation of students with significant disabilities. In the multilevel curriculum approach, students with disabilities and their peers participate in a shared activity. Each student has individually appropriate learning outcomes that are within the same curriculum area but that may be at grade level or below (or above) grade level (Campbell, Campbell, Collicott, Perner, & Stone, 1988; Peterson & Hittie, 2003). Students of different ability levels may be working on the same or different subject matter within the same academic area. In curriculum overlapping, students with disabilities and nondisabled peers participate together in an activity, but they pursue learning outcomes from different curriculum areas, including such broadly defined curriculum areas as social skills.

Multilevel Curriculum in Action

Let's go back to Ms. Santos's challenge of including Chris as an academic member of her class and see how she used multilevel curriculum. In class work for a social studies unit, Chris and his classmates studied the Revolutionary War. But Ms. Santos adapted Chris's level of learning outcomes to suit him: His goals were to become familiar with historical people, places, and events, whereas his classmates' goals were to demonstrate knowledge of political and economic factors that led to the war.

To reinforce students' learning, Ms. Santos created a Revolutionary War board game that drew on both the class's grade-appropriate learning goals and Chris's lower-level goals to advance in the game. The game board had colored spaces, and each color a student landed on corresponded to a stack of question cards related to the desired content, with blue cards for historical people, green cards for historical places, and so on. Ms. Santos and a special educator had set aside specially prepared cards for Chris with questions matched to his learning outcomes. The rest of the class drew cards matched to their goals.

Another player read aloud for Chris each question and the multiple-choice answers, which were given both verbally and with images. For example, the question, "What American Revolutionary War hero became the first president of the United States?" might be followed by the labeled images of George Washington and two other famous people. When Chris was learning new content, Ms. Santos made the distracter choices substantially different and included at least one absurd choice (such as George Washington, Abraham Lincoln, and LeBron James). As Chris became more proficient, she used distracter choices that were more difficult to spot. When Chris answered a question correctly, he rolled dice and moved forward. Although this activity focused on social studies, Chris also learned the social skill of taking turns and such math skills as counting.

Curriculum Overlapping in Action

Curriculum overlapping is a vital strategy for classrooms in which there are substantial differences between the learning outcomes most of the students are pursuing and the outcomes a student with a disability is pursuing.

For example, in a human biology unit, a group of four students might assemble a model of the human cardiovascular system. The primary goal of three students is to learn anatomical structures and their functions. The fourth student, who has significant disabilities, shares the activity, but has learning goals within the curriculum area of communications and social skills, such as learning to follow directions, taking turns, or making requests using a communication device.

One way to start planning for curriculum overlapping with a student who has significant disabilities is to make a simple matrix with the student's individually determined learning outcomes down the side and a list of regularly occurring classes or activities across the top. Team members can then identify where they should focus additional energy to ensure meaningful participation.

Ms. Santos and her team did this. They established cross-lesson routines through which Chris's individual learning outcomes could be embedded within many class activities. For example, Chris had a series of learning objectives involving communication and social skills, including matching to a sample; discriminating between different symbols and photos; following one- and two-step instructions; responding to questions; and describing events, objects, or emotions. Ms. Santos routinely embedded these skills in activities and lessons Chris participated in across different content areas as a form of curriculum overlapping.

While pursuing these learning outcomes, Chris might also work with the actual curricular content. For example, in a geography activity Chris might distinguish between maps of European countries, first discriminating between highly different pairs (a map of Italy paired with an image that is not a map); followed by slightly more similar pairs (a map of Greece and a map of China); followed by even more similar pairs (maps of France and Germany).

When first using multilevel curriculum and curriculum overlapping, teams often feel that they don't have enough for their student with a significant disability to do within the typical classroom activities. But as they persist in collaborative planning, seek input directly from the student, and involve classmates in problem solving, they find new opportunities for the student's meaningful participation and learning.

Although multilevel curriculum and curriculum overlapping are primarily ways to include students with disabilities, they also enable more meaningful participation for students functioning above grade level. Applying multilevel curriculum allows teachers to stretch their curriculum away from a "middle zone" in which all students share the same curricular content, level, and amount of work. The practices many people associate with differentiated instruction (Tomlinson, 2001) occur within the boundaries of this middle zone. Multilevel curriculum stretches the concept of differentiated instruction. With curriculum overlapping, the boundaries of curriculum planning expand even further to create effective learning situations for students working both far above and far below their peers.

In the interest of access to the general education curriculum, teachers and teams working with students with disabilities should first consider whether the student can pursue the same learning outcomes as classmates or whether multilevel curriculum and instruction will provide enough accommodation before using curriculum overlapping.

Making It Happen

Implementing either multilevel curriculum and instruction or curriculum overlapping requires time, collaboration, and creativity. But the reward is the authentic inclusion of students who function substantially below grade level. Approaching inclusive education this way contributes to a positive classroom culture, acknowledges differences, promotes acceptance, and provides opportunities for real-life problem solving.

Some claim that inclusion of students with certain disabilities is impossible because in many schools the curriculum is one-size-fits-all and differentiation is minimal or nonexistent. Although it is difficult to include a student with significant disabilities in such classes, this begs the question of whether one-size-fits-all classes are what we want for anyone. Instructional practices such as cooperative learning and differentiated instruction are often beneficial for general education students, too.

Students with disabilities bring educators a challenge to make our teaching practices more inclusive. Meeting the challenge invariably improves the way we teach the broader range of students who don't have disabilities.

References

Campbell, C., Campbell, S., Collicott, J., Perner, D., & Stone, J. (1988). Individualized instruction. *Education New Brunswick*, 3, 17–20.

Giangreco, M. F. (2006). Foundational concepts and practices for educating students with severe disabilities. In M. E. Snell & F. Brown (Eds.), *Instruction of students with severe disabilities* (6th ed., pp. 1–27). Upper Saddle River, NJ: Pearson Education/Prentice-Hall.

Peterson, J. M., & Hittie, M. M. (2003). *Inclusive teaching: Creating effective schools for all learners*. Boston: Allyn and Bacon.

Tomlinson, C. A. (2001). *How to differentiate instruction in mixed-ability classrooms* (2nd ed.). Alexandria, VA: ASCD.

Note

1. Ms. Santos is a composite of teachers I have observed who work with students with severe disabilities.

James M. Kauffman, Kathleen McGee,
and Michele Brigham  **NO**

Enabling or Disabling? Observations on Changes in Special Education

Schools need demanding and distinctive special education that is clearly focused on instruction and habilitation.[1] Abandoning such a conception of special education is a prescription for disaster. But special education has increasingly been losing its way in the single-minded pursuit of full inclusion.

Once, special education's purpose was to bring the performance of students with disabilities closer to that of their nondisabled peers in regular classrooms, to move as many students as possible into the mainstream with appropriate support.[2] For students not in regular education, the goal was to move them toward a more typical setting in a cascade of placement options.[3] But as any good thing can be overdone and ruined by the pursuit of extremes, we see special education suffering from the extremes of inclusion and accommodation.

Aiming for as much normalization as possible gave special education a clear purpose. Some disabilities were seen as easier to remediate than others. Most speech and language disorders, for example, were considered eminently remediable. Other disabilities, such as mental retardation and many physical disabilities, were assumed to be permanent or long-term and so less remediable, but movement *toward* the mainstream and increasing independence from special educators were clear goals.

The emphasis in special education has shifted away from normalization, independence, and competence. The result has been students' dependence on whatever special programs, modifications, and accommodations are possible, particularly in general education settings. The goal seems to have become the *appearance* of normalization without the *expectation* of competence.

Many parents and students seem to want more services as they learn what is available. Some have lost sight of the goal of limiting accommodations in order to challenge students to achieve more independence. At the same time, many special education advocates want all services to be available in mainstream settings, with little or no acknowledgment that the services are atypical. Although teachers, administrators, and guidance counselors are often willing and able to make accommodations, doing so is not always in students' best long-term interests. It gives students with disabilities what anthropologist Robert Edgerton called a cloak—a pretense, a cover, which actually fools no one—rather than actual competence.[4]

From *Phi Delta Kappan*, April 2004, pp. 613–620. Copyright © 2004 by Kappa Delta Pi. Reprinted by permission of Phi Delta Kappan and James M. Kauffman, Kathleen McGee, and Michele Bingham.

In this article, we discuss how changes in attitudes toward disability and special education, placement, and accommodations can perpetuate disability. We also explore the problems of ignoring or perpetuating disability rather than helping students lead fuller, more independent lives. Two examples illustrate how we believe good intentions can go awry—how attempts to accommodate students with disabilities can undermine achievement.

"But he needs resource. . . ." Thomas, a high school sophomore identified as emotionally disturbed, was assigned to a resource class created to help students who had problems with organization or needed extra help with academic skills. One of the requirements in the class was for students to keep a daily planner in which they entered all assignments; they shared their planner with the resource teacher at the beginning of class and discussed what academic subjects would be worked on during that period.

Thomas consistently refused to keep a planner or do any work in resource (he slept instead). So a meeting was set up with the assistant principal, the guidance counselor, Thomas, and the resource teacher. As the meeting was about to begin, the principal announced that he would not stay because Thomas felt intimidated by so many adults. After listening to Thomas' complaints, the guidance counselor decided that Thomas would not have to keep a planner or show it to the resource teacher and that the resource teacher should not talk to him unless Thomas addressed her first. In short, Thomas would not be required to do any work in the class! When the resource teacher suggested that, under those circumstances, Thomas should perhaps be placed in a study hall, because telling the parents that he was in a resource class would be a misrepresentation, the counselor replied, "But he *needs* the resource class."

"He's too bright. . . ." Bob, a high school freshman with Asperger's Syndrome, was scheduled for three honors classes and two Advanced Placement classes. Bob's IEP (individualized education program) included a two-page list of accommodations. In spite of his having achieved A's and B's, with just a single C in math, his mother did not feel that his teachers were accommodating him appropriately. Almost every evening, she e-mailed his teachers and his case manager to request more information or more help for Bob, and she angrily phoned his guidance counselor if she didn't receive a reply by the end of the first hour of the next school day.

A meeting was scheduled with the IEP team, including five of Bob's seven teachers, the county special education supervisor, the guidance counselor, the case manager, the principal, and the county autism specialist. When the accommodations were reviewed, Bob's mother agreed that all of them were being made. However, she explained that Bob had been removed from all outside social activities because he spent all night, every night, working on homework. The accommodation she demanded was that Bob have *no* homework assignments. The autism specialist agreed that this was a reasonable accommodation for a child with Asperger's Syndrome.

The teachers of the honors classes explained that the homework in their classes, which involved elaboration and extension of concepts, was even more essential than the homework assigned in AP classes. In AP classes, by contrast, homework consisted primarily of practice of concepts learned in class. The honors teachers explained that they had carefully broken their long assignments into segments, each having a separate due date before the final project, and they gave illustrations of their expectations. The director of special education explained the legal definition of accommodations (the mother said she'd never before heard that accommodations could not change the nature of the curriculum). The director also suggested that, instead of Bob's sacrificing his social life, perhaps it would be more appropriate for him to take standard classes. What Bob's mother was asking, he concluded, was not legal. She grew angry, but she did agree to give the team a "little more time" to serve Bob appropriately. She said she would "be back with her claws and broomstick" if anyone ever suggested that he be moved from honors classes without being given the no-homework accommodation. "He's too bright to take anything less than honors classes, and if you people would provide this simple accommodation, he would do just fine," she argued. In the end, she got her way.

Attitudes Toward Disability and Special Education

Not that many decades ago, a disability was considered a misfortune—not something to be ashamed of but a generally undesirable, unwelcome condition to be overcome to the greatest extent possible. Ability was considered more desirable than disability, and anything—whether a device or a service—that helped people with disabilities to do what those without disabilities could do was considered generally valuable, desirable, and worth the effort, cost, and possible stigma associated with using it.

The disability rights movement arose in response to the widespread negative attitudes toward disabilities, and it had a number of desirable outcomes. It helped overcome some of the discrimination against people with disabilities. And overcoming such bias and unfairness in everyday life is a great accomplishment. But the movement has also had some unintended negative consequences. One of these is the outright denial of disability in some cases, illustrated by the contention that disability exists only in attitudes or as a function of the social power to coerce.[5]

The argument that disability is merely a "social construction" is particularly vicious in its effects on social justice. Even if we assume that disabilities are socially constructed, what should that mean? Should we assume that socially constructed phenomena are not "real," are not important, or should be discredited? If so, then consider that dignity, civil rights, childhood, social justice, and nearly every other phenomenon that we hold dear are social constructions. Many social constructions are not merely near and dear to us, they are real and useful in benevolent societies. The important question is whether the idea of disability is useful in helping people attain dignity or whether it is more useful to assume that disabilities are not real (i.e., that, like social justice, civil rights, and other social constructions, they are fabrications that can be ignored when convenient). The denial of disability is sometimes expressed as an aversion to labels, so that we are cautioned not to communicate openly and clearly about disabilities but to rely on euphemisms. But this approach is counterproductive. When we are able only to whisper or mime the undesirable difference called disability, then we inadvertently increase its stigma and thwart prevention efforts.[6]

The specious argument that "normal" does not exist—because abilities of every kind are varied and because the point at which normal becomes abnormal is arbitrary—leads to the conclusion that no one actually has a disability or, alternatively, that everyone has a disability. Then, some argue, either no one or everyone is due an accommodation so that no one or everyone is identified as disabled. This unwillingness to draw a line defining something (such as disability, poverty, or childhood) is based either on ignorance regarding the nature of continuous distributions or on a rejection of the unavoidably arbitrary decisions necessary to provide special services to those who need them and, in so doing, to foster social justice.[7]

Another unintended negative consequence of the disability rights movement is that, for some people, disability has become either something that does not matter or something to love, to take pride in, to flaunt, to adopt as a positive aspect of one's identity, or to cherish as something desirable or as a badge of honor. When disability makes no difference to us one way or the other, then we are not going to work to attenuate it, much less prevent it. At best, we will try to accommodate it. When we view disability as a desirable difference, then we are very likely to try to make it more pronounced, not to ameliorate it.

Several decades ago, special education was seen as a good thing—a helpful way of responding to disability, not something everyone needed or should have, but a useful and necessary response to the atypical needs of students with disabilities. This is why the Education for All Handicapped Children Act (now the Individuals with Disabilities Education Act) was written. But in the minds of many people, special education has been transformed from something helpful to something awful.[8]

The full-inclusion movement did have some desirable outcomes. It helped overcome some of the unnecessary removal of students with disabilities from general education. However, the movement also has had some unintended negative consequences. One of these is that special education has come to be viewed in very negative terms, to be seen as a second-class and discriminatory system that does more harm than good. Rather than being seen as helpful, as a way of creating opportunity, special education is often portrayed as a means of shunting students into dead-end programs and killing opportunity.[9]

Another unintended negative consequence of full inclusion is that general education is now seen by many as the *only* place where fair and equitable treatment is possible and where the opportunity to learn is extended to all equally.[10] The argument has become that special education is good only as long as it is invisible (or nearly so), an indistinguishable part of a general education system that accommodates all students, regardless of their abilities or disabilities. Usually, this is described as a "unified" (as opposed to "separate") system of education.[11] Special education is thus something to be avoided altogether or attenuated to the greatest extent possible, regardless of a student's inability to perform in a general setting. When special education is seen as discriminatory, unfair, an opportunity-killing system, or, as one writer put it, "the gold-plated garbage can of American schooling,"[12] then it is understandable that people will loathe it. But this way of looking at special education is like seeing the recognition and treatment of cancer as the cause of the problem.

The reversal in attitudes toward disability and special education—disability from undesirable to inconsequential, special education from desirable to awful—has clouded the picture of what special education is and what it should do for students with disabilities. Little wonder that special education stands accused of failure, that calls for its demise have become vociferous, and that contemporary practices are often more disabling than enabling. An unfortunate outcome of the changing attitudes toward disability and special education is that the benefit of special education is now sometimes seen as freedom from expectations of performance. It is as if we believed that, if a student has to endure the stigma of special education, then the compensation should include an exemption from work.

Placement Issues

Placing all students, regardless of their abilities, in regular classes has exacerbated the tendency to see disability as something existing only in people's minds. It fosters the impression that students are fitting in when they are not able to perform at anywhere near the normal level. It perpetuates disabilities; it does not compensate for them.

Administrators and guidance counselors sometimes place students in programs for which they do not qualify, even as graduation requirements are increasing and tests are mandated. Often, these students' *testing* is modified although their *curriculum* is not. The students may then feel that they have beaten the system. They are taught that the system is unfair and that the only way to win is by gaming it. Hard work and individual responsibility for one's education are often overlooked—or at least undervalued.

Students who consistently fail in a particular curriculum must be given the opportunity to deal with the natural consequences of that fact as a means of learning individual responsibility. For example, social promotion in elementary and middle school teaches students that they really don't have to be able to do the work to pass. Students who have been conditioned to rely on social promotion do not believe that the cycle will end until it does so—usually very abruptly in high school. Suddenly, no one passes them on, and no one gives them undeserved credit. Many of these students do not graduate in four years. Some never recover, while other find themselves forced to deal with a very distasteful situation.

No one wants to see a student fail, but to alter any standard without good reason is to set that same student up for failure later in life. Passing along a student with disabilities in regular classes, pretending that he or she is performing at the same level as most of the class or that it doesn't really matter (arguing that the student has a legal "right" to be in the class) is another prescription for disappointment and failure in later life. Indeed, this failure often comes in college or on the job.

Some people with disabilities do need assistance. Others do not. Consider Deborah Groeber, who struggled through degenerative deafness and blindness. The Office of Affirmative Action at the University of Pennsylvania offered to intercede at the Wharton School, but Groeber knew that she had more influence if she spoke for herself. Today, she is a lawyer with three Ivy League degrees.[13] But not every student with disabilities can do or should be expected to do what Groeber did. Our concern is that too many students with disabilities are given encouragement based on pretense when they could do much more with appropriate special education.

Types of Accommodations

Two popular modifications in IEPs are allowing for the use of calculators and granting extended time on tests and assignments. Calculators can be a great asset, but they should be used when calculating complex problems or when doing word problems. Indiscriminate use of a calculator renders many math tests invalid, as they become a contest to see if buttons can be pushed successfully and in the correct order, rather than an evaluation of ability to do arithmetic or use mathematical knowledge.

Extended time on assignments and tests can also be a useful modification, but it can easily be misused or abused. Extended time on tests should mean *continuous* time so that a test is not studied for first and taken later. Sometimes a test must be broken into smaller segments that can be completed independently. However, this could put students with disabilities at a disadvantage, as one part of a test might help with remembering another part. Extensions on assignments need to be evaluated each time they are given, not simply handed out automatically because they are written into an IEP. If a student is clearly working hard, then extensions may be appropriate. If a student has not even been attempting assignments, then more time might be an avoidance tactic. Sometimes extended time means that assignments pile up and the student gets further and further behind. The result can then be overwhelming stress and the inability to comprehend discussions because many concepts must be acquired in sequence (e.g., in math, science, history, and foreign languages).

Reading tests and quizzes aloud to students can be beneficial for many, but great caution is required. Some students and teachers want to do more than simply read a test. Reading a test aloud means simply reading the printed words on the page *without* inflections that can reveal correct answers and without explaining vocabulary. Changing a test to open-notes or open-book, without the knowledge and consent of the classroom teacher, breaches good-faith test proctoring. It also teaches students dependence rather than independence and accomplishment. Similarly, scribing for a student can be beneficial for those who truly need it, but the teacher must be careful not to add details and to write only what the student dictates, including any run-on sentences or fragments. After scribing, if the assignment is not a test, the teacher should edit and correct the paper with the student, as she might do with any written work. But this must take place *after* the scribing.

How Misguided Accommodations Can Be Disabling

"Saving" a child from his or her own negative behavior reinforces that behavior and makes it a self-fulfilling prophecy. Well-intentioned guidance counselors often feel more responsibility for their students' success or failure than the students themselves feel. Sometimes students are not held accountable for their effort or work. They seem not to understand that true independence comes from *what* you know, not *whom* you know. Students who are consistently enabled and not challenged are never given the opportunity to become independent. Ann Bancroft, the polar explorer and dyslexic, claims that, although school was a torment, it was disability that forged her iron will.[14] Stephen Cannell's fear for other dyslexics is that they will quit trying rather than struggle and learn to compensate for their disability.[15]

Most parents want to help their children. However, some parents confuse making life *easier* with making life *better* for their children. Too often, parents feel that protecting their child from the rigors of academic demands is in his or her best interest. They may protect their child by insisting on curricular modifications and accommodations in assignments, time, and testing. But children learn by doing, and not allowing them to do something because they might fail is denying them the opportunity to succeed. These students eventually believe they are not capable of doing what typical students can do, even if they are. Sometimes it is difficult for teachers to discern what a student actually can do and what a parent has done until an in-class assignment is given or a test is taken. At that point, it is often too late for the teacher to do much remediation. The teacher may erroneously conclude that the student is simply a poor test-taker.

In reality, the student may have been "protected" from learning, which will eventually catch up with him or her. Unfortunately, students may not face reality until they take a college entrance exam, go away to college, or apply for a job. Students who "get through" high school in programs of this type often go on to flunk out of college. Unfortunately, the parents of these students frequently blame the college for the student's failure, criticizing the postsecondary institution for not doing enough to help. Instead, they should be upset both with the secondary institution for not preparing the child adequately for the tasks to come and with themselves for their own overprotection.

The Benefits of Demands

Many successful adults with disabilities sound common themes when asked about their ability to succeed in the face of a disability. Tom Gray, a Rhodes Scholar who has a severe learning disability, claims that having to deal with the hardest experiences gave him the greatest strength.[16] Stephen Cannell believes that, if he had known there was a reason beyond his control to explain his low achievement, he might not have worked as hard as he did. Today, he knows he has a learning disability, but he is also an Emmy Award-winning television writer and producer.[17] Paul Orlalea, the dyslexic founder of Kinko's, believes God gave him an advantage in the challenge presented by his disability and that others should work with their strengths. Charles Schwab, the learning-disabled founder of Charles Schwab, Inc., cites his ability to think differently and to make creative leaps that more sequential thinkers don't make as chief reasons for his success. Fannie Flagg, the learning-disabled author, concurs and insists that learning disabilities become a blessing *only if you can overcome them*.[18] Not every student with a disability can be a star performer, of course, but all should be expected to achieve all that they can.

Two decades ago, special educators thought it was their job to assess a student's achievement, to understand what the student wanted to do and what an average peer could do, and then to develop plans to bridge the gap, if possible. Most special educators wanted to see that each student had the tools and knowledge to succeed as independently as possible. Helping students enter the typical world was the mark of success for special educators.

The full-inclusion movement now insists that *every* student will benefit from placement in the mainstream. However, some of the modifications and accommodations now being demanded are so radical that we are doing an injustice to the entire education system.[19] Special education must not be associated in any way with "dumbing down" the curriculum for students presumed to be at a given grade level, whether disabled or not.

Counselors and administrators who want to enable students must focus the discussion on realistic goals and plans for each student. An objective, in-depth discussion and evaluation must take place to determine how far along the continuum of successfully completing these goals the student has moved. If the student is making adequate progress independently, or with minimal help, special education services might not be necessary. If assistance is required to make adequate progress on realistic goals, then special education may be needed. Every modification and every accommodation should be held to the same standard: whether it will help the student attain these goals—*not* whether it will make life easier for the student. Knowing where a student is aiming can help a team guide that student toward success.

And the student must be part of this planning. A student who claims to want to be a brain surgeon but refuses to take science courses needs a reality check. If a student is unwilling to attempt to reach intermediate goals or does not succeed in meeting them, then special education cannot "save" that student. At that point, the team must help the student revisit his or her goals. Goals should be explained in terms of the amount of work required to complete them, not whether or not the teacher or parent feels they are attainable. When goals are presented in this way, students can often make informed decisions regarding their attainability and desirability. Troy Brown, a university dean and politician who has both a doctorate and a learning disability, studied at home with his mother. He estimates that it took him more than twice as long as the average person to complete assignments. Every night, he would go to bed with stacks of books and read until he fell asleep, because he had a dream of attending college.[20]

General educators and special educators need to encourage all students to be responsible and independent and to set realistic expectations for themselves. Then teachers must help students to meet these expectations in a more and more independent manner. Special educators do not serve students well when they enable students with disabilities to become increasingly dependent on their parents, counselors, administrators, or teachers—or even when they fail to increase students' independence and competence.

Where We Stand

We want to make it clear that we think disabilities are real and that they make doing certain things either impossible or very difficult for the people who have them. We cannot expect people with disabilities to be "just like everyone else" in what they can do. . . .

In our view, students with disabilities *do* have specific short-comings and *do* need the services of specially trained professionals to achieve their potential. They *do* sometimes need altered curricula or adaptations to make their learning possible. If students with disabilities were just like "regular" students, then there would be no need whatever for special education. But the school experiences of students with disabilities obviously will not be—*cannot* be—just like those of students without disabilities. We sell students with disabilities short when we pretend that they are no different from typical students. We make the same error when we pretend that they must *not* be expected to put forth extra effort if they are to learn to do some things—or learn to do something in a different way. We sell them short when we pretend that they have competencies that they do not have or pretend that the competencies we expect of most students are not important for them.

Like general education, special education must push students to become all they can be. Special education must countenance neither the pretense of learning nor the avoidance of reasonable demands.

Notes

1. James M. Kauffman and Daniel P. Hallahan, *Special Education: What It Is and Why We Need It* (Boston: Allyn & Bacon, forthcoming).

2. Doug Fuchs et al., "Toward a Responsible Reintegration of Behaviorally Disordered Students," *Behavioral Disorders,* February 1991, pp. 133–47.

3. Evelyn Deno, "Special Education as Developmental Capital," *Exceptional Children,* November 1970, pp. 229–37; and Dixie Snow Huefner, "The Mainstreaming Cases: Tensions and Trends for School Administrators," *Educational Administration Quarterly,* February 1994, pp. 27–55.

4. Robert B. Edgerton, *The Cloak of Competence: Stigma in the Lives of the Mentally Retarded* (Berkeley, Calif.: University of California Press, 1967); idem, *The Cloak of Competence,* rev. ed. (Berkeley, Calif.: University of California Press, 1993); and James M. Kauffman, "Appearances, Stigma, and Prevention," *Remedial and Special Education,* vol. 24, 2003, pp. 195–98.

5. See, for example, Scot Danforth and William C. Rhodes, "Deconstructing Disability: A Philosophy for Education," *Remedial and Special Education,*

November/December 1997, pp. 357–66; and Phil Smith, "Drawing New Maps: A Radical Cartography of Developmental Disabilities," *Review of Educational Research,* Summer 1999, pp. 117–44.

6. James M. Kauffman, *Education Deform: Bright People Sometimes Say Stupid Things about Education* (Lanham, Md.: Scarecrow Education, 2002).

7. Ibid.

8. James M. Kauffman, "Reflections on the Field," *Behavioral Disorders,* vol. 28, 2003, pp. 205–8.

9. See, for example, Clint Bolick, "A Bad IDEA Is Disabling Public Schools," *Education Week,* 5 September 2001, pp. 56, 63; and Michelle Cottle, "Jeffords Kills Special Ed. Reform School," *New Republic,* 18 June 2001, pp. 14–15.

10. See, for example, Dorothy K. Lipsky and Alan Gartner, "Equity Requires Inclusion: The Future for All Students with Disabilities," in Carol Christensen and Fazal Rizvi, eds., *Disability and the Dilemmas of Education and Justice* (Philadelphia: Open University Press, 1996), pp. 144–55; and William Stainback and Susan Stainback, "A Rationale for Integration and Restructuring: A Synopsis," in John W. Lloyd, Nirbhay N. Singh, and Alan C. Repp, eds., *The Regular Education Initiative: Alternative Perspectives on Concepts, Issues, and Models* (Sycamore, Ill.: Sycamore, 1991), pp. 225–39.

11. See, for example, Alan Gartner and Dorothy K. Lipsky, *The Yoke of Special Education: How to Break It* (Rochester, N.Y.: National Center on Education and the Economy, 1989). For an alternative view, see James M. Kauffman and Daniel P. Hallahan, "Toward a Comprehensive Delivery System for Special Education," in John I. Goodlad and Thomas C. Lovitt, eds., *Integrating General and Special Education* (Columbus, Ohio: Merrill, 1993), pp. 73–102.

12. Marc Fisher, "Students Still Taking the Fall for D.C. Schools," *Washington Post,* 13 December 2001, p. B–1.

13. Elizabeth Tener, "Blind, Deaf, and Very Successful," *McCall's,* December 1995, pp. 42–46.

14. Christina Cheakalos et al., "Heavy Mettle: They May Have Trouble Reading and Spelling, but Those with the Grit to Overcome Learning Disabilities Like Dyslexia Emerge Fortified for Life," *People,* 30 October 2001, pp. 18, 58.

15. Ibid.

16. Ibid.

17. Stephen Cannell, "How to Spell Success," *Reader's Digest,* August 2000, pp. 63–66.

18. Cheakalos et al., op cit.

19. Anne Proffit Dupre, "Disability, Deference, and the Integrity of the Academic Enterprise," *Georgia Law Review,* Winter 1998, pp. 393–473.

20. Cheakalos et al., op cit.

POSTSCRIPT

Is Full Inclusion Always the Best Option for Children with Disabilities?

It is possible that research on inclusion to date has been inconclusive because researchers have focused on the wrong question. Much of the research in this area seems to have been designed to determine "once and for all" whether students with disabilities have better outcomes in segregated or inclusive educational programs. It is unlikely, however, that inclusion in all its forms will lead to better outcomes for all students and under all conditions. This has led some scholars to encourage researchers to ask more focused questions, such as, What types of students benefit from inclusion? What types of strategies are needed for inclusion to be effective? What types of training and belief systems do teachers need for inclusion to work? and What resources are associated with effective inclusive programs? Addressing these questions may help educators to learn more about when and why inclusion is effective or ineffective.

Some scholars have argued that deciding whether or not inclusion is the best option for students with disabilities is an ethical question and, therefore, not answerable by research. See, for example, "Inclusion Paradigms in Conflict," by Peter V. Paul and Marjorie E. Ward, *Theory Into Practice* (vol. 35, no. 1, 1996). These scholars argue that segregated education is by its very nature discriminatory because it denies students with disabilities access to the same experiences and opportunities afforded everyone else. Although these scholars see a role for empirical research, that role is not to learn whether inclusion should occur but rather how it should occur.

Readers interested in pursuing this topic further can turn to edited volumes by Dorothy K. Lipsky and Alan Gartner, *Inclusion and School Reform: Transforming America's Classrooms* (Paul H. Brookes, 1997) and Susan Stainback and William Stainback, *Inclusion: A Guide for Educators* (Paul H. Brookes, 1996) for histories of educational practices and legislation relating to students with disabilities. Suggestions for implementing inclusive educational practices can be found in "Rethinking Inclusion: Schoolwide Applications," by Wayne Sailor and Blair Roger, *Phi Delta Kappan* (March 2005). Discussions of barriers to inclusion can be found in "Barriers and Facilitators to Inclusive Education," by Jayne Pivik, Joan McComas, and Marc Laflamme, *Exceptional Children* (Fall 2002) and "Attitudes of Elementary School Principals toward the Inclusion of Students with Disabilities," by Cindy L. Praisner, *Exceptional Children* (Winter 2003). An argument against the proliferation of inclusive practices can be found in "The Oppression of Inclusion," by David A. Zera and Roy M. Seitsinger, *Educational Horizons* (Fall 2000). An argument for the value of inclusive practices can be found in "Self-Determination for Students with Intellectual Disabilities and Why I Want Educators to Know What It Means," by Susan Unok Marks, *Phi Delta Kappan* (September 2008). Finally, interesting insights into student perspecitives on inclusion can be found in "What Do Students Think about Inclusion," by Maury Miller, *Phi Delta Kappan* (January 2008).

ISSUE 4

Can Schools Close the Achievement Gap between Students from Different Ethnic and Racial Backgrounds?

YES: Carol Corbett Burris and Kevin G. Welner, from "Closing the Achievement Gap by Detracking," *Phi Delta Kappan* (April 2005)

NO: William J. Mathis, from "Bridging the Achievement Gap: A Bridge Too Far?" *Phi Delta Kappan* (April 2005)

ISSUE SUMMARY

YES: Carol Corbett Burris and Kevin G. Welner argue that the achievement gap between white students and African American and Hispanic students is a consequence of the overrepresentation of students from ethnic and racial minorities in low achieving-track classes. They argue that the watered-down curriculum and low expectations associated with low achieving-track classes prevent ethnic and racial minority students from achieving the same levels of academic success as white students.

NO: William J. Mathis argues that the achievement gap between white and African American and Hispanic students has been created by discriminatory social and political pressures that pervade all facets of life. He argues that it is, therefore, unreasonable to expect to eliminate the gap through curricular or other innovations in the schools. Mathis cites school vouchers as an example of a failed attempt to use schooling as a means of undoing the achievement gap.

In 2004, the nation witnessed the fiftieth anniversary of the U.S. Supreme Court's decision in *Brown v. the Board of Education,* which declared that the segregation of public schools according to race denied African American children the same educational opportunities as white children. Many educators and policy makers, however, did not view the anniversary as an occasion to celebrate, pointing to the continuing gap between the academic achievement of white students, on the one hand, and African American and Hispanic students, on the other. Put simply, compared to white students, African American and Hispanic students, on average, score lower on standardized achievement tests and tests of basic skills in mathematics and science, are more likely to leave school before graduating from high school, and are less likely to attend college. Although African American and Hispanic students are overrepresented among lower-income families in this country, the achievement gap cannot be fully explained by economic differences. Racial and ethnic differences in academic achievement remain even in comparisons of families with similar annual incomes.

What role do schools play in creating or maintaining this achievement gap? And what role should schools play in reducing or preventing the gap? Some critics of public education suggest that schools have created the gap through discriminatory practices and subtle forms of racism perpetrated by teachers, administrators, and support staff, such as having lower expectations for African American and Hispanic students and assigning them to low achieving-track or special education classes at substantially higher rates than their white peers. These critics also point out that the achievement gap actually widens over the school years, with African American and Hispanic students falling further and further behind their white peers as they move through the elementary to the middle and, eventually, the high school years. Critics suggest that this increasing gap is evidence that schools are causing, or at least contributing to, the problem. Indeed, President George W. Bush's controversial No Child Left Behind policy was based on the assumption that any student can succeed if given appropriate educational opportunities.

Many defenders of public education argue that it is not schools that are to blame for the existence of the achievement gap, but rather the broader social and economic conditions that create a wide array of disparities among different ethnic and racial groups. Years of discrimination, it is argued, have led to high rates of poverty among African American and Hispanic families, and thereby to less adequate material resources in homes, including books and other materials that support academic growth; more limited access to the health care and nutrition necessary to ensure optimal development; and exposure to a variety of hazardous conditions, from exposure to lead in paints to crime and violence, all of which interfere with learning. These defenders of public education point out that children who live in poverty begin school less well prepared (e.g., with fewer pre-literacy skills, such as the recognition that print encodes language or of specific letters) than their more affluent peers and thus, wider social forces rather than schooling is to blame for the achievement gap. Thus, it is unreasonable, according to critics, to expect that schools can overcome the pervasive social and economic barriers that exist before an African American or Hispanic child begins school and continue in his or her out-of-school hours.

In the first of the following selections, Carol Corbett Burris and Kevin G. Welner argue that the achievement gap between white students and African American and Hispanic students is a consequence of the over-representation of minority students in low achieving-track classes. Thus, for Burris and Welner, the desegregation ordered by the Supreme Court in *Brown v. the Board of Education* has not resulted in equal educational opportunities for all students. In the second selection, William J. Mathis argues that the discriminatory social and political pressures that have led to the achievement gap pervade all facets of life and thus cannot be overcome by curricular or other innovations in public schooling. He argues that this is why the achievement gap has persisted despite good-faith efforts by educators to reform curricula and policy, and he cites the school voucher program as an example of the failure of such school-based reforms.

YES

**Carol Corbett Burris and
Kevin G. Welner**

Closing the Achievement Gap
by Detracking

The most recent Phi Delta Kappa/Gallup Poll of the Public's Attitudes Toward the Public Schools found that 74% of Americans believe that the achievement gap between white students and African American and Hispanic students is primarily due to factors unrelated to the quality of schooling that children receive.[1] This assumption is supported by research dating back four decades to the Coleman Report and its conclusion that schools have little impact on the problem.[2] But is the pessimism of that report justified? Or is it possible for schools to change their practices and thereby have a strongly positive effect on student achievement? We have found that when all students—those at the bottom as well as the top of the "gap"—have access to first-class learning opportunities, all students' achievement can rise.

Because African American and Hispanic students are consistently overrepresented in low-track classes, the effects of tracking greatly concern educators who are interested in closing the achievement gap.[3] Detracking reforms are grounded in the established ideas that higher achievement follows from a more rigorous curriculum and that low-track classes with unchallenging curricula result in lower student achievement.[4] Yet, notwithstanding the wide acceptance of these ideas, we lack concrete case studies of mature detracking reforms and their effects. This article responds to that shortage, describing how the school district in which Carol Burris serves as a high school principal was able to close the gap by offering its high-track curriculum to all students, in detracked classes.

Tracking and the Achievement Gap

Despite overwhelming research demonstrating the ineffectiveness of low-track classes and of tracking in general, schools continue the practice.[5] Earlier studies have argued that this persistence stems from the fact that tracking is grounded in values, beliefs, and politics as much as it is in technical, structural, or organizational needs.[6] Further, despite inconsistent research findings,[7] many parents and educators assume that the practice benefits high achievers. This is partly because parents of high achievers fear that detracking and heterogeneous grouping will result in a "watered-down" curriculum and lowered learning standards for their children.

And so, despite the evidence that low-track classes cause harm, they continue to exist. Worse still, the negative achievement effects of such classes fall disproportionately on minority students, since, as noted above, African American and Hispanic students are overrepresented in low-track classes and underrepresented in high-track classes, even after controlling for prior measured achievement.[8] Socioeconomic status (SES) has been found to affect track assignment as well.[9] A highly proficient student from a low socioeconomic background has only a 50-50 chance of being placed in a high-track class.[10]

Researchers who study the relationship between tracking, race/ethnicity, and academic performance suggest different strategies for closing the achievement gap. Some believe that the solution is to encourage more minority students to take high-track classes.[11] Others believe that if all students are given the enriched curriculum that high-achieving students receive, achievement will rise.[12] They believe that no students—whatever their race, SES, or prior achievement—should be placed in classes that have a watered-down or remedial academic curriculum and that the tracking system should be dismantled entirely.[13] In this article, we provide evidence for the success of this latter approach. By dismantling tracking and providing the high-track curriculum to all, we can succeed in closing the achievement gap on important measures of learning.

Providing "High-Track" Curriculum to All Students

The Rockville Centre School District is a diverse suburban school district located on Long Island. In the late 1990s, it embarked on a multiyear detracking reform that increased learning expectations for all students. The district began replacing its tracked classes with heterogeneously grouped classes in which the curriculum formerly reserved for the district's high-track students was taught.

This reform began as a response to an ambitious goal set by the district's superintendent, William Johnson, and the Rockville Centre Board of Education in 1993: *By the year 2000, 75% of all graduates will earn a New York State Regents diploma.* At that time, the district and state rates of earning Regents diplomas were 58% and 38% respectively.

To qualify for a New York State Regents diploma, students must pass, at a minimum, eight end-of-course Regents examinations, including two in mathematics, two in laboratory sciences, two in social studies, one in English language arts, and one in a foreign language. Rockville Centre's goal reflected the superintendent's strong belief in the external evaluation of student learning as well as the district's commitment to academic rigor.

Regents exams are linked with coursework; therefore, the district gradually eliminated low-track courses. The high school eased the transition by offering students instructional support classes and carefully monitoring the progress of struggling students.

While the overall number of Regents diplomas increased, a disturbing profile of students who were not earning the diploma emerged. These students were more likely to be African American or Hispanic, to receive free or reduced-price lunch, or to have a learning disability. At the district's high school, 20% of all students were African American or Hispanic, 13% received free and reduced-price lunch, and 10% were special education students. If these graduates were to earn the Regents diploma, systemic change would need to take place to close the gaps for each of these groups.

Accelerated Mathematics in Heterogeneous Classes

On closer inspection of the data, educators noticed that the second math Regents exam presented a stumbling block to earning the diploma. While high-track students enrolled in trigonometry and advanced algebra in the 10th grade, low-track students did not even begin first-year algebra until grade 10.

In order to provide all students with ample opportunity to pass the needed courses and to study calculus prior to graduation, Superintendent Johnson decided that all students would study the accelerated math curriculum formerly reserved for the district's highest achievers. Under the leadership of the assistant principal, Delia Garrity, middle school math teachers revised and condensed the curriculum. The new curriculum was taught to all students, in heterogeneously grouped classes. To support struggling learners, the school initiated support classes called math workshops and provided after-school help four afternoons a week.

The results were remarkable. Over 90% of incoming freshmen entered the high school having passed the first Regents math examination. The achievement gap dramatically narrowed. Between the years of 1995 and 1997, only 23% of regular education African American or Hispanic students had passed this algebra-based Regents exam before entering high school. After universally accelerating all students in heterogeneously grouped classes, the percentage more than tripled—up to 75%. The percentage of white or Asian American regular education students who passed the exam also greatly increased—from 54% to 98%.

Detracking the High School

The district approached universal acceleration with caution. Some special education students, while included in the accelerated classes, were graded using alternative assessments. This 1998 cohort of special education students would not take the first ("Sequential I") Regents math exam until they had completed ninth grade. (We use year of entry into ninth grade to determine cohort. So the 1998 cohort began ninth grade in the fall of 1998.) On entering high school, these students with special needs were placed in a double-period, low-track, "Sequential I" ninth-grade math class, along with low-achieving new entrants. Consistent with the recommendations of researchers who have defended tracking,[14] this class was rich in resources (a math teacher, special education inclusion teacher, and teaching assistant). Yet the low-track culture of the class remained unconducive to learning. Students were disruptive, and teachers spent considerable class time addressing behavior management issues. All students were acutely aware that the class carried the "low-track" label.

District and school leaders decided that this low-track class failed its purpose, and the district boldly moved forward with several new reforms the following year. All special education students in the 1999 cohort took the exam in the eighth grade. The entire 1999 cohort also studied science in heterogeneous classes throughout middle school, and it became the first cohort to be heterogeneously grouped in ninth-grade English and social studies classes.

Ninth-grade teachers were pleased with the results. The tone, activities, and discussions in the heterogeneously grouped classes were academic, focused, and enriched. Science teachers reported that the heterogeneously grouped middle school science program prepared students well for ninth-grade biology.

Detracking at the high school level continued, paralleling the introduction of revised New York State curricula. Students in the 2000 cohort studied the state's new biology curriculum, "The Living Environment," in heterogeneously grouped classes. This combination of new curriculum and heterogeneous grouping resulted in a dramatic increase in the passing rate on the first science Regents exam, especially for minority students who were previously overrepresented in the low-track biology class. After just one year of heterogeneous grouping, the passing rate for African American and Hispanic students increased from 48% to 77%, while the passing rate for white and Asian American students increased from 85% to 94%.

The following September, the 2001 cohort became the first class to be heterogeneously grouped in *all subjects* in the ninth grade. The state's new multiyear "Math A" curriculum was taught to this cohort in heterogeneously grouped classes in both the eighth and ninth grades.

In 2003, some 10th-grade classes detracked. Students in the 2002 cohort became the first to study a heterogeneously grouped pre-International Baccalaureate (IB) 10th-grade curriculum in English and social studies. To help all students meet the demands of an advanced curriculum, the district provides every-other-day support classes in math, science, and English language arts. These classes are linked to the curriculum and allow teachers to pre- and postteach topics to students needing additional reinforcement.

Closing the Gap on Other Measures That Matter

New York's statewide achievement gap in the earning of Regents diplomas has persisted. In 2000, only 19.3% of all African American or Hispanic 12th-graders and 58.7% of all white or Asian American 12th-graders graduated with Regents diplomas. By 2003, while the percentage of students in both groups earning the Regents diploma increased (26.4% of African American or Hispanic students, 66.3% of white or Asian American students), the gap did not close.

In contrast, Rockville Centre has seen both an increase in students' rates of earning Regents diplomas and a decrease in the gap between groups. . . . For those students who began South Side High School in 1996 (the graduating class of 2000), 32% of all African American or Hispanic and 88% of all white or Asian American graduates earned Regents diplomas. By the time the cohort of 1999 graduated in 2003, the gap had closed dramatically—82% of all African American or Hispanic and 97% of all white or Asian American graduates earned Regents diplomas. In fact, . . . for this 1999 cohort (the first to experience detracking in all middle school and most ninth-grade subjects), the Regents diploma rate for the district's minority students surpassed New York State's rate for white or Asian American students.

In order to ensure that the narrowing of the gap was not attributable to a changing population, we used binary logistic regression analyses to compare the probability of earning a Regents diploma before and after detracking. In addition to membership in a detracked cohort, the model included socioeconomic and special education status as covariates. Those students who were members of the 1996 and 1997 cohorts were compared with members of the 1998–2000 cohorts. We found that membership in a cohort subsequent to the detracking of middle school math was a significant contributor to earning a Regents diploma. . . . In addition, low-SES students and special education students in the 2001 cohort also showed sharp improvement.

These same three cohorts (1998–2000) showed significant increases in the probability of minority students' studying advanced math courses. Controlling for prior achievement and SES, minority students' enrollment in trigonometry, precalculus, and Advanced Placement calculus all grew.[15] And as more students from those cohorts studied AP calculus, the enrollment gap decreased from 38% to 18% in five years, and the AP calculus scores significantly increased. . . .

Finally, detracking in the 10th grade, combined with teaching all students the pre-IB curriculum, appears to be closing the gap in the study of the IB curriculum. This year 50% of all minority students will study IB English and "History of the Americas" in the 11th grade. In the fall of 2003, only 31% chose to do so.

❦

Achievement follows from opportunities—opportunities that tracking denies. The results of detracking in Rockville Centre are clear and compelling. When all students were taught the high-track curriculum, achievement rose for all groups of students—majority, minority, special education, low-SES, and high-SES. This evidence can now be added to the larger body of tracking research that has convinced the Carnegie Council for Adolescent Development, the National Governors' Association, and most recently the National Research Council to call for the reduction or elimination of tracking.[16] The Rockville Centre reform confirms common sense: closing the "curriculum gap" is an effective way to close the "achievement gap."

Notes

1. Lowell C. Rose and Alec M. Gallup, "The 36th Annual Phi Delta Kappa/ Gallup Poll of the Public's Attitudes Toward the Public Schools," *Phi Delta Kappan,* September 2004, p. 49.

2. James Coleman et al., *Equality of Educational Opportunity* (Washington, D.C.: U.S. Government Printing Office, 1966).

3. Kevin G. Welner, *Legal Rights, Local Wrongs: When Community Control Collides with Educational Equity* (Albany: SUNY Press, 2001).

4. Clifford Adelman, *Answers in the Tool Box: Academic Intensity, Attendance Patterns, and Bachelor's Degree Attainment* (Washington, D.C.: Office of Educational Research, U.S. Department of Education, 1999); . . . Henry Levin, *Accelerated Schools for At-Risk Students* (New Brunswick, N.J.: Rutgers University, Center for Policy Research in Education, Report No. 142, 1988); Mano Singham, "The Achievement Gap: Myths and Realities," *Phi Delta Kappan,* April 2003, pp. 586–91; and Jay P. Heubert and Robert M. Hauser, *High Stakes: Testing for Tracking, Promotion, and Graduation* (Washington, D.C.: National Research Council, 1999).

5. Jeannie Oakes, Adam Gamoran, and Reba Page, "Curriculum Differentiation: Opportunities, Outcomes, and Meanings," in Philip Jackson, ed., *Handbook of Research on Curriculum* (New York: Macmillan, 1992), pp. 570–608.

6. Welner, op. cit.

7. Frederick Mosteller, Richard Light, and Jason Sachs, "Sustained Inquiry in Education: Lessons from Skill Grouping and Class Size," *Harvard Educational Review,* vol. 66, 1996, pp. 797–843; Robert Slavin, "Achievement Effects of Ability Grouping in Secondary Schools: A Best-Evidence Synthesis," *Review of Educational Research,* vol. 60, 1990, pp. 471–500; and James Kulik, *An Analysis of the Research on Ability Grouping: Historical and Contemporary Perspectives* (Storrs, Conn.: National Research Center on the Gifted and Talented, University of Connecticut, 1992).

8. Roslyn Mickelson, "Subverting Swann: First- and Second-Generation Segregation in Charlotte-Mecklenburg Schools," *American Educational Research Journal,* vol. 38, 2001, pp. 215–52; Robert Slavin and Jomills Braddock II, "Ability Grouping: On the Wrong Track," *College Board Review,* Summer 1993, pp. 11–17; and Welner, op. cit.

9. Samuel Lucas, *Tracking Inequality: Stratification and Mobility in American High Schools* (New York: Teachers College Press, 1999).

10. Beth E. Vanfossen, James D. Jones, and Joan Z. Spade, "Curriculum Tracking and Status Maintenance," *Sociology of Education,* vol. 60, 1987, pp. 104–22.

11. John Ogbu, *Black American Students in an Affluent Suburb* (Mahwah, N.J.: Erlbaum, 2003).

12. Levin, op. cit.; and Slavin and Braddock, op. cit.

13. Jeannie Oakes and Amy Stuart Wells, "Detracking for High Student Achievement," *Educational Leadership,* March 1998, pp. 38–41; and Susan Yonezawa, Amy Stuart Wells, and Irene Sema, "Choosing Tracks: 'Freedom of Choice' in Detracking Schools," *American Educational Research Journal,* vol. 39, 2002, pp. 37–67.

14. Maureen Hallinan, "Tracking: From Theory to Practice," *Sociology of Education,* vol. 67, 1994, pp. 79–91; and Tom Loveless, *The Tracking Wars: State Reform Meets School Policy* (Washington, D.C.: Brookings Institution Press, 1999).

15. Carol Corbett Burris, Jay P. Heubert, and Henry M. Levin, "Math Acceleration for All," *Educational Leadership,* February 2004, pp. 68–71.

16. Carnegie Council on Adolescent Development, *Turning Points: Preparing American Youth for the 21st Century* (New York: Carnegie Corporation, 1989); *Ability Grouping and Tracking: Current Issues and Concerns* (Washington, D.C.: National Governors Association, 1993); and National Research Council, *Engaging Schools: Fostering High School Students' Motivation to Learn* (Washington, D.C.: National Academies Press, 2004).

William J. Mathis

 **NO**

Bridging the Achievement Gap: A Bridge Too Far?

Seeking to cut off German access to the Rhine, Allied commanders dropped a small force of lightly armed paratroopers deep behind enemy lines. They were to seize a key bridge in Holland. Due to poor planning, inadequate support, overextended lines, and dropping the paratroopers into the middle of two crack Panzer divisions, the Allied venture was doomed.

It was a bridge too far.

Of course, the moral imperative was right. And of course, it is the moral obligation of all educators to bridge the achievement gap between rich and poor, between boys and girls, and between brown, black, and white. Half a century after *Brown v. Board of Education,* we can mark the great progress we have made. But the gap remains.

Some federal and state political leaders have made gung-ho proclamations about leaving no child behind. Yet they send in too few troops, too lightly supported, and with too little planning. The vaunted "historic investments" actually increase total education spending by less than 1%. The mandates were air-dropped into inner cities without social, community, school, or occupational networks to overcome the effects of ingrained poverty. The law then says the troops will be punished if they don't succeed.

If we are to bridge the achievement gap, then we must view our social and educational obligations in a far richer and more expansive light.

Are We Bridging the Gap?

There is some good news about the achievement gap. While the National Assessment of Educational Progress scores in reading and math have increased between four and six points over the past five years for white students, the scores for minority groups have increased six to 13 points during this same time period.[1] Likewise, college entrance rates have increased by 5% for white students over the past decade, while the rates for black students have increased by 12%. Increases for Hispanic students match those for white students.[2]

The achievement gap cannot be completely closed, however, by simply carrying out more intensely some program that zealous adherents claim will close it. Certainly, some whole-school reforms have shown positive long-term effects when administered consistently over time. Nevertheless, to deal

From *Phi Delta Kappan,* April 2005, pp. 590–593. Copyright © 2005 by Phi Delta Kappan. Reprinted by permission of Phi Delta Kappan and William J. Mathis, Ph.D.

effectively with the gap means that we must deal with the underlying problems of society.[3]

As any inner-city teacher can tell us (and many rural and suburban teachers as well), to pretend that schools can single-handedly overcome a lifetime of deprivation through a "whole-school action plan" or through rigorous and intensive adherence to a particular reading program is more an exercise in ritualistic magic than a realistic solution to social, economic, and personal problems.

Yet many politicians and educators contend—explicitly or implicitly and perhaps even complicitly—that the schools can and must go it alone. Four central fallacies are employed to argue that schools can do this job by themselves.

1. The fallacy of the successful example.

Countless profiles, filled with fine praise, have been written about successful schools. Typically, federal and state politicians stage a high-visibility media event to recognize a poor school that has registered high test scores despite the handicaps of poverty and inadequate facilities. . . . The media message is that, because this school has achieved success through hard work, all similarly situated schools can do the same. Thus closing the achievement gap requires no additional resources. It is simply a matter of will and effort.

Certainly, there are thousands of teachers, aides, and principals across our land who are genuine heroes. They do miraculous work in impossible circumstances. However, more than likely, these photo ops are created by a statistical fluke.

As is well known, average test scores for schools tend to distribute themselves along a normal curve (even if they are from criterion-referenced or mastery tests). So it is simple for someone to look at the test scores of all low-income, high-minority schools, identify the school at the top of the test-score distribution, and use it as an example of how well the reforms are working.

The problem is that these improvements are most often merely random fluctuations. Walt Haney showed that "Medallion" schools identified in one year in Massachusetts actually fell backwards in the following cycle.[4] Likewise, scores between fourth-graders this year and fourth-graders next year, in the same school, represent 70% test and cohort error and not learning effects.[5]

Thus, while examples of success can always be found, they do not mean that the level of educational or social support is adequate. In fact, these successful examples hide disparities and offer false promise.

2. The fallacy of the educational panacea.

Any number of professional development groups and reform networks advertise workshops with names like "Bridging the Achievement Gap." They are featured at national conventions, and high-ticket three-day workshops are offered in desirable locations. (Andy Hargreaves refers to them as "training cults."[6]) It is strongly implied that, if we attend the workshop and implement the program faithfully, all children will achieve mastery. While these workshops may well provide good, solid, organized instructional approaches, there is scant independent and accepted research evidence that such programs can successfully—by themselves—bridge the achievement gap.[7]

Unfortunately, testimonies about these programs come from educators and provide a rationale for politicians to ignore social inequities. They become the basis for claiming that schools are inefficient and wasteful. From here, it is a simple step to conclude that public schools are "failing."

3. The fallacy that "adequate yearly progress" on test scores decreases the true education gap.

The federal No Child Left Behind Act places increasing pressure on schools to make adequate yearly progress (AYP), but it is well known that schools with high concentrations of poor and minority students will fail to make AYP in disproportionate numbers. Schools with more wealthy student populations can (at least temporarily) escape being classified as failing, even though their rate of improvement may be far lower than that of schools with more poor and minority students.[8]

The result is educational apartheid. The more affluent schools can continue to provide a rich variety of educational and cultural opportunities with field trips, advanced studies, arts programs, and the like. The poor schools, however, find themselves increasingly trapped into a dull and spiritless routine of drill and practice, with the narrow objective of passing the examinations.[9] The effect is to widen some truly significant gaps.

4. The fallacy that vouchers bridge achievement gaps.

Although some folks sincerely believe that voucher systems, whether state or federal, will narrow achievement gaps, 30 years of national and international research show that there is no initial or long-term pattern of improvement in test scores with such systems. On the other hand, there is a substantial body of evidence that shows that social gaps increase as a result of vouchers.[10]

It is well established that poverty explains more of the variation in test scores than does any educational reform.[11] However, parents with lower levels of education and income are less likely to choose vouchers. Likewise, choice schemes tend to skim more advantaged students from underperforming schools.[12] The overall effect is to segregate schools and society to a greater extent rather than to bridge the gap.

The pressure to make AYP also offers schools the perverse incentive to select those students closest to proficiency and work to push them over the bar. There is less incentive to help those who are woefully behind. The result is that some students are seen as "helpable" and others are seen as less worthy of attention.[13] Since poverty is the main divider, AYP, combined with vouchers, creates incentives to leave our poorest and neediest children behind. Truly, this is a perverse incentive for a democratic nation.

Bridging the Achievement Gap

To be clear, external social forces and political misdeeds in no way relieve us of our responsibility to provide equality in education, to engage students, to align instruction to standards, to improve pedagogy, to employ diverse methods, to use formative assessments, to disaggregate data, and to track every student's progress. Effective schools remain essential for educational achievement. Yet, by themselves, these approaches cannot be completely successful. Six hours of instruction a day for 180 days a year cannot overcome the effects of a deprived and impoverished home environment for 18 hours a day and 365 days per year.

If we desire is to see all children succeed, we must invest in programs that are well outside the conventional ways of thinking about schools. We must address health, mobility, housing, nutrition, unemployment, family structure, medical and dental care, and a host of other factors.[14]

Within schools, early education programs, full day kindergarten, extensive summer programs, small class sizes, after-school programs, and adequate materials are essential. Furthermore, such support must continue throughout all the school years and not be confined solely to the early grades. Twenty-eight studies in 20 different states, conducted by a diverse group of sponsors and researchers, have shown an average increase of 30% in educational dollars will be needed if we are to provide an adequate education for all students.[15]

◆

If we are to bridge the achievement gap, educational leaders must adopt a broader vision of schooling and live that vision every day. They must take new leadership risks and engage the attention of state and federal legislators. They must expose the fallacies and advocate for comprehensive and democratic conceptions of education. Educational leadership is no longer just the safe (yet difficult) task of leading a faculty through a process of curriculum change.

Educational leaders must revise the definitions and solutions for leaving no child behind. They cannot passively let themselves be disempowered by simply accepting existing political formulations of the purpose of schools. They must be the public voice for the children who are left behind.

Educational leaders must therefore aggressively inform the public that narrow tests, adequate yearly progress targets, vouchers, and punishments will not—and cannot logically—constitute a system that will bridge the achievement gap. Instead, education must be seen as an integral part of the community and include a vast variety of human services and activities.

Bridging the achievement gap also means expanding our emphasis on civic virtues to equal that given to basic skills, and rejecting the fundamental premise that education is a business or commercial enterprise. It is an example of a "commons," owned and nourished by the citizenry, for the benefit and advancement of all groups. Its aim is to build a society that has no gaps.

Notes

1. Education Trust, "Education Watch: The Nation: Key Education Facts and Figures: Achievement, Attainment and Opportunity from Elementary School through College," Spring 2004, . . .

2. Jack Jennings and Madlene Hamilton, "What's Good about Public Schools." . . .

3. Geoffrey D. Borman and Gina M. Hewes, "The Long-Term Effects and Cost-Effectiveness of Success for All," *Educational Evaluation and Policy Analysis,* Winter 2002, pp. 243–66; and Richard Rothstein, *Class and Schools: Using Social, Economic, and Educational Reform to Close the Black-White Achievement Gap* (New York: Teachers College Press, 2004).

4. Walt Haney, "Lake Woebeguaranteed: Misuse of Test Scores in Massachusetts, Part I," *Educational Policy Analysis Archives,* 6 May 2002, . . .

5. Thomas J. Kane and Douglas O. Staiger, "Volatility in School Test Scores: Implications for School-Based Accountability Systems," unpublished paper, Hoover Institution, Stanford University, Stanford, Calif., 2001.

6. Andy Hargreaves, "Standardization and the End of the Knowledge Society," paper presented at the annual meeting of the American Educational Research Association, San Diego, April 2004.

7. Borman and Hewes, op. cit.

8. Robert L. Linn, "Accountability, Responsibility and Reasonable Expectations," *Educational Researcher,* October 2003, pp. 3–13.

9. Hargreaves, op. cit.

10. Henry Levin, "Educational Vouchers: Effectiveness, Choice and Costs," paper presented at the annual meeting of the American Economics Association, New Orleans, 1997.

11. Michael W. Apple, *Cultural Politics and Education* (New York: Teachers College Press, 1996).

12. Henry M. Levin, "Multiple 'Choice' Questions: The Road Ahead," in Noel Epstein, ed., *Who's in Charge Here? The Tangled Web of School Governance and Policy* (Washington, D.C.: Brookings Institution Press, 2004), pp. 246–47.

13. Michael W. Apple, "Creating Difference: Neo-Liberalism, Neo-Conservatism and the Politics of Education Reform," *Educational Policy,* January and March 2004, pp. 12–45.

14. Rothstein, chap. 5.

15. William J. Mathis, "Two Very Different Questions: The Cost of Leaving No Child Behind? Or, the Cost of Implementing 'No Child Left Behind'?," *Education Week,* 21 April, 2004, pp. 48, 33.

POSTSCRIPT

Can Schools Close the Achievement Gap between Students from Different Ethnic and Racial Backgrounds?

It would appear from the results described by Burris and Welner that the answer to our question should be a resounding "yes." After all, Burris and Welner describe what seem to be substantial improvements in several indicators of the academic achievement of the participating youth. It is important to recognize, however, that before we fully understand the effects of any educational intervention or curricular change, we must evaluate both the long-term effects and their generalizability. Maintaining the momentum of these curricular changes may be especially difficult because so many of the students may still experience the pernicious effects of ethnic and racial discrimination outside of school. So it will be important to continue to follow the achievement of the students experiencing the curricular change as well as cohorts of students who experience the curriculum in later years to determine the long-term effects of the change. Even if the effects last, we must still be concerned with whether the changes will lead to similar positive results if implemented in other school districts.

It is also important to point out that even if current school-based approaches turn out not to have lasting, transportable effects on the achievement gap, it is possible that more dramatic (i.e., far-reaching) changes could be successful. So, for example, perhaps extending the school year through the summer would help to reduce the achievement gap when coupled with the sorts of curricular changes described by Burris and Welner. In fact, there is considerable evidence that many of the benefits accrued during the school year by economically disadvantaged African-american and Hispanic students are "lost" during the summer, presumably because the pernicious effects of poverty overwhelm the benefits of schooling. Other changes might include having schools provide after-school care for students.

There are many interesting articles addressing the causes of, and the role of schools in reducing, the achievement gap, including "Education, Alone, Is a Weak Treatment," by James Gallagher, *Education Weekly* (July 1998); "The Linkages among Family Structure, Self-Concept, Effort, and Performance on Mathematics Achievement of American High School Students by Race," by Sharon A. O'Connor and Kathleen Miranda, *American Secondary Education* (2002); and "Class and the Classroom," by Richard Rothstein, *American School Board Journal* (October 2004). An excellent recent series of articles appeared in the *Phi Delta Kappan,* including the present selections. Other articles in that series are "A Wider Lens on the Black-White Achievement Gap," by

Richard Rothstein; "Reframing the Achievement Gap," by Robert Evans; and "Challenging Assumptions about the Achievement Gap," by Al Ramirez and Dick Carpenter. An interesting discussion of the decline in achievement during summer break is provided in "The Impact of Summer Setback on the Reading Achievement Gap," by Richard L. Allington and Anne McGill-Franzen, *Phi Delta Kappan* (September, 2003). And finally, highly recommended is *Savage Inequalities: Children in America's Schools,* by Jonathon Kozol (Crown, 1991), which eloquently describes the dramatically different school experiences of affluent and economically disadvantaged students and students of different races and ethnicities and the system of school funding that creates those differences.

ISSUE 5

Should Schools Try to Increase Students' Self-Esteem?

YES: Robert Sylwester, from "The Neurobiology of Self-Esteem and Aggression," *Educational Leadership* (February 1997)

NO: Maureen A. Manning, from "Self-Concept and Self-Esteem in Adolescents," *Principal Leadership* (February, 2007)

ISSUE SUMMARY

YES: Robert Sylwester, an emeritus professor of education at the University of Oregon, argues that self-esteem is rooted in brain biology and that low self-esteem can result in impulsive and violent actions. He sees schools as a particularly important mechanism for delivering the positive feedback and successes that are required for the development of high self-esteem.

NO: Maureen A. Manning, a school psychologist in the Maryland public schools, argues that self-esteem should not be targeted independent of academic skills. In particular, she believes that the best method to increase self-esteem is to improve student academic skills.

Believers in the self-esteem movement argue that students who feel good about themselves—those who have high self-esteem—will tackle academic tasks with fervor and will strive for excellence. In contrast, students who view themselves in a negative light—those who have low self-esteem—are thought to be at risk for academic failure. Students with low self-esteem will not be enthusiastic in the pursuit of academic goals, which will lead to failure, thereby further damaging their already low self-esteem. The curriculum must be designed to enhance self-esteem or at least not to diminish it. Many in the self-esteem movement believe that children in today's society frequently bring low self-esteem with them to the classroom due to outside factors, like poverty, divorce, and racial or class prejudice. Therefore, followers of the self-esteem movement argue, any effort at educational reform must include an affective component. This is often expressed with phrases such as "We must educate the whole child" and "The emotional side of learning is important too."

What does such a self-esteem-enhancing curriculum look like? The following are a few of the strategies that have been suggested for such a curriculum:

1. Teachers should praise all products produced by students. In other words, teachers should reward effort, regardless of the quality of the work.
2. Teachers should encourage students to value any contributions to the discussion that their classmates make because "there are no bad ideas."
3. Students should be allowed choices about what to study and how to display the knowledge they have acquired because such choices allow them to tailor the tasks to their strengths and, most important, to avoid failure. In fact, *all* classroom activities should be engineered to ensure success (or, conversely, to avoid failure) for all students.
4. Students who are least successful academically are most at risk for low self-esteem and thus most in need of praise, which is the primary tool for boosting self-esteem.

What is common to all of these strategies is the belief that praise and other forms of positive feedback (e.g., displaying student-generated products for all to see) must be used in a way that is not contingent on the quality of the products that students generate. In a sense, self-esteem is more important than achievement.

Few would question that low self-esteem can have undesirable long-term effects. Low self-esteem has been found to be related to a variety of later adjustment problems, including depression and delinquency. Nevertheless, many scholars and educators have become highly critical of the self-esteem movement. They argue that the pursuit of high self-esteem is a foolish, wasteful, and self-destructive enterprise that may end up doing more harm than good.

The dispute between supporters and critics of the self-esteem movement is illustrated in the following selections. In the first selection, Robert Sylwester argues that positive feedback is essential for developing healthy self-esteem, and he sees schools as an important mechanism for delivering such feedback. Moreover, he sees low self-esteem as having serious negative consequences for the individual at both a behavioral and a biological level, including heightened aggression and lowered levels of necessary brain chemicals. In the second selection, Maureen Manning argues that simply delivering praise will be ineffective in increasing student self-esteem. Instead, she argues that helping students identify and improve their academic weaknesses is necessary to make them feel better about themselves. In other words, the dispute between supporters and critics of the self-esteem movement revolves around whether they believe that boosting self-esteem leads to improved academic performance.

YES

Robert Sylwester

The Neurobiology of Self-Esteem and Aggression

Violent acts like gang-related murders, playground shootings, riots, suicides, and assaults in school are prominently featured in the news, but they aren't the norm in social interactions. Young males commit most of the physically violent acts, and 7 percent of the population commits 80 percent of all the violent acts. Thus, violence is a limited social pathology, but one that evolutionary psychologists seek to explain because of its distressing, even tragic, results. Since impulsive behavior can lead to reckless or violently aggressive behavior, we also seek to understand impulsivity. Many personal and social problems begin with an impulsive act—triggered perhaps by the aggressor's low level of self-esteem. Impulsivity, recklessness, violence—all these behaviors can negatively affect educational processes. Some recent related research developments in brain chemistry—particularly the effects of the neurotransmitter serotonin—shed light on educational practices.

Self-Esteem in a Hierarchy

Consider the following scenario—from the point of view of a neurobiologist studying social hierarchies or an evolutionary psychologist studying human behavior.

> A young man joins an athletic team in his freshman year of high school. He's thrilled just to make the team, even though he knows he's low in the hierarchy and won't get to play much in games. He's content for now because he also knows that the coaches and his teammates will note every successful act he makes in scrimmage, and so his playing time will come. He moves up the team hierarchy, substituting a few minutes here and there. His competition for most of this journey isn't the *alpha males* at the top of the hierarchy, but, rather, those who are competing with him for the next slot in the hierarchy.
>
> Over several years, his talent and that of his teammates will determine the level he achieves. He thus may settle for four years of comradeship, scrimmage, and limited game time because he realizes that's where he properly fits in the team hierarchy; or he may eventually bask in the celebrity afforded to him as one of the stars on the team. If the

From *Educational Leadership*, vol. 54, no. 5, February 1997. Copyright © 1997 by ASCD. Reprinted by permission. The Association for Supervision and Curriculum Development is a worldwide community of educators advocating sound policies and sharing best practices to achieve the success of each learner. To learn more, visit ASCD at www.ascd.org.

latter, he may seek to begin the sequence anew in a college team, and then perhaps a pro team. If the former, his memories and friendships will have to suffice—and he will seek success in other social arenas.

But what if he believes that he rates very high compared to the others—but the coaches don't agree, and won't give him a chance to play? Perhaps it's because of something he can't control, such as his height (or by extension, gender or race or whatever defines the *glass ceiling*). Imagine his frustration and rage. His opportunities don't match his sense of self.

It is adaptive for a social species (like humans) to develop a system that arranges groups into reasonably compatible hierarchical arrangements to perform various group tasks. The entire group benefits if survival-related tasks are assigned to those who are generally recognized to be the most capable. But things often don't work the way we'd like them to.

The Roots of Violent Aggression

The cognitive drive to move into our expected slot in the hierarchy is so strong that many people will do whatever it takes to achieve success. To continue with our sports scenario, if the frustration becomes too intense, a person may act impulsively or recklessly for any possible chance of success—and such risk-taking may on occasion escalate into aggressive and violent acts, which we may witness in news accounts of various sports, from baseball to Olympic-level figure skating.

Evolutionary psychology argues that each success enhances the level of the neurotransmitter *serotonin* in the brain—and so also our motor coordination and self-esteem. Failure and negative social feedback inhibit the effects of serotonin and lead to lower self-esteem and possible violence.

When young people see no hope to rise within mainstream society, they may create their own hierarchical gang cultures that provide them with opportunities to succeed within their counterculture's mores. Those among successful people in mainstream society who decry gang symbols and exclusionary turf areas should look to the high-status symbols they use to flaunt their success and to their exclusionary golf courses and walled communities. People in both mainstream cultures and countercultures have the same biological need to succeed; they all need a positive self-concept and self-esteem. Wealthy financiers have ruined small communities by closing moderately profitable plants for even greater profits elsewhere. Are such exploitative acts any less psychologically violent to the victims than the physical violence that erupts later in such communities from those whose plummeting serotonin levels suggest no vocational hope?

Recent research on stress (Sapolsky 1994) shows that in primate groups with a developed, stable hierarchy, those at the bottom (who had little control over events) experienced far more stress and stress-related illness than those at the top. Conversely, during periods in which the hierarchical structure was unstable and shifting, those currently at the top (whose power position was threatened) experienced the most stress and stress-related illness. This find-ing suggests that it is in the interest of the power elite (in community and classroom) to maintain social stability, and it is in the interest of the currently disenfranchised to create as much social instability (and classroom disruption) as possible in a desperate search for respect and success.

The fewer opportunities young people have to succeed in mainstream society, the more social instability we can expect. It is in our best interest to support inclusionary policies that promote social goals and to enhance the powerful role that schools can play in helping students to seek their dreams.

Our Brain and Social Systems

Our brain's complex collections of neural networks process our cognitive activity. Several dozen neurotransmitter and hormonal systems provide the key chemical substrate of this marvelous information-processing system. Neu-rotransmitter molecules, which are produced within one neuron, are released from that neuron's axon terminal into the synaptic gap, where they attach to receptors on the dendrites or surface of the next neuron in the information sequence.

Recent studies with human and nonhuman primates suggest that fluctu-ations in the neurotransmitter serotonin play an important role in regulating our level of self-esteem and our place within the social hierarchy. Researchers associate high serotonin levels in the brain with high self-esteem and social status and low serotonin levels with low self-esteem and social status. High serotonin levels are associated with the calm assurance that leads to smoothly controlled movements, and low serotonin levels with the irritability that leads to impulsive, uncontrolled, reckless, aggressive, violent, or suicidal behavior.

Evolutionary psychologists focus on the biological underpinnings of such educationally significant concepts as self-esteem, impulsivity, and aggres-sion and on the effects of drugs like Prozac. If genetics and fluctuations in biochemical systems combine to trigger aggression, for example, one could argue that chronically aggressive people have a reduced capacity for free will and thus are not (legally) responsible for their acts. Further, if courts mandate medical treatments for such people, the policy could be viewed as governmen-tal *mind control*. The social implications of this research are profound and wide ranging. For example, in determining responsibility for an aggressive act, how important are the negative effects of the aggressor's life experiences and the events that triggered the aggression?

Wright (1995) suggests that social feedback creates fluctuations from our basal serotonin levels, and these fluctuations help determine our current level of self-esteem. Thus, serotonin fluctuations are adaptive in that they help primates to negotiate social hierarchies, to move up as far as circumstances permit, and to be reasonably content at each stage, as our earlier sports sce-nario suggests. Social success elevates our self-esteem (and serotonin levels), and each such elevation further raises our social expectations, perhaps to try for a promotion or leadership role we hadn't considered when we were lower on the hierarchy.

A biological system of variability in self-esteem prepares and encourages us to reach and maintain a realistic level of social status. A high or low level of self-esteem (and serotonin) isn't innate and permanent. Successful people may tumble percipitously in social status, self-esteem, and serotonin levels when they retire or are discharged and thereby may experience a rapid reduction in positive social feedback. This doesn't mean that the serotonin system developed to help low-status people endure their fate for the good of all. Evolutionary psychology argues that natural selection rarely designs things for the good of the group. But the serotonin system provides us with a way to cope in a bad social situation—to be content to play a group role that is consistent with our current limitations. The human serotonin system seems to function similarly in males and females in the important roles it plays in regulating self-esteem and impulse control.

The Role of Drugs and Nutrition

Is is possible to stimulate the serotonin system when conditions become so averse in a person's life that self-esteem and serotonin levels plummet into the depths of depression? Drugs such as Prozac (a fluoxetine antidepressant) can produce an elevation in the effects of serotonin that often enhances a person's self-esteem; this increased optimism and happier mood leads to the positive social feedback that allows the natural system to take over again in time and to function effectively. Think of jump-starting a dead car battery—a few miles of driving will reenergize the battery, and it can then function on its own.

People often use alcohol when they feel low, and alcohol does increase serotonin levels. Thus, it can temporarily help to raise our mood and self-esteem—but chronic alcohol use depletes a brain's store of serotonin, and so it makes matters even worse by further impairing the impulse control system.

Nutrition may provide another avenue to serotonin elevation. Prolonged periods of stress increase our brain's need for serotonin. Nutrition researchers have discovered a connection between serotonin/carbohydrate levels and emotionally driven eating disorders that emerge out of family stress, premenstrual syndrome, shift work, seasonal mood changes, and the decision to stop smoking. Wurtman and Suffes (1996) propose nondrug diet adaptations that could solve some of these problems.

Prescription and other drugs can provide only a temporary chemical boost in self-esteem, and diets require a certain level of self-control. The best support for a serotonin deficiency is probably the natural system of positive social feedback that we have evolved over millennia.

Educational Implications

If positive social feedback is nature's way of regulating the serotonin system so that both an inexperienced substitute football player and the team's star can work together comfortably and effectively, then positive feedback in the classroom is a powerful social device for helping us to assess and define ourselves (self-concept) and to value ourselves (self-esteem). Serotonin research adds biological support to some educational practices that enhance self-esteem—and these practices don't require a prescription or an ID card that proves you are 21 years old.

- Portfolio assessments encourage self-examination in students and enhance student self-concept and self-esteem. Journals, creative artwork, and other forms of reflective thought can produce the same results.
- When students have many opportunities to work together in groups, they may experience success in both leading and supporting roles. Positive self-esteem can develop at any level in a work group, if the problem is challenging and the group values the contributions of all.
- Many school conflicts arise because an impulsive, reckless act escalates into aggression. We have tended to view these events only in negative terms—as misbehavior, as something to be squashed. But what if we used positive group strategies to help students study such behavior and discover how to reduce it? David and Roger Johnson (1995) provide practical cooperative learning strategies for conflict resolution that are consistent with neurobiological research.
- Emmy Werner's four-decade longitudinal study of seriously at-risk children who matured into resilient, successful adults found that they received unconditional love from family or nonfamily mentors, who encouraged their curiosity, interests, and dreams and assigned them responsibilities that helped them to discover their strengths and weaknesses (Werner and Smith 1992). We can also provide this support in the classroom—and parents, guardians, and other community members can help.

Cognitive science research is now providing some welcome biological support for practices that many educators have felt were simply right, even though these strategies take more instructional time and energy and result in less precise evaluations. Serotonin was identified as a neurotransmitter at about the time that Werner began her studies of resilient at-risk children in 1955—with no hint of the powerful biological substrate of her research. That kind of research is now becoming available to us. Let's use it.

References

Johnson, D., and R. Johnson. (1955). *Reducing School Violence Through Conflict Resolution.* Alexandria, Va.: ASCD.

Sapolsky, R. (1994). *Why Zebras Don't Get Ulcers: A Guide to Stress, Stress-Related Diseases, and Coping.* New York: Freeman.

Werner, E., and R. Smith. (1992). *Overcoming the Odds: High Risk Children from Birth to Adulthood.* Ithaca, N.Y.: Cornell University Press.

Wright, R. (March 13, 1995). "The Biology of Violence." *The New Yorker:* 68–77.

Wurtman, J., and S. Suffes. (1996). *The Serotonin Solution: The Potent Brain Chemical That Can Help You Stop Bingeing, Lose Weight, and Feel Great.* New York: Fawcett Columbine.

Maureen A. Manning

 **NO**

Self-Concept and Self-Esteem in Adolescents

Deena had repeated 6th grade and was in danger of failing 9th grade. She was tall for her age and often bullied her younger, smaller classmates. The school counselor placed Deena in a self-esteem group and taught lessons from a popular self-esteem curriculum.

When the counselor noticed Deena's behavior becoming progressively worse, she consulted with the school psychologist, who suggested that the school support team review Deena's academic and social needs to determine what skill deficits might be contributing to her behavior, rather than assuming that her self-esteem was the primary problem.

Although Deena did not have a learning disability, she did struggle with reading. The team determined that Deena's self-esteem was adequate but that her reading difficulties contributed to a low academic self-concept. They recommended that the reading specialist provide corrective reading strategies. Two months later, Deena was passing two of her four core classes and her discipline referrals had decreased by 40%.

Self-Concept and Self-Esteem

Teachers, administrators, and parents commonly voice concerns about students' self-esteem. Its significance is often exaggerated to the extent that low self-esteem is viewed as the cause of all evil and high self-esteem as the cause of all good. Promoting high self-concept is important because it relates to academic and life success, but before investing significant time, money, and effort on packaged programs, principals should understand why such endeavors have failed and what schools can do to effectively foster students' self-esteem and self-concept.

Although the terms *self-concept* and *self-esteem* are often used interchangeably, they represent different but related constructs. *Self-concept* refers to a student's perceptions of competence or adequacy in academic and non-academic (e.g., social, behavioral, and athletic) domains and is best represented by a profile of self-perceptions across domains. *Self-esteem* is a student's overall evaluation of him- or herself, including feelings of general happiness and satisfaction. Schools are most likely to support students' positive self-esteem by implementing strategies that promote their self-concept.

Development of Self-Concept

Students frequently display a decline in self-concept during elementary school and the transition to middle level. This decrease represents an adaptive reaction to the overly positive self-perceptions that are characteristic of childhood. Young children tend to overestimate their competence because they lack the cognitive maturity to critically evaluate their abilities and to integrate information from multiple sources. As students develop, they better understand how others view their skills and better distinguish between their efforts and abilities. As a result, their self-perceptions become increasingly accurate.

As students transition from middle level to high school, their self-concept gradually grows. Increasing freedom allows adolescents greater opportunities to participate in activities in which they are competent, and increased perspective-taking abilities enable them to garner more support from others by behaving in more socially acceptable ways.

Myths and Misunderstandings

Many myths and misunderstandings about self-concept and self-esteem persist despite a wealth of empirical evidence that "self-esteem per se is not the social panacea that many people once hoped it was."

Self-Concept and Academic Achievement
Self-concept is frequently positively correlated with academic performance, but it appears to be a *consequence* rather than a cause of high achievement. This suggests that increasing students' academic skills is a more effective means to boost their self-concept than vice versa.

Self-Concept and Aggression
Another popular assumption is that aggressive students have low self-concept and use aggression as a means of raising it. Substantial research contradicts this assumption, showing that many aggressive students express adequate, if not inflated, self-concept.

Self-Concept, Depression, and Use of Illegal Substances
Low self-concept is often considered a defining characteristic of depression, but the evidence for this is weak. Similarly, although some evidence suggests that low self-concept may be a weak risk factor for smoking in girls, the relationship between self-concept and the use of alcohol and illegal drugs has little support.

Baumeister et at. (2003) suggest that self-concept is "not a major predictor or cause of almost anything" (p. 37). Principals are advised not to focus on self-concept in hopes of preventing or remediating children's academic or interpersonal problems but rather to focus on building students' competencies and self-perceptions, which in turn will promote their self-concept and, ultimately, self-esteem.

Preventing Low Self-Concept

Effective prevention targets the primary antecedents of self-worth, namely perceived success in areas in which students desire success and approval from significant others. Although these two factors are highly related, excesses in one area cannot compensate for deficits in the other because the effects are additive rather than compensatory.

Promoting Competence in Domains of Importance

To view themselves positively, students must feel competent in domains that they deem important. Two domains that educators greatly influence are academics and behavior. For students who highly value these two domains—most adolescents—steady messages of academic and behavioral incompetence (e.g., poor grades, retention, public reprimands, and suspension) are likely to result in low self-concept.

Self-perceived physical appearance has the strongest relationship to overall self-esteem, whereas self-perceived athletic competence has the weakest relationship. Given adolescents' tendency to base their perceptions of attractiveness on media figures, schools should help students understand that it is unrealistic and unhealthy to adopt such standards and should reinforce healthier values.

Perceptions of competence in domains that are valued by significant others also contribute to overall self-esteem. Parents often value scholastic competence and behavioral conduct, whereas peers often value physical appearance, social competence, and athletic competence. Students may feel incompetent in domains valued by others without necessarily feeling bad about themselves: self-esteem may be protected if students feel competent in areas that they value and discount the importance of the domains others value. Principals should consider the extent to which non-academic areas of competence—technical, artistic/creative, and practical—receive recognition in their schools.

Enhancing Support from Significant Others

Support from parents and peers is particularly important to students' self-concept. When students are young, parental approval is more predictive of self-concept than approval from peers. The influence of peers increases over the course of development, but the influence of parents does not decline. Students' perception of the support they receive is even more important to self-concept than the actual support given.

School staff members can help parents and peers be more effective "supporters" by providing suggestions and opportunities for appropriate positive reinforcement, and they can help students learn to be more aware of the support they receive. Although the direct effects of teacher support on student self-concept remain unstudied, close relationships with teachers increase students' academic and social skills and may therefore indirectly enhance self-concept.

Interventions

The interventions for a student who is considered to have tow self-concept should be based on an accurate assessment of the student's deficits and targeted to the student's individual needs.

Packaged Programs

Avoid packaged programs that promise to boost self-concept. They do not work.

Assumptions

Do not assume that students with deficits or difficulties in academics, behavior, or other domains have low self-esteem, even if they are bullying others, receiving low grades, or showing symptoms of depression.

Assessments

Assess students' self-concept using theoretically sound, empirically validated instruments before investing time, money, and effort trying to correct deficits that may not exist. Use the results of the assessment to determine whether intervention is warranted and, if so, whether it should be directed toward the classroom, the student, the home, or a combination thereof. Trained school mental health professionals should conduct and interpret these assessments and work with the student support team to implement and evaluate interventions.

Placement Decisions

Ensure that special education teams do not make placement decisions on the basis of the *presumed* effects of a particular setting on self-concept. Although inclusive settings are often assumed to protect self-concept by reducing the stigmatization associated with placement in a separate special education classroom, two recent meta-analyses fail to support this, at least for students with learning disabilities.

The two reviews also failed to support the opposite assumption, that inclusive settings may be more damaging to students' self-concept because of negative comparisons with higher-achieving peers. Students are most likely to experience enhanced self-concept when they are placed in an academic setting where they find the greatest success.

Interventions

Interventions should be individualized but generally should involve building students' skills in areas in which they have deficits. For example, students who express low academic self-concept and experience reading difficulties may benefit from interventions designed to build their literacy skills. Students do not have to experience success in every possible domain to develop adequate or high self-concept. They simply must experience success in a few domains that they value.

Students may benefit from learning skills that not only increase their competence in areas of importance but also help them gain more support from others. Interventions that promote academic competence and better behavior will not only further core education objectives and school success but also can engender higher levels of parent support and consequently student self-concept. It is important that schools also address domains that are valued by peers. Students who lack attributes in these domains may benefit from interventions that address these areas such as social skills training or nutrition and exercise programs. In some cases, it may be most effective to help students reevaluate the importance they attach to particular sources of support. For example, students may need to discount the importance of the support they lack from the popular crowd and focus on the support they receive from others.

Sometimes students lack accurate perceptions of the skills or support they have. In such cases, students may benefit from therapeutic techniques that help them see that they are more competent or more supported than they believe. Research supports the effectiveness of cognitive-behavioral techniques for modifying children's self-perceptions when used by properly trained individuals. Principals should consult school psychologists and counselors trained in cognitive-behavioral interventions regarding the use of such techniques.

Classroom Interventions

Classroom interventions, such as peer tutoring and cooperative learning, may promote self-concept by increasing students' academic skills and perceptions of social support. Teachers can use appropriate positive feedback to maintain positive self-concept. Praise, recognition, and encouragement are strong determinants of positive self-perceptions.

Teachers can prevent or reduce feelings of low self-concept by reducing social comparison cues in the classroom. Helping students change the point of reference they use when judging their abilities may help them change their self-perceptions. Encouraging students to focus on how much they have improved over time instead of focusing on how their peers are doing is a simple way of avoiding negative self-perceptions and low motivation.

Teachers also can promote self-concept by fostering supportive relationships among students. Students' perceptions of their classroom as a caring community are positively related to their academic, social, and global self-concepts. The relationship between sense of community and academic self-concept is particularly pronounced in high-poverty schools. Schoolwide interventions that develop students' sense of belonging, eliminate bullying, and promote prosocial values and self-discipline can be effective.

Conclusion

Self-concept and self-esteem are among the most widely discussed but misunderstood constructs in education. The good news is that principals do not need to invest already-stretched resources in another program. In fact, most schools already address positive self-concept and self-esteem through their efforts to build students' academic and social competencies and create environments in which students feel supported. The challenge is to reframe the understanding of self-concept so that adults are focusing on the right strategies to foster students' sense of competence and self-worth.

POSTSCRIPT

Should Schools Try to Increase Students' Self-Esteem?

Critics of the self-esteem movement have amassed considerable evidence indicating that students who are rewarded for mediocre work or unduly praised for succeeding at trivial tasks not only fail to benefit but may actually be harmed. Some argue that the self-esteem movement has produced students who are afraid to take on challenging academic tasks because they fear failure and embarrassment. Other critics suggest that the self-esteem movement may produce students who are arrogant and egotistical. Roy Baumeister, a particularly vocal critic of the self-esteem movement, has suggested that in some instances inflated self-esteem may be associated with a penchant for bullying and violence. See "Should Schools Try to Boost Self-Esteem? Beware the Dark Side," *American Educator* (Summer 1996). In short, the critics' message is that academic standards must come first. Students should be praised, but only when they earn it—when they meet the expectations of teachers, school administrators, and the community. Only then, critics argue, will student self-evaluations be realistic and, thus, "healthy."

But should this message be extended to all students? Supporters of the self-esteem movement argue that many students are so ill-prepared for even the most basic academic tasks that they face constant failure and, thus, threats to self-esteem at every turn. These students include those with emotional and behavioral problems, those with learning disabilities or intellectual disabilities and those from severely economically disadvantaged backgrounds. Supporters also argue that many children leave school at the end of the day bound for impoverished homes and neighborhoods that have been "written off" by society and do nothing to help self-esteem. It is such "at-risk" students who supporters say benefit from the self-esteem movement. These students need a chance to succeed and to feel competent before they are required to tackle the challenge of a higher set of academic standards. Indeed, Sylwester implies that a failure to provide such opportunities will ensure that these students will continue to fail and might even lead them to resort to violence or other antisocial behaviors. Empirical studies of this claim, however, have yet to be conducted.

Readers interested in articles about the concept of self-esteem and its development should turn to "Processes Underlying the Construction, Maintenance, and Enhancement of the Self-Concept of Children," by Susan Harter, in Jerry Suls and G. Greenwald, eds., *Psychological Perspectives on the Self, Vol. 3* (Lawrence Erlbaum, 1986). To learn more about the negative consequences of self-esteem, see "Psychological Risk Factors Contributing to Adolescent Suicide Ideation," by Susan Harter and D. B. Marold, in Gil G. Noam and Sophie Borst, eds., *Children, Youth, and Suicide: Developmental Perspectives* (Jossey-Bass, 1992).

There are many readable critiques of the self-esteem movement in addition to the paper by Roy Baumeister cited above. These include "Praise That Doesn't Demean, Criticism That Doesn't Wound," by Adele Faber and Elaine Mazlish with Lisa Nyberg and Rosalyn Anstine Templeton, *American Educator* (Summer 1995), "Self-Esteem and Excellence: The Choice and the Paradox," by Barbara Lerner, *American Educator* (Summer 1996), and "The Perils and Promises of Praise," by Carol S. Dweck, *Educational Leadership* (October 2007). Finally, techniques for enhancing self-esteem in the classroom can be found in "Implementing a Successful Affective Curriculum," by Susan J. Wood, *Theory into Practice* (November 1996); "Self-Esteem: Its Effect on the Development and Learning of Children with EBD," by Andrew Margerison, *Support for Learning* (vol. 11, no. 4, 1996); and *Guide to Human Development for Future Educators,* by Leonard Abbeduto and Stephen N. Elliott (McGraw-Hill, 1998).

ISSUE 6

Should Character Education Define the Values We Teach Students?

YES: Merle J. Schwartz, Alexandra Beatty, and Eileen Dachnowicz, from "Character Education: Frill or Foundation?" *Principal Leadership* (December, 2006)

NO: Pamela Bolotin Joseph and Sara Efron, from "Seven Worlds of Moral Education," *Phi Delta Kappan* (March, 2005)

ISSUE SUMMARY

YES: Merle J. Schwartz, Alexandra Beatty, and Ellen Dachnowicz, who are all affiliated with Character Education Partnership in Washington, DC, argue that identifying and teaching core values such as civic engagement and virtue can improve academic performance, school climate, and individual character.

NO: Pamela Bolotin Joseph, a faculty member at Antioch University, and Sara Efron, a faculty member at National-Louis University, argue for a broader moral curriculum, one that goes beyond character education to include cultural competence and a commitment to peace, justice, and social action.

U.S. society is in a state of moral decay, or so say many government officials, politicians, and religious leaders. And, indeed, there are many alarming trends reflecting a tendency of citizens to harm or devalue themselves and others. Crime, violence, and high-risk behaviors (e.g., drug and alcohol abuse) are more common today than they were a few decades ago. In the past, concerns about the moral state of society typically led to a renewed interest in—and dedication to—society's children, who were seen as the hope for the future. What is unique about today's disintegration of the social order is that many of the crimes, acts of violence, and problem behaviors of greatest concern are those perpetrated by children and youth. Perhaps even more startling are the acts of violence committed by children against other children *at school*. In addition to the acts of violence, many social commentators point with concern and outrage to increases in teenage pregnancy, drug and alcohol abuse, gambling, and other problem activities. It often seems that every new report disseminated by the media suggests that children are engaging in risky or criminal behaviors at younger and younger ages.

Many social critics have argued that the solution to this problem is to teach morality, or values in school. These critics suggest that schools rather than families must be the source of moral education because the American family is itself in disarray. As evidence that many families are poorly prepared to conduct the requisite moral education, critics point to the increasing divorce rate, the fact that the majority of American children live for at least some part of their lives in a single-parent home, and the decline in the amount of time that parents spend with their children. In fact, many believe that this so-called disintegration of the American family is largely responsible for what they see as the dismal moral state of today's youth.

Calls for the inclusion of a moral agenda in the school curriculum harken back to the early history of education in the United States. Prior to the twentieth century, moral education, which often took the form of inculcating a system of values and beliefs reflective of a particular religious ideology, was commonplace. In fact, the Bible was often the primary textbook not only for the curriculum of values but also for the more strictly academic curriculum. It was not until recently that the debate about the separation of church and state led to a more secular and, some would say, less moral curriculum. This movement away from explicit instruction in religiously derived morality was greatly hastened in the 1960s and 1970s by a rejection of "traditional" values and authority and an increased emphasis on personal freedom and autonomy. In more recent years, the increasing cultural diversity of U.S. schools has facilitated the adoption of moral relativism, a belief that there are differences across cultures (and perhaps even between individuals within a culture) with regard to the systems of values held and that all those systems should be seen as equally valid and moral.

Should schools once again incorporate morality into their agendas? What should this moral curriculum look like? Whose values should it reflect? Have American schools really stopped teaching moral values, or have they simply been teaching values that are at odds with the values held by those who call for a return to morality? These are some of the questions that shape the debate reflected in the following selections. In the first selection, Merle Schwartz, Alexandra Beatty, and Eileen Dachnowicz describe several successful character education programs that not only inculcated specific moral traits and values in students but also improved academic performance. These programs stress the use of role models of, and reinforcement for, engaging in specific behaviors thought to be critical for the functioning of a democratic society such as ours. In the second selection, Pamela Bolotin Joseph and Sara Efron argue that the traits and behaviors at the center of character education represent only one possible instantiation of moral education. Joseph and Efron suggest that equally important as the values of moral education are behaviors and modes of thought derived from non-mainstream or non-U.S. cultures, an ethic of caring and nurturing, an orientation toward peace, an inclination toward social action, and a commitment to justice and ethical inquiry.

YES ↵

Merle J. Schwartz, Alexandra Beatty, and Eileen Dachnowicz

Character Education: Frill or Foundation?

Accountability. The word resounds in states, districts, and schools as educational programs come under close scrutiny. Proof of academic performance often serves as the litmus test for maintaining instructional practices and programs. Just as the national focus on academic improvement has gained momentum, so too has another movement calling for character education. Educators find themselves caught in the middle, questioning whether character education is just another passing fad or a valid educational initiative that will positively affect student performance as well as attitude.

Although character education has gained momentum at the elementary school level and has made considerable strides in middle level schools, high school faculties are still less than enthusiastic about adopting it. It is easy to see how some teachers, long exhausted from serving as the custodians of the prevailing education fashion, look skeptically at this movement. Faced with the formidable challenge of high-stakes testing, they wonder how they can prepare their students for state standardized tests as well as the SAT and AP exams and still find time to accent ethical qualities. Some teachers may listen wistfully to success stories in which character education has transformed school culture. Many can easily point out that a lack of ethical values seems to be the root of many of the problems in schools.

What Does Science Say?

The Character Education Partnership (CEP), a national advocacy group for character education in Washington, DC, aims to help educators and policymakers make informed decisions about character education by identifying and describing strategies that work. Each year for the past nine years, CEP has recognized approximately 10 elementary and secondary schools as National Schools of Character because of their exemplary implementation of character education. Through reading thousands of applications and visiting more than 180 award-winning schools, CEP has collected a wealth of effective strategies and also observed a correlation between the effective implementation of character education and improved school culture and academic advancement.

From *Principal Leadership,* December 2006, pp. 25–30. Copyright © 2006 by National Association of Secondary School Principals. Reprinted by permission. For more information about NASSP programs and services, visit www.principals.org.

Interviews and record reviews of middle level and high school award winners showed that character education had positive effects on discipline, student and faculty member morale, and student performance. For example, Kennedy Middle School in Eugene, OR, showed a 15% improvement in meeting or exceeding the state's academic benchmarks and a 65% decrease in discipline referrals. Halifax (PA) Middle School reported not only the elimination of vandalism but also a total change in student attitude toward academic success. In addition to improved disciplinary statistics, high school winners—such as South Carroll High School in Sykesville, MD, and Cranford (NJ) High School—have reported a steady increase in their SAT averages. Site visitors observed that school size and geographical location did not appear to be the contributing factor to the school's success. Eleanor Roosevelt High School in Greenbelt, MD, which has nearly 3,000 students, and private New Hampton (NH) School, which has 325, have benefited from character education.

The outcomes of character education, however, are difficult to measure. Most studies either have referred to the results of specific commercial programs or have relied heavily on anecdotal accounts. But two recent studies of character education programs, funded largely by the John Templeton Foundation, provide evidence of their effectiveness—and describe strategies that will help middle level and high school educators who want to initiate or improve character education in their schools.

These data-driven studies approach character education scientifically from two different perspectives. The first explores the character education initiatives in 24 high schools that have received recognition for excellence; the second study examines 69 research studies on 33 specific character education programs to provide empirical evidence of what works in character education. The two studies fit together like pieces of a puzzle to confirm what many have long argued: effective character education not only improves school climate and student behavior but also can lead to academic improvement.

What Is Character Education?

The phrase *character education* does not refer to a single approach or even a single list of the values that are taught in character education programs. *Character education* is often the umbrella term that describes concerted efforts to teach a number of qualities, such as civic virtues, respect and responsibility, social and emotional learning, empathy and caring, tolerance for diversity, and service to the community. Citizens need training in each of these areas to develop the moral and ethical stamina that enables them to contribute positively to a democratic society. Because a democratic society depends on a citizenry that shares such values as justice, fairness, responsibility, and caring, many believe that it is the obligation of schools, both public and private, to teach such values.

Lickona and Davidson (2005) point out that strength of character is necessary for the development of civic character: "Becoming a person of civic character, for example, requires the development of ethical thinking, moral agency, and a battery of social and emotional skills" (p. 178). Individual research on character and civic education adds additional characteristics to the definition of *character*. In emphasizing the role of living in an increasingly globalized economy. Nordgren (2002) exhorts schools to foster highly effective teamwork and shared decision making because people's lives are intertwined in a shrinking world.

Although some schools and districts choose commercial programs so staff members and families will be on the same page as far as language and goals are concerned, many schools have developed homegrown programs that address their students' specific needs. Some are comprehensive, and others are a compilation of books, Web sites, and other resources that educators can mine for ideas.

All character education programs share the following goals:

- Increasing students' awareness of moral and ethical questions
- Affecting students' attitudes regarding such questions
- Affecting students' actions.

Some programs target specific behaviors—they aim to reduce rates of disciplinary action, cheating, teen pregnancy, drug use, and the like. Others may aim to promote positive behaviors, such as community involvement and civic participation. Still others focus on developing skills or fostering complex thinking about ethical issues—and many incorporate multiple goals.

The boundaries of character education are imprecise. These goals overlap with those for other efforts, such as civic education programs and service-learning programs. By 2002, however, roughly three-fourths of the states were actively encouraging their versions of character education; 14 states mandated some form of it, another 14 encouraged it through legislation, and another 10 supported it in other ways.

Does It Work? Can We Tell?

Lickona and Davidson (2005) document a three-part effort to identify practices that seem to hold promise for character education at the secondary level. Beginning with a broad review of the literature on adolescent development, high school reform, and character education, the authors developed a framework for thinking about the characteristics of high schools that integrate ethics and excellence. First, they identified 24 high schools that had received external recognition for excellence. The schools, ranging in size from 300 to 4,300 students, were drawn from every section of the country and included public and private schools in rural, suburban, and urban settings. The researchers examined each school closely to ascertain successful strategies and develop generalizations about effective practice that is based on those strategies. Using focus groups, classroom observations, interviews, and analyses of program materials and archival data, the team developed portraits of the schools and their practices.

The findings are organized around the "promising practices" that the team identified as most effective for developing both individuals with key character traits and an ethical learning community. The authors present their findings in the form of six principles for developing such a community:

1. Develop shared purpose and identity. Explicit expectations for personal behavior as well as academic achievement—such as an honor code, a school motto, and school traditions—provide important direction for students.
2. Align practices with desired outcomes and relevant research. Offering staff members and parents specific guidance about research-based strategies for meeting designated goals reinforces a school's efforts.
3. Have a voice; take a stand. Allowing students to have a voice in the classroom and in school affairs—as well as listening to faculty and staff members, parents, and community members—contributes to excellence and ethics in a school.
4. Take personal responsibility for continuous self-development. Adult members of the school community can set an example for students by promoting the need to strive for excellence and to engage in self-reflection. Thus, a culture of excellence and fostering personal responsibility is created in classrooms and schoolwide.
5. Practice collective responsibility for excellence and ethics. In a community that values ethics and excellence, adults and students intervene right away when others need support to succeed or do the right thing.
6. Grapple with tough issues. Collective responsibility for an ethical learning community entails confronting institutional practices or issues that are at odds with the school's commitment to excellence and ethics.

Promising practices also buttress the "eight strengths of character" identified as integral to "smart and good high schools":

• Lifelong learner and critical thinker
• Diligent and capable performer_
• Socially and emotionally skilled person
• Ethical thinker
• Respectful and responsible moral agent
• Self-disciplined person who pursues a healthy lifestyle
• Contributing community member and democratic citizen
• Spiritual person engaged in crafting a life of noble purpose.

After assessing their own school's needs, educators can select from a host of proven instructional strategies, high school reform designs, professional development opportunities, curricular structures, media literacy resources, study skills programs, team challenges, and academic initiatives that they can replicate in their own schools. The report concludes with a question-and-answer section that offers practical advice for initiating or implementing character education programs in schools that have a wide range of concerns.

For teachers who perceive character education as another frill that interferes with the real business of education, namely academic growth, this study shows that teaching ethical values goes hand-in-hand with academic per-formance. A headmaster of a small, private school interviewed for the study summed up his vision: "'To have an engaging school, you need three things: teachers ready to teach, students ready to learn, and something important to teach.'" Lickona and Davidson's study provides practitioners with verified strategies for character education that have worked in shaping high schools of excellence, strategies that middle level and high school educators can adapt to the needs of their schools.

Berkowitz and Bier (2005), the authors of the second study, look at exist-ing research on character education programs "to help practitioners to be more effective in fostering the development of students' character" (p. 23). They began with a fairly broad definition of *character education:* "any school-based K–12 initiatives either intended to promote the development of some aspect of student character or for which some aspect of student character was measured as a relevant outcome variable" (p. 3). They sought to address four questions:

- For which programs is there research demonstrating effectiveness?
- What are the characteristics of effective programs?
- What do schools generally do that is effective?
- What are the effects of specific character education practices?

To answer the first question, Berkowitz and Bier identified 109 research studies that were potentially relevant and found that 69 of them provided sci-entifically sound evidence that 33 of the programs studied were effective. This list of programs provided the basis for answering the second question. The team developed lists of pedagogical strategies and other characteristics of the 33 programs for which there was some evidence of successful outcomes and col-lected data about how prevalent these strategies were. The question about the effectiveness of these strategies was more difficult to address, and the authors suggest that support for additional research on that question is needed.

On the question of the outcomes of character education, the team found an overall success rate of 51%—approximately half the time, positive change was found to result from the program studied. Among the areas in which the researchers noted the greatest degree of positive change were sociomoral cognition (thinking about ethical and moral issues), prosocial behaviors and attitudes, sexual behavior, problem-solving skills, and drug use. Moreover, the researchers found that cooperative learning and class discussions of moral issues were the most effective practices for producing academic and social outcomes.

From this review, Berkowitz and Bier (2005) concluded that, when effec-tively implemented, character education programs of many kinds can have a significant impact on young people and that the effects can be quite long last-ing. They identified features that were characteristic of effective programs:

- Professional development. All 33 of the effective programs identified incorporated ongoing professional development.
- Peer interaction. All 33 also incorporated strategies for fostering peer interaction, such as discussion, role playing, and cooperative learning.

- Direct teaching and skill training. Many of the programs included direct instruction about character as well as teaching specific intrapersonal (e.g., self-management) and interpersonal (e.g., conflict resolution) skills and capacities.
- Explicit agenda. More than half the programs studied use specific language about character, morality, values, or ethics.
- Family and community involvement. Including parents and other community members—as recipients of character education and as participants in the design and delivery of the programs—was a common strategy.
- Models and mentors. Both peer and adult role models foster character development.
- Integration into academic curricula. Nearly half of the effective programs are integrated with academic curricula in some way, most often through social studies and language arts curricula.
- Multiple strategies. Virtually all of the effective programs use a multi-strategy approach, rather than relying on a single model or tool.

How Does It Add Up?

These two studies offer a wealth of detail and descriptions that enrich the picture of how and why particular strategies stand out as effective. The data presented in the two studies indicate that character education initiatives affect student attitudes and behavior, thus setting the stage for improved academic performance.

They also take different but equally important approaches to the challenge of drawing conclusions about what works in character education. What is interesting in comparing the studies is that despite the difference in focus, there was similarity in identifying earmarks of fruitful character education programs at the secondary level, including:

- Goals should be both explicit and ambitious
- Professional development is necessary
- The whole school community should be involved, and everyone should have a voice
- Adults need to be role models.

Transforming the culture of a middle level or high school is not easy. As these studies point out, however, through careful planning, professional development, and involvement of all members of the school community, character education becomes far more than a passing fad; it is the road map to building a caring school culture, a safer and more-nurturing environment, and a more responsible and responsive student body, all of which lay the foundation for improved academic performance.

**Pamela Bolotin Joseph
and Sara Efron**

 **NO**

Seven Worlds of Moral Education

In his striking critique of character education, Alfie Kohn suggests that educators might want to "define our efforts to promote children's social and moral development as an *alternative*" to character education.[1] In this article, we address Kohn's question "What does the alternative look like?" by describing the aims, practices, advantages, and difficulties of seven worlds of moral education—of which character education is only one. Lastly, we consider why character education should be the dominant approach to moral education in the United States when there are inspiring alternatives.

Viewing moral education as comprising various "moral worlds" helps us to imagine classrooms and schools that consistently support the beliefs, values, and visions that will shape students into adults and determine the world they will make. In such environments, moral education is a coherent endeavor created with purpose and deliberation. Educators in moral worlds believe that they must create a process through which young people can learn to recognize values that represent prosocial behaviors, engage in actions that bring about a better life for others, and appreciate ethical and compassionate conduct.

We describe below the moral worlds of character education, cultural heritage, caring community, peace education, social action, just community, and ethical inquiry. These worlds do not exist in isolation, nor are their purposes diametrically opposed; they may, in fact, share several characteristics. Classrooms and schools can also create coherent hybrid approaches that combine aspects of several moral worlds. Nonetheless, to clarify and foster conversations about moral education, we explore these approaches to social and ethical development as distinct moral worlds.

Character Education

The moral world of character education rests on the conviction that schooling can shape the behavior of young people by inculcating in them the proper virtues. Proponents of this world argue that children need clear directions and good role models and, implicitly, that schools should shape character when families are deficient in this task. Advocates also recommend giving students numerous opportunities to do good deeds, such as taking part in service learning, which they believe will eventually lead to moral habits. Moreover, character educators believe in establishing strong incentives for good behavior.[2]

To no small extent, *The Book of Virtues,* by William Bennett, influences many character education programs. The virtues Bennett describes are "self-discipline, compassion, responsibility, friendship, work, courage, perseverance, honesty, loyalty, and faith." Another strong influence is Character Counts, a coalition that posits "six pillars of character": 1) be honest; 2) treat others with respect; 3) do what you are supposed to do; 4) play by the rules; 5) be kind; and 6) do your share to make your school and community better. Communities have also developed their own sets of traits or rules that guide character education programs.[3]

How do schools create a moral world using character traits as starting points? First, modeling virtuous behavior is a key component of character education programs—teachers, administrators, and students are instructed to be role models. Many schools call attention to character traits in public forums and displays such as assemblies, daily announcements, bulletin boards, and banners, as well as in the study of history and literature. School 18 in Albany, New York, uses "positive reinforcement of good character traits" through a Kids for Character program. "Students who are 'caught' doing something that shows good character have their names posted where the entire school community can see. Then, each Friday, those students are called to the office to receive a reward."[4]

Schools may emphasize a different character trait each month in curricular content and assemblies. In the Kent City Schools in Ohio, November is "compassion" month. In social studies classes, students "study those who immigrated to this country at great personal sacrifice, develop a school or community service project, and research the Underground Railroad and consider how people extended help to those escaping slavery." Self-control is the trait for December. In physical education classes, students "devise an exercise chart to help monitor personal fitness." In language arts, they "keep a personal journal of times self-control was used." And in math classes, they "graph the number of times students hand in assignments on time." Teachers may also infuse their classroom management strategies and lessons with respect for aspects of character.[5]

A strength of the character education moral world is educators' belief that it is their responsibility to form character rather than remain indifferent to their students' moral development. Another positive aspect of this approach is the goal of proponents to infuse character education throughout the curriculum and school environment in order for students to experience the consistency of a moral world both academically and socially.

However, character education raises a number of critical questions that its advocates have not satisfactorily addressed. Are behavioral traits in fact the same as moral character? Do displays of virtues or desired traits truly encourage moral behavior? Does the posting of character traits on banners and bulletin boards result in a "marquee mentality" and therefore not reach the hearts and minds of young people? Is character education merely indoctrination of dominant cultural standards that may not represent the values of diverse communities? And finally, do the values chosen by character educators reflect the status quo and encourage compliance with it?[6]

Cultural Heritage

Like character education, the moral world of cultural heritage emphasizes values. These values, however, are not those of the mainstream but, instead, are drawn from the traditions of nondominant cultures. Unlike character education, there are no underlying assumptions that schools may have better values than those of communities and families or that schools need to instill character traits in children that may run counter to students' own cultural values. In the cultural heritage moral world, the spheres of school, home, and community are interconnected. Parents, elders, and cultural leaders educate children within and outside the walls of the school. Moreover, students learn cultural traditions and values not through direct instruction but by deep understanding of and participation in the culture's arts and ceremonies.

One embodiment of the cultural heritage world is the values instruction offered in Afrocentric schools. For example, the mission statement of the African American Academy for Accelerated Learning in Minneapolis affirms the importance of "reconnecting African American families to their cultural heritage, spirituality and history." The mission of the African American Academy, a public school in Seattle, is to instruct students in a way that "embraces the history, culture and heritage of African and African American people by studying and putting into practice the seven principles of Nguzo Saba: Umoja (Unity), Kujichagulia (Self-Determination), Ujima (Collective Work and Responsibility), Ujamaa (Cooperative Economics), Nia (Purpose), Kuumba (Creativity), and Imani (Faith)." Afrocentric schools emphasize parent involvement. In a report to the Kansas City Missouri Board of Education, the African Centered Education Task Force affirmed the African proverb "It takes an entire village to raise just one child" by giving parents an essential role in African-centered schools as "partners of the village."[7]

Native American schools that teach language, customs, and history also create the moral world of cultural heritage. In Native American education, cherished values include "respect [for] people and their feelings, especially respecting elders, and living in harmony with nature." Schools are imbued with a "sense of empathy and kinship with other forms of life" and a belief that "there should be no division between school climate and culture and family and community climate and culture." Parents and elders are present throughout the school, and students and teachers are expected to be in the community and the natural environment as well as in the classroom. The Tulalip Heritage School in Washington State (jointly sponsored by the public school district, the Boys and Girls Club, and the Tulalip Tribe) transmits its ethos to the students by having them learn the stories of ancestors, cultivating respect for Native American culture and "respect for one another," and recognizing the importance of community. The NAWAYEE Center School, an alternative high school in Minneapolis, offers cultural classes that "include art, spirituality, family, community, and oral traditions" but also strives to ensure that "American Indian cultural values and beliefs are modeled and integrated throughout the entire curriculum."[8]

The cultural heritage moral world has a number of advantages. Cultural heritage schools demonstrate respect for the cultures of their students by not just paying lip service to cultural diversity but being seriously committed to the sustenance of cultures. Partnerships with communities and meaningful parent involvement create active stakeholders in these schools and foster greater commitment to education. Continuity between the culture of the home and that of the school allows for moral instruction to use familiar patterns of communication, both verbal and nonverbal. As they learn through culturally congruent education, students do not experience a disjunction between their families' and schools' moral instruction. Furthermore, students have opportunities to learn more about their communities' moral values through the study of their history and culture, so moral learning is embedded within academic scholarship.[9]

A difficulty in implementing this model of moral education is its dependence on educators who come from the students' cultures or who themselves have deep knowledge of the culture. Districts clearly must do all that is possible to attract such educators and to sponsor community members in teacher preparation programs. Also, although all schools benefit from parents' and elders' participation, a fully realized moral world of cultural heritage would be most desired in certain schools or districts in which a significant percentage of the students are from one ethnic culture. it is crucial, however, to be sensitive to the concerns of the community. This model of moral education cannot be imposed upon a community, but it should be provided if the community so desires. Moreover, a focus on the cultural heritage of a community in no way precludes the need to learn the skills required for success in the dominant culture. Indeed, all the schools mentioned here also have a strong academic focus.

Caring Community

The caring community emphasizes the ethic of care—nurturing, closeness, emotional attachment, and respectful, mutually supportive relationships. This moral world also focuses on the social and emotional health of all its community members. As the individuals in the classroom and the school begin to feel like a family, the school's institutional image is replaced by that of a home. Educators' moral influence stems from their caring relationships with students, parents, and one another. In the caring community, students are not rewarded for individual empathic actions; instead, these behaviors are considered the norm of the classroom culture.[10]

Accounts of schools as caring communities describe how teachers, administrators, parents, and students feel that they are members of a community. In these schools, class size is small, teachers are mentored, and all staff members feel and demonstrate genuine concern for students. In the classroom, nurturing peer relationships develop as students care for one another through informal and planned activities and structures such as buddy systems.[11]

In academics, the theme of caring is introduced through service learning projects and the study of literature that accentuates interpersonal and intercultural understanding. The classroom environment features discussions and cooperative learning activities and is defined not by rules but by how students feel about being in the class and being with one another. For example, at the Russ School in California, children developed a list of "Ways We Want to Be in Room Eight" as their classroom rules rather than a list of prohibitions.[12]

Inclusiveness is another theme in the caring community, as schools welcome and nurture diverse populations, including special education students. For instance, when the Lincoln Center Middle School in Milwaukee chose to become a caring community, it expressed caring by selecting students by means of a lottery for all who were interested in its arts-based curriculum rather than by holding auditions or having specific admissions requirements. This moral world also features schoolwide activities that involve parents and community members. Moreover, families and school personnel communicate with one another about students' academic progress, social development, and emotional health.[13]

The caring community has numerous benefits for students. Researchers from the Developmental Studies Center Child Development Project report that children educated in such schools perceive their classrooms as fair, safe, caring places that are conducive to learning. Once more, students "with a strong sense of community [are] more likely to act ethically and altruistically, develop social and emotional competencies, avoid drug use and violent behavior, and [be] academically motivated." Emotional well-being is the catalyst for moral development in the caring community. As students feel respected and cared for in loving classroom and school environments, they are less likely to act out "from feelings of inferiority, cynicism, or egocentrism that blind them to others' feelings." Furthermore, students who are nurtured are more likely to expand their sphere of caring from friends, teachers, and families to others in their communities.[14]

Difficulties for educators who wish to create a caring community occur when school culture—large class size, disruptive pullout programs, and a history of not welcoming families—thwarts the building of caring relationships. Although educators may strive to create a caring classroom, students and teachers may feel "uncared for" when the school environment is hostile. Unfortunately, the students most in need of caring often have schools whose resources cannot support this moral world.[15]

Peace Education

The moral world of peace education stems from an ethic of care that extends beyond the classroom. Moral commitments underpinning peace education include valuing and befriending the Earth, living in harmony with the natural world, recognizing the interrelatedness of all human and natural life, preventing violence toward the Earth and all its peoples, and learning how to create and live in a culture of peace. Peace education promotes "awareness of the interdependence of all things and a profound sense of responsibility for the fate of the planet and for the well-being of humanity."[16]

The components of peace education include:

- conflict resolution—developing skills and appreciation for nonviolent problem solving;
- peace studies—examining the causes of war and its prevention and participating in activities that focus on the meaning of peace and raise peace awareness;
- environmental education—developing an appreciation of and the desire to inquire into the interrelationships of humans, their cultures, their surroundings, and all forms of life;
- global education—recognizing the interdependent nature of the world and studying problems and issues that cut across national boundaries; and
- human rights education—learning about the universal rights of human beings and strengthening respect for fundamental freedoms.[17]

Although many U.S. schools teach violence-reduction skills, few create a holistic moral world that makes a connection between peaceful personal behaviors and promoting peace throughout the world. Maria Montessori's belief that education can contribute to world peace has been a profound influence on some schools that emphasize her vision. One World Montessori School in California is an example of a school devoted to peace as an ultimate moral goal. In its K–8 peace curriculum, "teachers assist the children in developing a common language of peace and work on their own communication, peace making, and peace keeping skills."[18]

Another school that teaches for peace and interconnectedness is the Global Village School in California, which develops materials for home-schoolers. Its "Peacemakers" course "presents role models who work to enact nonviolent social change and concrete examples of such successfully enacted change." And the peace awareness curriculum of the New School at South Shore, a public primary school in Seattle, is inspired by the school's mission to "view each child as a bright spirit on a magnificent journey in our quest to contribute powerfully to the healing of humanity and Mother Earth." The goal of the Environmental and Adventure School, a public school in Washington State, is to develop responsible citizens who are stewards of the Earth. This school's mission is based on the belief that "when students are out in their environment and learn to respect and care for their surroundings, they also learn to respect and care for their classmates and teachers." The theme of "interdependent relationships—people and environments" is woven into the junior high school curriculum both in the classroom and in the many natural settings nearby.[19]

Peace educators teach that all lives and actions matter and that students are connected to all of life through a vision of peace, harmony, and Earth stewardship. Peace educators aim to create "moral sensitivity to others in the immediate classroom [and] concern for local communities and for all life on the planet." Thus the greatest advantage of this moral world is that it nourishes students' desire for personal meaning in increasingly violent times. An academic benefit is that peace education can be integrated into a stimulating curriculum that covers all disciplines, including science, language, and history.[20]

Creating an integrated peace education curriculum is difficult within traditional education systems in which content is taught in discrete disciplines. The greatest hurdle to creating this moral world, however, is the potential for conflict with community values. Undoubtedly, teaching about justice, sustainability, and peace challenges the prevailing world view in the U.S. by promoting values that confront uncontrolled economic development, consumerism, and militarism.

Social Action

In the moral world of social action, the values of justice and compassion guide a curriculum focused on the political nature of society. Educators believe that students are both empathic human beings and social agents who are capable of effecting change by critically examining unjust situations and participating in political processes. Teachers encourage students to ask, "What should I be paying attention to in my world?" The social action approach taps students' idealism for bringing about a better world—to "heal, repair and transform the world."[21]

Students are encouraged to generate ideas, negotiate subject matter, and find learning resources outside of the school setting. They venture into the community to gather documents, conduct interviews, and make observations. Teachers believe that their role is to confront students' ignorance or prejudices by helping the students to understand both privilege and oppression and by cultivating a "critical consciousness" of the perspectives of others.[22]

An example of this moral world occurred at Nova Alternative High School, a public school in Seattle. A junior who works with a human rights group told her classmates and teachers about the difficult situation in East Timor. In response, students began meeting once a week to study East Timor's history, politics, and culture and to raise money for Kay Rala, a small high school in Manatuto that "was burned to the ground by Indonesian soldiers in the late 1990s." Rather than donating money to a charity, the Seattle students established direct contact with Kay Rala and developed a fund-raising system with the students in East Timor. The Seattle students raised thousands of dollars for the school. The student whose concerns sparked the project reported that her "world [had] opened up"—helping her "not only to see people who are less fortunate but instead of accepting dreary situations, to change them."[23]

Another account of the social action moral world is from a fifth-grade class in Aurora, Colorado. When her students were studying the Civil War, teacher Barbara Vogel explained to her pupils that slavery was not merely a defunct system from a bygone era in American history but that people in Sudan and elsewhere were enslaved in the present day. Although the children were horrified and distraught, Vogel did not try to comfort them or to rationalize such horrors. Instead, she sought to channel their feelings of concern and outrage into social action by helping her students start a letter-writing campaign to bring this dire situation to the public's attention. When their letters did not change the fate of Sudanese slaves, the children raised money to buy freedom for a few slaves. As newspapers publicized the children's efforts, donations came in from around the world, and the class eventually purchased the freedom of more than 1,000 people. The class even developed a website to encourage others to stop slavery in Sudan.[24]

A highlight of the social action world is its Integrated curriculum—rich in academic, social, and political knowledge—which reflects the moral concerns of children and adolescents. Educators report that students learn to view themselves as social and political beings with the right to access the systems of influence in communities and the larger world. Through involvement in social action, students come to believe in themselves as moral agents.[25]

Creating this moral world is not without challenges. Teachers are responsible for creating an atmosphere in which students feel comfortable voicing their moral concerns and ensuring that students' ideas are not dismissed. Also, it requires a contemporary, integrated curriculum not constrained by rigid disciplinary boundaries. Moreover, despite the opportunities to make a difference, the social action moral world requires students to encounter misery and critically analyze the reasons for unjust acts and conditions. Accordingly, can students resist pessimism when they cannot easily change the world?

Just Community

In the just community moral world, classrooms and schools become democratic settings that provide students with opportunities to deliberate about moral dilemmas and to participate in cooperative decision making. Students, teachers, and administrators openly discuss and address matters of mutual concern, construct the school community's policies and rules through procedures that are viewed as fair and just, and resolve moral conflicts. In the process of building community, students gain perspectives on the principles of justice and fairness by experiencing moral deliberations and by applying the principles to real and specific problems in the school community.[26]

The just community model, based on the ideas of Lawrence Kohlberg, holds that the goal of moral education is the enhancement of students' development from lower to higher stages of moral reasoning. Advocates for the just community assert that students influence their own moral development by deliberating about and seeking to resolve moral conflicts. Social interactions—i.e., lived moral dilemmas—advance learners' moral judgment as students clarify and refine their thoughts while listening and responding to other points of view. In such environments, "teachers and students engage in philosophical deliberation about the good of the community." Teachers can prepare even young students to participate in a just community by encouraging them to think about rules not as "immutable laws" but as constructed moral guidelines necessary for living in a community.[27]

Two examples of just community schools are in New York State: the Pablo Neruda Academy for Architecture and World Studies in the Bronx and the Scarsdale Alternative School. Both public high schools emphasize students' deliberation about moral dilemmas within real-world situations—freedom combined with responsibility, cooperation over competition, and "how to balance the needs of individuals with those of the community." Features of these schools include community meetings, in which decisions are made about essential school policy; fairness committees, in which conflicts among students or students and teachers are resolved; and advisories, in which students discuss their own problems and plan the agendas for community meetings.[28]

An advantage of the just community is its unequivocal naming of justice as a safeguard of individuals' rights and the community's well-being. The ideal of democracy is both a moral standard and a guiding light, raising awareness of good citizenship within a moral context. Finally, students learn that their views and actions make a difference because their moral inquiries do not seek to resolve hypothetical situations or to prepare them for life outside of school but are focused on the school itself.[29]

One problem with the just community approach is that it takes a great deal of time for students to develop real trust among themselves and to deliberate about and resolve issues. Another difficulty is that most teachers have not been trained to facilitate "an apprenticeship in democracy." Finally, truly democratic school cultures with shared authority have been exceedingly rare, and this moral world cannot exist without students' uninhibited conversations and real decision-making authority.[30]

Ethical Inquiry

In the world of ethical inquiry, moral education is a process by which students engage in "moral conversation" centered on dilemmas. Also influenced by Lawrence Kohlberg's theories, this ethical inquiry approach to moral education is grounded on the premise that deliberation promotes students' moral development. Within respectful, egalitarian, and carefully facilitated discussions, teachers invite students to investigate values or actions and to imagine alternatives. In this world, students consider "how human beings should act," "life's meaning and the human place in the world," "the sources of evil and suffering," and "universal existential concerns and ways of knowing such as the meaning of friendship, love, and beauty."[31]

Teachers guide discussions on the moral dilemmas embedded within subjects across the curriculum. Springboards for ethical inquiry include literature, history, drama, economics, science, and philosophy. In particular, students learn about the consequences of making moral decisions and how fictional characters and real people make choices when aware that a moral question is at stake. Through this process of inquiry, students ponder the effects that moral, immoral, and amoral actions have on themselves and others, empathize with and appreciate the perspectives of others (their classmates as well as fictional characters or historical figures), and construct their understanding of what it means to be a moral human being.[32]

There are numerous accounts of how teachers integrate moral inquiry into their literature, social studies, and science classroom—illustrating that most topics have ethical dimensions. Teachers also use published curricula, such as Philosophy for Children, that provide stories and other media for ethical deliberation. Facing History and Ourselves, a curriculum about 20th-century genocide, focuses on teaching middle and high school students "the meaning of human dignity, morality, law, citizenship, and behavior." This curriculum aims to help students learn to reason morally as they think about their individual decisions and behavior toward others.[33]

A value of the ethical inquiry world is that it is not an "add-on" program but rather a way to integrate genuine moral deliberation into all academic areas—becoming a norm of the classroom culture. Ethical inquiry provides opportunities for students to appreciate others' viewpoints and to bring different perspectives into their own deliberations—important skills for democratic citizenship. This moral world also capitalizes on the process of identity development, making the search for moral identity an explicit goal.[34]

Because it is a process of inquiry and negotiation, a criticism of ethical inquiry is that it does not explicitly teach values. Teachers act as important intellectual role models who care about their students' ideas and their construction of personal ethics, but they do not overtly advocate particular moral standards. Another concern is ethical inquiry's cognitive approach to moral education. Educators do not guide students to help others or to bring about a better society but instead trust that students who think ethically will actively participate in the world beyond the classroom.

Choosing a Moral World

Our description of seven worlds of moral education reveals that there is "no perfect world." All moral worlds have their limitations, and educators face challenges no matter which approach they take to moral education. How then do we select a moral world for classrooms and schools?

Educators face hard choices, but choose they must, as these seven worlds hold dissimilar assumptions about what constitutes best practice for moral education. These worlds also reveal different conceptions of learners. They posit that moral educators can think about students as material to be shaped, as feelers with emotional needs, as thinkers whose judgments can be stimulated, or as villagers who learn from elders. Indeed, these moral worlds hold different understandings of *morality* itself. Does morality mean having good character, nurturing peers, caring for those who suffer (those both near and far), or being stewards of the Earth?

Serious ethical deliberation about the aims and practices of moral education cannot be avoided. It would be a mistake to try to create an approach to moral education that represents the "best of all worlds," because forming an amalgam of many approaches is more likely to result in a haphazard environment in which students receive conflicting messages. Moral educators need to decide on one approach or to create a thoughtfully considered hybrid that has clear aims and coherent practices. Too often, consideration of moral education (as well as any aspect of education) focuses only on the inadequate question of what works rather than on what we define as our utmost hopes for our students and the society in which they will live. When we ask the moral question, not merely the operational one, we allow ourselves to imagine our students having lives of meaning, taking part in genuine and peaceful relationships, and living without violence, cynicism, and despair.

The most popular world of moral education at present is character education. Numerous politicians, organizations, and boards of education advocate its implementation. Yet, as we explore these seven moral worlds, we see that character education has the most limited vision of morality and moral education—despite its advocates' good intentions.

How do we compare naming "the trait of the month" to teaching children to have a deep appreciation for peace and for sustaining the Earth? Why should we select stories in the hope that students will assimilate certain values or emulate heroes when we can teach literature as a springboard for pondering moral dilemmas and developing moral identities? Why should we settle for posting the names of "good" children on a bulletin board when we can aim to create loving, familial classrooms or a village of moral educators? How do we equate mandated service learning with a thought-fully conceived student-led effort of social action, not only to alleviate suffering but also to stop cycles of poverty and injustice?

We question why the dominant approach to moral education consists of the practice of giving rewards to students just for following rules and for occasional acts of kindness. Instead, should we not help students to engage in profound ethical deliberation, revere peace, be cared for and be caring, and develop as moral agents who can repair the world? Why are these not among the endorsed goals of moral education?

In conclusion, the other six moral worlds hold more humane, imaginative, and profound visions of morality and moral education than those of character education. These compelling alternatives deserve serious consideration on the part of educators.

References

1. Alfie Kohn, "How Not to Teach Values: A Critical Look at Character Education," *Phi Delta Kappan,* February 1997, p. 436.

2. Thomas Lickona, *Educating for Character: How Our Schools Can Teach Respect and Responsibility* (New York: Bantam, 1991); Kevin Ryan and Karen E. Bohlin, *Building Character in Schools: Practical Ways to Bring Moral Instruction to Life* (San Francisco: Jossey-Bass, 1999), p. 11; and Edward A. Wynne and Kevin Ryan, *Reclaiming Our Schools: A Handbook on Teaching Character, Academics, and Discipline* (New York: Macmillan,1993).

3. William J. Bennett, *The Book of Virtues: A Treasury of Great Moral Stories* (New York: Simon & Schuster, 1993). The six ethical values of the Character Counts Youth Ethics Initiative can be found at. . . . The Kent City Schools in Ohio developed a list of character virtues: cooperation, self-control, trustworthiness, tolerance, compassion, commitment and dedication, work ethic and responsibility, respect for self and others, fairness and justice, and respect for our community and environment, which is available at. . . .

4. For information on the School 18 program, see. . . .

5. For information on these and other character activities, see. . . .

6. See J. Wesley Null and Andrew J. Milson, "Beyond Marquee Morality: Virtue in the Social Studies," *Social Studies,* May/June 2003, pp. 119–22; Don Jacobs, "The Case for the Inclusion of an Indigenous Perspective in Character Education," paper presented at the annual meeting of the American Educational Research Association, New Orleans, April 2002; and David Purpel, "The Politics of Character Education," in idem, ed., *Moral Outrage in Education* (New York: Peter Lang, 1999), pp. 83–97.

7. For more information on these examples, visit . . . ; . . . ; . . . ; and. . . .

8. In this article, we focus on examples from Indian schools that are not strictly tribal schools. For example, see Sandra M. Stokes, "Curriculum for Native American Students: Using Native American Values," *Reading Teacher,* vol. 50, 1997, pp. 576–84; Angayuqaq Oscar Kawagley and Ray Barnhardt, "Education Indigenous to Place: Western Science Meets Native Reality," in Gregory A. Smith and Dilafruz R. Williams, eds., *Ecological Education in Action: On Weaving Education, Culture, and the Environment* (Albany: State University of New York Press, 1998), pp. 117–40; G. Mike Charleston, "Toward True Native Education: A Treaty of 1992: Final Report of the Indian Nations at Risk Task Force," *Journal of American Indian Education,* Winter 1994, pp. 1–23; and Washington Education Association, "Tulalip Heritage School: Linking Cultures and Generations," 9 November 2000, available at. . . . For information on the Center School, see. . . .

9. For discussions on culturally relevant moral education, see Cynthia Ballenger, "Because You Like Us: The Language of Control," *Harvard Educational Review,* vol. 62, 1992, pp. 199–208; Peter Murrell, "Afrocentric Immersion: Academic and Personal Development of African American Males in Public Schools," in Theresa Perry and James W. Frazer, eds., *Freedom's Plow: Teaching in the Multicultural Classroom* (New York: Routledge, 1993), pp. 231–59.

10. Nel Noddings, *The Challenge to Care in Schools* (New York: Teachers College Press, 1992); and Jane Roland Martin, *The Schoolhome: Rethinking Schools for Changing Families* (Cambridge: Harvard University Press, 1992).

11. Victor Battistich et al., "Students and Teachers in Caring Classroom and School Communities," paper presented at the annual meeting of the American Educational Research Association, New Orleans, April 1994; and Rick Weissbourd, "Moral Teachers, Moral Students," *Educational Leadership,* March 2003, pp. 6–11.

12. Lynn H. Doyle and Patrick M. Doyle, "Building Schools as Caring Communities: Why, What, and How?," *The Clearing House,* May/June 2003, pp. 259–61; and Jean Tepperman, "Schooling as a Caring Community," *Children's Advocate,* September/October 1997, available at. . . .

13. Doyle and Doyle, op. cit.

14. Eric Schaps, "Creating a School Community," *Educational Leadership,* March 2003, pp. 31–33.

15. Ibid.; and Weissbourd, op. cit.

16. Ian M. Harris, Mary Lee Morrison, and Timothy Reagan, *Peace Education,* 2nd ed. (Jefferson, N.C.: McFarland & Company, 2002); "What Is Peace Education?," in *A Teachers' Guide to Peace Education* (New Delhi, India:

United Nations Educational, Scientific, and Cultural Organization, 2001), available at . . . ; Frans C. Verhagen, "The Earth Community School: A Back-to-Basics Model of Secondary Education," *Green Teacher,* Fall 1999, pp. 28–31; William Scott and Chris Oulton, "Environmental Values Education: An Exploration of Its Role in the School Curriculum," *Journal of Moral Education,* vol. 27, 1998, pp. 209–24; and American Montessori Society, "AMS Position Paper: Holistic Peace Education," available at. . . .

17. Mary Lee Morrison, "Peace Education in Theory and Practice," *Delta Kappa Gamma Bulletin,* Fall 2002, pp. 10–14.

18. For information on the One World Montessori School, see. . . .

19. For more information on these examples, see . . . and. . . .

20. Morrison, op. cit.

21. Peter McLaren, *Life in Schools: An Introduction to Critical Pedagogy in the Foundations of Education* (New York: Longman, 1989); and Henry Giroux, *Border Crossings: Cultural Works and the Politics of Education* (New York: Routledge, 1993), p. 104.

22. Pamela Bolotin Joseph and Mark Windschill, "Fostering a Critical and Caring Classroom Culture," *Social Education, Middle Level Learning Supplement,* May/June 1999, pp. 14–15.

23. Regine Labossiere, "Nova Sister-School Class Aids East Timor Students," *Seattle Times,* 13 October 2003, p. B-3.

24. See David Field, "Freedom Writers," *Teacher Magazine on the Web,* February 1999; Nat Hentoff, "Fifth-Grade Freedom Fighters," *Washington Post,* 1 August 1998, p. A-15; Mindy Sink, "Schoolchildren Set Out to Buy Freedom for Slaves," *New York Times,* 2 December 1998, p. B-14; and Richard Woodbury, "The Children's Crusade," *Time,* 21 December 1998, p. 44.

25. Joseph and Windschitl, op. cit.

26. Lawrence Kohlberg, *The Psychology of Moral Development: Moral Stages and the Life Cycle,* vol. 2 (San Francisco: Harper & Row, 1984).

27. Clark Power, "Building Democratic Community: A Radical Approach to Moral Education," in William Damon, ed., *Bringing in a New Era in Character Education* (Palo Alto, Calif.: Hoover Institution, 2002), pp. 1–32; and Elsa K. Weber, "Rules, Right and Wrong, and Children," *Early Childhood Education Journal,* Winter 2000, pp. 107–11.

28. For more information on these examples, see . . . ; and . . .

29. Sara Efron, "Beyond Character Education: Democracy as a Moral Goal," *Critical Issues in Teacher Education,* vol. 8, 2000, pp. 20–28.

30. Barbara J.Thayer-Bacon, "Democratic Classroom Communities," *Studies in Philosophy and Education,* vol. 15, 1996, pp. 333–51; F. Clark Power, "Building Democratic Community: A Radical Approach to Moral Education," in Damon, pp. 129–48; and Edward R. Mikel, "Deliberating Democracy," in Pamela Bolotin Joseph et al., eds., *Cultures of Curriculum* (Mahwah, N.J.: Lawrence Erlbaum, 2000), pp. 115–35.

31. Robert J. Nash, *Answering the "Virtuecrats": A Moral Conversation on Character Education* (New York: Teachers College Press, 1997); and Katherine G. Simon, *Moral Questions in the Classroom: How to Get Kids to Think Deeply About Real Life and Their Schoolwork* (New Haven, Conn.: Yale University Press, 2001), pp. 37–38.

32. Joe Winston, "Theorising Drama as Moral Education," *Journal of Moral Education,* December 1999, pp. 459–71; Vaille Dawson, "Addressing Controversial Issues in Secondary School Science," *Australian Science Teachers Journal,* November 2001, pp. 38–44; and Larry R. Johannessen, "Strategies for Initiating Authentic Discussion," *English Journal,* September 2003, pp. 73–79.

33. Linda Leonard Lamme, "Digging Deeply: Morals and Ethics in Children's Literature," *Journal for a Just and Caring Education,* October 1996, pp. 411–20; Steven Wolk, "Teaching for Critical Literacy in Social Studies," *Social Studies,* May/June 2003, pp. 101–6; Lena Green, "Philosophy for Children: One Way of Developing Children's Thinking," *Thinking,* vol. 13, no. 2, 1997, pp. 20–22; . . . ; Margot Stern Strom, Martin Sleeper, and Mary Johnson, "Facing History and Ourselves: A Synthesis of History and Ethics in Effective History Education," in Andrew Garrod, ed., *Learning for Life: Moral Education Theory and Practice* (Westport, Conn.: Praeger, 1992), pp. 131–53; and Melinda Fine, "Facing History and Ourselves: Portrait of a Classroom," *Educational Leadership,* December 1991, pp. 44–49.

34. Constance M. Perry, "How Do We Teach What Is Right?: Research and Issues in Ethical and Moral Development," *Journal for a Just and Caring Education,* October 1996, pp. 400–10; and Ruth W. Grant, "The Ethics of Talk: Classroom Conversation and Democratic Politics," *Teachers College Record,* Spring 1996, pp. 470–82.

POSTSCRIPT

Should Character Education Define the Values We Teach Students?

Can we answer the question posed for this issue by gathering and evaluating data through empirical research? In one respect, the answer is yes. It certainly would be possible to compare the relative effectiveness of two curricula—one including a character education component and the other with a strictly academic focus or with a broader moral focus such as that proposed by Joseph and Efron—in achieving the hoped-for moral qualities in students. In any such study, of course, care would need to be taken to ensure that the students, classes, or schools compared were identical in all respects save the moral dimensions of the curricula.

In another respect, however, the question may not simply be answerable by empirical data. It simply may not be possible to reach consensus on what the objectives of a moral education should be. Ultimately, decisions about the content of any moral education curriculum will be decided not by recourse to empirical investigation or by considerations of universal acceptance but rather by the beliefs and values of those who have the power to make decisions about the schools; namely, government leaders, the educational establishment that trains teachers, and the people who develop and administer the curriculum. Because access to these positions of power has been limited until recently to those of the majority culture, it is likely that the moral values contained in most educational programs will reflect to a very large degree those of the majority culture.

There are several thought-provoking books on the issues surrounding moral education, including *The Nature of Human Values* by Milton Rokeach (Free Press, 1973) and *How to Raise a Moral Child: The Moral Intelligence of Children* by Robert Coles (NAL/Dutton, 1998). The November 1993 issue of the journal *Educational Leadership* is devoted to a consideration of these issues and contains articles from authors in a variety of disciplines. Other worthwhile articles on moral education include "The Death of Character Education," by Timothy Rusnak and Frank Ribich, *Educational Horizons* (Fall 1997); "A Comprehensive Model of Values Education and Moral Education," by Howard Kirschenbaum, *Phi Delta Kappan* (June 1992); and "Creating a Curriculum for Character Development: A Case Study," by Andrew J. Milson, *The Clearing House* (November/December 2000). Provocative articles by Thomas Lickona include "Religion and Character Education," *Phi Delta Kappan* (September 1999) and "Character-Based Sexuality Education: Bringing Parents into the Picture," *Educational Leadership* (October 2000). An interesting case study of moral education "in action" is provided by James Traub in "The Moral

Imperative," *Education Digest* (Winter 2005). Psychological perspectives on the development of morality in children can be found in *Essays on Moral Development, Vol. 1,* by Lawrence Kohlberg (Harper & Row, 1981) and *Helping Clients Forgive* by Robert D. Enright and Richard Fitzgibbons (American Psychological Association, 2000). Also recommended is *In a Different Voice: Psychological Theory and Women's Development* by Carol Gilligan (Harvard University Press, 1982). An interesting historical treatment of moral education is provided by Hunter Brimi in "Academic Instructors or Moral Guides? Moral Education in America and the Teacher's Dilemma," *The Clearing House* (January/February 2009).

Internet References . . .

Jean Piaget Society

Established in 1970, the Jean Piaget Society (JPS) is an international organization of scholars and teachers who are interested in constructivist approaches to human development and the application of these approaches to education. The JPS holds symposia and publishes books that focus on research, theory, and education.

http://www.piaget.org

Association for Behavior Analysis

The Association for Behavior Analysis is an international organization that promotes scientific inquiry into and clinical applications of the concepts and theories of behaviorism. The organization publishes scientific journals and books, holds conferences, and promotes information exchange among its members.

http://www.abainternational.org

Howard Gardner on Multiple Intelligences

This site contains links to personal information and to many papers written by Dr. Gardner as well as his responses to frequently asked questions about the theory.

http://www.howardgardner.com/MI/mi.html

Education-World

A Web site of resources for educators that includes links to numerous professional societies and organizations that have developed educational content domains, including the National Council of Teachers of Mathematics, National Council of Teachers of English, and National Academies of Sciences.

http://www.education-world.com/standards/national/

James S. McDonnell Foundation

The James S. McDonnell Foundation provides funding for research in the behavioral and biomedical sciences. This site includes articles of general interest about current research, including research in the neurosciences and its application to education.

http://www.jsmf.org

Theories of Learning and Their Implications for Educational Practice

*S*ince the 1990s there has been increasing dissatisfaction among politicians, parents, and educators with the performance of students in U.S. schools. Rightly or wrongly, the blame for the shortcomings of students has been placed squarely on the shoulders of teachers (and on the shoulders of those who train and supervise them). This has led to an increasing number of calls for reform of how and what teachers should teach. The criticisms and resulting proposals for reform have revolved around various theoretical controversies about teaching and learning that have characterized the field of educational psychology. Some of these controversies have been ongoing in the field for many years, such as the dispute about whether reinforcement facilitates or hinders learning. Other controversies have emerged more recently, such as the dispute about the pedagogical implications of research on brain structures and processes, the dispute about the educational value of constructivist approaches to learning and development, and arguments about the potential impact of adopting explicit and uniform educational standards. In this section, we consider these controversies within the context of teaching and learning in the classroom.

- Should Schools Adopt a Constructivist Approach to Education?

- Does Reinforcement Facilitate Learning?

- Can Howard Gardner's Theory of Multiple Intelligences Transform Educational Practice?

- Will a Push for Standards and Accountability Lead to More Motivated Students?

- Do Recent Discoveries about the Brain and Its Development Have Implications for Classroom Practice?

ISSUE 7

Should Schools Adopt a Constructivist Approach to Education?

YES: Mark Windschitl, from "The Challenges of Sustaining a Constructivist Classroom Culture," *Phi Delta Kappan* (June 1999)

NO: E. D. Hirsch, Jr., from "Reality's Revenge: Research and Ideology," *American Educator* (Fall 1996)

ISSUE SUMMARY

YES: Mark Windschitl, a member of the faculty in the department of curriculum and instruction at the University of Washington, argues in favor of constructivism, a child-centered approach to education that is defined by student participation in hands-on activities and extended projects that are allowed to "evolve" in accordance with the students' interests and initial beliefs.

NO: E. D. Hirsch, Jr., a professor in the School of Education at the University of Virginia, Charlottesville, argues that child-centered approaches have failed and points to research demonstrating the superiority of fact-based, teacher-centered approaches.

Observation of any school classroom in the United States at any point in history would reveal, to no one's surprise, a teacher (or teachers) and a varying number of students. In fact, although many other people, including administrators, parents, and even politicians, participate directly or indirectly in the educational process, most people view the teacher-student relationship as the primary determinant of what students accomplish in school. But the relationship between teachers and students has changed dramatically over the past few decades. In the 1950s, for example, the relationship was very much dominated by the teacher. He or she exerted a high degree of control over what students did at nearly every point throughout the day. In this teacher-centered approach, the teacher disseminated the "facts" to be learned to the students, typically within the context of a lecture. The teacher ensured that students would learn the facts by requiring that they listen carefully and engage in various highly structured, drill-and-practice activities. In recent years, however, students have come to exert considerably more control over the educational process and the teacher-student relationship. In many classrooms today, students are much more likely to be "doing" rather than "listening." This doing is often in the form of participation in an extended project of some form, such as building a Civil War-era town or collecting and cataloging insects. The teacher may assign these projects, but it is the students who shape the projects to suit their own interests as well as the discoveries that they make along the way. Although labeled in different ways (e.g., project-based, discovery learning, hands-on learning), the hallmark of this constructivism approach is a high degree of self-directed student activity.

Concerns about student achievement, especially as compared to student achievement in other industrialized nations, have led some scholars and administrators to begin calling for a return to a more teacher-centered, fact-based approach to education. Critics have argued that the constructivist approach is inefficient; that is, because children "waste time" with incorrect "discoveries" before arriving at the correct one, there often is not enough time to teach them all of the content that should be mastered. Other critics assert that some children never make the correct discoveries on their own and thus require greater teacher control and a more systematic introduction of the skills to be mastered. Finally, critics argue that acquisition of higher-order modes of thought applicable to a broad range of problems will not emerge without mastery of the rich networks of facts that constitute the domains of mathematics, physics, chemistry, and the like.

Supporters of the constructivist approach, however, are not without responses to these criticisms. They counter that a fact-based, teacher-centered approach is itself inefficient because of the sheer number of facts that compose any meaningful domain and because the "facts" change with new discoveries. This means, they argue, that the only lasting education is one that promotes higher modes of thought and action rather than storage of facts. Supporters also suggest that many attempts to implement a constructivist approach fail only because they do not go far enough; they merely insert a few student-initiated projects into an otherwise teacher-centered system. Finally, supporters argue that the well-documented decline in student interest in academic tasks that occurs throughout the school years is the result of a teacher-centered orientation. They point to numerous examples of constructivist classrooms in which students appear to be highly engaged in the academic life of the classroom.

In the following selection, Mark Windschitl argues for constructivism over a fact-based, teacher-centered approach to education. He also argues that constructivism is not merely a set of instructional practices but a way of thinking about the nature of child development and schooling. Successfully implementing this approach, he says, requires a fundamental change in the "culture" of the school, a change that affects not only how children are taught but how they are assessed, how classrooms are physically organized, how activities are scheduled, and how teaching is evaluated. In the second selection, E. D. Hirsch, Jr., argues that supporters of constructivist and other child-centered approaches have ignored empirical research, which, he argues, favors the use of a fact-based, teacher-centered approach.

YES

Mark Windschitl

The Challenges of Sustaining a Constructivist Classroom Culture

Ms. Hughes' sixth-grade classroom is a noisy place, and if you come to visit you may have a hard time finding her. Today, students are clustered in small groups, bent over note cards and diagrams they have assembled in order to determine whether they can design a habitat that can support Australian dingoes and marmosets.

The students have just participated in three days of discussion and reading about interrelationships among mammals. They are divided into four groups, each of which has negotiated with Ms. Hughes to devise a complex problem to work on that reflects their interests and abilities. One group chose a design problem: creating a habitat for a local zoo that will support at least three kinds of mammals naturally found in the same geographic area.

The students are now engaged for the next two weeks on this project. They find and share dozens of resources, many of which are spread out on tables and on the floor around the room. Allen brings to class a video he shot at the zoo last week so that everyone can see what different habitats look like. Michelle loads a CD-ROM on mammals that she brought from home, and James donates one of his mother's landscape architecture books for ideas on how to diagram spaces and buildings.

During the next two weeks, these students will develop an understanding of how mammal species interact with one another, cope with the environment, and follow the natural cycles of reproduction. Concepts such as "competition for resources" and "reproductive capacity"—whose definitions in other classes might have been memorized—arise instead from a meaningful and multifaceted context. These concepts are built on the experiences of the students and are essential, interconnected considerations in the success of the habitat design. This is one of the many faces of the constructivist classroom.

A growing number of teachers are embracing the fundamental ideas of constructivist learning—that their students' background knowledge profoundly affects how they interpret subject matter and that students learn best when they apply their knowledge to solve authentic problems, engage in "sense-making" dialogue with peers, and strive for deep understanding of core ideas rather than recall of a laundry list of facts. Unfortunately, much of the public conversation about constructivism has been stalled on its philosophical contrasts with more traditional approaches to instruction. Constructivists have offered varying descriptions of how classrooms can be transformed, usually framed in terms of these contrasts. And although these descriptions have prompted educators to reexamine the roles of teachers, the ways in which students learn best, and even what it means to learn, the image of what is possible in constructivist classrooms remains too idealized.

To all the talk about theory, educators must add layers of dialogue about real classroom experiences and concerns about those experiences. An essential part of this dialogue is the articulation of the pedagogical, logistical, and political challenges that face educators who are willing to integrate constructivism into their classroom practice. The new discourse shifts the emphasis from comparisons between constructivism and traditional instruction to the refinement of constructivist practices in real classrooms. This frank conversation about challenges is equally valuable for sympathetic administrators—being informed and reflective about these issues is a necessary prerequisite to offering support for the classroom teacher.

In this article, I characterize and categorize these challenges and describe the kinds of administrative support necessary to create and sustain a culture of constructivist teaching in schools. First, however, it is necessary to examine constructivism as a philosophy on which a systemic classroom culture can be based rather than to view it as a set of discrete instructional practices that may be inserted into the learning environment whenever necessary. The challenges I describe here are challenges precisely because they cause us to reconsider and dare us to change the comfortable (and often unstated) norms, beliefs, and practices of the classroom culture we are so familiar with. Constructivism is more than a set of teaching techniques; it is a coherent pattern of expectations that underlie new relationships between students, teachers, and the world of ideas.

Constructivism as Culture

Constructivism is premised on the belief that learners actively create, interpret, and reorganize knowledge in individual ways. These fluid intellectual transformations occur when students reconcile formal instructional experiences with their existing knowledge, with the cultural and social contexts in which ideas occur, and with a host of other influences that serve to mediate understanding. With respect to instruction, this belief suggests that students should participate in experiences that accommodate these ways of learning. Such experiences include problem-based learning, inquiry activities, dialogues with peers and teachers that encourage making sense of the subject matter, exposure to multiple sources of information, and opportunities for students to demonstrate their understanding in diverse ways.

However, before teachers and administrators adopt such practices, they should understand that constructivism cannot make its appearance in the classroom as a set of isolated instructional methods grafted on to otherwise traditional teaching techniques. Rather, it is a culture—a set of beliefs, norms, and practices that constitute the fabric of school life. This culture, like all other cultures, affects the way learners can interact with peers, relate to the teacher, and experience the subject matter. The children's relationships with teachers, their patterns of communication, how they are assessed, and even their notion of "what learning is good for" must all be connected, or the culture risks becoming a fragmented collection of practices that fail to reinforce one another. For example, the constructivist belief that learners are capable of intellectual autonomy must coincide with the belief that students possess a large knowledge base of life experiences and have made sense out of much of what they have experienced. These beliefs are linked with the practice of problem-based learning within relevant and authentic contexts and with the norm of showing mutual respect for one another's ideas in the classroom.

Portraying the constructivist classroom as a culture is important because many challenges for the teacher emerge when new rituals take root or when familiar norms of behavior are transformed into new patterns of teacher/ student interaction.[1] By contrast, if discrete practices that have been associated with constructivism (cooperative learning, performance assessments, hands-on experiences) are simply inserted as special activities into the regular school day, then it remains business as usual for the students. Teachers and students do not question their vision of learning, no one takes risks, and hardly a ripple is felt.

Throughout this article then, challenges become apparent when we question the fundamental norms of the classroom—the images and beliefs we hold of teachers and students, the kinds of discourse encouraged in the classroom, the way authority and decision making are controlled, and even what "counts" as learning. I begin with a subtle but powerful influence on classroom instruction.

Images of Teaching: The Chains That Bind Us

Most of us are products of traditional instruction; as learners, we were exposed to teacher-centered instruction, fact-based subject matter, and a steady diet of drill and practice.[2] Our personal histories furnish us with mental models of teaching, and these models of how we were taught shape our behavior in powerful ways. Teachers use these models to imagine lessons in their classrooms, develop innovations, and plan for learning.[3] These images serve to organize sets of beliefs and guide curricular actions.[4] Teachers are more likely to be guided not by instructional theories but by the familiar images of what is "proper and possible" in classroom settings.[5]

Unfortunately, the signs and symbols of teacher-centered education and learning by transmission, which are likely to be a part of teachers' personal histories, persist in classrooms today.[6] In this environment, it is assumed that the more quiet and orderly the classrooms are, the more likely it is that learning is taking place. Individual desks face the front of the room, where the teacher occupies a privileged space of knowing authority; students work individually on identical, skill-based assignments to ensure uniformity of learning. Value statements are embedded everywhere in this environment.

Constructivist teachers envision themselves emerging boldly from the confines of this traditional classroom culture, but the vision first requires critical reflection. Teachers must ask themselves, "Is my role to dispense knowledge or to nurture independent thinkers? How do I show respect for the ideas of the students? Am I here to learn from the students?" Teachers must struggle to develop a new, well-articulated rationale for instructional decisions and cannot depend on their previous teaching or learning experiences for much help in shaping their choice of methods; shifting the centers of authority and activity in accordance with this rationale requires persistence. For example, teachers can be uncomfortable with their apparent lack of control as students engage with their peers during learning activities and may be unwilling to allow supervisors who visit the classroom to observe this kind of environment. Teachers may reconsider their ideas of student-centered learning in favor of conforming to the more traditional images of the teacher as the hub of classroom discourse and attention.[7]

New Demands on the Teacher

Constructivist instruction, especially that which is based on design tasks or problem solving, places high demands on the teacher's subject-matter understanding. The teacher must not only be familiar with the principles underlying a topic of study but must also be prepared for the variety of ways these principles can be explored.

For example, if students are studying density in science class, the teacher must support the understanding of one group of students who want to approach the concept from a purely abstract, mathematical perspective as they construct tables, equations, and graphs to develop their knowledge. In this case, the teacher must understand these different representations of information and how they are interrelated. Another group of students may plan to recount the story of the *Titanic,* emphasizing the role that density played in the visibility of the iceberg, the ballast of the ship, and the sinking itself. Here, the teacher must be intellectually agile, able to apply his or her mathematical understanding of density to a real-life, inevitably more complex situation.

Teachers in different subject areas may allow students varying degrees of latitude in exploring content and will differ in how they accept student "constructions" of core curricular ideas. Mathematics is characterized by rule-based propositions and skills that may be open to discovery via many experiential pathways. Most forms of mathematics problems, however, have only one right answer. And if students are allowed to explore problems by their own methods, teachers may find it difficult to see exactly how the students are making sense of the problem-solving process—not all constructions are created equal. Science and social studies present the same challenges, although science is less axiomatic than mathematics, and the issues explored in social studies are open to wider interpretation. Dealing with the "correctness" of student constructions is an ongoing concern, and the arguments have barely been introduced here, but reflection on these issues helps teachers develop a critical awareness of disciplinary "truths" and the viability of various ways of knowing the world.

In addition to the necessity for flexible subject-matter knowledge, constructivism places greater demands on teachers' pedagogical skill. Crafting instruction based on constructivism is not as straightforward as it seems. Educators struggle with how specific instructional techniques (e.g., lecture, discussion, cooperative learning, problem-based learning, inquiry learning) fit into the constructivist model of instruction. Regardless of the particular techniques used in instruction, students will always construct and reorganize knowledge rather than simply assimilate information from teachers or textbooks. The question is not whether to use lecture or discussion, but how to use these techniques to complement rather than dominate student thinking. For example, constructivist principles suggest that students should experience the ideas, phenomena, and artifacts of a discipline before being exposed to formal explanations of them. Students might begin units of instruction in science class by manipulating a pendulum, in math class by constructing polygons, or in social studies by reading letters from Civil War battlefields. Only after these experiences do teachers and students together suggest terminology, explanations, and conceptual organization.

Even though designing instruction is important, constructivist teaching is less about the sequencing of events and more about responding to the needs of a situation.[8] Teachers must employ a sophisticated range of strategies to support individual students' understandings as they engage in the problem-based activities that characterize constructivist classrooms. These strategies include scaffolding, in which the task required of the learner is strategically reduced in complexity; modeling, in which the teacher either thinks aloud about or acts out how she would approach a problem; and coaching, guiding, and advising, which are loosely defined as providing learners with suggestions of varying degrees of explicitness.[9] The teacher is challenged to select the proper strategy and implement it with skill.

Problem-based activities exemplify another core value of the constructivist culture—collaboration. Students are witness to and participate in one another's thinking. Learners are exposed to the clear, cogent thinking of some peers as well as to the inevitable meandering, unreflective thought of others. Students do require training to function effectively in these groups.[10] However, even with training, many capable students are simply not interested in helping their peers, and negative consequences of group work—such as bickering, exclusion, and academic freeloading—are common.[11] These consequences can be minimized if the teacher is familiar with the principles of cooperative learning. And so, having students work together requires that the teacher have additional competencies in cooperative learning strategies and management skills particular to decentralized learning environments.

A final pedagogical challenge involves independent student projects. Depending on the degree of structure the teacher imposes in a classroom, students will have some latitude in choosing problems or design projects that relate to the theme under study. Often, students determine with the teacher suitable criteria for problems and for evidence of learning. Negotiation about criteria prompts questions such as: Is the problem meaningful? Important to the discipline? Complex enough? Does it relate to the theme under study? Does it require original thinking and interpretation, or is it simply fact finding? Will the resolution of this problem help us acquire the concepts and principles fundamental to the theme under study? Because curricular materials are often filled with prepared questions and tasks, teachers seldom have occasion to introduce their students to this idea of "problems about problems." Clearly, teachers must develop their own ability to analyze problems by reflecting on the nature of the discipline and refining their ideas through extended dialogue with colleagues and experiences with students.

Logistical and Political Challenges

Effective forms of constructivist instruction call for major changes in the curriculum, in scheduling, and in assessment.[12] When students are engaged in problem solving and are allowed to help guide their own learning, teachers quickly find that this approach outgrows the 50-minute class period. This situation often means that the teacher will have to negotiate with administrators and other teachers about the possibilities of block scheduling and integrating curricula. If teachers can team with partners from other subject areas, they can extend the length of their class periods and develop more comprehensive themes for study that bridge the worlds of science, social studies, math, and the arts.

The purpose of integrated curricula and extended class periods is to allow students to engage in learning activities that will help them develop deep and elaborate understandings of subject matter. These understandings may be quite different in nature from student to student. Thus there is a need for forms of assessment that allow students to demonstrate what they know and that connect with rigorous criteria of excellence. These are not the paper-and-pencil, objective tests in which learners recognize rather than generate answers or create brief responses to questions in which they have little personal investment. Rather, students are required to produce journals, research reports, physical models, or performances in the forms of plays, debates, dances, or other artistic representations. Assessing these products and performances requires well-designed, flexible rubrics to maintain a link between course objectives and student learning. Designing these rubrics (through negotiation with students) builds consensus about what "purpose" means in a learning activity, about the nature of meaningful criteria, and about how assessments reflect the efficacy of the teacher as a promoter of understanding.

The final and perhaps most politically sensitive issue confronting teachers is that the diversity of understandings emerging from constructivist instruction does not always seem compatible with state and local standards. For example, student groups engaged in science projects on photosynthesis may have radically different approaches to developing their understanding of this phenomenon. One group may choose to focus on chemical reactions at the molecular level while another group may examine how oxygen and carbon dioxide are exchanged between animals and plants on a global scale. These two groups will take disconcertingly divergent paths to understanding photosynthesis.

This kind of project-based learning must be skillfully orchestrated so that, however students choose to investigate and seek resolutions to problems, they will acquire an understanding of key principles and concepts as well as the critical thinking skills that are assessed on standardized tests. Proponents of project-based learning have demonstrated that these kinds of learning outcomes are entirely possible.[13] Artful guidance by the teacher notwithstanding, it can be unsettling for teachers to reconcile the language of "objectives, standards, and benchmarks" with the diversity of understandings that emerge in a constructivist classroom.

Conclusions and Recommendations

How does a school community support the instructional expertise, academic freedom, and professional collaboration necessary to sustain a constructivist culture? First, a core group of committed teachers must systematically investigate constructivism in order to understand its principles and its limitations. The ideas behind constructivism seem intuitive and sensible, but teachers and administrators must go beyond the hyperbole and the one-shot-workshop acquaintance with constructivism. Interested faculty members should conduct a thorough reading campaign, and at least one or two teachers should extend their experience by participating in advanced workshops, attending classes, and witnessing how constructivist cultures operate in other schools. Stipends and released time can be provided for a cadre of lead teachers to attend classes, do extra reading, adapt curriculum, and offer their own workshops to fellow teachers. Workshop topics could include the constructivist implementation of cooperative learning, scaffolding techniques, problem-based learning, or multifaceted assessment strategies.

The faculty members must openly discuss their beliefs about learners and about their roles as teachers. If these beliefs are left unexamined or unchallenged, then individuals have feeble grounding for their personal philosophies. Just as problematically then, everyone operates on different, untested assumptions. And all decisions about curriculum, instruction, and assessment are built on such assumptions.

Personal philosophies of education are particularly important when constructivism is used to furnish underlying principles—important because constructivism means risk taking and a divergence from business as usual. Sooner or later, teachers will be asked, "Why do you teach that way?" Whatever form that question takes, teachers must be able to justify the choices they make. This task will not be as intimidating if the teacher has mindfully linked the aspects of his or her constructivist philosophy to the various dimensions of classroom experience and to the larger goals of education.

The process of making these beliefs explicit can also strengthen teachers' resolve to move beyond the traditional images of what is proper and possible in the classroom. It can make clear to them the characteristics and limitations of the system that encouraged images of teachers as dispensers of information and students as passive recipients of knowledge. Accordingly, teachers must try to arrive at a new vision of their role. This vision must include serving as a facilitator of learning who responds to students' needs with a flexible understanding of subject matter and a sensitivity to how the student is making sense of the world.

Teachers and their principals must be prepared to go on record with these beliefs in discussions with parent groups and the school board. Educators should always have a rationale for what and how they teach; however, because constructivism is so contrary to historical norms, it is even more important in this case that the rationale be well founded, coherent, and applicable to the current school context. Community members will undoubtedly be suspicious of teaching methods that are so different from the ones they remember as students and that sound too much like a laissez-faire approach to learning.

Administrators must also take the lead in supporting a "less is more" approach. The compulsion to cover material is antithetical to the aim of constructivist instruction—the deep and elaborate understanding of selected core ideas. Textbooks, which are often the de facto curriculum, have become encyclopedic, and administrators should make teachers feel secure about using a variety of other resources. They should also provide funds to purchase alternative classroom materials. Furthermore, administrators must be open to suggestions for block scheduling and for integrating curricula, perhaps even arranging for interested teachers to be placed together in team-teaching situations that are premised on the constructivist approach.

To strengthen the school's position on accountability, assessment specialists who understand constructivism can be brought in to connect local standards with instruction and with evidence that learning is taking place. Teachers will undoubtedly appreciate assistance in investigating and evaluating a variety of assessment strategies.

The list of challenges I have described here is not exhaustive. There are certainly others, and the challenges outnumber the solutions at the moment. But articulating these challenges is a significant step in helping educators create and sustain a classroom culture that values diversity in learning and offers a new vision of the roles of teachers and learners—the culture of constructivism.

Notes

1. Pam Bolotin-Joseph, "Understanding Curriculum as Culture," in Pam Bolotin-Joseph, Stevie Bravman, Mark Windschitl, Edward Mikel, and Nancy Green, eds., *Cultures of Curriculum* (Mahwah, N.J.: Erlbaum, forthcoming).

2. Thomas Russell, "Learning to Teach Science: Constructivism, Reflection, and Learning from Experience," in Kenneth Tobin, ed., *The Practice of Constructivism in Science Education* (Hillsdale, N.J.: Erlbaum, 1993), pp. 247–58.

3. Corby Kennison, "Enhancing Teachers' Professional Learning: Relationships Between School Culture and Elementary School Teachers' Beliefs, Images, and Ways of Knowing" (Specialist's thesis, Florida State University, 1990).

4. Kenneth Tobin, "Constructivist Perspectives on Teacher Learning," in idem, ed., pp. 215–26; and Kenneth Tobin and Sarah Ulerick, "An

Interpretation of High School Science Teaching Based on Metaphors and Beliefs for Specific Roles," paper presented at the annual meeting of the American Educational Research Association, San Francisco, 1989.

5. Kenneth Zeichner and Robert Tabachnick, "Are the Effects of University Teacher Education Washed Out by School Experience?," *Journal of Teacher Education*, vol. 32, 1981, pp. 7–11.

6. Adriana Groisman, Bonnie Shapiro, and John Willinsky, "The Potential of Semiotics to Inform Understanding of Events in Science Education," *International Journal of Science Education*, vol. 13, 1991, pp. 217–26.

7. James H. Mosenthal and Deborah Ball, "Constructing New Forms of Teaching: Subject Matter Knowledge in Inservice Teacher Education," *Journal of Teacher Education*, vol. 43, 1992, pp. 347–56.

8. David Lebow, "Constructivist Values for Instructional Systems Design: Five Principles Toward a New Mindset," *Educational Technology, Research, and Development*, vol. 41, no. 3, 1993, pp. 4–16.

9. Jeong-Im Choi and Michael Hannafin, "Situated Cognition and Learning Environments: Roles, Structures, and Implications for Design," *Educational Technology, Research, and Development*, vol. 43, no. 2, 1995, pp. 53–69.

10. David W. Johnson, Roger T. Johnson, and Karl A. Smith, *Active Learning: Cooperation in the College Classroom* (Edina, Minn.: Interaction Book Company, 1991).

11. Robert E. Slavin, *Cooperative Learning* (Boston: Allyn and Bacon, 1995).

12. Phyllis Blumenfeld et al., "Motivating Project-Based Learning: Sustaining the Doing, Supporting the Learning," *Educational Psychologist*, vol. 26, 1991, pp. 369–98.

13. Ibid.

E. D. Hirsch, Jr.

 **NO**

Reality's Revenge: Research and Ideology

The first step in strengthening education in America is to avoid the premature polarizations that arise when educational policy is confused with political ideology. In the United States today, the hostile political split between liberals and conservatives has infected the public debate over education—to such an extent that straight thinking is made difficult.

. . . I would label myself a political liberal and an educational conservative, or perhaps more accurately, an educational pragmatist. Political liberals really ought to oppose progressive educational ideas because they have led to practical failure and greater social inequity. The only practical way to achieve liberalism's aim of greater social justice is to pursue conservative educational policies.

That is not a new idea. In 1932, the Communist intellectual Antonio Gramsci, writing from jail (having been imprisoned by Mussolini), was one of the first to detect the paradoxical consequences of the new "democratic" education, which stressed "life relevance" and other naturalistic approaches over hard work and the transmission of knowledge. Il Duce's educational minister, Giovanni Gentile, was, in contrast to Gramsci, an enthusiastic proponent of the new ideas emanating from Teachers College, Columbia University, in the United States.[1] . . .

Gramsci saw that to denominate such methods as phonics and memorization of the multiplication table as "conservative," while associating them with the political right, amounted to a serious intellectual error. That was the nub of the standoff between the two most distinguished educational theorists of the political Left—Gramsci and Paulo Freire. Freire, like Gramsci a hero of humanity, devoted himself to the cause of educating the oppressed, particularly in his native Brazil, but his writings also have been influential in the United States. Like other educational progressivists, Freire rejected traditional teaching methods and subject matters, objecting to the "banking theory of schooling," whereby the teacher provides the child with a lot of "rote-learned" information. The consequence of the conservative approach, according to Freire, is to numb the critical faculties of students and to preserve the oppressor class. He called for a change of both methods and content—new content

From *American Educator* by E. D. Hirsch, Jr., Fall 1996, pp. 4–6–31–46. Copyright © 1996 by E. D. Hirsch, Jr. Reprinted with permission of the American Educator, the quarterly journal of the American Federation of Teachers AFL-CIO, and E. D. Hirsch, Jr.

that would celebrate the culture of the oppressed, and new methods that would encourage intellectual independence and resistance. In short, Freire, like other educational writers since the 1920s, associated political and educational progressivism.

Gramsci took the opposite view. He held that political progressivism demanded educational conservatism. The oppressed class should be taught to master the tools of power and authority—the ability to read, write, and communicate—and to gain enough traditional knowledge to understand the worlds of nature and culture surrounding them. Children, particularly the children of the poor, should not be encouraged to flourish "naturally," which would keep them ignorant and make them slaves of emotion. They should learn the value of hard work, gain the knowledge that leads to understanding, and master the traditional culture in order to command its rhetoric, as Gramsci himself had learned to do.

In this debate, history has proved Gramsci to be the better theorist and prophet. Modern nations that have adopted Gramscian principles have bettered the condition and heightened the political, social, and economic power of oppressed classes of people. By contrast, nations (including our own) that have stuck to the principles of Freire have failed to change the social and economic status quo. . . .

The educational standpoint from which this article is written may be accurately described as neither "traditional" nor "progressive." It is pragmatic. Both educational traditionalists and progressivists have tended to be far too dogmatic, polemical, and theory-ridden to be reliable beacons for public policy. The pragmatist tries to avoid simplifications and facile oppositions. Thus, this article will argue that the best guide to education on a large scale is observation of practices that have worked well on a large scale, coupled with as exact an understanding as possible of the reasons why those practices have succeeded in many different contexts. . . .

What Is Higher-Order Thinking?

The goal of present-day educational reformers is to produce students with "higher-order skills" who are able to think independently about the unfamiliar problems they will encounter in the information age, who have become "problem solvers" and have "learned how to learn," and who are on their way to becoming "critical thinkers" and "lifelong learners." The method advocated for achieving these "higher-order skills" is "discovery learning," by which students solve problems and make decisions on their own through "inquiry" and "independent analysis" of "real-world" projects—what [William Heard] Kilpatrick in the 1920s called the "project method."

The oft-repeated goal of the educational community—to inculcate general thinking skills—is not, however, soundly based in research. And that is stating the point too mildly. The idea that school can inculcate abstract, generalized skills for thinking, "accessing," and problem solving, and that these skills can be readily applied to the real world is, bluntly, a mirage. So also is the hope that a thinking skill in one domain can be readily and reliably transferred to other domains.

Yet broad-gauged thinking abilities do exist. Most of us know well-educated people, even some not very bright ones, who have high general competence, can think critically about diverse subjects, can communicate well, can solve a diversity of problems, and are ready to tackle unfamiliar challenges. The belief that our schools should regularly produce such people appeals to both experience and common sense. If the goal didn't make apparent sense, it could hardly have retained its attractiveness to the educational community and the general public. Rightly understood, then, the goal of general competence does define one important aim of modern education. The task is not to change that goal but to interpret it accurately so that it corresponds to the nature of real-world competency and can actually be achieved.

Two traditions in cognitive psychology are useful for understanding the nature of the critical-thinking, problem-solving skills that we wish to develop in our students. One tradition has studied the characteristic differences between expert and novice thinking, sometimes with the practical goal of making novices think more like experts as fast as possible.[2] Another tradition has investigated the differences between accurate and inaccurate thinking of the everyday newspaper-reading, bargain-hunting sort that all of us must engage in as non-experts.[3] Both sorts of study converge on the conclusion that, once basic underlying skills have been automated, the almost universal feature of reliable higher-order thinking about any subject or problem is the possession of a broad, well-integrated base of background knowledge relevant to the subject. This sounds suspiciously like plain common sense (i.e., accurate everyday thinking), but the findings entail certain illuminating complexities and details that are worth contemplating. Moreover, since the findings run counter to the prevailing fact-disparaging slogans of educational reform, it will be strategically useful to sketch briefly what research has disclosed about the knowledge-based character of higher-order thinking.

The argument used by educators to disparage "merely" factual knowledge and to elevate abstract, formal principles of thought consists in the claim that knowledge is changing so rapidly that specific information is outmoded almost as soon as it has been learned. This claim goes back at least as far as Kilpatrick's *Foundations of Method* (1925). It gains its apparent plausibility from the observation that science and technology have advanced at a great rate in this century, making scientific and technological obsolescence a common feature of modern life. The argument assumes that there is an analogy between technological and intellectual obsolescence. Educators in this tradition shore up that analogy with the further claim that factual knowledge has become a futility because of the ever-growing quantity of new facts. The great cascade of information now flowing over the information highway makes it pointless to accumulate odd bits of data. How, after all, do you know which bits are going to endure? It is much more efficient for students to spend time acquiring techniques for organizing, analyzing, and accessing this perpetual Niagara of information.

Like the tool metaphor for education, the model of acquiring processing techniques that would be permanently useful—as contrasted with acquiring mere facts that are soon obsolete—would be highly attractive if it happened to be workable and true. But the picture of higher thinking skills as consisting of all-purpose processing and accessing techniques is not just a *partly* inadequate metaphor—it is a totally misleading model of the way higher-order thinking actually works. Higher thought does not apply formal techniques to looked-up data; rather, it deploys diverse relevant cues, estimates, and analyses from pre-existing knowledge. The method of applying formal techniques to looked-up data is precisely the inept and unreliable problem-solving device used by novices. As a model of real-world higher-order thinking, the picture is not simply inaccurate—it reverses the realities. It describes the lower-order thinking of novices, not the higher-order thinking of experts.

A useful illustration of the point is presented by Jill Larkin and Ruth Chabay in a study of the ways in which novices and experts go about solving a simple physics problem.[4] The problem Larkin and Chabay set up is (in simple terms) to find out how much friction there is between a sled and the snow-covered ground when a girl is pulling her little brother through the snow at a constant rate. The brother and the sled together weigh 50 pounds. The sister is pulling with a force of 10 pounds, and she pulls the rope at an angle of 30 degrees from the horizontal. What is the coefficient of friction? The typical novice tries to solve the problem by applying formal equations that can be looked up in a book, thus dutifully following the tool principle of problem solving. The student finds that the applicable formula is $f = {}_u N$, where f is force, N is the "normal force" (which is usually equal to weight), and $_u$ is the coefficient of friction, which is the quantity to be solved. The novice sees that $f = {}_u = \times 50$. The student assumes that $f = 10$, the force exerted by the girl. So $10 = {}_u \times 50$ and $_u = {}^{10}/_{50}$, which equals .2. The answer is wrong, not because the equation or the math is wrong but because the novice doesn't know enough about real-world physics to know how to connect the formula to the problem. The novice's procedure illustrates not just the inappropriateness of the formalistic model but also the bankruptcy of the claim that students need only learn how to look things up—so-called "accessing skills." In this typical case, the skill of looking things up simply lends spurious exactitude to the student's misconceptions.

The expert physicist goes about the problem differently. He or she analyzes the critical components of the situation before looking up equations and makes two critical observations before even bothering with numbers. The first observation is that the sled is going at a constant speed, so that, in effect, there is no net residue of forces acting on the sled; there is an exact balance between the force exerted horizontally by the girl's pull and the force exerted against that pull by friction. If there had been some difference in the two forces, then the sled would speed up or slow down. So the answer has got to be that the friction is exactly equal to the horizontal component of the force exerted by the girl. The physicist also sees that since the rope is pulled at 30 degrees, part of the girl's 10 pounds of force is vertical. The answer is going to be that the friction equals the *horizontal* force of the girl's pull, which is going to be the 10 pounds minus its vertical component. The structure of the answer is solved on the basis of multiple cues and relevant knowledge, before any formulas are looked up and applied. Larkin and Chabay make the following comment (which is much more to our purpose than the details of the physics involved):

> Scientists' problem solving starts with redescribing the problem in terms of the powerful concepts of their discipline. *Because the concepts are richly connected with each other, the redescribed problem allows cross-checking among inferences to avoid errors* [author's emphasis].[5]

An important feature of higher-order thinking is this "cross-checking among inferences," based on a number of "richly connected" concepts. In higher-order thinking, we situate a problem in mental space on analogy with the way we situate ourselves in physical space—through a process of cross-checking or triangulation among relevant guideposts in our landscape of pre-existing knowledge. If we look at a problem from a couple of different angles, using a couple of different cues, and if our different estimates converge, we gain confidence in our analysis and can proceed with confidence. If, on the other hand, there is some dissonance or conflict between our cues, then warning signals go up, and we figure out which approach is more probable or fruitful. The procedure is clearly a very different and far more reliable mode of thinking than the error-prone method of applying formal techniques to looked-up data.

The example also illustrates the implausibility of the claim that school-based information quickly grows outdated. How outmoded will the knowledge used to solve the sled problem become? A philosopher of science, Nicholas Rescher, once observed that the latest science is in a sense the least reliable science, because, being on the frontier, it is always in dispute with other, rival theories—any of which may emerge victorious. Accordingly, reasoned Rescher, the most reliable physics is "stone-age-physics": If you throw the rock up, it is going to come down. For most problems that require critical thought by the ordinary person regarding ethics, politics, history, and even technology, the most needed knowledge is usually rather basic, long-lived, and slow to change. True, just as physics is under revision at the frontier, so American history before the Civil War is constantly under revision in certain details (e.g., did Abraham Lincoln have an affair with Ann Rutledge?). But behind the ever-changing front lines, there is a body of reliable knowledge that has not changed, and will not change very much, and that serves very well as a landscape to orient us in mental space. It is true that, over time, the content of the most significant and useful background knowledge for today's world does change. But I have never seen a carefully reasoned defense of the repeated assertion that, in the new age, factual knowledge is changing so fast as to make the learning of significant information useless. Probably, no carefully reasoned defense of this mindless claim could be mounted.

The physics example from Larkin and Chabay, if viewed in isolation, might be taken to show that higher-order thinking depends on abstract concepts rather than on factual details. But most research indicates that while the thinking activities through which we reach conclusions and solve problems are not crowded with literally remembered facts, neither are they made up of abstract concepts alone. The models, cues, and schemas through which we think critically are neither pure concepts nor a literal recall of data but a complex and varied combination of concepts, estimates, and factual examples. The key trait to remember about higher-order thinking is its mixed character, consisting of operational facility and domain-specific knowledge.

Some of the most useful studies of higher-order thinking have been concerned with improving our ability to make intelligent and accurate estimates on which to base decisions in our ethical, economic, and civic lives.[6] Since most of us cannot remember, and do not want to take the time to learn, all the details of the U.S. budget deficit and similar matters, we follow political and economic debates with a degree of impressionism that leaves many of us open to slogans and demagoguery. What kind of critical thinking can improve our ability to reach accurate conclusions on such issues? How can we protect ourselves and our students from oversimplifications, lies, and scapegoating conspiracy theories?

It is hard to see why a generalized skepticism, unsupported by accurate knowledge, is superior to a generalized credulity, similarly unsupported. Indeed, uninformed, generalized skepticism expresses itself as a form of credulity, despite our inclination to call I'm-from-Missouri postures "critical thinking." Our best hope for intelligent civic thought lies in our ability to make good ballpark estimates that are close enough to truth to make our decisions well informed and sound. But life is too short, and learning too arduous, for all citizens to memorize a lot of economic and demographic data. Our current yearly government budget deficit—is it around $30, $300, or $3,000 per American family? Sure, we could look it up, but few of us will. If we can't make an intelligent estimate from the knowledge we already have, we usually won't make an intelligent estimate at all. A lot of higher-order thinking involves our ability to make these sorts of estimates, and to make them well. How do some people manage to do it? And how can we all learn how to do it? From answers to those questions, what implications can be deduced for the K–12 curriculum?

The best research on this subject shows that neither fact-filled memorization nor large conceptual generalizations are effective modes of education for higher-order thinking about the complexities of the modern world. On the other hand, it has been shown that accurate factual estimates are necessary for understanding many issues. . . .

The breadth-depth issue will always be with us and will always require compromises and common sense. The particular compromise one makes will depend upon subject matter and goals. In practice, an appropriate compromise has been reached by self-taught, well-informed people and by the fortunate students of particularly able teachers. One well-tested teaching method, already followed by many good books and teachers, provides students with a carefully chosen but generous sampling of factual data that are set forth in a meaningful web of inferences and generalizations about the larger domain. Researchers have shown that such generally selective factual instruction leads to accurate inferences not directly deducible from the literal facts that were taught. The mechanisms by which we are able to use these selective exemplifications in order to make remarkably accurate factual guesses about untaught domains are a subject of vigorous current research.

Whatever the underlying psychological mechanisms prove to be, research has demonstrated that the teaching of a generous number of carefully chosen exemplary facts within a meaningful explanatory context is a better method for inducing insightful thinking than is any proposed alternative. These alternatives include (1) the teaching of the whole factual domain, (2) the teaching of the general principles only, and (3) the teaching of a single example in great depth (the less-is-more theory). None of these methods is as effective for inducing effective real-world thinking as sampling well-selected and consistent facts in a carefully prepared explanatory context.[7] This careful-sampling method works well even when (as usually happens) the literal details of the taught facts are not memorized by students and cannot be retrieved accurately from memory after a period of several months. Nonetheless, a strong improvement in accurate thinking persists if students have once been taught a carefully chosen sample of the factual data.

This finding has strong implications for curriculum making. The conclusion from cognitive research shows that there is an unavoidable interdependence between relational and factual knowledge and that teaching a broad range of factual knowledge is essential to effective thinking both within domains and among domains. Despite the popularity of the anti-fact motif in our progressive education tradition, and despite its faith in the power of a few "real-world" projects to educate students "holistically" for the modern world, no state board or school district has yet abandoned the principle of requiring a broad range of different subject matters in elementary school. Across the land, there are still universal requirements for mathematics, science, language arts, and social studies.

Is this curricular conservatism a mere residue of traditional thinking, or does it indicate that common sense has not been defeated by Romantic theory? I favor the latter hypothesis. Despite the vagueness of state and district guidelines, their continued parceling out of schooling into different subject matters, against continued pleas for a more "integrated" and holistic approach, shows an implicit understanding that breadth of knowledge is an essential element of higher-order thinking. School boards have rightly assumed that the mental landscape needs to be broadly surveyed and mapped in order to enable future citizens to cope with a large variety of judgments. No effective system of schooling in the world has abandoned this principle of subject-matter breadth in early schooling.

For later schooling, however, a good deal of evidence—marshaled in the superb research of John Bishop of Cornell—shows that in the last two years of high school, and later on, the balance of utility shifts in favor of deeper and more narrowly specialized training as the best education for the modern world.[8] This finding means that breadth in earlier schooling is all the more essential to developing adequate higher-order thinking and living skills in our citizens-to-be. If schooling is going to become more and more specialized in later life, it is ever more important to map out the wider intellectual landscape accurately and well in the earlier years. Otherwise, we shall produce not critical thinkers but narrow, ignorant ones, subject to delusion and rhetoric. This danger was uppermost in Jefferson's mind when he advocated teaching of human history in early years. In our age, the same argument holds for the domains connected with mathematics, science, technology, and communication skills. A wide range of knowledge and a broad vocabulary supply entry wedges into unfamiliar domains, thus truly enabling "lifelong learning," as well as the attainment of new knowledge and greater depth as needed. The unmistakable implication for modern education is that, instead of constantly deferring the introduction of challenging and extensive knowledge, we need to be taking the opposite tack by increasing both the challenge and the breadth of early education.

Consensus Research on Pedagogy

A consensus regarding the most effective teaching methods has emerged from three independent sources whose findings converge on the same pedagogical principles. This pattern of independent convergence (a kind of intellectual triangulation) is, along with accurate prediction, one of the most powerful, confidence-building patterns in scientific research. There are few or no examples in the history of science (none that I know of) when the same result, reached by three or more truly independent means, has been overturned. . . .

The independent convergence on the fundamentals of effective pedagogy that exists today is less mathematical but nonetheless compelling. The same findings have been derived from three quite different and entirely independent sources: (1) small-scale pairings of different teaching methods; (2) basic research in cognition, learning, memory, psycholinguistics, and other areas of cognitive psychology; and (3) large-scale international comparative studies. The findings from all three sources are highly consistent with each other regarding the most effective pedagogical principles. Because real-world classroom observations are so completely affected by so many uncontrolled variables, the most persuasive aspect of the current picture is the congruence of the classroom-based observations with cognitive psychology—which is currently our best and most reliable source of insight into the processes of learning.

In presenting these findings, my strategy will be briefly to go through some of the classroom studies and summarize their points of agreement. Then, I will relate those points to findings in cognitive psychology. Finally, I will comment on their congruence with the results of international comparisons. . . .

New Zealand studies   In a series of "process-outcome" studies between 1970 and 1973, researchers from the University of Canterbury in New Zealand found that time spent focused on content and the amount of content taught were more important factors than the teacher behaviors that were used to teach the content.[9] . . .

"Follow through" studies   Jane Stallings and her colleagues observed and evaluated results from 108 first-grade classes and fifty-eight third-grade classes taught by different methods. Programs having strong academic focus rather than programs using the project-method approach produced the highest gains in reading and math. Brophy and Good summarize the Stallings findings as follows: "Almost anything connected with the classical recitation pattern of teacher questioning (particularly direct, factual questions rather than more open questions) followed by student response, followed by teacher feedback, correlated positively with achievement." As in the New Zealand studies, students who spent most of their time being instructed or guided by their teachers did much better than students who did projects or were expected to learn on their own.[10]

Brophy-Evertson studies Between 1973 and 1979, Brophy and his colleagues conducted a series of studies in which they first determined that some teachers got consistently good results over the years, and others consistently bad ones. They made close observations of the teacher behaviors associated, respectively, with good and bad academic outcomes. Teachers who produced the most achievement were focused on academics. They were warm but businesslike. Teachers who produced the least achievement used a "heavily affective" approach and were more concerned with the child's self-esteem and psychic well-being than with academics. They emphasized warmth, used student ideas, employed a democratic style, and encouraged student-student interaction. The researchers further found that learning proceeded best when the material was somewhat new and challenging, but could also be assimilated relatively easily into what students already knew. The biggest contrast was not between modes of academic instruction but between all such instruction and "learner-centered" "discovery learning," which was ineffective. Paradoxically, the students were more motivated and engaged by academic-centered instruction than by student-centered instruction.

In 1982, Brophy and his colleagues summarized some of their later findings on the effective teaching of beginning reading. These were the most salient points:

1. Sustained focus on content.
2. All students involved (whole-class instruction dominates).
3. Brisk pace, with easy enough tasks for consistent student success.
4. Students reading aloud often and getting consistent feedback.
5. Decoding skills mastered to the point of over learning (automaticity).
6. In the course of time, each child asked to perform and getting immediate, nonjudgmental feedback.[11]

Good-Grouws studies For over a decade, Good and Grouws pursued process-outcome studies that support the Brophy-Evertson findings. Their 1977 summary contained the following points:

1. The best teachers were clearer.
2. They introduced more new concepts, engaged in less review.
3. They asked fewer questions.
4. Their feedback to the students was quick and nonevaluative.
5. They used whole-class instruction most of the time.
6. They were demanding and conveyed high expectations.[12]

The Gage studies   N. L. Gage and his colleagues at Stanford University have produced a series of process-outcome studies from the 1960s to the 1980s. These results, consistent with the above, are summarized in the following points of advice to teachers:

1. Introduce material with an overview or analogy.
2. Use review and repetition.
3. Praise or repeat student answers.
4. Be patient in waiting for responses.
5. Integrate the responses into the lesson.
6. Give assignments that offer practice and variety.
7. Be sure questions and assignments are new and challenging, yet easy enough to allow success with reasonable effort.[13]

Other studies   In 1986, Rosenshine and Stevens listed five other "particularly praiseworthy" studies of effective teaching modes, all of which came to similar conclusions. They summarize these conclusions as follows:

1. Review prerequisite learning.
2. Start with a brief statement of goals.
3. Introduce new material in small steps.
4. Maintain clarity and detail in presentation.
5. Achieve a high level of active practice.
6. Obtain response and check for understanding (CFU).
7. Guide student practice initially.
8. Give systematic, continual feedback.
9. Monitor and give specific advice during seatwork.[14]

The Brophy-Good summary   In their final summation of research in this area, Brophy and Good make a comment worth quoting directly. They draw two chief conclusions from reviewing all of this research:

> One is that academic learning is influenced by the amount of time students spend in appropriate academic tasks. The second is that students learn more efficiently when their teachers first structure new information for them and help them relate it to what they already know, and then monitor their performance and provide corrective feedback during recitation, drill, practice, or application activities. . . . There are no shortcuts to successful attainment of higher-level learning objectives. Such success will not be achieved with relative ease through discovery learning by the student. Instead, it will require considerable instruction from the teacher, as well as thorough mastery of basic knowledge and skills that must be integrated and applied in the process of "higher-level" performance. Development of basic knowledge and skills to the level of automatic and errorless performance will require a great deal of drill and practice. Thus drill and practice activities should not be slighted as "low level." They appear to be just as essential to complex and creative intellectual performance as they are to the performance of a virtuoso violinist.[15]

Before I go on to discuss correlations between these findings and research in cognitive psychology, I will digress to make an observation connecting these results to student motivation. While common sense might have predicted the *academic* superiority of structured, whole-class instruction over less academically focused, learner-centered instruction, it was unexpected that these studies should have demonstrated the *motivational* superiority of instruction centered on content rather than on students. Why is academically focused instruction more engaging and motivating to young learners than learner-centered instruction?

I know of no research that explains this finding, but I shall hazard the guess that individualized, learner-centered instruction must be extremely boring to most students most of the time, since, by mathematical necessity, they are not receiving individualized attention most of the time. It may also be the case that the slow pace and progress of less structured teaching may fail to engage and motivate students. A teacher must be extraordinarily talented to know just how to interact engagingly with each individual child. Given the strong motivation of young children to learn about the adult world, the best way to engage them is by a dramatic, interactive, and clear presentation that incidentally brings out the inherent satisfaction in skill mastery and interest in subject matter.

There is also a basis in cognitive psychology for the finding that students should be taught procedural skills to the point of "over learning." "Over learning" is a rather unfortunate term of art, since intuitively it seems a bad idea to overdo anything. But the term simply means that students should become able to supply the right answer or to follow the right procedure very fast, without hesitation. Through practice, they become so habituated to a procedure that they no longer have to think or struggle to perform it. This leaves their highly limited working memory free to focus on other aspects of the task at hand. The classroom research cited above simply reported that teachers who followed the principle of over learning produced much better results. Cognitive psychology explains why. . . .

The classroom studies also stressed the importance of teaching new content in small incremental steps. This is likewise explained by the limitations of working memory, since the mind can handle only a small number of new things at one time. A new thing has to become integrated with prior knowledge before the mind can give it meaning, store it in memory, and attend to something else. New learnings should not be introduced until feedback from students indicates that they have mastered the old learnings quite well, though not, as in the case of procedural skills, to the point of over learning. Research into long-term memory shows why this slow-but-sure method of feedback and review works best: "Once is not enough" should be the motto of long-term memory, though nonmeaningful review and boring repetition are not good techniques. The classroom research cited above indicated that the best teachers did not engage in incessant review. Memory studies suggest that the best approach to achieving retention in long-term memory is "distributed practice." Ideally, lessons should spread a topic over several days, with repetitions occurring at moderately distant intervals. . . . This feature of learning explains the importance of a deliberate pace of instruction, as all the classroom studies showed. Whatever practical arrangements are chosen for classroom learning, the principle of content rehearsal is absolutely essential for fixing content in long-term memory. Until that fixation occurs, content learning cannot be said to have happened.

That receiving continual feedback from the students is essential to good teaching is a robust finding in all the studies, and also gets support from research into both short-term and long-term memory. Feedback indicates whether the material has been learned well enough to free short-term (i.e., working) memory for new tasks. Moreover, the process of engaging in question-answer and other feedback practices constitutes content rehearsal, which also helps achieve secure learning in memory. Good teachers seem to be implicitly aware of this double function of question asking—that is, simultaneous monitoring and rehearsing.

Finally, research in cognitive psychology supports the finding that classes should often begin with a review or an analogy that connects the new topic with knowledge students already have. Psycholinguistic studies have shown that verbal comprehension powerfully depends on students' relevant background knowledge and particularly on their ability to apply that knowledge to something new.[16] Meaningful understanding seems to be equivalent to joining the new knowledge to something already known. Other psycholinguistic studies show that comprehension is enhanced when clues are offered at the beginning of a written passage indicating the overall character and direction of the passage. One needs to have a sense of the whole in order to predict the character of the parts and the way they fit with each other. Just as holistic, generic clues are important for the reader's comprehension of a written passage, such clues are similarly important for the student's understanding in the classroom. This psycholinguistic principle shows why a summary at the beginning of a class can give students the right "mindset" for assimilating the new material.[17]

These few principles concerning working memory, long-term memory, and the best prior conditions for meaningful learning explain the effectiveness of almost all the practices that were found to be effective in the classroom studies. Their congruence with mainstream psychology was well observed by Rosenshine and Stevens when they stated that research in cognitive psychology

> helps explain why students taught with structured curricula generally do better than those taught with either more individualized or discovery learning approaches. It also explains why young students who receive their instruction from a teacher usually achieve more than those who are expected to learn new materials and skills on their own or from each other. When young children are expected to learn on their own, particularly in the early stages, the students run the danger of not attending to the right cues, or not processing important points, and of proceeding on to later points before they have done sufficient elaboration and practice.[18]

Now I shall turn to some data from international studies on classroom practice. The fullest such research has been conducted by Harold Stevenson and his several colleagues in the United States, China, Japan, and Taiwan, who observed 324 Asian and American mathematics classrooms divided between first grade and fifth grade. Each classroom was studied for more than twenty hours by trained observers who took voluminous notes. . . .

In light of the contrast in outcomes, it is no surprise that the activities that typically occur in Asian classrooms follow the effective pedagogical principles deduced from small-scale American studies and from cognitive psychology. By contrast, the activities that typically occur in American classrooms run counter to those research findings. . . .

To illustrate the agreement between the small-scale intranational studies and the international studies, I shall first summarize the small-scale research findings in each category, then the corresponding findings from the international studies.

Social Atmosphere

Small-scale intranational studies In the best classrooms, the social atmosphere was warm and supportive, but at the same time businesslike and focused on the job at hand. By contrast, the worst-performing classrooms were "heavily affective," with a lot of verbal praise and self-esteem talk. In the best classes, the teacher was respectful to students but demanded good discipline as well as hard work. In the worst, the atmosphere was less ordered and disciplined.

International studies The most frequent form of evaluation used by American teachers was praise, a technique that is rarely used in either Taiwan or Japan. Praise cuts off discussion and highlights the teacher's role as the authority. It also encourages students to be satisfied with their performance rather than informing them about where they need improvement. Chinese and Japanese teachers have a low tolerance for errors, and when they occur, they seldom ignore them. Discussing errors helps to clarify misunderstandings, encourage argument and justification, and involve students in the exciting quest of assessing the strengths and weaknesses of the various alternative solutions that have been proposed.[19]

Initial Orientation

Small-scale intranational studies The teacher first reviews the knowledge prerequisite to the new learning and orients the class to what is in store. One good way is to introduce the material with an overview or analogy connecting it with previous knowledge and to present a brief statement of goals for the day's class.

International studies The Asian teacher stands in front of the class as a cue that the lesson will soon start. The room quiets. "Let us begin," says the teacher in Sendai. After brief reciprocal bows between pupils and teacher, the teacher opens the class with a description of what will be accomplished during the class period. From that point until the teacher summarizes the day's lesson and announces, "We are through," the Japanese elementary school class—like those in Taiwan and China—consists of teacher and students working together toward the goals described at the beginning of the class. . . .

Pace

Small-scale intranational studies   The best teachers introduce new material in small, easily mastered steps setting a deliberate but brisk pace, not moving ahead until students show that they understand. Better results come from teachers who move forward with new concepts, have higher expectations, and provide review, but not "incessant review."

International studies   The pace is slow, but the outcome is impressive. Japanese teachers want their students to be reflective and to gain a deep understanding of mathematics. Each concept and skill is taught with great thoroughness, thereby eliminating the need to teach the concept again later. Covering only a few problems does not mean that the lesson turns out to be short on content. In the United States, curriculum planners, textbook publishers, and teachers themselves seem to believe that students learn more effectively if they solve a large number of problems rather than if they concentrate their attention on only a few.[20]

Clarity

Small-scale intranational studies   The most effective teachers were not just clearer but more focused on the content or skill goal, asked questions but fewer of them, and kept the focus by continually integrating student responses into the lesson. A useful tool for clarity in presentation: an end-of-class summary review indicating where the lesson went and what it did.

International studies   Irrelevant interruptions often add to children's difficulty in perceiving lessons as a coherent whole. In American observations, the teacher interrupted the flow of the lesson with irrelevant comments, or the class was interrupted by someone else in 20 percent of all first-grade lessons and 47 percent of all fifth-grade lessons. In Sendai, Taipei, and Beijing, interruptions occurred less than 10 percent of the time at both grade levels. Coherence is also disrupted by frequent shifting from one topic to another within a single lesson. Twenty-one percent of the shifts within American lessons were to different topics (rather than to different materials or activities), compared with only 5 percent in the Japanese lessons. Before ending the lesson, the Asian teacher reviews what has been learned and relates it to the problem she posed at the beginning of the lesson. American teachers are much less likely than Asian teachers to end lessons in this way. . . .

Managing and Monitoring

Small-scale intranational studies   In the most effective teaching, whole-class instruction is used most of the time. The teacher obtains responses and checks for understanding for each student, ensuring that each child gets some feedback and that all students stay involved. While feedback to the students is frequent, it is not incessant. The teacher is patient in waiting for responses. Student answers are often repeated for the class. Many effective teachers make constructive, nonevaluative use of student errors, working through how they were made. Students are more engaged and motivated in these classrooms than in student-centered ones.

International studies   Chinese and Japanese teachers rely on students to generate ideas and evaluate the correctness of the ideas. The possibility that they will be called upon to state their own solution keeps Asian students alert, but this technique has two other important functions. First, it engages students in the lesson, increasing their motivation by making them feel they are participants in a group process. Second, it conveys a more realistic impression of how knowledge is acquired. American teachers are less likely to give students opportunities to respond at such length. Although a great deal of interaction appears to occur in American classrooms—with students and teachers posing questions and giving answers—American teachers generally ask questions that are answerable with a yes or a no or a short phrase. They seek a correct answer and continue calling on students until one produces it.[21]

Drill and Practice

Small-scale intranational studies   Two kinds of practice are needed, corresponding to two objects of learning—content and skills. For content, new concepts are discussed and reviewed until secure in the memory. Procedural skills are mastered to the point of overlearning (automaticity). Guided practice should be part of whole-class instruction before seatwork occurs. Small-group seatwork generally works better than individual seatwork, but seatwork per se is used rather sparingly for both content and skills. Supervision and feedback are provided during seatwork.

International studies   When children must work alone for long periods of time without guidance or reaction from the teacher, they begin to lose focus on the purpose of their activity. Asian teachers assign less seatwork than American teachers; furthermore, they use seatwork differently. Asian teachers tend to use short, frequent periods of seatwork, alternating between discussing problems and allowing children to work problems on their own. When seatwork is embedded within the lesson, instruction and practice are tightly woven into a coherent whole. Teachers can gauge children's understanding of the preceding part of the lesson by observing how they solve practice problems. Interspersing seatwork with instruction in this way helps the teacher assess how rapidly she can proceed through the lesson. American teachers, on the other hand, tend to relegate seatwork to one long period at the end of the class, where it becomes little more than a time for repetitious practice. . . . American teachers often do not discuss the work or its connection to the goal of the lesson, or publicly evaluate its accuracy.[22] . . .

. . . [C]onsensus [research into teacher effectiveness] among present-day reformers is well summarized by Zemelman, Daniels, and Hyde in their 1993 book, *Best Practice*.

> In virtually every school subject, we now have recent summary reports, meta-analyses of instructional research, bulletins from pilot classrooms, and landmark sets of professional recommendations. Today there is a strong consensus definition of Best Practice, of state-of-the-art teaching in every critical field. . . . Whether the recommendations come from the National Council of Teachers of Mathematics, the Center for the Study of Reading, the National Writing Project, the National Council for the Social Studies, the American Association for the Advancement of Science, the National Council of Teachers of English, the National Association for the Education of Young Children, or the International Reading Association, the fundamental insights into teaching and learning are remarkably congruent. Indeed on many key issues, the recommendations from these diverse organizations are unanimous.

Zemelman, Daniels, and Hyde then list twenty-five "LESS" and "MORE" admonitions on which all these organizations agree. Among them are the following:

- LESS whole-class teacher-directed instruction
- LESS student passivity, sitting, listening, receiving
- LESS attempts by teachers to cover large amounts of material
- LESS rote memorization of facts and details
- LESS stress on competition and grades
- MORE experiential, inductive, hands-on learning
- MORE active learning with all the attendant noise of students doing, talking, collaborating
- MORE deep study of a smaller number of topics
- MORE responsibility transferred to students for their work: goal-setting, record-keeping, monitoring, evaluation
- MORE choice for students, e.g., picking their own books, etc.
- MORE attention to affective needs and varying cognitive styles of students
- MORE cooperative, collaborative activity.[23]

The authors praise the current consensus on these "child-centered" principles for being "progressive, developmentally appropriate, research based, and eminently teachable." These claims are not, however, "research based" in the way the authors imply. Quite the contrary. No studies of children's learning in mainstream science support these generalizations. With respect to effective learning, the consensus in research is that their recommendations are worst practice, not "best practice."

This Alice in Wonderland reversal of reality has been accomplished largely by virtue of the rhetorical device that I have called "premature polarization." Discovery learning is labeled "progressive," and whole-class instruction "traditional.". . . It overlooks, for instance, the different pedagogical requirements for procedural learning and content learning and thus neglects the different pedagogical emphases needed at the different ages and stages of learning. Effective procedural learning requires "overlearning," and hence plenty of practice. Content learning is amenable to a diversity of methods that accommodate themselves to students' prior knowledge, habits, and interests.

What the international data show very clearly is that both procedural and content learning are best achieved in a focused environment that preponderantly emphasizes whole-class instruction but that is punctuated by small-group or individualized work. Within that focused context, however, there are many good roads to Rome. The classroom observations of Stevenson and his colleagues bring home the ancient wisdom of integrating both direct and indirect methods, including inquiry learning, which encourages students to think for themselves, and direct informing, which is sometimes the most effective and efficient mode of securing knowledge and skill. A combination of show and tell, omitting neither, is generally the most effective approach in teaching, as it is in writing and speaking.

The only truly general principle that seems to emerge from process-outcome research on pedagogy is that focused and guided instruction is far more effective than naturalistic, discovery, learn-at-your-own-pace instruction. But within the context of focused and guided instruction, almost anything goes, and what works best with one group of students may not work best with another group with similar backgrounds in the very same building. Methods must vary a good deal with different age groups. Within the general context of focused and guided instruction, my own general preference, and one followed by good teachers in many lands, is for what might be called "dramatized instruction." The class period can be formed into a little drama with a beginning, middle, and end, well directed but not rigidly scripted by the teacher. The beginning sets up the question to be answered, the knowledge to be mastered, or the skill to be gained; the middle consists of a lot of back-and-forth between student and student, student and teacher; and the end consists of a feeling of closure and accomplishment. . . .

The focused narrative or drama lies midway between narrow drill and practice (which has its place) and the unguided activity of the project method (which may also occasionally have a place). Sir Philip Sidney argued (in 1583!) that stories are better teachers than philosophy or history, because philosophy teaches by dull precept (guided instruction) and history teaches by uncertain example (the project method).[24] The story, however, joins precept and example together, thus teaching and delighting at the same time. . . .

Excellent classroom teaching has a narrative and dramatic feel even when there is a lot of interaction between the students and the teacher—it has a definite theme, and a beginning, middle, and end. This teaching principle holds even for mathematics and science. When every lesson has a well-developed plot in which the children themselves are participants, teaching is both focused and absorbing. The available research is consistent with this scheme, though it by no means says that thoughtful sequencing, plotting, and dramatizing of learning activities are the exclusive or whole key to good pedagogy. For many elementary learnings, repeated practice has to be an integral part of the plot.

That recent psychological research should yield insights that confirm what . . . Sidney said about stories should probably make us more, not less, confident in the results of this recent research. Education is as old as humanity. The breathless claim that technology and the information age have radically changed the nature of the education of young children turns out to be, like most breathless claims in education, unsupported by scholarship. Nor should current studies surprise us when they show that a naturalistic approach, lacking a definite story line and a sharp focus, has the defect Sidney saw in history as a teacher of humankind: it "draweth no necessary consequence." There is a modest place for discovery learning, just as there is for drill and practice. But research indicates that, most of the time, clearly focused, well-plotted teaching is the best means for "[holding] children from play and old men from the chimney corner."

Notes

1. For comments on Gentile's views and for basic insights into Gramsci's ideas about education, I am grateful to Entwistle, *Antonio Gramsci*. Additional commentary may be found in Broccoli, *Antonio Gramsci e l'educazione come egemonia;* Scuderi, *Antonio Gramsci e il problema pedagogico;* and De Robbio, *Antonio Gramsci e la pedagogia dell'impegno.* For modern data showing that Gramsci is right in holding that traditional schooling greatly improves the academic competencies of low achievers, see K. R. Johnson, and Layng, "Breaking the Structuralist Barrier," 1475–90.

2. Larkin et al., "Models of Competence in Solving Physics Problems," 317–48. Schoenfeld and Hermann, "Problem Perception and Knowledge Structure in Expert and Novice Mathematical Problem Solvers," 484–94.

3. Some work in this tradition: Tversky and Kahneman, "Availability," 207–32; Collins, *Human Plausible Reasoning;* and Fischoff, "Judgment and Decision Making," 153–87.

4. Larkin and Chabay, "Research on Teaching Scientific Thinking," 158.

5. Ibid., 150–72.

6. Kunda and Nisbett, "The Psychometrics of Everyday Life," 195–224.

7. Brown and Siegler, "Metrics and Mappings," 531. But see also Scardamalia and Bereiter, "Computer Support for Knowledge-Building Communities," 265–83; and Scardamalia, Bereiter, and Lamon, "CSILE: Trying to Bring Students into World 3," 201–28.

8. Bishop, *Expertise and Excellence.*

9. The data from the New Zealand study and most other studies cited here are taken from the excellent review by Brophy and Good, who conducted some of the most significant research into effective teaching methods. See Brophy and Good, "Teacher Behavior and Student Achievement," 328–75. Some of the New Zealand work is described in Nuthall and Church, "Experimental Studies of Teaching Behaviour." The importance of this kind of research was well argued by Gilbert T. Sewall in his *Necessary Lessons*, especially pages 131–33. Sewall cites highly similar findings from the British researcher Neville Bennett in N. Bennett, *Teaching Styles and*

Pupil Progress. For an explanation why progressive methods like discovery learning have not worked well in teaching science, see Walberg, "Improving School Science in Advanced and Developing Countries," 625–99.

10. Stallings and Kasowitz, *Follow Through Classroom Evaluation*, 1972–1973.

11. Brophy and Evertson, *Learning from Teaching*. Anderson, Evertson, and Brophy, *Principles of Small-Group Instruction in Elementary Reading*.

12. Good and Grouws, "Teacher Effects," 49–54.

13. Gage, *The Scientific Basis of the Art of Teaching*.

14. Rosenshine and Stevens, "Teaching Functions," 376–91.

15. Brophy and Good, "Teacher Behavior and Student Achievement," 338.

16. Spiro, "Cognitive Processes in Prose Comprehension and Recall"; and Anderson and Shifrin, "The Meaning of Words in Context."

17. Bransford and Johnson, "Contextual Prerequisites for Understanding," 717–26. Spiro, "Cognitive Processes in Prose Comprehension and Recall."

18. Rosenshine and Stevens, "Teaching Functions," 379.

19. Stevenson and Stigler, *The Learning Gap*, 191.

20. Ibid., 194.

21. Ibid., 190.

22. Ibid., 183.

23. Zemelman, Daniels, and Hyde, *Best Practice*, 4–5.

24. Sidney, *An Apology for Poetry*.

POSTSCRIPT

Should Schools Adopt a Constructivist Approach to Education?

Hirsch points to dozens of studies that he believes demonstrate the superiority of a teacher-centered, fact-based approach. Why, then, do Windschitl and other constructivists adhere so firmly to their position? How can they ignore the empirical evidence amassed by Hirsch? In fact, interpreting the studies that Hirsch cites is not so straightforward. Many of these studies are correlational, involving comparisons between existing classrooms exemplifying the different approaches. In a correlational study, the researcher has no control over factors such as the assignment of students or teachers to one approach or the other or the ways in which the two approaches are implemented. This means that it is often difficult to discern whether differences in student achievement have been caused by differences in pedagogical approach or by preexisting differences that were beyond the control of the researchers. In addition, constructivists would argue that many of the so-called constructivist classrooms examined in these studies did little more than insert a few hands-on activities into an otherwise teacher-centered classroom. They would question whether the classrooms that were evaluated really provided a fair test of the impact constructivism has on student learning and achievement. An even more vexing problem in interpretation, however, is that the two approaches appear to value very different types of outcomes for students. The teacher-centered, fact-based approach values a large quantity of decontextualized skills and facts, whereas the constructivist approach values the acquisition of more particular forms of knowing and acting. In other words, the two approaches seem to be designed to teach very different things. This raises the possibility that deciding between them cannot be done solely by relying on empirical data. Instead, we must decide what outcomes are most valuable for students—large collections of facts and skills or the particular modes of thought and action described by the constructivists. Only when that is decided can empirical research be carried out to determine whether the teacher-centered approach, the constructivist approach, or some other approach is best suited to reaching those outcomes in a timely and cost-effective manner.

Complicating matters further is the fact that both the teacher-centered approach and the constructivist approach are composed of many elements, and it may turn out to be that some elements of each may be most effective. In fact, this possibility has been suggested by a number of cognitive scientists, including David Perkins, codirector of Harvard Project Zero. In an insightful paper, "Teaching for Understanding," *American Educator* (vol. 17, no. 3, 1993),

Perkins criticizes the drill-and-practice strategy for not providing students the means of knowing how to apply the facts that they have memorized to solve meaningful problems. At the same time, he acknowledges that deep understanding of any domain of knowledge demands that certain critical facts be mastered, although he stresses that real understanding ultimately requires that students recognize the relationships among these facts. Perkins is also critical of the constructivist approach for underestimating the sophistication of the cognitive capabilities of even the youngest children. This underestimation, he argues, often leads constructivists to withhold material that children could and should master early in their schooling. Perkins further criticizes constructivists for focusing so completely on the concept of hands-on activities that they ignore the possibility that verbal discourse can also be used to actively engage students in the material to be mastered. At the same time, however, he acknowledges that deep understanding of a domain—in the sense of recognizing the relationships among critical facts and being able to apply those facts to solve a range of meaningful problems—requires the active, extended engagement with tasks and materials that is characteristic of the hands-on constructivist approach. Perkins maintains that the goal for students should be deep understanding of the domains of knowledge we value and that this will require an approach that blends elements of both the teacher-centered and the constructivist approach.

Readers interested in learning more about the psychological theories underlying constructivist education should see Leonard Abbeduto and Stephen N. Elliott, *Guide to Human Development for Future Educators* (McGraw-Hill, 1998); "Constructing Scientific Knowledge in the Classroom," by R. Driver et al., *Educational Researcher* (vol. 23, no. 7, 1994); *In Search of Understanding: The Case for Constructivist Classrooms* by Jacqueline G. Brooks and Martin G. Brooks (Association for Supervision & Curriculum Development, 1993); and "Piaget's Equilibration Theory and the Young Gifted Child: A Balancing Act," by Leonora M. Cohen and Younghee M. Kin, *Roeper Review* (1999). Readers interested in reading original papers by developmental psychologist Jean Piaget, from whose work the constructivist approach has grown most directly, can turn to the collection *The Essential Piaget: An Interpretive Reference and Guide,* edited by Howard E. Gruber and Jacques J. Voneche (Jason Aronson, 1995). Articles that provide illustrations of constructivist classrooms are "How to Build a Better Mousetrap: Changing the Way Science Is Taught Through Constructivism," by Thomas R. Lord, *Contemporary Education* (Spring 1998); "Constructivist Theory in the Classroom," by Mary M. Bevevino, Joan Dengel, and Kenneth Adams, *The Clearing House* (May/June 1999); and "Constructivism: Science Education's 'Grand Unifying Theory,'" by Alan Colburn, *The Clearing House* (September/October 2000). See also "The Role of Assessment in a Learning Culture," by Lorrie A. Shepard, *Educational Researcher* (October 2000) for an interesting article on the place of assessment in the constructivist classroom.

ISSUE 8

Does Reinforcement Facilitate Learning?

YES: Tashawna K. Duncan, Kristen M. Kemple, and Tina M. Smith, from "Reinforcement in Developmentally Appropriate Early Childhood Classrooms," *Childhood Education* (Summer 2000)

NO: Charles H. Wolfgang, from "Another View on 'Reinforcement in Developmentally Appropriate Early Childhood Classrooms,'" *Childhood Education* (Winter 2000/2001)

ISSUE SUMMARY

YES: Tashawna K. Duncan, Kristen M. Kemple, and Tina M. Smith from the School of Teaching and Learning at the University of Florida, argue that reinforcement has a long history of successful application in the classroom. They dismiss concerns that it lowers intrinsic motivation or that it is ethically equivalent to paying children to learn. They do acknowledge, however, that reinforcement must be integrated with a consideration of the developmental and unique needs of each child.

NO: Charles H. Wolfgang, a professor of early childhood education, admits that reinforcement and other techniques derived from behaviorist theory do control children's behavior in the short term. He asserts, however, that such techniques do little to encourage internalization of the types of standards that will ultimately lead children to behave effectively and appropriately in a range of situations in the future.

During the first half of the twentieth century, American psychology was dominated by *behaviorism*. Although expressed in a number of seemingly distinct theories, the fundamental assumption of behaviorism—that the behavior of any organism is controlled by forces that are external to it—has remained constant across its many manifestations. In Ivan Pavlov's theory of *classical conditioning*, a dog reflexively salivates in response to the sound of a bell that was previously paired with the delivery of food. In B. F. Skinner's theory of *operant conditioning*, a thirsty rat presses a bar when a light flashes because this results in the delivery of a few drops of water. In these examples, the organism's behavior is controlled by some feature of the world around it—the sound of a bell, the flash of light, the delivery of food or water. Despite its apparent complexity and the addition of a conscious mind, behaviorists have traditionally argued that human behavior, like the behavior of animals, is also controlled by external forces.

The influence of behaviorism has extended far beyond academic psychology to include the American classroom. This influence can be traced most directly to the work of Skinner (1904–1990), who emphasized the role of *reinforcement* in his theory of operant conditioning. According to Skinner, an event serves as reinforcement if it is contingent on an organism's response to a stimulus and increases the future likelihood of that response. If, for example, a student who is praised consistently by his teacher for completing assignments on time begins to meet deadlines with increasing frequency over time, the teacher's praise would be a reinforcer. It is important to note that, according to Skinner, we cannot know in advance whether praise, a gold star, a good grade, or any other stimulus will be reinforcing. In fact, he argued that we can only know that something is reinforcing if we observe that it leads to an increase in the target behavior. This was a critical point for Skinner. He felt that all too often teachers, parents, and cognitive psychologists expend too much effort "guessing" about what is going on inside a student's head: Is the student motivated? Will the student see my overture as positive or negative? Because we can never know for sure what is going on in another person's mind, Skinner believed that it is far more productive to analyze the consequences of a student's behavior. In short, according to Skinner, we can control a student's behavior by changing its consequences—removing the reinforcement for behaviors we see as negative and providing reinforcement for behaviors we see as positive.

In recent decades, the dominance of behaviorism in psychology and education has been challenged by *constructivist* approaches. Constructivist approaches envision a more active role for the student in learning, with either his or her mental action on the world or participation in interactions with a more highly skilled partner being the catalyst for change. Perhaps most important, these approaches are based on the belief that the student has a natural curiosity and inclination to try and master the problems posed in and out of the classroom. In constructivist theories, there is no need to posit a role for external reinforcement.

In the following selections, the debate about reinforcement is played out in the context of a discussion about early childhood education. In the first selection, Tashawna K. Duncan, Kristen M. Kemple, and Tina M. Smith side with Skinner and argue that reinforcement is an effective technique for producing positive changes in young children's behavior. They also argue that it is ethically acceptable when integrated into an approach that is sensitive to each child's individual needs and developmental level. In the second selection, Charles H. Wolfgang argues that reinforcement controls children's behavior in the short term but can have long-term negative consequences for child outcomes, including a failure to develop the internal resources needed to inhibit maladaptive behaviors.

Tashawna K. Duncan, Kristen M.
Kemple, and Tina M. Smith

Reinforcement in Developmentally Appropriate Early Childhood Classrooms

Each day from 10:30 to 11:00, the children in Mrs. Kitchens's 1st-grade classroom are expected to sit silently in their desks and copy words from the chalkboard into their notebooks. Children who finish early are required to remain silently in their seats. After five minutes has passed, Mrs. Kitchens assesses whether every child in the class has been behaving according to the rules. If they have been, she makes a check mark on the chalkboard and announces, "Good! There's a check." If even one child has violated the rules, she announces "no check." At the end of the week, if 20 or more checks have accrued on the board, the whole group is awarded an extra-long Friday recess period. This longed-for reward is rarely achieved, however.

Five-year-old Rodney has recently joined Mr. Romero's kindergarten class. On his first day in his new class, Rodney punched a classmate and usurped the tricycle the other boy was riding. On Rodney's second day in the class, he shoved a child off a swing and dumped another out of her chair at the snack table. In an effort to deal with Rodney's problematic behavior, Mr. Romero is taking a number of steps, including making sure that Rodney knows the classroom rules and routines, helping Rodney learn language and skills to resolve conflicts, exploring ways to make Rodney feel welcome and a special part of the class, and arranging for a consultation with a special education specialist to see if support services would be appropriate. Mr. Romero is concerned for the emotional and physical safety of the other children, and he believes that Rodney will have a hard time making friends if his reputation as an aggressor is allowed to solidify. He feels the need to act fast. Deciding that a system of reinforcement, along with other strategies, may help Rodney control his aggressive behavior, Mr. Romero implements a token reinforcement system. Rodney earns a ticket, accompanied by praise, for each 30-minute period during which he does not behave aggressively. At the end of the day, Rodney can trade a specified number of earned tickets for his choice of small toys.

The above examples illustrate two teachers' efforts to use the behavioral strategy of reinforcement—with varying degrees of appropriateness. In Mrs. Kitchens's class, reinforcement is being used as a means to get children to sit still and be quiet in the context of a developmentally inappropriate lesson. In an effort to keep children "on task," Mrs. Kitchens substitutes a control tactic for a meaningful and engaging curriculum. Mr. Romero, on the other hand, is making efforts to identify and address the reasons for Rodney's behavior. Furthermore, he believes that Rodney's behavior is so detrimental to himself and to the other children that additional measures must be used to achieve quick results and restore a sense of psychological safety in the classroom community. Mr. Romero utilizes a variety of strategies in the hopes of creating lasting change in Rodney's behavior.

Inclusion of Children with Special Needs

The trend toward including children with disabilities in early childhood education settings is growing (Wolery & Wilbers, 1994). As greater numbers of children with disabilities participate in early childhood programs, teachers are faced with the challenge of expanding their repertoire of teaching and guidance practices to accommodate the needs of children with diverse abilities and needs. To this end, teachers responsible for the care and education of diverse groups of young children are encouraged to examine their beliefs about their role in promoting children's development and learning, and to explore their understanding of developmentally appropriate practices as outlined by the National Association for the Education of Young Children (NAEYC) (Bredekamp & Copple, 1997).

Recent federal legislation requires that children be educated in the "least restrictive environment." This means that, to the maximum extent possible, the setting in which children with special needs are educated should be the same as that in which typically developing children are educated, and that specialized services should be provided within the regular classroom (Thomas & Russo, 1995).

Early Childhood Education and Early Childhood Special Education

Most early childhood teachers have little or no training in early childhood special education. Historically, differences have existed between teachers who work with young children with disabilities and teachers who work with typically developing children, including different educational preparation, separate professional organizations, and reliance on different bodies of research (Wolery & Wilbers, 1994). As both groups of children are increasingly cared for and educated in the same programs, early childhood educators and early childhood special educators are called upon to work in collaboration to ensure that children receive individually appropriate education. This collaborative effort requires that all teachers have familiarity with and respect for the philosophy and practices of both disciplines.

Historically, early childhood special education has had stronger roots in behavioral psychology and applied behavior analysis than has early childhood education. As Wolery and Bredekamp (1994) noted, developmentally appropriate practices (DAP) (as outlined by NAEYC) have their roots primarily in maturational and constructivist perspectives. While current early childhood special education practices also tend to be rooted in constructivist perspectives, the additional influence of cultural transmission perspectives (including behaviorist models of learning) is evident. Given their diverse origins, it should not be surprising that the two disciplines would advocate, on occasion, different practices (Wolery & Bredekamp, 1994). This potential tension is exemplified in an editor's note found in the recent NAEYC publication *Including Children With Special Needs in Early Childhood Programs* (Wolery & Wilbers, 1994). Carol Copple (the series' editor) stated,

> Certainly early childhood educators are well aware of the limits of behaviorism as the sole approach to children's learning and are wary of overreliance on rewards as a motivational technique. From this vantage point, some readers may have a negative first response to some of the techniques described in this chapter. Although we must be aware of the limitations and pitfalls of such methods, I urge readers to keep an open mind about them. . . . They are not for every situation, but when used appropriately, they often succeed where other methods fail. (Wolery & Wilbers, 1994, p. 119)

The current authors hope that readers will be open to considering the judicious use of methods of reinforcement described in this article. When included as part of a total developmentally appropriate program and used after careful assessment of individual needs, these methods can be important tools for implementing *individually* appropriate practice.

Developmentally Appropriate Practice

In 1987, NAEYC published *Developmentally Appropriate Practice in Early Childhood Programs Serving Children From Birth to Age 8* (Bredekamp, 1987), which was revised and published in 1997 as *Developmentally Appropriate Practice in Early Childhood Programs* (Bredekamp & Copple, 1997). Many have argued that DAP provides an appropriate educational context for the inclusion of young children with disabilities, assuming that the interpretations of DAP guidelines leave room for adaptations and extensions to meet the child's specific needs (Bredekamp, 1993; Carta, 1995; Carta, Atwater, Schwartz, & McConnell, 1993; Carta, Schwartz, Atwater, & McConnell, 1991; Wolery & Bredekamp, 1994; Wolery, Strain, & Bailey, 1992; Wolery, Werts, & Holcombe-Ligon, 1994). For some young children, this may mean the use of behavioral strategies, such as planned programs of systematic reinforcement. In fact, the current DAP guidelines do not identify reinforcement systems as inappropriate practice. Some early childhood educators, however, view many forms of reinforcement as completely unacceptable. If inclusion is to succeed, it may be necessary for teachers to consider using such strategies for particular children in particular circumstances.

While reinforcement through use of stickers, privileges, and praise is *not* identified as developmentally *inappropriate* practice, it does become inappropriate when used in exclusion of other means of promoting children's engagement and motivation, and when used indiscriminately (for the wrong children, and/or in the wrong situations). Children's active engagement is a guiding principle in both DAP and early childhood special education (Carta et al., 1993). As Carta et al. (1993) have pointed out, however, many young children with disabilities are less likely to engage spontaneously with materials in their environments (Peck, 1985; Weiner & Weiner, 1974). The teacher's active encouragement is needed to help such children become actively involved in learning opportunities. A principal goal of early intervention is to facilitate young children's active engagement with materials, activities, and the social environment through systematic instruction (Wolery et al., 1992). Such instruction may include use of reinforcement as incentives.

Behavioral Strategies in Early Childhood Education

Behavioral theory holds that behaviors acquired and displayed by young children can be attributed almost exclusively to their environment. Several behavioral strategies are employed by early childhood teachers to facilitate children's learning, including the use of praise and external rewards. However, practitioners often fail to identify these strategies in their repertoire and dismiss, out of hand, their use in the classroom. Misunderstandings may exist concerning the appropriate use and potential effectiveness of these strategies for young children. As a result, they are not always well accepted in the early childhood community (Henderick, 1998; Rodd, 1996; see also Strain et al., 1992).

A review of contemporary literature suggests that behavioral strategies are appropriate for creating and maintaining an environment conducive to growth and development (e.g., Peters, Neisworth, & Yawkey, 1985; Schloss & Smith, 1998). Research has demonstrated that behavioral strategies are successful in school settings with various diverse populations, including those with young children (Kazdin, 1994). Furthermore, while many such "best practices" are unrecognized by early childhood professionals, they are grounded in behavioral theory (Strain et al., 1992).

The Use of Positive Reinforcement

Positive reinforcement is perhaps the strategy most palatable to educators who are concerned about the misuse of behavioral strategies. A particular behavior is said to be positively reinforced when the behavior is followed by the presentation of a reward (e.g., praise, stickers) that results in increased frequency of the particular behavior (Schloss & Smith, 1998). For example, Stella has been reluctant to wash her hands before lunch. Mrs. Johnson begins consistently praising Stella when she washes her hands by saying, "Now your hands are nice and clean and ready for lunch!" Stella becomes more likely to wash her hands without protest. In this case, we can say that Stella's handwashing behavior has been positively reinforced.

Most frequently, positive reinforcement strategies are used to teach, maintain, or strengthen a variety of behaviors (Zirpoli, 1995). Although some early childhood teachers may be reluctant to endorse the use of reinforcement, they often unknowingly employ reinforcement strategies every day in their classroom (Henderick, 1998; Wolery, 1994).

Types of Reinforcers

Reinforcers frequently used by teachers generally fall within one of three categories: social, activity, or tangible. These three categories can be viewed along a continuum ranging from least to most intrusive. Social reinforcers are the least intrusive, in that they mimic the natural consequences of positive, prosocial behavior. At the other end of the continuum are tangible reinforcers. Tangible reinforcers involve the introduction of rewards that ordinarily may not be part of the routine. In selecting a reinforcer, the goal is to select the least intrusive reinforcer that is likely to be effective. If reinforcers other than social ones are necessary, teachers should develop a plan to move gradually toward social reinforcers. The following sections describe each category of reinforcers and how they can be used effectively within the context of developmentally appropriate practice.

Social reinforcers. Teachers employ social reinforcers when they use interpersonal interactions to reinforce behaviors (Schloss & Smith, 1998). Some commonly used social reinforcers include positive nonverbal behaviors (e.g., smiling) and praise (Alberto & Troutman, 1990; Sulzer-Azaroff & Mayer, 1991). Because they are convenient, practical, and can be highly effective, social reinforcers are the most widely accepted and frequently used type of reinforcer in the early childhood classroom (Sulzer-Azaroff & Mayer, 1991). One means of effectively reinforcing a child's behavior via social reinforcement is by using a "positive personal message" (Gordon, 1974; Kostelnik, Stein, Whiren, & Soderman, 1998). For example, Ms. Tarrant says, "Sally, you put the caps back on the markers. I'm pleased. Now the markers won't get dried up. They'll be fresh and ready when someone else wants to use them." This positive personal message reminds Sally of the rule (put the caps on the markers) at a time when Sally has clear and immediate proof that she is able to follow the rule. The personal message pinpoints a specific desirable behavior, and lets the child know why the behavior is appropriate. When used appropriately, social reinforcers have been shown to enhance children's self-esteem (Sulzer-Azaroff & Mayer, 1991). When used in tandem with less natural (e.g., tangible) reinforcers, social reinforcers have been shown to enhance the power of those less natural reinforcers (Sulzer-Azaroff & Mayer, 1991).

Of the various types of social reinforcers, praise is used most frequently and deliberately by teachers (Alberto & Troutman, 1990). In recent years, several articles have been published on the topic of praise (Hitz & Driscoll, 1988; Marshall, 1995; Van der Wilt, 1996). While praise has the potential to enhance children's self-esteem, research has demonstrated that certain kinds of praise may actually lower children's self-confidence, inhibit achievement, and make children reliant on external (as opposed to internal) controls (Kamii, 1984; Stringer & Hurt, 1981, as cited in Hitz & Driscoll, 1988). These authors have drawn distinctions between "effective praise" (sometimes called "encouragement") and "ineffective praise." Effective praise is consistent with commonly held goals of early childhood education: promoting children's positive self-concept, autonomy, self-reliance, and motivation for learning (Hitz & Driscoll, 1988).

Effective praise is specific. Instead of saying, "Justin, what a lovely job you did cleaning up the blocks," Mrs. Constanz says, "Justin, you put each block in its place on the shelf." In this case, Mrs. Constanz leaves judgment about the *quality* of the effort to the child. By pinpointing specific aspects of the child's behavior or product (rather than using vague, general praise), Mrs. Constanz communicates that she has paid attention to, and is genuinely interested in, what the child has done (Hitz & Driscoll, 1988).

Effective praise generally is delivered privately. Public uses of praise, such as, "I like the way Carlos is sitting so quietly," have a variety of disadvantages. Such statements are typically intended to manipulate children into following another child's example. In the example, the message was, "Carlos is doing a better job of sitting than are the rest of you." With time, young children may come to resent this management, and resent a child who is the frequent recipient of such public praise (Chandler, 1981; Gordon, 1974). As an alternative, the teacher could whisper the statement quietly to Carlos, and/or say to the other children, "Think about what you need to do to be ready to listen." As individual children comply, the teacher may quickly acknowledge each child, "Caitlin is ready, Tyler is ready; thank you, Nicholas, Lakeesha, and Ali . . ." (Marshall, 1995).

Another characteristic of effective praise is that it emphasizes improvement of process, rather than the finished product. As Daryl passes out individual placemats to his classmates, he states their names. Mrs. Thompson says, "Daryl, you are learning more names. You remembered Tom and Peg today." She could have said, "Daryl, you are a great rememberer," but she chose not to, because Daryl knows that he did not remember everyone's name, and tomorrow he may forget some that he knew today. In this example, Mrs. Thompson's praise is specific and is focused on the individual child's improvement.

Activity reinforcers. Teachers employ activity reinforcers when they use access to a pleasurable activity as a reinforcer (Sulzer-Azaroff & Mayer, 1991). Some commonly used and effective activity reinforcers include doing a special project, being a classroom helper, and having extra free-choice time (Sulzer-Azaroff & Mayer, 1991). When using activity reinforcers, teachers create a schedule in which an enjoyable activity follows the behavior they are trying to change or modify (Sulzer-Azaroff & Mayer, 1991). Teachers often use such activity reinforcers unknowingly. Following social reinforcers, activity reinforcers are the most frequently used (Alberto & Troutman, 1990), probably because teachers view them as more convenient and less intrusive than tangible reinforcers (Sulzer-Azaroff & Mayer, 1991). When used appropriately, activity reinforcers can modify a wide variety of behaviors. The following examples illustrate the appropriate use of activity reinforcers.

In Miss Annie's class, a brief playground period is scheduled to follow center clean-up time. Miss Annie reminds the children that the sooner they have the centers cleaned up, the sooner they will be able to enjoy the playground. It appears that the playground time is reinforcing children's quick clean-up behavior: They consistently get the job done with little dawdling.

As part of a total plan to reduce Christopher's habit of using his cupped hands to toss water out of the water table, Mrs. Jackson has told Christopher that each day he plays without throwing water out of the table, he may be table washer after snack time (which Christopher delights in doing). This strategy was implemented following efforts to help Christopher develop appropriate behavior through demonstrations and by redirecting him with water toys chosen specifically to match his interests.

Tangible reinforcers.   Teachers sometimes employ tangible reinforcers, such as stickers and prizes, to strengthen and modify behavior in the early childhood classroom. Tangible reinforcers are most often used to modify and maintain the behavior of children with severe behavior problems (Vaughn, Bos, & Schumm, 1997).

Stacey, who has mild mental retardation, is a member of Miss Hamrick's preschool class. She rarely participates during free-choice activities. Miss Hamrick has tried a variety of strategies to increase Stacey's engagement, including using effective praise, making sure a range of activity options are developmentally appropriate for Stacey, modeling appropriate behaviors, and implementing prompting strategies. None of these strategies appear to work. Aware of Stacey's love of the TV show "Barney," Miss Hamrick decides to award Barney stickers to Stacey when she actively participates. Stacey begins to participate more often in classroom activities.

One major advantage of tangible reinforcers is that they almost always guarantee quick behavioral change (Alberto & Troutman, 1990), even when other strategies (including other types of reinforcers) fail. Although the use of tangible reinforcers can be very effective, their use in early childhood classrooms has been highly controversial. Many early childhood teachers have concerns about the use of tangible reinforcers and believe that they cannot be used appropriately in the early childhood classroom. Such reinforcers often are intrusive, and their effective use requires large amounts of teacher time and commitment.

Given these disadvantages, when using tangible reinforcers teachers should gradually move toward using more intangible, less intrusive reinforcers (Henderick, 1998). Teachers can accomplish this goal by accompanying all tangible reinforcers with social reinforcers (e.g., praise). Later, as children begin to exhibit the desired behavior consistently, the teacher may begin to taper off the use of tangible reinforcers while maintaining the use of social reinforcers. Eventually, the teacher will no longer need to award tangible reinforcers after the desired behavior occurs. In time, the teacher also should be able to fade out the use of social reinforcers, and the children will begin to assume control over their own behaviors.

Questions Frequently Asked about Reinforcement Strategies

The following is a discussion of some of the most common concerns about reinforcement strategies, particularly tangible ones.

Are reinforcers bribes? Some have described reinforcement strategies as bribery (Kohn, 1993). Kazdin (1975) argues that such characterizations misconstrue the concepts of reinforcement and bribery:

> Bribery refers to the illicit use of rewards, gifts, or favors to pervert judg-
> ment or corrupt the conduct of someone. With bribery, reward is used
> for the purpose of changing behavior, but the behavior is corrupt, illegal
> or immoral in some way. With reinforcement, as typically employed,
> events are delivered for behaviors which are generally agreed upon to
> benefit the client, society, or both. (p. 50)

Kazdin's arguments point to clear distinctions between bribery and giving reinforcement for appropriate behaviors. No one would doubt that receiving pay for work is reinforcing, but few would suggest it is bribery. The difference may lie in the fact that bribes usually are conducted in secret for an improper purpose.

Does the use of reinforcers lower intrinsic motivation?   Intrinsic motivation refers to motivation that comes from within the child or from the activity in which the child is involved. Thus, an intrinsically motivated child would engage in an activity for its own sake (Eisenberger & Cameron, 1996). For example, external rewards frequently are used to motivate children extrinsically.

Some researchers have suggested that the use of reinforcers undermines intrinsic motivation (Kohn, 1993; Lepper & Greene, 1975). Lepper & Greene (1975) conducted a series of experiments on the effects of offering a child a tangible reward to engage in an initially interesting task in the absence of any expectation of external rewards. The results of their experiments suggested that extrinsic rewards can lower intrinsic motivation (Lepper & Greene, 1975). Therefore, when reinforcement is withdrawn after increasing a particular behavior, an individual may engage in an activity less often than before the reinforcement was introduced (Eisenberger & Cameron, 1996). Recent research offers alternative conclusions. After conducting a meta-analysis of over 20 years of research, Cameron and Pierce (1994) concluded that a tangible reward system contingent on performance will not have a negative effect on children's intrinsic motivation. In fact, they propose that external rewards, when used appropriately, can play an invaluable role in increasing children's intrinsic motivation (Cameron & Pierce, 1994, 1996; see also Eisenberger & Cameron, 1996, 1998).

Although the evidence is still inconclusive, the results do suggest that negative effects of rewards occur under limited conditions, such as giving tangible rewards without regard to performance level. For example, if a teacher rewards a child regardless of performance, the child's intrinsic motivation may diminish for the particular activity. When external rewards are contingent on a child's performance, however, they can be used to enhance the child's intrinsic motivation for the particular activity. This is true because the positive or negative experiences surrounding an activity or task are likely to influence whether the activity is perceived as intrinsically enjoyable or unpleasurable (Eisenberger & Cameron, 1996). Therefore, the authors advocate the use of external reinforcement for behaviors that, for a particular child, are not currently intrinsically reinforcing. For example, children who hit other children to obtain desired toys may find getting what they want to be more intrinsically reinforcing than positive social behavior. In this case, the introduction of external reinforcers for prosocial behavior is unlikely to diminish intrinsic motivation.

By using reinforcement, are teachers "paying" children to learn?   Some argue that rather than being "paid" to behave a certain way or complete certain tasks, children should do these things simply because they are the right thing to do (Harlen, 1996; Schloss & Smith, 1998; Sulzer-Azaroff & Mayer, 1991). Children's individual differences (e.g., ability levels) often require teachers to use a number of strategies to meet each child's individual needs. An important goal of early childhood education is to move children toward behaving appropriately for moral reasons; in other words, "because it is the right thing to do." Strong evidence exists, however, that the behavior of preschoolers and primary grade children is largely controlled by external factors (Bandura, 1986; Walker, deVries, & Trevarthen, 1989). The move from external control to internalized "self-discipline" is only gradually achieved during this age. Adults can help children learn to behave in appropriate ways for moral reasons by combining developmentally appropriate explanations with carefully chosen consequences (see Kostelnik et al., 1998).

Must teachers use reinforcement "equally"?   It is important that early childhood teachers recognize children's unique differences (Bredekamp & Copple, 1997) and structure the early childhood classroom environment so that it meets each child's individual needs. This does not mean, however, that all children will be treated the same or even equally. In fact, the premise that all children should be treated equally is incongruent with developmentally appropriate practices (Zirpoli, 1995; see also Bredekamp & Copple, 1997). Early childhood teachers must recognize that all children are unique and develop at different rates (Bredekamp & Copple, 1997); therefore, some children may require special accommodations.

Using Reinforcers Effectively

Sometimes, reinforcement strategies fail because they are implemented incorrectly. Early childhood teachers should consider general guidelines when using reinforcers in their classroom. Furthermore, the teacher must fully understand the behavior and the function it serves for the child before beginning a reinforcement program.

Once a decision has been made to use reinforcement strategies, teachers must carefully consider implementation to ensure that the strategies are effective and to minimize any potential effects on the child's intrinsic motivation. This process can be viewed as consisting of four states: 1) behavior identification, 2) selection of reinforcers, 3) implementation, 4) and evaluation and fading.

Behavior identification.   In identifying the behavior, it is important to be as clear and objective as possible about the exact nature of the behavior, as well as about the times and settings under which the plan will be implemented. For example, while running in the classroom setting is dangerous, it is an important developmental activity outside the classroom. In order for the strategy to be successful, the child must understand not only "what" is being targeted, but also "when" and "where."

Selection of reinforcers.   The selection of reinforcers is a crucial step, because a successful reinforcer must be more powerful than the intrinsic reward of engaging in the behavior. However, the reinforcement plan also must be as naturalistic as possible. Tangible reinforcers should be used only as a last resort, either because other classes of reinforcers have been unsuccessful or because it is necessary to eliminate a behavior immediately (e.g., ones that are dangerous to the child or others). Social reinforcers should be considered first, by following the guidelines for effective praise. If praise is unsuccessful, teachers may want to consider using an activity reinforcer. One way to select activity reinforcers is to think about the following question: If given complete free choice in the classroom, what would this child choose to do?

Another very important consideration in the selection of reinforcers involves understanding the function that the challenging behavior is serving. For example, many preschoolers engage in challenging behaviors in order to gain attention. If children are not given more appropriate ways to obtain needed attention, the program is unlikely to be successful.

Implementation.   In the implementation stage, the child receives the reinforcer contingent upon the appropriate behavior. Intitially, the child may need to receive reinforcement very frequently if the challenging behavior occurs frequently. As the child's behavior improves, the time between rewards can be extended. Another strategy is to "shape" the child's behavior, which teachers can do by breaking down the desired behavior into small steps. Each step is then reinforced on each occurrence. Teachers move to the next step only when the previous one is mastered (Schloss & Smith, 1998). Activity or tangible reinforcers should be accompanied by social praise.

Evaluation and fading.   Before beginning the intervention, base line observations need to be made so that any improvement can be systematically evaluated. As the program is implemented, the teacher will want to continue keeping records. As the child's behavior improves, the reinforcement should be phased out. This can be done by reducing the frequency of the reinforcer and beginning to rely on social praise more often than on tangible or activity reinforcers. If the child begins to revert to "bad habits," the program can be adjusted.

When Are Reinforcers Appropriate?

Reinforcement strategies, when used appropriately, can have numerous benefits. They are not, however, a cure-all. In the introductory example, Mrs. Kitchens attempted to use reinforcement as a substitute for appropriate practice. Rather than attempting to rely on reinforcement as a primary means of motivation and management, teachers may incorporate such strategies within the context of a developmentally appropriate program. Use of reinforcement certainly cannot substitute for a teacher establishing a warm, nurturing, and enticing classroom with developmentally appropriate materials, activities, and interactions (Wolery, 1994). Within such developmentally appropriate contexts, reinforcement strategies provide teachers with an effective means to help those children who require additional assistance in meeting particular behavioral, cognitive, and social goals. In all cases, the reinforcement strategy must be ethically definsible, compliant with all relevant school policies (Wolery & Bredekamp, 1994), and consistent with the program's philosophy.

Decisions about individual appropriateness are not always easy to make. Teachers must take into consideration all relevant factors bearing on the appropriateness of the strategy selected. Teachers are better equipped to make these assessments when they have solid knowledge of typical and atypical child development; are well acquainted with the needs, capabilities, and personalities of the children in their care; and are familiar with a wide continuum of strategies. Furthermore, they also must consider the student's familial and cultural experiences, the expectations and experiences of the student's family, and the mores of the society in which the student interacts (Bredekamp & Copple, 1997). The DAP guidelines (Bredekamp & Copple, 1997) emphasize the importance of children's cultural backgrounds. Developmentally appropriate practices should not discriminate against children from diverse backgrounds; rather, they should level the playing field (see Bredekamp & Copple, 1997). Therefore, when considering the use of various reinforcement strategies, teachers must consider the whole child, including his or her abilities, special needs, personality, and cultural background.

When a teacher works with young children who present a broad range of abilities, challenges, and cultural values, it is particularly important that he or she be an adaptive and thoughtful problem-solver, while respecting children's individuality. A widened range of acceptable options from which to choose, coupled with a keen sense of individual and situational needs, can empower teachers to make good decisions for a diversity of young children.

References

Alberto, P. A., & Troutman, A. C. (1990). *Applied behavior analysis for teachers* (3rd ed.). Columbus, OH: Merrill.

Bandura, A. (1986). *Social foundations of thought and action: A social cognitive theory.* Englewood Cliffs, NJ: Prentice-Hall.

Bredekamp, S. (1987). *Developmentally appropriate practice in early childhood programs serving children from birth through age eight.* Washington, DC: National Association for the Education of Young Children.

Bredekamp, S. (1993). The relationship between early childhood education and early childhood special education: Healthy marriage or family feud? *Topics in Early Childhood Special Education, 13*(3), 258–273.

Bredekamp, S., & Copple, C. (1997). *Developmentally appropriate practice in early childhood programs* (Rev. ed.). Washington, DC: National Association for the Education of Young Children.

Cameron, J., & Pierce, W. D. (1994). Reinforcement, reward, and intrinsic motivation: A meta-analysis. *Review of Educational Research, 64,* 363–423.

Cameron, J., & Pierce, W. D. (1996). The debate about rewards and intrinsic motivation: A meta-analysis. *Review of Educational Research, 66,* 39–51.

Carta, J. (1995). Developmentally appropriate practice: A critical analysis as applied to young children with disabilities. *Focus on Exceptional Children, 27*(8), 1–14.

Carta, J. J., Atwater, J. B., Schwartz, I. S., & McConnell, S. R. (1993). Developmentally appropriate practices and early childhood special education: A reaction to Johnson & McChesney Johnson. *Topics in Special Education, 13,* 243–254.

Carta, J. J., Schwartz, I. S., Atwater, J. B., & McConnell, S. R. (1991). Developmentally appropriate practice: Appraising its usefulness for young children with disabilities. *Topics in Early Childhood Special Education, 11*(1), 1–20.

Chandler, T. A. (1981). What's wrong with success and praise? *Arithmetic Teacher, 29*(4), 10–12.

Eisenberger, R., & Cameron, J. (1996). Detrimental effects of reward: Reality or myth. *American Psychologist, 51*(11), 1153–1166.

Eisenberger, R., & Cameron, J. (1998). Reward, intrinsic interest, and creativity: New findings. *American Psychologist, 53*(6), 676–679.

Gordon, T. (1974). *Teacher effectiveness training.* New York: Wyden.

Harlen, J. C. (1996). *Behavior management strategies for teachers: Achieving instructional effectiveness, student success, and student motivation; every teacher and every student can!* Springfield, IL: C.C. Thomas.

Henderick, J. (1998). *Total learning: Development curriculum for the young child.* Columbus, OH: Merrill.

Hitz, R., & Driscoll, A. (1988). Praise or encouragement? *Young Children, 43*(5), 6–13.

Kamii, C. (1984). The aim of education envisioned by Piaget. *Phi Delta Kappan, 65*(6), 410–415.

Kazdin, A. E. (1975). *Behavior modification in applied settings.* Pacific Grove, CA: Brooks/Cole.

Kazdin, A. E. (1994). *Behavior modification in applied settings* (5th ed.). Pacific Grove, CA: Brooks/Cole.

Kohn, A. (1993). *Punished by rewards: The trouble with gold stars, incentive plans, A's, praise and other bribes.* New York: Houghton Mifflin.

Kostelnik, M. J., Stein, L. C., Whiren, A. P., & Soderman, A. K. (1998). *Guiding children's social development* (2nd ed.). New York: Delmar.

Lepper, M. R., & Greene, D. (1975). When two rewards are worse than one: Effects of extrinsic rewards on intrinsic motivation. *Phi Delta Kappan, 56*(8), 565–566.

Marshall, H. H. (1995). Beyond "I like the way...." *Young Children, 50*(2), 26–28.

Peck, C. (1985). Increasing opportunities for social control by children with autism and severe handicaps: effects on student behavior and percieved classroom climate. *Journal of the Association for Persons with Severe Handicaps, 10*(4), 183–193.

Peters, D., Neisworth, J. T., & Yawkey, T. D. (1985). *Early childhood education: From theory to practice.* Monterey, CA: Brooks/Cole.

Rodd, J. (1996). *Understanding young children's behavior: A guide for early childhood professionals.* New York: Teachers College Press.

Schloss, P. J., & Smith, M. A. (1998). *Applied behavior analyses in the classroom* (Rev. ed.). Boston: Allyn and Bacon.

Strain, P. S., McConnell, S. R., Carta, J. J., Fowler, S. A., Neisworth, J. T., & Wolery, M. (1992). Behaviorism in early intervention. *Topics in Early Childhood Special Education, 12*(1), 121–141.

Sulzer-Azaroff, B., & Mayer, G. R. (1991). *Behavior analysis for lasting change.* New York: Harcourt Brace.

Thomas, S. B., & Russo, C. J. (1995). *Special education law: Issues and implications for the 90's.* Topeka, KS: National Organization on Legal Problems of Education.

Van der Wilt, J. (1996). Beyond stickers and popcorn parties. *Dimensions of Early Childhood, 24*(1), 17–20.

Vaughn, S., Bos, C. S., & Schumm, J. S. (1997). *Teaching mainstreamed, diverse, and at-risk students in the general education classroom.* Boston: Allyn and Bacon.

Walker, L. J., DeVries, B., & Trevarthen, S. D. (1989). Moral stages and moral orientations in real-life and hypothetical dilemmas. *Child Development, 58*(3), 842–858.

Weiner, E. A., & Weiner, B. J. (1974). Differentiation of retarded and normal children through toy-play analysis. *Multivariate Behavioral Research, 9*(2), 245–257.

Wolery, M. (1994). *Including children with special needs in early childhood programs.* Washington, DC: National Association for the Education of Young Children.

Wolery, M., & Bredekamp, S. (1994). Developmentally appropriate practices and young children with disabilities: Contextual issues in the discussion. *Journal of Early Intervention, 18,* 331–341.

Wolery, M., Strain, P. S., & Bailey, D. (1992). Reaching potentials of children with special needs. In S. Bredekamp & T. Rosegrant (Eds.), *Reaching potentials: Appropriate curriculum and assessment for young children. Vol. 1* (pp. 92–111). Washington, DC: National Association for the Education of Young Children.

Wolery, M., Werts, M. G., & Holcombe-Ligon, A. (1994). Current practices with young children who have disabilities: Issues in placement, assessment and instruction. *Focus on Exceptional Children, 26*(6), 1–12.

Wolery, M., & Wilbers, J. S. (1994). Introduction to the inclusion of young children with special needs in early childhood programs. In M. Wolery & J. S. Wilbers (Eds.), *Including children with special needs in early childhood programs* (pp. 1–22). Washington, DC: National Association for the Education of Young Children.

Zirpoli, T. J. (1995). *Understanding and affecting the behavior of young children.* Englewood Cliffs, NJ: Merrill.

Charles H. Wolfgang

 **NO**

Another View on "Reinforcement in Developmentally Appropriate Early Childhood Classrooms"

In the Summer 2000 issue of *Childhood Education*, the article written by Tashawna Duncan, Kristen Kemple, and Tina Smith supports reinforcement as a developmentally appropriate practice (Bredekamp & Copple, 1997). In the present article, the author contrasts the Duncan-Kemple-Smith position with another view: How to use developmental theory to inform us of appropriate strategies for dealing with young children in the classroom. The use of behavioral techniques such as reinforcers often can produce desired behavior changes. Behavior modification through the use of reinforcers, however, is a superficial effort to lead the child down the road of development without using the road map of developmental theory, which views the child's actions with regard to developmental constructs.

Let's take the Duncan-Kemple-Smith example. *"Five-year-old Rodney has recently joined Mr. Romero's kindergarten class. On his first day in his new class, Rodney punched a classmate and usurped the tricycle the other boy was riding. On Rodney's second day in the class, he shoved a child on a swing and dumped another out of her chair at the snack table"* (Duncan, Kemple, & Smith, 2000, p. 194). In essence, the authors support behavioral theory and advocate addressing Rodney's negative actions through the use of social reinforcers (e.g., praise, and similar teacher attention), *activity reinforcers* (e.g., earning use of a toy such as a tricycle with "good" behavior), and *tangible reinforcers* (e.g., stickers). Unfortunately, applying reinforcers to extinguish Rodney's "aggression" overlooks the context of how children develop.

The developmentalist, by contrast, would attempt to change Rodney's antisocial behaviors by trying to understand his developmental needs—specifically, what may be causing such behaviors in the first place. As this is Rodney's first day in his new class, the first question for the developmentalist, knowing the literature on attachment and separation fears (Mahler, 1970, 1975; Speers, 1970a, 1970b), would be: Did the teacher help Rodney make a gradual transition from home to school, and allow time for him to bond with his new teacher and become comfortable in this strange new world of the kindergarten classroom? The developmentalists may use supportive actions to help the child make a successful transition (Jervis, 1999). In Rodney's case, the teacher could have made home visits, giving

Rodney a chance to meet his teacher on his own "turf"; permitted Rodney to bring a "transitional object" (his cuddle toy or his "Linus" blanket) (Wolfgang & Wolfgang, 1999); and encouraged a parent to stay in the class the first day or two so that Rodney could "wean" himself from parental support.

Developmentalists may, in fact, view Rodney's aggressive actions as *heroic* attempts to get his needs met in a strange new world. The developmentalist might ask: Are there enough tricycles (or similar favorite items) that would permit him to play in parallel form as a developmental step into associative and cooperative play? (Parten, 1971). Or is the playground developmentally appropriate? Are back-and-forth swings, because of the preoperational child's inability to understand movement between states, or states vs. transformations (Piaget & Inhelder, 1958), appropriate at the kindergarten level? Is the organization of snacks and the arrangement of chairs done in such a manner that certain chairs (e.g., those that allow children to sit with the teacher) are favored, thus causing competition? In viewing Rodney's aggressive behaviors, a developmentalist also would ask: Are the environment, procedures, rules, and daily activities developmentally appropriate for this child, especially when we have children with special needs in our classroom?

The teacher who is armed with a repertoire of *social reinforcers*, *activity reinforcers*, and *tangible reinforcers*, and who uses them daily as the general mode of guidance for children, is missing an opportunity to understand how a child's actions may give us insight into his developmental needs. When we have a medical visit, the doctor says, "Where does it hurt?" We show where the pain is, and the doctor then considers each ailment suggested by pain in that location. Similarly, "punching, pushing, and taking others' possessions" should prompt us to learn about this child's developmental needs, to draw on our knowledge to give meaning to the child's "symptoms," and to use developmentally appropriate practices.

Rather than administering a reinforcer to change the child's behavior, the developmental teacher asks: How does that child separate and bond? Can he cuddle with supportive adults, such as the teacher? How does he eat and handle himself at snack or at rest time? Can he handle demanding activities such as finger painting, water play, or painting? Can he do socio-dramatic play? How do his social skills relate to typical developmental stages? Can he express his needs with words while under pressure in a social situation? (Wolfgang, 1977; Wolfgang & Wolfgang, 1999). These questions can be posed only from within an understanding of certain developmental theories—Mahler's theories of bonding and attachment (1970, 1975), Anna Freud's developmental lines (1968, 1971), play research and theory (Erikson, 1950; Freud, 1968; Peller, 1969; Smilansky, 1969), and Parten's social stages (1971).

Considering Rodney from a Developmentally Appropriate Perspective

Young children who do not feel empowered or do not believe they will get their needs met begin to deal with their world in an automatic, reflexive manner.

They may respond through verbal aggression (swearing or using bathroom talk), physical aggression (punching, pushing, and taking others' possessions), or passivity (flat, expressionless behavior accompanied by excessive thumb sucking, masturbation, or even self-abusive activities, such as striking their own head) (Wolfgang, 1977).

Children slowly "learn to be the cause" of events in their world over the first three years of life. The young infant attaches to a significant person, then begins a gradual separation process: first learning causality as a baby by throwing a spoon in order to get others to pick it up, acting upon objects during toddlerhood by opening all the kitchen cabinet doors and banging on pots and pans, and using language to achieve a goal in late toddlerhood by asking mommy for something. Thus, the child becomes socially adaptive. If development went well during these first three years, children will enter kindergarten expecting the best, with the confidence that they can master what lies before them. If this development has not gone well, they may enter kindergarten as Rodney did—by "punching, pushing, and taking others' possessions."

In behavioral theory, we address children's inappropriate behavior by moving away when the child acts out; otherwise, we would be reinforcing the behavior by attending to them. For example, we may ignore a child when he cries, in an effort to eliminate the crying. Developmentalists take just the opposite approach. The kindergarten teacher's first goal should be to rebond with Rodney, then gradually teach him to channel his energy (aggression is simply misdirected energy) from the body to the toy, from the toy to play, and from play to work (Freud, 1968).

On the third day of school, the developmental teacher would direct Rodney into a host of activities that permit him to divert his aggression (energy) from his body into the toy (pounding at the carpentry table, pounding with clay, or pursuing aggressive play themes in the safe, make-believe world of small animal toys). At the same time, the teacher would attempt to bond with Rodney (even to the point of cuddling him), so that he would begin to realize that he can depend on this caring adult to help get what he needs (Wolfgang, 1977; Wolfgang & Wolfgang, 1999).

Instead of permitting Rodney to have the tricycle after he goes for a period of time without pushing or hitting as a reinforcement (*activity reinforcers*), the developmental teacher might allow Rodney to use a tricycle whenever he wants, because it is an excellent outlet for his energy. Thus, Rodney can transfer his aggression from other children to the toy. The teacher may tape his picture or name to a chair at snack time so that he will know that this seat will always be reserved for him, and thus know that he does not need to fight for one.

Next, after Rodney has aggressively used the carpentry equipment, clay, or the make-believe rubber animal toys (such as lions and tigers), the teacher would help him cross the bridge into "making something" with the clay, or "making a story" with the animals. He then will move from the toy to play. Once he learns isolated play (Parten, 1971), the teacher can encourage others to join him; he will then move from parallel to associative play, and then to cooperative play (Smilansky, 1968; Smilansky & Shefatya, 1990), whereby he becomes a role-player with others and practices the social skills of give-and-take.

Rodney pushes, shoves, and hits because he does not yet have the social skills to work with others and to get his needs met. Reinforcing "good" behavior does not teach him the developmental skills he needs to function. Through role-play (as in socio-dramatic play), the child moves from isolated play into cooperation with others, which requires sophisticated social and language skills. Rodney, through such play, would be empowered and, therefore, would not need the teacher reinforcements, or control. He can develop effective adaptive skills.

As part of their advice for Rodney's teacher, Duncan, Kemple, and Smith write, *"Mr. Romero is concerned for the emotional and physical safety of the other children, and he believes that Rodney will have a hard time making friends if his reputation as an aggressor is allowed to solidify. He feels the need to act fast. Deciding that a system of reinforcement, along with other strategies, may help Rodney control his aggressive behavior, Mr. Romero implements a token reinforcement system. Rodney earns a ticket, accompanied by praise, for each 30-minute period during which he does not behave aggressively. At the end of the day, Rodney can trade a specified number of earned tickets for his choice of small toys"* (p. 194).

While it is certainly necessary to protect the other children and ensure fairness, the authors' advice fails to incorporate developmentally appropriate practice. At circle time, and possibly even before Rodney has arrived, a teacher using a developmentalist approach would have discussed Rodney's arrival with the other kindergarten children to help them develop empathy for Rodney, who is, after all, getting accustomed to a new place. The teacher could ask the children to think about how Rodney might feel, why he might push and shove and take other children's toys, and why the teacher might need to do special things for this new person. Young children can understand these concepts, and as they watch the developmental teacher guiding the "misbehaving" child they will become secure in the knowledge that the teacher will not punish them for similar actions. Thus, they can learn to master their own aggressive impulses as they watch Rodney strive for self-control and social skills.

The Duncan-Kemple-Smith article includes a short review of studies (e.g., Schloss & Smith, 1998; Zirpoli, 1995) demonstrating that reinforcers are effective in eliminating unwanted behaviors in early childhood settings. It is often true that behavioral techniques are powerful and effective when they are used with the narrow goal of changing a particular behavior. These brief targeted studies, however, do not answer the following questions: Should this behavior be extinguished? What caused the behavior in the first place? What are the new behaviors that result when this behavior is extinguished? There is no doubt that an experienced behavioral teacher using reinforcers can extinguish Rodney's aggression.

What happens, however, if we return the next month to observe Rodney and find that new problem behaviors have developed? In short, targeting one behavior obscures the perspective on the dynamic aspect of human behavior and the interdependence of social, emotional, and cognitive development. When we narrow our view of children's growth to one observable behavior, we lose the holistic view of the child.

Another Look at Specific Behavioral Techniques

In light of recommended developmentally appropriate practices, behavioral constructs of reinforcement raise some concerns.

Social Reinforcers (e.g., praise and similar teacher attention). The narrow behavioral nature of a social reinforcer, such as teacher praise and attention, boxes the teacher into scripted behavior when used with young children. Teacher attention toward the child should be based on the teacher's insights into, and empathy with, the child's real development needs, as well as on an understanding of the necessary steps for the child to gradually gain autonomy.

Activity Reinforcers (e.g., earning use of a toy with "good" behavior). In a developmental classroom, there are no activities, materials, and toys that are considered "treats." Instead, these items and processes are basic to the educational developmental model itself. One example of activity reinforcers from the Duncan, Kemple, and Smith article shows the teacher reminding the children that they must first clean up before they are permitted to go out to the playground. No one can disagree with the need to teach young children to clean up; with a child like Rodney, however, cleaning up will only come after he has become a co-player and a worker with others. This will take time. He should never be barred from a play activity, especially during his first days of kindergarten. Following the developmental construct of Anna Freud (1968), activities on the playground, with the guidance of an informed developmental teacher, are exactly what Rodney needs to help him gain control of his own behavior and attain true maturity. The developmentally appropriate classroom does not use toys, materials, and activities as "activity treats" or *activity reinforcers*; all toys, materials, and activities are there to contribute to children's development.

Tangible Reinforcers (e.g., stickers). One kindergarten teacher once stated, "My students would kill for a sticker." Because Rodney does not yet have the developmental social skills to function at an age-appropriate level, he will miss out on such tangible reinforcers as stickers and feel resentment and anger toward those who do receive them. In fact, Rodney may push and hit to get a sticker. The use of stickers as a tangible reinforcer may achieve short-term success, but bring about unintended, long-term consequences for the children who do not, as yet, have the social skills to merit the reward.

Conclusion

The behavioral constructs of social reinforcers, activity reinforcers, and tangible reinforcers can be learned quickly by beginning teachers of young children, provide them with feelings of empowerment and control, and may help, in the short term, to curb children's aggressive behavior. It may be helpful, however, to view aggression from a developmental point of view—as children's attempts to adapt to new situations. Behavioral techniques that shape and change children's surface behaviors without placing these behaviors within a developmental context may, in the long run, interfere with the child's developmental needs and cause much harm.

References

Bredekamp, S., & Copple, C. (1997). *Developmentally appropriate practice in early childhood programs* (Rev. ed.). Washington, DC: National Association for the Education of Young Children.

Duncan, T. K., Kemple, K. M., & Smith, T. M. (2000). Reinforcement in developmentally appropriate early childhood classrooms. *Childhood Education, 76,* 194–203.

Erikson, E. (1950). *Childhood and society.* New York: Norton Press.

Freud, A. (1968). *Normality and pathology in childhood: Assessments of development.* New York: International Universities Press.

Freud, A. (1971). *The ego and the mechanisms of defense.* New York: International Universities Press.

Jervis, K. (1999). *Separation: Strategies for helping two- to four-year-olds.* Washington, DC: National Association for the Education of Young Children.

Mahler, M. S. (1970). *On human symbiosis and the vicissitudes of individuation.* New York: International Universities Press.

Mahler, M. S. (1975). *The psychological birth of the human infant.* New York: Basic Books.

Parten, M. B. (1971). Social play among preschool children. In R. E. Herron & B. Sutton-Smith (Eds.), *Child's play* (pp. 83–95). New York: John Wiley & Sons.

Peller, L. E. (1969). Libidinal phases, ego development and play. In *Psychoanalytic study of the child, no. 9* (pp. 178–197). New York: International Universities Press.

Piaget, J., & Inhelder, B. (1958). *The growth of logical thinking: From childhood to adolescence.* New York: Basic Books.

Smilansky, S. (1969). *The effects of sociodramatic play on disadvantaged preschool children.* New York: John Wiley & Sons.

Smilansky, S. J., & Shefatya, L. (1990). *Facilitating play: Medium for promoting cognitive, social-emotional and academic development in young children.* Gaithersburg, MD: Psychosocial & Educational Publishing.

Speers, R. W. (1970a). Recapitulation of separation-individuation processes when the normal three-year-old enters nursery school. In J. McDevitt (Ed.), *Separation-individuation: Essays in honor of Margaret Mahler* (pp. 38–67). New York: International Universities Press.

Speers, R. W. (1970b). *Variations in Separation—Individuation and implications for play abilities and learning as studied in the three-year-old in nursery school.* Pittsburgh, PA: University of Pittsburgh Press.

Wolfgang, C. H. (1977). *Helping aggressive and passive preschoolers through play.* Columbus, OH: Charles E. Merrill Publishing.

Wolfgang, C. H., & Wolfgang, M. E. (1999). *School for young children: Developmentally appropriate practices.* Boston: Allyn and Bacon.

POSTSCRIPT

Does Reinforcement Facilitate Learning?

It is perhaps surprising to many readers that there is still controversy about the effectiveness of reinforcement. After all, haven't psychologists been studying reinforcement for nearly a century? And haven't parents, teachers, and other adults been using rewards (and punishments) in one form or another to control children's behavior for even longer? Why, then, have we failed to answer the question, Does reinforcement facilitate learning? In part, it has been difficult to answer this question because, when we carefully analyze the concept of reinforcement, it turns out to be a bit slippery. Recall that, according to B. F. Skinner, it cannot be known whether or not a stimulus or an event is a reinforcer prior to observing its effects on an individual's behavior. We may have hunches or educated guesses about what a child might find reinforcing—money, a gold star, candy, a special outing—but we cannot know for certain until we observe the desired changes in the child's behavior. If we do not observe those changes, we may have guessed wrong and need to try some other stimulus or event. At first glance, this seems reasonable. Suppose, however, that we test another potential reinforcer, and another, and another, and still do not observe the desired change in behavior. Should we search indefinitely for the reinforcer? Or might it be that the behavior in question is controlled less by factors that are external to the child and more by internal factors, such as the child's interests, motives, and inclinations? This is the dilemma that many parents, teachers, and researchers face at one time or another. Unfortunately, there is no empirical means of determining whether we should keep searching for a reinforcer or whether the behavior in question is controlled by internal factors. As a result, some scholars, practitioners, and even parents adhere almost religiously to a belief in the power of reinforcement, whereas others dismiss reinforcement as a useless and, perhaps, even morally offensive concept.

Readers interested in pursuing the topic of reinforcement can turn to a number of excellent summaries of behaviorist theories, including *An Introduction to Theories of Learning*, 6th ed., by B. R. Hergenhan and Matthew H. Olson (Prentice Hall, 2001). A critique of reinforcement and its many manifestations in the classroom can be found in Alfie Kohn's *Punished by Rewards: The Trouble with Gold Stars, Incentive Plans, A's, and Other Bribes* (Houghton Mifflin, 1993) and *Beyond Discipline: From Compliance to Community* (Association for Supervision and Curriculum Development, 1996). Interesting discussions on the issue of grades as reinforcement can be found in "Let's End the Grading Game," by Clifford Edwards and Laurie Edwards, *The Clearing House* (May–June 1999) and "Can Grades Be Helpful and Fair?" by Dennis Munk and William Bursuck, *Educational Leadership* (December 1997/January 1998).

ISSUE 9

Can Howard Gardner's Theory of Multiple Intelligences Transform Educational Practice?

YES: **Seana Moran, Mindy Kornhaber, and Howard Gardner,** from "Orchestrating Multiple Intelligences," *Educational Leadership* (September 2006)

NO: **Perry D. Klein,** from "Multiplying the Problems of Intelligence by Eight: A Critique of Gardner's Theory," *Canadian Journal of Education* (vol. 22, no. 4, 1997)

ISSUE SUMMARY

YES: Seana Moran, a graduate student at Harvard University, Mindy Kornhaber, an associate professor of education at the Pennsylvania State University, and Howard Gardner, the long-time Harvard University faculty member who originally proposed the theory of multiple intelligences, argue that the theory can transform the ways in which teachers teach and students view themselves.

NO: Perry D. Klein, a member of the Faculty of Education at the University of Western Ontario, argues that although a number of diverse pedagogical practices have been inspired by Gardner's theory, the theory is really too broad to be particularly informative about education.

$\mathbf{F}$or the better part of the twentieth century, scholars, policymakers, and lay-people have debated the nature of intelligence. This issue considers one theory of the nature of intelligence that has been embraced by educators around the United States; namely, the theory of multiple intelligences proposed by Howard Gardner.

The centerpiece of Gardner's theory is the idea of independent domains (components, or modules) of cognitive ability, which he refers to as frames of mind. Gardner has proposed, at various times, that there are seven, eight, or even nine intelligences. These are separate areas of ability in the sense that a person can do well in one area but not in another. In fact—although Gardner relies on other forms of evidence as well—the most compelling evidence supporting the existence of independent intelligences comes from cases of people with special talents (e.g., musical prodigies who are otherwise "average") or with a circumscribed loss or limitation of abilities (e.g., savants, who are highly skilled painters, musicians, etc., despite having autism, intellectual disability, or another pervasive disability). The intelligences proposed by Gardner include the linguistic, spatial, and logical-mathematical. These are the forms of intelligence that are most directly assessed by IQ tests, such as the Stanford-Binet. Also included on Gardner's list, however, are less traditional intelligences: bodily-kinesthetic, musical, interpersonal, intrapersonal, and the most recently proposed intelligences of the naturalist and the existentialist. These latter intelligences are unlikely to be measured in a meaningful way by current IQ tests.

Gardner's theory has inspired calls for dramatic changes in education. Here are but a few examples of the changes called for in the name of the theory of multiple intelligences:

1. Education has focused too narrowly on tasks that fall within the linguistic and logical-mathematic intelligences. The scope of education should be expanded to value and nurture the development of the other intelligences as well.
2. Recent calls for a return to "basic skills" will only lead to a further narrowing of the scope of education and will marginalize many children whose talents fall within Gardner's nontraditional intelligences.
3. Evaluations of each intelligence should be made regularly so as to measure the effectiveness of educational efforts. Traditional psychometric methods of assessment are likely to be inadequate and should be replaced by more product-oriented methods, such as student portfolios of their classroom work.
4. Education must extend beyond the classroom and include nontraditional experiences, such as apprenticeships, mentorships, and participation in community-based volunteer programs.
5. Education should be structured to allow students to make discoveries on their own and to construct their own knowledge. A teacher-centered, fact-based, drill-and-practice approach bypasses the discovery process and, thus, is to be avoided.
6. Students may differ in how they approach the same academic content. Those differences should be honored and even encouraged.

Although the response from educators has been largely positive, some have been critical of Gardner's claims and have wondered whether or not the theory really has any significant implications for educational practice. The two selections that follow take very different views about the educational importance of the theory. In the first selection, Seana Moran and her colleagues argue that the theory of multiple intelligences dictates that teachers should create lessons and activities that engage and challenge all the intelligences so that all students will benefit, albeit in different ways depending on each student's profile of relative strengths and weaknesses. In the second selection, Perry D. Klein argues that although a number of diverse pedagogical practices have been inspired by Gardner's theory, the theory is really too broad to be particularly informative about education.

190

YES ↵

Seana Moran, Mindy Kornhaber, and Howard Gardner

Orchestrating Multiple Intelligences

Education policymakers sometimes go astray when they attempt to integrate multiple intelligences theory into schools. They mistakenly believe that teachers must group students for instruction according to eight or nine different intelligence scores. Or they grapple with the unwieldy notion of requiring teachers to prepare eight or nine separate entry points for every lesson.

Multiple intelligences theory was originally developed as an explanation of how the mind works—not as an education policy, let alone an education panacea. Moreover, when we and other colleagues began to consider the implications of the theory for education, the last thing we wanted to do was multiply educators' jobs ninefold. Rather, we sought to demonstrate that because students bring to the classroom diverse intellectual profiles, one "IQ" measure is insufficient to evaluate, label, and plan education programs for all students.

Adopting a multiple intelligences approach can bring about a quiet revolution in the way students see themselves and others. Instead of defining themselves as either "smart" or "dumb," students can perceive themselves as potentially smart in a number of ways.

Profile Students, Don't Score Them

Multiple intelligences theory proposes that it is more fruitful to describe an individual's cognitive ability in terms of several relatively independent but interacting cognitive capacities rather than in terms of a single "general" intelligence. Think of LEGO building blocks. If we have only one kind of block to play with, we can build only a limited range of structures. If we have a number of different block shapes that can interconnect to create a variety of patterns and structures, we can accomplish more nuanced and complex designs. The eight or nine intelligences work the same way.

The greatest potential of a multiple intelligences approach to education grows from the concept of a *profile* of intelligences. Each learner's intelligence profile consists of a combination of relative strengths and weaknesses among the different intelligences: linguistic, logical-mathematical, musical, spatial, bodily-kinesthetic, naturalistic, interpersonal, intrapersonal, and (at least provisionally) existential (Gardner, 2006).

Most people have jagged profiles; they process some types of information better than other types. Students who exhibit vast variation among their intelligences—with one or two intelligences very strong and the others relatively weak—have what we call a *laser* profile. These students often have a strong area of interest and can follow a clear path to success by developing their peak intelligences. Given the ubiquity of high-stakes testing, educators' challenge with laser-profile students is deciding whether to accentuate the students' strengths through advanced opportunities to develop their gifts or to bolster their weak areas through remediation so that they can pass the tests. Policy and funding currently favor the second option unless the student is gifted in the traditional academic areas.

Other students have a *searchlight* profile: They show less pronounced differences among intelligences. The challenge with searchlight-profile students is to help them choose a career and life path. Time and resource limitations often preclude developing all intelligences equally, so we need to consider which intelligences are most likely to pay off for a particular student. Policy and funding currently favor developing primarily linguistic and logical-mathematical intelligences at the expense of the others.

Intelligences are not isolated; they can interact with one another in an individual to yield a variety of outcomes. For example, a successful dancer must combine musical, spatial, and bodily-kinesthetic intelligences; a science fiction novelist must use logical-mathematical, linguistic, interpersonal, and some existential intelligences; an effective trial lawyer must combine linguistic and interpersonal intelligences; a skillful waiter uses linguistic, spatial, interpersonal, and bodily-kinesthetic intelligences; and a marine biologist needs strong naturalistic and logical-mathematical intelligences. In the education setting, the different intelligences can interact in two ways: within the student and across students.

An Internal Orchestra

Just as the sounds of string, woodwind, and percussion instruments combine to create a symphony, the different intelligences intermix within a student to yield meaningful scholastic achievement or other accomplishments. And as in an orchestra, one intelligence (instrument) in an individual can interfere with others, compensate for others, or enhance others.

Interference.   Intelligences may not always work in harmony; sometimes they create discord. For example, even a student who has good social skills (strong interpersonal intelligence), may have trouble making friends if she cannot talk with others easily because she has weak linguistic intelligence. Another student who loves to read and receives frequent praise in English class may sit in the back row and bury her head in a novel during math class, where she feels less confident. Thus, her linguistic strength is a bottleneck for the development of her logical-mathematical intelligence. A third student's weakness in intrapersonal intelligence, which makes it difficult for him to regulate his moods or thoughts, may prevent him from completing his math homework consistently and thus mask his strong logical-mathematical intelligence.

Compensation. Sometimes one intelligence compensates for another. A student may give great class presentations because he can effectively use his body posture and gestures even though his sentence structure is somewhat convoluted. That is, his bodily-kinesthetic intelligence compensates for his linguistic limitations. (We can think of more than one U.S. president who fits this profile.) Or a student may earn a high mark on a paper for writing with a powerful rhetorical voice, even though her argument is not quite solid: Her linguistic intelligence compensates for her logical-mathematical limitations.

Enhancement. Finally, one intelligence may jump-start another. Strong spatial intelligence may improve a student's ability to conceptualize a mathematical concept or problem. This was certainly the case with Einstein. Strong musical intelligence may stimulate interest and playfulness in writing poetry. Understanding how intelligences can catalyze one another may help students—and teachers—make decisions about how to deploy the intellectual resources they have at their disposal.

The profile approach to multiple intelligences instruction provides teachers with better diagnostic information to help a particular student who is struggling. Before providing assistance, we need to ask *why* the student is having difficulty. For example, consider three beginning readers who have trouble comprehending a story. The first is struggling because of poor reading comprehension skills (a linguistic intelligence challenge). The second has poor social understanding of the dynamics among the story's characters (an interpersonal intelligence challenge). The third has such strong spatial intelligence that he has trouble seeing beyond the physical pattern of the letter symbols (a challenge that Picasso, for example, faced in his early years). More reading practice, which is often the default intervention, may not help all of these students.

A student's potential is not the sum of his or her intelligence "scores," as some multiple intelligence inventory measures on the market imply. If one intelligence is a bottleneck for others, then the student's overall potential may be lower than the straight sum. If intelligences are compensating for or enhancing one another, the student's overall potential may be higher than the straight sum. Intelligences have multiplicative as well as additive effects.

An Effective Ensemble

Intelligences can also work across students. The information explosion has greatly escalated the amount of information that each person must assimilate and understand—frequently beyond what we can handle by ourselves. Work teams, institutional partnerships, and interdisciplinary projects have increasingly become the norm. These ensembles support individuals as they seek to learn, understand, and perform well.

Multiple intelligences theory encourages collaboration across students. Students with compatible profiles (exhibiting the same patterns of strengths and weaknesses) can work together to solidify and build on strengths. For example, two students highly capable in storytelling can support each other by moving beyond the basics of plot to explore and develop twists in the narrative. A group of students who are skilled in numerical computation might extend a statistics lesson beyond mean, median, mode, and range to understand correlation or regression.

Students with complementary profiles (in which one student's weak areas are another student's strengths) can work together to compensate for one another. Such students can approach material in different but equally valid ways. For example, a student who is strong in logical-mathematical intelligence and sufficient in spatial intelligence might be able to translate abstract math problems into dance choreography or sculpture contexts to make them understandable to a student with strong spatial and bodily-kinesthetic intelligences.

Provide Rich Experiences

The eminent psychologist L. S. Vygotsky (1978) emphasized that *experience*—the idiosyncratic way each individual internalizes the environment's information—is important in both cognitive and personality development. If we give all students the same material, each student will have a different experience according to his or her background, strengths, and challenges. Thus, to promote learning across student intelligence profiles, teachers need to offer students rich experiences—activities in which they can engage with the material personally rather than just absorb it in an abstract, decontextualized way.

Rich experiences enable students to learn along several dimensions at once—socially, spatially, kinesthetically, self-reflectively, and so on. Often, these experiences cross subject-area lines. At Searsport Elementary School in Searsport, Maine, a 5th grade teacher who had strong storytelling abilities and an avid interest in history joined forces with her colleague, an expert in hands-on science, to develop an archaeology unit. Students studied history and geography as well as scientific method and archaeology techniques. They investigated local history, conducted a state-approved archaeological dig, identified and classified objects, and displayed the artifacts in a museum exhibit that met real-world curatorial standards (Kornhaber, Fierros, & Veenema, 2004).

Rich experiences also provide diagnostic information. Teachers can observe student performances to find root causes of misunderstandings and to figure out how students can achieve superior understandings. One small group of 2nd and 3rd graders in Chimene Brandt's class at Pittsburgh's McCleary Elementary School produced a mural depicting a rainy street scene. Their spatial portrayal of material was ambiguous: The connection to the unit's topic of rivers and the lesson's topic of the water cycle laws was not obvious. The students' understanding came through linguistically, however, when they presented in class how the water from the street would evaporate, condense into clouds, and again produce rain. By giving the students multiple ways to express the concepts, Brandt was able to confirm that the students understood the material even though their linguistic skills outstripped their spatial skills (Kornhaber, Fierros, & Veenema, 2004).

Two programs exemplify how rich experiences can serve as venues for developing and assessing multiple intelligences. The first, Project Spectrum, is an interactive assessment process for preschool children developed in the 1980s at

Harvard Project Zero (Gardner, Feldman, & Krechevsky, 1998). This process eval-
uates each intelligence directly, rather than funneling the information through
a linguistic paper-and-pencil test. Spatial orientation and manipulation tasks
evaluate spatial intelligence; group tasks evaluate interpersonal intelligence; self-
assessments paired with the other assessments evaluate intrapersonal intelligence.
Project Spectrum environments do not segment tasks strictly into one intelligence or another. Instead, they set up situations in which a student can interact
with rich materials—and teachers can observe these interactions—to see which
intelligences come to the fore and which are relegated to the background.

A naturalist's corner provides biological specimens for students to touch
and move (using bodily-kinesthetic intelligence), arrange (naturalistic), create
relationships among (logical-mathematical), tell stories about (linguistic), or
even compare themselves with (intrapersonal). In a storytelling area, students
can tell tales (linguistic), arrange props and character figurines (spatial and possibly bodily-kinesthetic), make characters interact (interpersonal), and design
their own storyboards (spatial). Fifteen other activities provide opportunities
for evaluating intelligences through reliable scoring rubrics that have been
used widely in early childhood education in the United States, Latin America,
Europe, and Asia (Gardner, Feldman, & Krechevsky, 1998).

Another environment providing rich experiences using a multiple intelligences approach is the Explorama at Danfoss Universe, a science park in
Nordborg, Denmark. . . . Designed according to multiple intelligences theory,
this interactive museum is used by people of all ages—from school groups to
corporate teams. The designers have devised separate exhibits, games, and challenges for each intelligence and for numerous combinations of intelligences.
One experience asks participants to balance themselves (bodily-kinesthetic);
another asks them to balance in a group (bodily-kinesthetic and interpersonal).
A computer program encourages participants to add, subtract, or combine
different musical qualities and see on screen how the tone frequencies change,
tapping into musical, spatial, and logical-mathematical intelligences.

Three activities deserve particular attention for their innovativeness in
assessing several intelligences concurrently and in emphasizing intelligences
that are often neglected in mainstream academic testing. One game involves
manipulating a joystick to control a robot that can lift and move a cube to
a target space. When played alone, this exhibit primarily assesses bodily-
kinesthetic and spatial intelligence. But when two to four people each control
a different joystick—one that controls the left wheel of the robot, another that
controls the right wheel, another that raises the cube, and another that lowers
the cube—they must coordinate their play to accomplish the task, employing
linguistic, logical-mathematical, and interpersonal intelligences.

Another game has two players sitting opposite each other at a table, with
a ping-pong ball in the center. Each player tries to move the ball toward the
opponent by relaxing. Relaxing reduces the player's stress level, creating alpha
waves in the brain that sensors pick up to move the ball forward. This task
requires self-control, and thus taps into intrapersonal intelligence. However,
the players must also employ interpersonal intelligence, paying attention to
each other and trying to produce more alpha waves than the opponent does.

A third notable Explorama activity is a computerized questionnaire in which participants assess their own intelligence profiles. Participants take the self-assessment before entering the Explorama and again after they have engaged in the various activities and tasks. Participants thus get an idea of how well they know their own capabilities. They also can compare their self-assessments before and after the Explorama experience to learn whether their self-perceptions stayed constant or changed. This process develops participants' intrapersonal intelligence.

Get Personal

The orientation toward profiles, interactions, and experience emphasizes a need to develop, in particular, the two personal intelligences.

Intrapersonal intelligence involves knowing yourself—your talents, energy level, interests, and so on. Students who strengthen their intrapersonal intelligence gain a better understanding of areas in which they can expect to excel, which helps them plan and govern their own learning.

Interpersonal intelligence involves understanding others through social interaction, emotional reactions, conversation, and so on. An individual's interpersonal intelligence affects his or her ability to work in groups. Group projects can create environments for students to improve their interpersonal intelligence as they develop other skills and knowledge.

Donna Schneider, a 3rd grade teacher at the John F. Kennedy Elementary School in Brewster, New York, developed a real-world publishing company in her classroom: "Schneider's Ink." Each spring when the school puts on performances and events, Schneider's 3rd graders create programs, banners, advertisements, and other publicity materials for their clients, the sponsoring teachers. Each student assumes a different job—editor, sales manager, typist, accountant, customer service representative, or designer. Before taking on a given position, each student writes a resumé and cover letter, obtains letters of recommendation, and is interviewed by the teacher. Students explore their own strengths and become aware of how those strengths can enable them to succeed in various jobs.

Schneider's Ink also engages students' interpersonal intelligence. For example, the quality-control manager, who is responsible for handling customer complaints, has to work with both clients and the editor to review problems. As company employees, the students juggle simultaneous print orders, coordinating the sequencing of tasks among themselves to produce high-quality work on time. They must understand others through social interaction, emotional reactions, and conversation. Through this process, students acquire a better understanding of the interdependence of individual strengths (Kornhaber, Fierros, & Veenema, 2004).

Building Active Learners

The multiple intelligences approach does not require a teacher to design a lesson in nine different ways so that all students can access the material. Rather, it involves creating rich experiences in which students with different intelligence profiles can interact with the materials and ideas using their particular combinations of strengths and weaknesses.

Often, these experiences are collaborative. As the amount of information that students—and adults—must process continues to increase dramatically, collaboration enables students to learn more by tapping into others' strengths as well as into their own. In ideal multiple intelligences instruction, rich experiences and collaboration provide a context for students to become aware of their own intelligence profiles, to develop self-regulation, and to participate more actively in their own learning.

References

Gardner, H. (2006). *Multiple intelligences: New horizons*. New York: Basic Books.

Gardner, H., Feldman, D. H., & Krechevsky, M. (Eds.). (1998). *Project Zero frameworks for early childhood education: Volume 1. Building on children's strengths: The experience of Project Spectrum*. New York: Teachers College Press.

Kornhaber, M., Fierros, E., & Veenema, S. (2004). *Multiple intelligences: Best ideas from research and practice*. Boston: Pearson.

Vygotsky, L. S. (1978). *Mind in society: The development of higher psychological processes*. Cambridge, MA: Harvard University Press.

Perry D. Klein  **NO**

Multiplying the Problems
of Intelligence by Eight

Howard Gardner introduced the theory of multiple intelligences (MI) in his book *Frames of Mind* (1983). In place of the traditional view that there is one general intelligence, he contended that there are seven, each operating in a specific cultural domain: linguistic, logical-mathematical, spatial, bodily-kinesthetic, musical, interpersonal, and intrapersonal. Since then, Gardner (1995) has tentatively added "the intelligence of the naturalist," which includes the ability to understand living things and to use this knowledge productively, as in farming. Each intelligence has its own core set of operations and supports specific activities. Spatial intelligence, for example, mentally represents and transforms objects, and underpins navigation, mechanics, sculpture, and geometry. Because the intelligences are independent, most individuals show an uneven profile, with some intelligences greater than others (Gardner, 1983, 1993b; Gardner & Hatch, 1989).

MI has swept education in the 15 years since its inception. ERIC [Education Resource Information Clearinghouse] citations favourable to the theory run into the hundreds, including some in prestigious or widely circulating journals (e.g., Armstrong, 1994; Gardner, 1994, 1995; Gardner & Hatch, 1989; Nelson, 1995). Most authors cite MI theory as an egalitarian alternative both to the theory that there is one general intelligence, and also to the practice of teaching a curriculum that emphasizes language and mathematics. They recommend innovations ranging from planning units of study that span each intelligence (Wallach & Callahan, 1994), to enriching education for gifted or learning-disabled students in their areas of strength (Hearne & Stone, 1995; Smerechansky-Metzger, 1995), to using virtual reality to educate each intelligence (McLellan, 1994).

However, few authors have systematically evaluated MI theory. D. Matthews (1988) argued in favour of it, noting that gifted students usually excel in a single domain, such as mathematics or music. Other authors have suggested friendly revisions, such as the need for a "moral" intelligence, clarification of the theory or its implications, more evidence, or recognition of other educational concerns (Boss, 1994; Eisner, 1994; Levin, 1994). Some researchers in the psychometric tradition have rejected MI theory outright, claiming that Gardner's intelligences correlate positively with I.Q. and therefore are

From *Canadian Journal of Education*, vol. 22 no. 2, 1997, pp. 377–394. Copyright © 1997 by Canadian Society for the Study of Education. Reprinted by permission of ProQuest LLC.

factors of general intelligence (Brand, 1996; Sternberg, 1983). Morgan (1992) noted the same positive correlations, and added that several of Gardner's intelligences canno t be conceptually distinguished from one another. Instead, Morgan interpreted these "intelligences" as cognitive styles. In the most sustained critique of MI, Ericsson and Charness (1994) suggested that expert performances are based on highly specific skills developed largely through extended deliberate practice, rather than on broad abilities.

Conceptual Problems

If someone were to ask, "Why is Michael a good dancer?," the MI answer would be "Because he has high bodily-kinesthetic intelligence." If the questioner then asked, "What is bodily-kinesthetic intelligence?," the answer would be "[It] is the ability to use one's body in highly differentiated and skilled ways, for expressive as well as goal-directed purposes . . . [and] to work skillfully with objects" (Gardner, 1983, p. 206). This explanation, however, is circular: the definition of bodily-kinesthetic intelligence is virtually a definition of dance, so the explanation says, in effect, that Michael is a good dancer because he is a good dancer. In fact, the explanation is less informative than the original question, which at least identified the type of physical activity in which Michael excels. MI's reliance on this sort of explanation makes the theory tautological, and, therefore, necessarily true (Smedslund, 1979). It also makes it trivial.

On the other hand, ascribing an achievement to an "intelligence" has a series of far-from-trivial implications. It means that performances are expressions of moderately general abilities, such as bodily-kinesthetic intelligence, rather than either very general abilities, such as general intelligence, or very specific skills, such as knowing how to dance. It also implies that whereas Michael may be better at dance than at other physical activities, his high "bodily-kinesthetic intelligence" should give him an advantage in these areas as well. Conversely, he need not be good at non-physical tasks, such as writing poems or solving mathematics problems. Furthermore, ascribing some level of achievement to an ability such as an "intelligence," rather than to an acquisition, such as "knowledge," suggests that this level will be relatively stable over time, and that its origins may be innate (Gardner, 1995).

Gardner (1983) goes even further, claiming that the "intelligences" are modules (pp. 55–56, 280–285) in approximately the sense proposed by Fodor (1983) or Allport (1980). Modules are neural structures that quickly process particular kinds of content. Colour vision, speech perception, and facial recognition have all been ascribed to modules. Each module is "computationally autonomous," meaning that it carries out its operations independently, and, for the most part, does not share resources with other modules. This autonomy implies that the internal workings of one module are not available to others, although the "output" of one module can become the "input" of another. In short, the implication of modularity for MI theory is that the mind is made up of seven (or eight) innate mechanisms, each of which works largely independently to handle one kind of content.

However, this independence makes the theory insufficient to account for some familiar experiences. Most activities involve several intelligences (Gardner, 1983, p. 304). Dance is both musical and physical; conversation is both linguistic and interpersonal; and solving a physics problem is both spatial and logical-mathematical. Modularity perse is not the problem, because the output of one module can become the input of another. But Gardner has defined the intelligences of MI in terms of their differing content, which raises the question of how they could exchange information. . . .

The phenomenon of intentionality drives this problem home. As Husserl (1962/1977) observed, our mental acts are *about* something, so they include two poles: the intending act ("noesis"), and the intended object ("noema"). Often, MI theory assigns the intending act and intended object to different "intelligences." Many intending acts express logical-mathematical intelligence: inferring, classifying, hypothesizing, counting, calculating, and so on. But the objects of these intentions are assigned to other intelligences. They include material things ("spatial intelligence"), other people ("interpersonal intelligence"), physical activities ("bodily-kinesthetic intelligence"), personal experience ("intrapersonal intelligence"), music ("musical intelligence") and living things ("naturalist's intelligence"). These other intelligences carry out their own operations. Consequently, MI theory makes it difficult to understand how people can use logic and mathematics to think *about* anything. . . .

The "strong" claim that humans have several distinct intelligences is difficult to defend, and Gardner sometimes presents MI theory in a "weak" form. He has written that it is "less a set of hypotheses and predictions than it is an organized framework" (Gardner, 1994, p. 578). He has allowed that the components of each intelligence can dissociate or uncouple (Gardner, 1983, p. 173). He also acknowledges that pairs of intelligences may "overlap" or be correlated (Gardner & Walters, 1993a, pp. 41–42). Finally, he has suggested that "many people can evaluate their intelligences and plan to use them together in certain putatively successful ways" (p. 43), leaving some room for an executive that spans the intelligences.

These concessions risk, however, returning Gardner to the first problem of MI theory: triviality. If the intelligences extensively exchange information, cooperate in activities, or share a common executive, then there is little warrant for characterizing them as independent entities. Of course, Gardner could claim that although the intelligences are distinct, in practice they always work together. However, this concession makes the multiplicity of the intelligences a distinction without a difference, and invites the reply that the system as a whole is one single intelligence, and specific abilities, such as spatial reasoning, are mere components of this intelligence. . . .

Empirical Problems
Exceptional Populations

Gardner views the existence of groups that he believes to be high or low in one specific intelligence as part of the evidence for MI. The first of these are the geniuses: Yehudi Menuhin illustrates exceptional musical intelligence; Babe Ruth, outstanding bodily-kinesthetic intelligence; and Barbara McClintock, outstanding logical-mathematical intelligence (Gardner, 1993b). However, the abilities of Gardner's candidates do not appear to correspond to the categories of MI theory. Many excel in more than one domain: Barbara McClintock's work spanned the logical-mathematical and natural domains (pp. 19–20), Virginia Woolf's, the linguistic and intrapersonal domains (pp. 24–25), and Albert Einstein's, the spatial and the logical-mathematical domains (Gardner, 1993a, pp. 104–105). It is to be expected that if the intelligences are independent, then some individuals will excel in two or more domains, but if Gardner fails to show that most achieve excellence in one specific domain, then his claim that the intelligences are independent is threatened. Conversely, Gardner does not show that any of the geniuses excel throughout one of the domains defined by MI theory; instead, each seems to excel on some smaller subset of activities within a domain. Unless Gardner can show that most geniuses perform relatively well throughout a domain, then the notion that the intelligences are integrated structures is threatened. Generally, the difficulty with Gardner's discussion of genius is that many psychological theories imply some way of categorizing individuals of exceptional ability; he has not yet shown that MI theory fits the data better than other theories.

The argument from genius could be bolstered by a second special population: prodigies. Gardner acknowledges that an individual's level of each intelligence is the result of both "nature" and "nurture." Furthermore, if outstanding individuals were to show exceptional abilities at a very early age, and these abilities were specific to domains, then it could be inferred that the structures of MI theory are "biopsychological potential[s]" (Gardner & Walters, 1993a, p. 36). But a competing theory would hold that prodigies appear in various fields because societies divide activities in specific ways and enculturate individuals accordingly. Gardner never tells the reader enough about any one case to indicate which alternative is more plausible. For example, he implies that Pablo Picasso was genetically prepared for prodigy, but later adds that no work he did prior to age 9 has survived (Gardner, 1993a, pp. 138–146). This kind of fragmentary anecdotal evidence raises a "chicken-and-egg" question: Is early tutoring a response to early talent, or vice versa? Howe (1990) has noted that children with exceptional abilities intensely explore and practise in their area of interest, observe models, and receive tutoring from an early age. In one historical study, Fowler (1986) found that of 24 outstanding mathematicians, 21 received special stimulation in mathematics before the age of 5, and several before the age of 3. Another objection to Gardner's view is that the talents of many prodigies simply do not fit the categories of MI theory; instead, they reflect the importance of specific enculturation. Talent at chess is a prime example. Thus, although the achievements of these children are impressive and difficult to explain, they do not establish the eight discrete "biopsychological potentials" that MI theory requires. And given that prodigy is rare, even among the most accomplished members of a field (Bloom, 1985; Feldman, 1986), this phenomenon is probably not a useful touchstone for educational practice.

In any case, exceptional accomplishments may not be based on the domain-wide abilities Gardner proposes. For example, he claims that excellence in chess expresses spatial intelligence (Gardner, 1983, pp. 192–195). But chess is one of the most-researched human cognitive activities, and general abilities, spatial or otherwise, seem to contribute little to its mastery (Ericsson & Smith, 1991). Chess masters are no better than other persons at spatial tasks, except at recognizing strategically significant board arrangements (Chase & Simon, 1973; Pfau & Murphy, 1988). Highly ranked players are less likely to work in professions that involve solving spatial problems, such as engineering, than they are to work in professions in the humanities, such as writing (de Groot, 1978; Elo, 1978). A defender of MI might counter that there are many domains of spatial abilities, and an individual who excels in one need not excel in others. But as this rebuttal tacitly concedes, if this were the case, then there is no reason to speak of a general "spatial intelligence" in the first place.

The third exceptional population Gardner discusses are savants, individuals who do one thing exceptionally well, such as calculating large products mentally, stating the day of the week for any given calendar date, or playing a piano piece after a single hearing. These include "idiot savants," many of whom are autistic. Savantry could support the coherence and independence of the intelligences if it were shown to embody one high intelligence in an otherwise average or low profile. However, savants usually do not excel across an entire domain. For example, hyperlexic autistic readers decode print better than other children their age, but because their comprehension is poor (Snowling & Frith, 1986), they could not be said to show high linguistic intelligence.

Gardner interprets autism as a limitation on intrapersonal intelligence (Gardner & Walters, 1993b, p. 25). However, its effects are not limited to this domain. Sloboda, Hermelin, and O'Connor (1985) described NP, a musical autistic savant, who could accurately play a piece on the piano after one hearing. Interestingly, 24 hours later, NP played the same piece in a way that sounded "metronomic in the extreme" (p. 165). Most autistic savants have difficulty planning and monitoring the use of their exceptional skills, which may explain why many cannot find employment in their areas of special interest (Frith, 1989). It appears that autism, primarily an impairment in intrapersonal understanding, affects other "intelligences," showing that these are not independent, but affects only some aspects of each intelligence, suggesting that they are not coherent entities.

Like the achievements of geniuses, those of savants are probably not based on the general operations that Gardner posits. Instead, these achievements rely on knowledge and skills specific to particular activities. When autistic savants replay a piece of music after one hearing, the errors they make are reversions to forms typical of the piece's genre, which indicates that they rely on matching the new tune to the repertoire of melodic forms they already know (Sloboda et al., 1985). Similarly, a case study of a non-autistic mathematical savant showed that through thousands of hours of practice she had learned the characteristics of a huge repertoire of numbers, recognizing at a glance, for instance, that 720 equals 6 factorial (i.e., $6 \times 5 \times 4 \times 3 \times 2 \times 1$). She had also learned a collection of computational algorithms. This knowledge allowed her quickly to fit a routine to the numbers in most questions, and to solve those questions efficiently. In contrast, her basic cognitive processes did not differ from those of other adults (Jensen, 1990).

MI researchers also cite learning disabilities as evidence for their theory (Gardner & Hatch, 1989). The most common of these disabilities is dyslexia. Most dyslexic students have difficulty discriminating sounds in language, matching them to letters, and combining them to form words; some appear to have difficulty recalling word images (Patterson, Marshall, & Coltheart, 1985). However, because many dyslexic students equal their normal classmates in aspects of language other than reading, such as listening comprehension (Mosberg & Johns, 1994; Torgesen, 1988), dyslexia affects a range of abilities too narrow to comprise "linguistic intelligence." Another learning disability, Gerstmann syndrome, initially seems to represent difficulties in spatial reasoning (Gardner, 1983, p. 156). But its symptoms include problems in distinguishing left from right, making mathematical computations, and recognizing and remembering finger contact. Because these difficulties involve logical-mathematical and bodily-kinesthetic intelligence, Gerstmann syndrome corresponds to a broader set of abilities than does spatial intelligence. Indeed, I was not able to identify a single learning disability that maps onto an intelligence of MI theory. . . .

Studies Concerning Transfer of Learning

If, as Gardner suggests, the core of each "intelligence" consists of knowledge and procedures that operate across a wide domain, then it would make sense to build school curricula around these cores. The "Right Start" program illustrates this approach in mathematics. Griffin, Case, and Siegler (1994) researched the concepts central to understanding Grade 1 arithmetic. Then they created a set of mathematical games and activities, and engaged students in discussions that highlighted these concepts. As a result, the children's understanding of number improved dramatically compared with a control group, and transferred to a variety of new quantitative activities, such as telling time and predicting the behaviour of a balance scale. The Right Start results are impressive. However, to support MI theory, it is necessary to show that students' gains transferred across the logical-mathematical domain, but not further (e.g., to spatial tasks).

Moreover, other kinds of transfer research bear on MI theory quite differently. When students articulate and elaborate on a concept, this helps them to apply it to new problems, a phenomenon called "high road transfer" (Brown & Kane, 1988; Chi & Bassok, 1989). Similarly, when teachers explicitly state the rules for solving a problem, this articulation adds significantly to the value of examples alone in helping students to transfer these rules to new content (Cheng, Holyoak, Nisbett, & Oliver, 1986; Fong, Krantz, & Nisbett, 1986). This transfer of strategies across domains is difficult to explain within MI theory. Even more problematic is the role of language in moving information within and among other "intelligences." Gardner (1983) is aware of transfer across domains, and notes that it is problematic, but does not attempt to reconcile this transfer with the notion of autonomous intelligences, except by alluding to "waves of symbolization" (pp. 306–309). In this sense, research on transfer is a double-edged sword for MI theory.

Psychometric Research

Gardner also relies on statistical research. Factor analysis is a procedure that can be used to tease out themes appearing within, or across, tests. Several factors similar to Gardner's intelligences have emerged in such analyses, including linguistic (Wiebe & Watkins, 1980), spatial (Gustafsson, 1984), and social factors (Rosnow, Skleder, Jaeger, & Rind, 1994). But this kind of research provides shaky support for MI. First, the factors in these studies typically are not independent, but instead correlate positively with one another, a fact that has been used to argue both for the existence of general intelligence and against MI (Brand, 1996; Sternberg, 1983). Although Gardner has replied that this evidence comes almost entirely from tests of logical-mathematical or linguistic intelligence (Gardner & Walters, 1993a, p. 39), it is important to note that spatial tasks correlate substantially with verbal tasks even when performance measures are used (Wechsler, 1974). Second, each factor splits into several smaller factors, each of these narrower than the intelligences of MI theory. For instance, in a review of "visual perception" abilities (similar to Gardner's "spatial intelligence"), Carroll (1993) examined 230 data sets. The factors of visual perception found in each study varied in number from one to six, which Carroll grouped into five categories "despite much difficulty" (p. 309). These results can be accommodated by theories of intelligence that recognize both general and specific components, but they present difficulties for MI theory, which recognizes only one level of structure.

Surprisingly, a re-examination of Gardner's own assessment research also challenges MI theory. He and his colleagues have developed assessment tasks based on authentic activities in several different domains. According to MI theory, students' performances on activities derived from the same intelligences should show high correlations, and activities derived from different intelligences should show low correlations, or none at all. However, in two studies with primary school children, several pairs of tasks that were supposed to represent independent intelligences correlated strongly, and those that were supposed to represent the same intelligences failed to correlate significantly, except for two number tasks (Gardner & Hatch, 1989; Gardner & Krechevsky, 1993). In both studies, the researchers interpreted these patterns as evidence against the existence of a single general intelligence. However, they failed to acknowledge that these same findings also weigh crucially against MI theory.

Experimental Studies

If the mind is composed of independent modules, as MI theory claims, then individuals should be able to carry out two activities that call on different intelligences at the same time, without one interfering with the other. Conversely, if two activities call on the same intelligence, then the speed or accuracy of at least one activity should suffer. Several studies have explored these possibilities using spatial and verbal tasks, and have shown that these predictions are largely true (e.g., Barton, Matthews, Farmer, & Belyavin, 1995; Liu & Wickens, 1992).

The picture is more complex, however, than MI theory would predict. First, verbal and visual tasks disrupt one another somewhat, indicating that they share some kind of resource, possibly an executive that switches attention between them (Logie, Zucco, & Baddeley, 1990). Second, experimental research indicates that people can translate information from verbal to visual form, or vice versa (Conrad, 1964; Holding, 1992, 1993; N. N. Matthews, Hunt, & MacLeod, 1980), which limits the notion that various kinds of knowledge are handled by separate intelligences. Most importantly, other "intelligences" seem to rely on linguistic or spatial resources: mathematical tasks interfere with verbal tasks (Logie & Baddeley, 1987; Logie et al., 1990), and verbal tasks interfere with musical tasks for novices (Pechmann & Mohr, 1992). Similarly, switching attention among sounds originating from different locations interferes with spatial tasks (Smyth & Scholey, 1994). . . .

Pedagogical Problems

One response to these criticisms could be to claim that even though MI theory is conceptually and empirically weak, it remains a useful framework for teaching. But this is far from clear. Interpretations have been so diverse that Kornhaber has noted that "one reason for the success of MI is that educators can cite it without having to do anything differently" (cited in Gardner, 1994, p. 580). Some practices based on the theory are no doubt misinterpretations. Reiff (1996), for example, has suggested that if a child is weak in one intelligence, he or she can be taught "through" another. Because this view assumes that the same material can be learned using a variety of modes, it could be called the "learning styles" interpretation. Whether this view is true or false, it is essentially the opposite of Gardner's (1995) theory. If each intelligence operates on a different domain, and represents a specific kind of content, then only rarely can a given piece of knowledge be presented in different ways for different intelligences.

A second common interpretation of MI theory claims that schools currently overemphasize linguistic and logical-mathematical knowledge, so curricula ought to be changed to balance the intelligences more equally. Educators could plan units of study that include activities to engage each intelligence (Hoerr, 1994; Wallach & Callahan, 1994), or that give a more prominent place to the arts (Deluca, 1993). Balanced programming and MI theory are obviously compatible, but one does not entail the other. The notion that there are eight intelligences does not imply that school should be the institution responsible for developing all of them. Conversely, if educators choose to offer balanced programming, they do not require Gardner's theory for justification, which is why such alternative systems as Waldorf schools long predated MI theory.

A more elaborate version of the balanced programming proposal suggests educators should assess children's intelligences, then provide programs that include remediation in their areas of weakness, and enrichment in their areas of strength (Gardner & Walters, 1993b, p. 31; Hearne & Stone, 1995; Hoerr, 1994). This approach is appealing, but presents practical problems. The first, already noted, is that despite several years of effort, MI researchers have not yet developed reliable methods for assessing the intelligences. The second problem is that growing class sizes in many jurisdictions, multiplied by the supposed existence of eight intelligences, and the many levels at which children could operate in each of these intelligences, would yield an explosion in the workload of the teachers who would have to plan and deliver these programs.

Gardner favours a general education in primary school. His preferences for the middle elementary years are less clear, in that he mentions "mastering the crucial literacies," but stresses "early specialization" in areas chosen by each child and family, and informed by an assessment of his or her intelligences (Gardner, 1993b, pp. 194–196). Later, students would pursue a broader education during adolescence. This preference for specialization in middle childhood may contradict the political goals of MI theory. Gardner (1993b) has criticized conventional education, particularly in its use of intelligence testing, as ethnocentric and elitist, or "'Westist,' 'Testist,' and 'Bestist'" (p. 12). But, arguably, specialization represents a subtle kind of streaming. Opportunities for activities of various kinds are not allocated to all preschool children equally. Choosing specialties on the basis of the "intelligences" they have acquired by age 7 could potentially exacerbate these inequalities. And although Gardner wishes that society valued all intelligences equally, it does not. Mathematics, particularly, serves as a "gate-keeping" subject for admission to advanced study in many highly paid professions (Gainen, 1995). Therefore, contrary to Gardner's good intentions, his suggestions could lead to a hardening of traditional categories of privilege.

Some educators have claimed that a benefit of the MI framework is that children learn to identify their own "areas of strength," and some schools now issue report cards based on the theory (see Hanson, 1995; Hoerr, 1994; Wallach & Callahan, 1994). However, there is good reason to predict that these practices will backfire. The converse of being "high" in some intelligences is being "mediocre" or "low" in others. Students who believe that they are low in an ability often avoid activities that call on it, even when they might learn from the effort (Covington, 1992; Palmquist & Young, 1992). Paradoxically, students' beliefs that they are high in an ability can lead to the same result in the long run. Those who attribute their achievements to such ability approach tasks with confidence. But, when they encounter a problem that they cannot solve easily, they often quit. Apparently, their theory that achievement reflects ability leads them to interpret failure as a lack of this ability. In contrast, students who attribute achievement to effort, learning, and the application of appropriate strategies are more likely to persist when "the going gets tough," and to recover after initial failure (Dweck & Leggett, 1988).

These objections invite the fundamental pedagogical question: Is MI the right *kind* of theory for education? Although Gardner stresses the differences between general intelligence and multiple intelligences, the two frameworks nevertheless share fundamental characteristics that limit their relevance to teaching. Both identify cognitive structures far too broad to be useful for interpreting any specific educational tasks. For instance, the knowledge that basketball relies on "bodily-kinesthetic intelligence" tells a coach nothing about the skills that her players need to learn. Because both general intelligence and MI are theories of ability rather than theories of knowledge or learning, they offer only a static interpretation of children's performance; knowing that a student is high in "musical intelligence" provides no clues about how to enrich his music education; knowing that he is low in musical intelligence provides no clues about how to remedy it. Of course, both general intelligence theorists and MI theorists agree that both education and experience can affect ability (e.g., Neisser et al., 1996), and Gardner has argued for innovative practices, such as expert mentoring in settings outside of school. But learning is not the focus of ability theories, and the positive innovations Gardner advocates derive from other research traditions, such as sociocultural theory, rather than from MI itself (e.g., Gardner, Kornhaber, & Krechevsky, 1993).

Conclusion

In examining the nature of intelligence, Gardner and his colleagues have used a wider set of tools than have traditional psychometric researchers. They have contended compellingly that the arts are as much intellectual activities as are writing, mathematics, and science (Gardner, 1982). MI researchers have drawn educators' attention to an alternative to the theory of general intelligence. And Gardner (1983, p. 297) is admirably willing to consider criticisms of his own framework. However, I contend that MI theory offers a level of analysis neither empirically plausible nor pedagogically useful.

A promising alternative to this kind of research focuses on the knowledge and strategies that children and adults use in carrying out various, specific activities. Such analyses are already being carried out in areas as diverse as drawing (Cox, 1992), argument comprehension (Chambliss, 1995), and volleyball (Allard & Starkes, 1980). Innovative projects have explored the creation of classroom communities in which students collaborate to construct knowledge in areas such as science, mathematics, and interdisciplinary studies (e.g., McGilly, 1994). Such research seems likely to prove more relevant than ability theories in setting curricular goals and interpreting students' learning.

References

Allard, F., & Starkes, J. L. (1980). Perception in sport: Volleyball. *Journal of Sport Psychology, 2*, 22–33.

Allport, D. A. (1980). Patterns and actions: Cognitive mechanisms are content specific. In G. Claxton (Ed.), *Cognitive psychology: New directions* (pp. 26–64). London: Routledge & Kegan Paul.

Armstrong, T. (1994). Multiple intelligences: Seven ways to approach curriculum. *Educational Leadership, 52*(3), 26–28.

Barton, A., Matthews, B., Farmer, E., & Belyavin, A. (1995). Revealing the basic properties of the visuospatial sketchpad: The use of complete spatial arrays. *Acta Psychologica, 89*, 197–216.

Bloom, B.S. (Ed.). (1985). *Developing talent in young people*. New York: Ballantine.

Boss, J. A. (1994). The anatomy of moral intelligence. *Educational Theory, 44,* 399–416.

Brand, C. (1996). *The g factor: General intelligence and its implications*. New York: John Wiley.

Brown, A. L., & Kane, M. J. (1988). Preschool children can learn to transfer: Learning to learn and learning from example. *Cognitive Psychology, 20,* 493–523.

Carroll, J. B. (1993). *Human cognitive abilities: A survey of factor-analytic studies*. Cambridge: Cambridge University Press.

Chambliss, M. J. (1995). Text cues and strategies successful readers use to construct the gist of lengthy written arguments. *Reading Research Quarterly, 30,* 778–807.

Chase, W. G., & Simon, H. A. (1973). The mind's eye in chess. In W. G. Chase (Ed.), *Visual information processing* (pp. 215–281). New York: Academic Press.

Cheng, P. W., Holyoak, K. J., Nisbett, R. E., & Oliver, L. M. (1986). Pragmatic versus syntactic approaches to training deductive reasoning. *Cognitive Psychology, 18,* 293–328.

Chi, M. T. H., & Bassok, M. (1989). Learning from examples via self-explanations. In L. B. Resnick (Ed.), *Knowing, learning, and instruction: Essays in honour of Robert Glaser* (pp. 251–282). Hillsdale, NJ: Erlbaum.

Conrad, R. (1964). Acoustic confusions in immediate memory. *British Journal of Psychology, 55,* 75–84.

Covington, M. V. (1992). *Making the grade: A self-worth perspective on motivation and school reform*. Cambridge: Cambridge University Press.

Cox, M. (1992). *Children's drawings*. London: Penguin Books.

de Groot, A. D. (1978). *Thought and choice in chess* (2nd ed.). The Hague: Mouton.

Deluca, L. S. (1993). The arts and equity. *Equity and Excellence in Education, 26*(3), 51–53.

Dweck, C. S., & Leggett, E. L. (1988). A social cognitive approach to motivation and personality. *Psychological Review, 95,* 256–273.

Eisner, E. W. (1994). Commentary: Putting multiple intelligences in context: Some questions and observations. *Teachers College Record, 95,* 555–560.

Elo, A. E. (1978). *The rating of chess players, past and present*. New York: Arco.

Ericsson, K. A., & Charness, N. (1994). Expert performance: Its structure and acquisition. *American Psychologist, 49,* 725–747.

Ericsson, K. A., & Smith, J. (1991). Prospects and limits of the empirical study of expertise: An introduction. In K. A. Ericsson & J. Smith (Eds.), *Toward a general theory of expertise: Prospects and limits* (pp. 1–38). Cambridge: Cambridge University Press.

Feldman, D. H. (1986). *Nature's gambit: Child prodigies and the development of human potential*. New York: Basic Books.

Fodor, J. A. (1983). *The modularity of mind: An essay of faculty psychology*. Cambridge, MA: MIT Press.

Fong, G. T., Krantz, D. H., & Nisbett, R. E. (1986). The effects of statistical training on thinking about everyday problems. *Cognitive Psychology, 18*, 253–292.

Fowler, W. (1986). Early experiences of great men and women mathematicians. In W. Fowler (Ed.), *Early experience and the development of competence* (New Directions for Child Development No. 32, pp. 87–109). San Francisco: Jossey-Bass.

Frith, U. (1989). *Autism: Explaining the enigma*. Oxford: Basil Blackwell.

Gainen, J. (1995). Barriers to success in quantitative gatekeeper courses. *New Directions for Teaching and Learning, 61*, 5–14.

Gardner, H. (1982). *Art, mind, and brain: A cognitive approach to creativity*. New York: Basic Books.

Gardner, H. (1983). *Frames of mind: The theory of multiple intelligences*. New York: Basic Books.

Gardner, H. (1993a). *Creating minds: Anatomy of creativity as seen through the lives of Freud, Einstein, Picasso, Stravinsky, Eliot, Graham, and Gandhi*. New York: Basic Books.

Gardner, H. (1993b). *Multiple intelligences: The theory in practice*. New York: Basic Books.

Gardner, H. (1994). Intelligences in theory and practice: A response to Elliot W. Eisner, Robert J. Sternberg, and Henry M. Levin. *Teachers College Record, 95*, 576–583.

Gardner, H. (1995, November). Reflections on multiple intelligences: Myths and messages: *Phi Delta Kappan, 77*, 200–203, 206–209.

Gardner, H., & Hatch, T. (1989). Multiple intelligences go to school: Educational implications of the theory of multiple intelligences. *Educational Researcher, 18*(8), 4–9.

Gardner, H., Kornhaber, M., & Krechevsky, M. (1993). Engaging intelligence. In H. Gardner, *Multiple intelligences: The theory in practice* (pp. 231–248). New York: HarperCollins.

Gardner, H., & Krechevsky, M. (1993). The emergence and nurturance of multiple intelligences in early childhood: The Project Spectrum approach. In H. Gardner, *Multiple intelligences: The theory in practice* (pp. 86–111). New York: Basic Books.

Gardner, H., & Walter, J. (1993a). Questions and answers about multiple intelligences theory. In H. Gardner, *Multiple intelligences: The theory in practice* (pp. 35–48). New York: Basic Books.

Gardner, H., & Walters, J. (1993b). A rounded version. In H. Gardner, *Multiple intelligences: The theory in practice* (pp. 13–34). New York: Basic Books.

Griffin, S. A., Case, R., & Siegler, R. S. (1994). Right start: Providing the central conceptual prerequisites for first formal learning of arithmetic to students at risk for failure. In K. McGilly (Ed.), *Classroom lessons: Integrating cognitive theory and classroom practice* (pp. 25–49). Cambridge, MA: MIT Press.

Gustafsson, J. E. (1984). A unifying model for the structure of intellectual abilities. *Intelligence, 8*, 179–203.

Hanson, R. M. (Executive Producer). (1995). *How are kids smart? Multiple intelligences in the classroom: Teachers' Version* [Videotape]. Port Chester, NY: National Professional Resources.

Hearne, D., & Stone, S. (1995). Multiple intelligences and underachievement: Lessons from individuals with learning disabilities. *Journal of Learning Disabilities, 28,* 439–448.

Hoerr, T. R. (1994). How the New City School applies the multiple intelligences. *Educational Leadership, 52*(3), 29–33.

Holding, D. H. (1992). Theories of chess skill. *Psychological Research, 54,* 10–16.

Holding, D. H. (1993). Sharing verbal and visuospatial resources in working memory. *Journal of General Psychology, 120,* 245–256.

Howe, M. J. A. (1990). *The origins of exceptional abilities.* Oxford: Blackwell.

Husserl, E. (1977). *Phenomenological psychology: Lectures, summer semester,* 1925 (J. Scanlon, Trans.). The Hague: Martinus Nijhoff. (Original work published 1962)

Jensen, A. R. (1990). Speed of information processing in a calculating prodigy. *Intelligence, 14,* 259–274.

Levin, H. M. (1994). Commentary: Multiple intelligence theory and everyday practice. *Teachers College Record, 95,* 570–575.

Liu, Y., & Wickens, C. D. (1992). Visual scanning with or without spatial uncertainty and divided and selective attention. *Acta Psychologica, 79,* 131–153.

Logie, R. H., & Baddeley, A. D. (1987). Cognitive processes in counting. *Journal of Experimental Psychology: Learning, Memory, and Cognition, 13,* 310–326.

Logie, R. H., Zucco, G. M., & Baddeley, A. D. (1990). Interference with visual short-term memory. *Acta Psychologica, 75,* 55–74.

Matthews, D. (1988). Gardner's multiple intelligence theory: An evaluation of relevant research literature and a consideration of its application to gifted education. *Roeper Review, 11,* 100–104.

Matthews, N. N., Hunt, E. B., & MacLeod, C. M. (1980). Strategy choice and strategy training in sentence-picture verification. *Journal of Verbal Learning and Verbal Behavior, 19,* 531–548.

McGilly, K. (Ed.). (1994). *Classroom lessons: Integrating cognitive theory and classroom practice.* Cambridge, MA: MIT Press.

McLellan, H. (1994). Virtual reality and multiple intelligences: Potentials for higher education. *Journal of Computing in Higher Education, 5,* 33–66.

Morgan, H. (1992). *An analysis of Gardner's theory of multiple intelligence.* Paper presented at the Annual Meeting of the Eastern Educational Research Association. (ERIC Document Reproduction Service No. ED 360 088)

Mosberg, L., & Johns, D. (1994). Reading and listening comprehension in college students with developmental dyslexia. *Learning Disabilities Research and Practice, 9,* 130–135.

Neisser, U., Boodoo, G., Bouchard, T. J., Jr., Boykin, A. W., Brody, N., Ceci, S. J., Halpern, D. F., Loehlin, J. C., Perloff, R., Sternberg, R. J., & Urbina, S. (1996). Intelligence: Knowns and unknowns. *American Psychologist, 51,* 77–101.

Nelson, K. (1995). Nurturing kids' seven ways of being smart. *Instructor, 105,* 26–30, 34.

Palmquist, M., & Young, R. (1992). The notion of giftedness and student expectations about writing. *Written Communication, 9,* 137–168.

Patterson, K. E., Marshall, J. C., & Coltheart, M. (Eds.). (1985). *Surface dyslexia: Neuro-psychological and cognitive studies of phonological reading.* Hillsdale, NJ: Lawrence Erlbaum.

Pechmann, T., & Mohr, G. (1992). Interference in memory for tonal pitch: Implications for a working-memory model. *Memory and Cognition, 20,* 314–320.

Pfau, H. D., & Murphy, M. D. (1988). Role of verbal knowledge in chess skill. *American Journal of Psychology, 101,* 73–86.

Reiff, J. C. (1996). Bridging home and school through multiple intelligences. *Childhood Education, 72*(3), 164–166.

Rosnow, R. L., Skleder, A. A., Jaeger, M. E., & Rind, B. (1994). Intelligence and the epistemics of interpersonal acumen: Testing some implications of Gardner's theory. *Intelligence, 19,* 93–116.

Sloboda, J. A., Hermelin, B., & O'Connor, N. (1985). An exceptional musical memory. *Music Perception, 3,* 155–170.

Smedslund, J. (1979). Between the analytic and the arbitrary: A case study of psychological research. *Scandinavian Journal of Psychology, 20,* 129–140.

Smerechansky-Metzger, J. A. (1995). The quest for multiple intelligences. *Gifted Child Today, 18*(3), 12–15.

Smyth, M. M., & Scholey, K. A. (1994). Interference in immediate spatial memory. *Memory and Cognition, 22,* 1–13.

Snowling, M., & Frith, U. (1986). Comprehension in "hyperlexic" readers. *Journal of Experimental Child Psychology, 42,* 392–415.

Sternberg, R. J. (1983). How much gall is too much gall? A review of *Frames of mind: The theory of multiple intelligences. Contemporary Education Review, 2,* 215–224.

Torgesen, J. K. (1988). Studies of children with learning disabilities who perform poorly on memory span tasks. *Journal of Learning Disabilities, 21,* 605–612.

Wallach, C., & Callahan, S. (1994). The 1st grade plant museum. *Educational Leadership, 52*(3), 32–34.

Wechsler, D. (1974). *Manual for the Wechsler Intelligence Scale for children—Revised.* New York: The Psychological Corporation.

Wiebe, M. J., & Watkins, E. O. (1980). Factor analysis of the McCarthy Scales of Children's Abilities on preschool children. *Journal of School Psychology, 18,* 154–162.

POSTSCRIPT

Can Howard Gardner's Theory of Multiple Intelligences Transform Educational Practice?

It may not be possible to answer the question posed by this issue for several years. In part, this reflects the fact that Gardner's theory of multiple intelligences has been proposed relatively recently and is still evolving. It also reflects the fact that Gardner's theory, like many other psychological theories, was originally formulated as a description of an important dimension of the human mind and was not intended as a theory of pedagogy. This means that there is considerable theoretical and empirical work to be done before the educational implications of the theory are completely understood. Unfortunately, there is considerable pressure to reform our educational system now. This has led to a number of initiatives that claim to have been inspired by Gardner's theory but that, on careful analysis, have little to do with the theory. Some reformers, for example, have used Gardner's theory to advocate teaching to accommodate a variety of learning styles, including differences between left- and right-brain learners, verbal and visual-spatial learners, and reflective and intuitive learners. See "Multiple Intelligences: Seven Keys to Opening Closed Minds," by Shirley E. Jordan, *NASSP Bulletin* (November 1996). Other reformers have advocated the creation of formal tests for each of the proposed intelligences.

It is also important to recognize that there is not universal support for Gardner's view of intelligence among scholars of the human mind. Many continue to point to the ubiquitous correlations that exist between a wide range of tasks that most of us would agree must tap "intelligence." See "Spearman's g and the Problem of Educational Equality," by Arthur R. Jensen, *Oxford Review of Education* (vol. 17, no. 2, 1991).

Readers interested in pursuing Gardner's writings on intelligence are encouraged to read *The Unschooled Mind: How Children Think and How Schools Should Teach* (Basic Books, 1991), *Multiple Intelligences: The Theory into Practice* (Basic Books, 1993), and *Multiple Intelligences: New Horizons* (Basic Books, 2006). An example of an adoption of a multiple intelligences-inspired curriculum can be found in "It's No Fad: Fifteen Years of Implementing Multiple Intelligences," by Thomas R. Hoerr, *Educational Horizons* (Winter 2003). The reader who is interested in alternative conceptions of intelligence should also seek out work by Robert Sternberg, including; *Successful Intelligence* (Plume, 1997); "Raising the Achievement of All Students: Teaching for Successful Intelligence," *Educational Psychology Review* (December 2002); "The Theory of

Successful Intelligence as a Basis for Gifted Education," coauthored by Elena Grigorenko, *Gifted Child Quarterly* (vol. 46, no. 4, 2002); and "Recognizing Neglected Strengths," *Educational Leadership* (September 2006). A series of articles in a special issue of the *Teachers College Record* (January 2004) provides an excellent summary of the current state of the theory and its applications. Particularly useful in this issue are "Multiple Intelligences Theory after 20 Years," by Branton Shearer and "Multiple Intelligences: Its Tensions and Possibilities," by Elliot W. Eisner.

ISSUE 10

Will a Push for Standards and Accountability Lead to More Motivated Students?

YES: Lauren B. Resnick, from "From Aptitude to Effort: A New Foundation for Our Schools," *American Educator* (Spring 1999)

NO: Kennon M. Sheldon and Bruce J. Biddle, from "Standards, Accountability, and School Reform: Perils and Pitfalls," *Teachers College Record* (Fall 1998)

ISSUE SUMMARY

YES: Lauren B. Resnick, a professor of psychology at the University of Pittsburgh, presents a plan for reforming American schools. One critical feature of the plan is clear achievement standards set for all students, not just those who are assumed to have the highest academic aptitude. Such standards, Resnick argues, will motivate students to work harder and, thus, increase achievement by all students.

NO: Kennon M. Sheldon and Bruce J. Biddle, both members of the faculty in the department of psychology at the University of Missouri, argue that the mission of schooling must be to create "lifelong, self-directed learners"—adults who enjoy learning for its own sake. They argue that an emphasis on standards is inconsistent with this mission because it rewards (and punishes) students and teachers for achieving a narrowly defined set of outcomes.

The past two decades have been punctuated with frequent calls for the reform of the U.S. educational system. In part, these calls have been sparked by cross-national comparisons of educational achievement. These comparisons have consistently shown that U.S. students are falling behind those in other nations in their mastery of the content in fundamental academic domains, most notably mathematics and science. Many of the plans for reform have included the adoption of a set of standards that would specify the content and skills that students should master, typically on a grade-by-grade basis. In some plans, standards would be set at the level of the individual school district. In other plans, the standards would be common across all districts within a state, or possibly even across all schools within the United States.

Strong proponents of the standards movement argue that much of the failure of U.S. schools can be traced to the fact that teachers and schools have too much freedom over what content to teach and when it is taught. More moderate standards proponents suggest that teachers are overwhelmed by the sheer amount of content that they *could* teach and that they lack a sound, shared basis for making decisions. Less charitable standards proponents suggest that teachers have simply made bad choices—choices motivated by a particular political agenda or ideological stance—that have led them to waste their time teaching content in the social and affective domains at the expense of content in more traditional academic domains, such as science and mathematics. Proponents of standards have also suggested that the freedom provided teachers and schools over the curriculum has resulted in *a priori* decisions about what content falls within the ability of a particular student or group of students. The result is that teachers hold unnecessarily low expectations for certain students or groups of students and, thus, "water down" the curriculum, thereby ensuring that those students will fail to acquire meaningful academic skills.

Proponents of standards also point to a number of successes as evidence of the need for even wider adoption of this reform. Mike Schmoker and Robert J. Marzano, for example, in "Realizing the Promise of Standards-Based Education," *Educational Leadership* (March 1999), provide the following examples of the "promise of standards":

1. In Maryland's Frederick County, alignment of the curriculum with standards in the state-wide assessment led to a dramatic increase in assessed performance, with the result being that the district moved to the "highest tier" of Maryland schools.
2. Teachers in Glendale Union High School in Arizona all adopted the same curriculum, which was designed to meet end-of-the-year assessed standards in each subject area. Average student performance improved in nearly every course.

Critics of the standards movement, however, have suggested that short-term gains on outcome measures (typically, standardized tests of achievement) may hide deeper failures. Some argue that the gains in achievement are nothing more than the result of teachers "teaching to the test." Still other critics suggest that the standards proposed have a decidedly "back-to-basics" orientation—an orientation that will lead to drill-and-practice-oriented instruction and student rote memorization rather than true understanding.

In the following selections, another point of disagreement between the supporters and critics of the standards movement is considered. In the first selection, Lauren B. Resnick argues that standards can motivate students to put forth more effort and that such effort can lead to increased aptitude. In the second selection, Kennon M. Sheldon and Bruce J. Biddle argue that standards (or any system of external control) will lead to a decrease in students' motivation to engage in learning for its own sake.

YES

Lauren B. Resnick

From Aptitude to Effort:
A New Foundation for Our Schools

Two challenges face American education today: We must raise overall achievement levels, and we must make opportunities for achievement more equitable. The importance of both derives from the same basic condition—our changing economy. Never before has the pool of developed skill and capability mattered more in our prospects for general economic health. And never before have skill and knowledge mattered as much in the economic prospects for individuals. There is no longer a welcoming place in low-skill, high-wage jobs for people who have not cultivated talents appropriate to an information economy. The country, indeed each state and region, must press for a higher overall level of such cultivated talents. Otherwise, we can expect a continuation of the pattern of falling personal incomes and declining public services that has characterized the past twenty years.

The only way to achieve this higher level of skill and ability in the population at large is to make sure that all students, not just a privileged and select few, learn skills that our society requires. Equity and excellence, classically viewed as competing goals, must now be treated as a single aspiration.

To do this will require a profound transformation of our most basic assumptions about the conditions that enable people to learn. What we learn is a function both of our talents—our aptitude for particular kinds of learning— and of how hard we try—our effort. But what is the relationship between aptitude and effort? Are they independent of each other, and, if so, which is more important? Do strengths in one compensate for weaknesses in the other? Or does one help to create the other?

Facing Up to Our Aptitude-Oriented Education System

Historically, American education has wavered between the first and second of these possibilities, the independent and the compensatory. But it has never seriously considered the third possibility—that effort can create ability. Early in this century, we built an education system around the assumption that aptitude is paramount in learning and that it is largely hereditary. The system was oriented toward selection, distinguishing the naturally able from the less

As seen in *American Educator* (Spring 1999). Originally published in *Daedalus,* vol. 124, no. 4 (Fall 1995), pp. 55–62. Copyright © 1995 by the American Academy of Arts and Sciences. Reprinted by permission of MIT Press Journals.

able and providing students with programs thought suitable to their talents. In other periods, most notably during the Great Society reforms, we worked on a compensatory principle, arguing that special effort, by an individual or an institution, could make up for low aptitude. The third possibility—that effort actually creates ability, that people can become smart by working hard at the right kinds of learning tasks—has never been taken seriously in America or indeed in any European society, although it is the guiding assumption of education institutions in societies with a Confucian tradition.

Although the compensatory assumption is more recent in the history of American education, many of our tools and standard practices are inherited from the earlier period in which aptitude reigned supreme. As a result, our schools largely function as if we believed that native ability is the primary determinant in learning, that the "bell curve" of intelligence is a natural phenomenon that must necessarily be reproduced in all learning, that effort counts for little. Consider the following examples: (1) IQ tests or their surrogates determine who will have access to the enriched programs for the "gifted and talented." This curriculum is denied to students who are judged less capable. (2) Our so-called achievement tests are normed to compare students with one another rather than with a standard of excellence, making it difficult to see the results of learning, and, in the process, actively discouraging effort: Students stay at about the same relative percentile rank, even if they have learned a lot, so why should they try hard? (3) We group students, sometimes within classrooms, and provide de facto different curricula to different groups. As a result, some students never get the chance to study a high-demand, high-expectation curriculum. (4) College entrance is heavily dependent on tests that have little to do with the curriculum studied and that are designed—like IQ tests—to spread students out on a scale rather than to define what one is supposed to work at learning. (5) Remedial instruction is offered in "pullout" classes, so that students who need extra instruction miss some of the regular learning opportunities. (6) We expect teachers to grade on a curve. If every student gets an A or a B, we assume that standards are too low. We seldom consider the possibility that the students may have worked hard and succeeded in learning what was taught.

These are commonplace, everyday, taken-for-granted features of the American educational landscape. They are institutionalized expressions of a belief in the importance of aptitude. These practices are far more powerful than what we might say about effort and aptitude. Their routine, largely unquestioned use continues to create evidence that confirms aptitude-based thinking. Students do not try to break through the barrier of low expectations because they, like their teachers and parents, accept the judgment that aptitude matters most and that they do not have the right kinds of aptitude. Not surprisingly, their performance remains low. Children who have not been taught a demanding, challenging, thinking curriculum do not do well on tests of reasoning or problem solving, confirming our original suspicions that they did not have the talent for that kind of thinking. The system is a self-sustaining one in which hidden assumptions are continually reinforced by the inevitable results of practices that are based on those assumptions.

Organizing for Effort

It is not necessary to continue this way. Aptitude is not the only possible basis for organizing schools. Educational institutions could be built around the alternative assumption that effort actually creates ability. Our education system could be designed primarily to foster effort. What would such a system look like? How might it work? There are five essential features of an effort-oriented education system: (1) clear expectations for achievement, well understood by everyone, (2) fair and credible evaluations of achievement, (3) celebration and payoff for success, (4) as much time as is necessary to meet learning expectations, and (5) expert instruction. Let us consider each of these features and what the implications may be.

1. Clear expectations.   Achievement standards—publicly announced and meant for everyone—are the essential foundation of an equitable, effort-oriented education system. If students are to work hard, they need to know what they are aiming for. They need not only to try hard, but also to point their efforts in a particular direction. To direct their efforts, students need to know what they are trying to learn, what the criteria of "good" performance are. Artists building a portfolio of work engage in a continuous process of self-evaluation—aided, when they are fortunate, by friendly but critical teachers and peers. If clear standards of achievement existed, elementary and secondary students could work that way, too, building portfolios of work that they continually evaluate, eventually submitting their best work for external "jurying" to see whether it meets the standards they have been working toward.

An equitable standards system must not just make the goals clear but must also set the same expectations for all students. In the absence of publicly defined standards, our inherited assumptions about aptitude lead us to hold out lower expectations for some children than for others. We will go on doing this as long as official standards of achievement do not exist. The best remedy, the equitable solution, is to set clear, public standards that establish very high minimum expectations for everyone, providing a solid foundation for effort by students and teachers alike.

2. Fair and credible evaluations.   If I am to put out serious effort, I need to know that I will be evaluated fairly, and that those evaluations will be honored and respected. But there is more to fairness than the simple absence of bias in tests and examinations: Fair evaluations are also transparent. Students know their content in advance; they can systematically and effectively study for such an evaluation. In America today, students rarely have the experience of studying hard to pass an examination that they know counts in the world and for which they have been systematically prepared by teachers who themselves understand what is to be examined.

Local tests and exams, usually made up by teachers and administered at the end of teaching units or marking periods, may appear to contradict my claim. Students can study for those, and they are clearly related to the taught curriculum. But, especially for students from poor schools, those tests do not really "count." They are not credible to the world at large. It is understood that an A or a B in an inner-city school does not equal the same grade in an upscale suburban or private school.

A credible evaluation system, one that will evoke sustained effort by students and teachers throughout the system, must evaluate students from all kinds of schools against the same criteria. It must include some externally set exams graded by people other than the students' own teachers, along with an external quality control of grades based on class work (as in an audited portfolio grading system, for example). Neither of these is a new idea. Some version of external exams and audited class work is used in virtually every country except ours as the basis for diplomas, university entrance, and employment. Joined with the other elements of an effort-oriented system, this kind of evaluation system constitutes a strategy for optimizing both equity and excellence in our schools.

3. Celebration and the payoff for success.   Hard work and real achievement deserve celebration. And celebration encourages future effort. An education system that actively tries to promote effort will make sure that its schools organize visible, important events highlighting the work students are doing and pointing clearly to achievements that meet the publicly established standards of quality. There are many options for organizing celebrations. School-community nights can become occasions for displaying work, organizing exhibitions, and putting on performances. Local newspapers and radio and television stations can be recruited to publish exemplary student work or otherwise mark achievements. Community organizations can be asked to participate. It is critical that these celebrations include people who matter to the students, and that what is celebrated is work that meets or is clearly en route to meeting the established standards.

For older students, celebration alone may no longer be enough to sustain effort. Adolescents are increasingly concerned with finding their way into adult roles. They will want to see connections between what they are accomplishing in school and the kinds of opportunities that will become available to them when they leave school. This is why many today advocate some kind of high school credential that is based on specific achievements and that is honored for entrance into both college and work. Celebration coupled with payoff will keep the effort flowing; achievement will rise accordingly.

4. Time and results—inverting the relationship.   Schools today provide roughly equal instructional time to all students: a certain number of hours per day, days per year, and years of schooling. As much instruction and learning as can be fitted into that time is offered. Then, at the end of the prescribed period of study, some kind of evaluation takes place. The spread of results confirms the assumptions about aptitude of American schooling.

What if, instead of holding time fixed and allowing results to vary, we did the opposite: set an absolute standard of expectation and allowed time (and the other resources that go with it) to vary? That arrangement would recognize that some students need more time and support than others but would not change expectations according to an initial starting point. Everyone would be held to the same high minimum. Effort could really pay because all students would know that they would have the learning opportunities they need to meet the standards.

Allowing time to vary does not have to mean having young people remain indefinitely in school, repeating the same programs at which they failed the year before. We already know that this kind of additional time produces very little. Instead, schools and associated institutions would need to offer extra learning opportunities early on. For example, pullout instruction could be replaced with enriched, standards-oriented after-school, weekend, and summer programs. Churches, settlement houses, Scouts, 4-H clubs, and other youth service organizations could be asked to join with the schools in providing such programs. A results-oriented system of this kind would bring to all American children the benefits that some now receive in programs organized by their parents and paid for privately.

5. *The right to expert instruction.*   I have been arguing that we ought to create the right to as much instruction as each child needs. That is what the time-results inversion is about. But an equitable system requires more than that. It requires expert instruction for all children. We are far from providing that. With notable exceptions, the best teachers, and, therefore, the best instruction, gravitate to the schools that teach children with the fewest educational problems. Children who start out with the greatest need for expert instruction are the ones least likely to get it.

That will not do. An effort-oriented system that sets high expectations for all will create a demand—indeed, a right—to expert instruction. To fulfill that demand, it will be necessary to create enhanced instruction expertise up and down the teaching force, so that there is enough expert instruction to go around. This means that new forms of professional development, for teachers now in the force as well as for those preparing to enter the field, are an essential ingredient of the standards and effort revolution.

From Effort to Ability

My proposal is, in some respects, a radical one. The effort-oriented education that I am calling for—a system in which everyone in the schools knows what they are working toward, in which they can see clearly how they are doing, and in which effort is recognized in ways that people value—is based on assumptions about the nature of human ability that are very different from those that predominate today. But in other respects, my proposal is a practical and feasible one. It calls for a return in institutional practice to values that most Americans subscribe to: effort, fair play, the chance to keep trying. Most of the elements of the proposal—standards, exams, celebrations of achievement, extended time for those who want to meet a higher standard, expert instruction, and professional development—already exist somewhere in our educational practice. These elements need to be brought together in a few major demonstrations that show the possibilities of effort-oriented practices. Just as aptitude-oriented practices have created evidence that confirms our assumptions about aptitude, so a few effort-oriented demonstrations can begin to create evidence of the power of effort to create ability. As evidence accumulates, beliefs will begin to change, and we can, perhaps, look forward to education in America that is equitable in the deepest sense of the word because it creates ability everywhere.

Kennon M. Sheldon and
Bruce J. Biddle

 **NO**

Standards, Accountability, and School Reform: Perils and Pitfalls

Calls for tough, universal academic standards, more use of national tests, and greater accountability, backed by strong "rewards" or "consequences," are frequently heard in current debates about educational reform. Proponents of such actions seem to assume that problems in American schools occur because educators are not sufficiently focused on the bottom-line issue of student performance. To solve such problems, according to this view, we need to set higher standards for students, assess students' performance with standardized tests, and reward or punish students, their teachers, and their schools, depending on whether those standards are met.

Many aspects of this perspective are problematic. One of the most questionable is the use of tangible rewards or punishments to promote better performance by students and their teachers. As we shall show, many perils can arise when politicians try to graft sanctioning systems onto the educational process. Enthusiasm for the use of such systems seems to reflect a top-down view of human enterprise, in which leaders try to maximize productivity by assigning rote tasks to their followers and ensuring their task performance through the provision of rewards or punishments. This hierarchical view was promoted in the first half of the twentieth century by advocates such as F. W. Taylor and Henry Ford and seemed at that time to be a good way to think about the employees who would staff assembly lines.[1] But today's assembly lines are more often staffed by computerized robots, and advanced thinking in the business world now stresses the need for employee flexibility, creativity, and an ability to transcend intraorganizational boundaries.[2]

This does not mean that accountability and incentive systems will disappear completely from the business world. Businesses tend to have a single, easy-to-measure bottom line: economic profit. Given such a goal, explicit reward and punishment systems can sometimes be useful tools for motivating people to perform tedious, difficult, or dangerous (though profitable) tasks, although we would argue that businesses also pay a hidden price when they over-stress such systems. However, education is a different matter: schools are not businesses run for profit, teachers are not assembly-line workers, and students are not commodities to be turned out with specific skills installed and ready to take their place on the assembly lines of America. Rather, schools are complex organizations, with many goals, whose success is often hard to

From *Teachers College Record*, vol. 100, no. 1, Fall 1998, pp. 164–180. Copyright © 1998 by Columbia University Teachers College. Reprinted by permission via Copyright Clearance Center.

measure. Teachers must cope with a role that is demanding, complex, and moral, and students must be considered as works-in-progress, with multiple interests, unique goals and perspectives,[3] and the enduring potential to construct and reconstruct both themselves and their social worlds—if that potential is not squandered.[4]

Thus, we argue that a key goal of modern education must be to create a population of lifelong, self-directed learners: adults who possess sophisticated interests, an enduring receptivity to new challenges and growth, and a willingness to adapt to the changing needs of the workplace and society-at-large. However, a good deal of research suggests that the practice of bribing or punishing students (and teachers) in order to motivate performance will only thwart this goal. Although such incentives can be used to boost superficial performance in the short run, they are also likely to create an educational climate that alienates teachers from teaching and students from learning. Thus, proposals for educational reform that stress tangible sanctions for performance . . . are not merely questionable, they are disasters waiting to happen.

Our task here is to examine this research and to discuss its implications for current debates about educational reform. Most of the studies we review reflect the concepts and ideas of Deci and Ryan's Self-Determination Theory, so we begin with a general overview of the theory.[5] We next describe four examples of research that support the theory. Finally, we consider what these ideas suggest about the probable effects of simple-minded accountability systems and discuss better strategies for educational reform.

Self-Determination Theory

Self-Determination Theory begins with the concept of intrinsic motivation. *Intrinsically-motivated* behaviors are actions carried out because people enjoy doing them. (In contrast, *externally-motivated* behaviors are engaged in to earn a tangible reward or avoid a punishment.) A huge literature now documents the relative advantages of intrinsic motivation. Although externally-motivated persons can demonstrate impressive feats of short-term, rote learning, intrinsically motivated learners retain such rote material longer, demonstrate a stronger understanding of both rote and more complex material, and demonstrate greater creativity and cognitive flexibility.[6] This happens because intrinsically-motivated persons are more wholly engaged and absorbed in their activities, bringing more of their previous knowledge and integrative capacities to bear in their pursuit of new understanding and mastery.[7]

The concept of intrinsic motivation is also integral to a central philosophical position in the life sciences: the organismic perspective. In this view, humans are assumed to be inherently active, with a natural motivation to explore and assimilate their environments. As they do so, they develop new cognitive structures and abilities.[8] This does not mean that their interests cannot be guided. Indeed, those interests can be channelled, expanded, and stimulated by sensitive mentors who are able to respond to the needs of those who learn. It follows that promoting student interests in socially valued topics through such means is one of the key tasks facing education.[9]

However, the literature makes it clear that states of intrinsic motivation are fragile; they are easily undermined by factors such as concrete rewards, surveillance, contingent praise, and punitive sanctions.[10] The common denominator connecting such factors is that they tend to move the "perceived locus of causality" for the activity outside the person's phenomenal self and into the external environment. When this happens, the person feels like a "pawn," rather than an "origin."[11] And once a person begins to feel like a pawn, it is difficult for him or her to reclaim the self-directed initiative and sense of involvement that promote maximal learning, creativity, and performance.

The organismic perspective makes sharply different assumptions than operant theory, in which people are thought to be inherently passive—acting only to relieve biological drives or secondary motives that have been set up through prior conditioning. Ironically, however, the research we discuss below indicates that operant theory's pessimistic assumptions about human nature *can become true* if people are treated in controlling ways. Thus, before endorsing new top-down initiatives for educational reform, it is very important to consider their potential for depriving students and teachers of intrinsic motivation.

Of course, not all of the things that students and teachers must do are "fun" and enjoyable. Almost all students, for example, will find that learning the multiplication table or a foreign-language vocabulary are dull tasks. Students also have their own unique interests and talents, which may not converge with the particular materials a teacher offers in the classroom. Although teachers should try to make materials interesting for most students, it is unlikely that they can meet the unique needs of everyone. When they cannot, they may instead promote a second positive form of motivation specified in Self-Determination Theory—*identified motivation*. A person has identified motivation when he or she willingly chooses to perform a behavior despite the fact that it is not intrinsically interesting. To illustrate, consider the person who goes to the dentist each year for an annual checkup. This behavior is unlikely to be enjoyable, but the person engages in it because it is thought to be important and valuable. As is the case with intrinsically motivated behavior, the perceived locus of causality for identified motivation also resides within the person's phenomenal self. This is because he or she feels "in charge" and that he or she made the decision to engage in the behavior.

It follows that if we want to produce long-term, self-directed learning among students, our schools should not only promote intrinsic motivation for specific topics but should also help to create identified motivation for life-long learning. This means that students should leave school with the belief that learning is important and valuable, and they should be willing to seek more education without being prodded or forced, even when that education is not intrinsically interesting. From this perspective, a second key task of education is that of helping students to *internalize* the value of learning.

According to Self-Determination Theory, this is often easily accomplished because humans have a natural propensity to take in the values promoted by mentors and authorities. Thus, in their efforts to assimilate and adapt to their environments, students are often willing to be shown which goals and motives are important and may then internalize such ideas. The theory asserts that authorities (i.e., educators) can best facilitate this internalization process by providing support for students' feelings of autonomy.

Three techniques associated with autonomy support have been identified, and all three have been shown to promote increased identification when activities are not intrinsically motivating.[12] Specifically, when asking students to perform such activities, authorities can: (1) acknowledge and validate the person's perspective ("I understand that this may not seem like a lot of fun, and that's O.K."); (2) provide choice whenever possible ("If you'd rather not do it that way, you can choose to do it this way"); and (3) provide a rationale when choice provision is impossible ("It's important to learn these multiplication facts by heart because many of the more interesting things we will do later depend on this knowledge"). When teachers present activities in such ways, students are able to connect their sense of self to the activity and thus are more likely to identify with it. In contrast, when teachers are controlling, that is, dictatorial, coercive, punitive, or uninterested in students' ideas, internalization is forestalled.[13]

The two useful forms of motivation we have discussed (intrinsic and identified) may also be contrasted with two less desirable forms. *Externally motivated* behaviors are those that are done largely or solely to obtain a reward or avoid a punishment. In performing them, the person assigns little value to the activity and feels little or no sense of involvement in doing it. To illustrate: factory workers may perform jobs they consider boring, exhausting, or dangerous, provided they are paid sufficiently. Needless to say, external motivation tends to involve "have to's" and "must's" and is often characterized by cynicism or resignation, where the perceived "locus of causality" lies outside the person.

Finally, *introjected motivation* occurs when persons force themselves to do an activity in order to avoid guilt or anxiety, or in order to protect or shore up their sense of self-esteem. For example, a person may have a bad case of flu and ought to stay in bed, but decides to attend a scheduled meeting because of an earlier promise that he or she would attend. Introjected motivation involves "should's" and "ought's" and is often characterized by feelings of internal pressure; here, the perceived locus of causality also does not lie fully within the person.

Various studies have shown that external and introjected motivation are common among students when teachers are controlling or when they try to use tangible rewards and punishments.[14] Furthermore, research has indicated that neither of these latter forms of motivation promotes the type of deeper conceptual learning that we desire in students and that neither is likely to generate behavior that persists for long in the absence of external prods and support.[15] What this means, then, is that the use of tangible rewards and punishments tends to defeat the goals of creating student interests in both subject matter and self-directed, lifelong learning. Similarly, when teachers are faced by sanctioning systems that generate only external or introjected motivation, they are likely to experience resentment and loss of morale, to engage in superficial conformity, and (eventually) to quit their jobs as teachers.[16]

Specific Studies Applying These Ideas

These ideas suggest that accountability systems can and often do create negative forces that are inimical to key goals of education. In order to illustrate these ideas more concretely, we describe here the results of four specific studies.

The first study, conducted by Deci, examined the effects of two types of instructional sets upon the performance of teachers asked to teach students about spatial relations puzzles.[17] In one condition, teachers were told, "Your role is to facilitate the student's learning how to work with the puzzles. There are no performance requirements; your job is simply to help the student learn to solve the puzzles." In the other condition teachers were told, "Your role is to ensure that the student learns to solve the puzzles. It is a teacher's responsibility to make sure that students perform up to standards." Thus, the study provided two very different types of instructional set: one in which student understanding was the goal; the other which stressed the need for students to perform "up to standards."

The investigators found sharp differences in the ways in which teachers behaved given these two conditions. Specifically, teachers in the "performance standards" condition talked more and used more controlling strategies (i.e., they issued more "should" statements and made more criticisms of students). Furthermore, they let students solve far fewer puzzles on their own. Although students in this condition completed more puzzles, only in four percent of cases were they allowed to solve the puzzles by themselves. In contrast, students in the "learning only" condition solved 30 percent of completed puzzles by themselves and rated the teacher as promoting greater understanding. Thus, although students with controlling teachers may have appeared to accomplish more, they actually learned less because their teachers were, in essence, doing the puzzles for them. Findings such as these surely challenge the vaunted "advantages" of telling teachers they must make sure their students meet higher performance standards!

Grolnick and Ryan made a related point in a study of reading performance outcomes among fifth-grade children.[18] Specifically, they examined the effects of three types of task-set on students' ability to comprehend the conceptual meaning of a reading passage. Students in the first, *nondirected* condition were told simply, "After you are finished, I'll be asking you some questions." Grading and evaluation were not mentioned. In effect, students were "turned loose" to find their own ways of becoming interested in the material.

Students in a second, *directed* (but noncontrolling) condition were told, "After you're finished, I'm going to ask you some questions about the passage. It won't really be a test, and you won't be graded on it. I'm just interested in what children can remember from reading passages." This manipulation focused students' attention on the goal of learning without emphasizing an ensuing test, thus inviting them to develop identified motivation for the task.

In contrast, students in a third, *controlling* condition were told, "After you are finished, I'm going to test you on it. I'm going to see how much you can remember. You should work as hard as you can because I'll be grading you on the test to see if you're learning well enough." This manipulation was designed, of course, to give students an external locus of causality for their learning. (In effect they were led to believe, "I'm doing this reading largely or solely because of the upcoming test.")

As expected, students given the first, nondirected instructions indicated the most *interest* in the text and felt the least *pressure*. Conversely, students in the third, or controlling, condition felt the most pressure and indicated the least interest. In addition, post-testing showed that students in the controlling condition had the poorest conceptual *understanding* of the material taught, and although they displayed a high level of recall for *rote material* from the reading lesson when tested immediately afterward, they also experienced a large drop in rote recall when retested eight days later. In contrast, nondirected students showed the strongest conceptual understanding of the material they had read and forgot very little of its rote details. In effect, these students had engaged in deeper processing of the information and had integrated that information more fully with their preexisting knowledge.

Interestingly, students in the second, directed (but noncontrolling) condition displayed respectable levels of both understanding and rote recall. This indicates that directive teaching is not necessarily problematic, but it can become a problem when it crosses the line into a controlling mode. And as the first study we reviewed suggests, this threshold is more likely to be crossed when teachers feel pressures from above to ensure that their students perform to high standards.

Of course, teachers do not necessarily become more controlling when performance pressure is imposed from above.[19] Some teachers may have the skills and insights to resist temptations to "bludgeon" their students into learning. There is, however, another way in which top-down performance pressures can generate detrimental effects—when they prompt politicians, education officials, or parents to impose tangible rewards and punishments on students for their performance. Various studies[20] have shown that, when left to their own devices, children will select tasks that are neither too easy nor too hard—tasks just above their current level of skills and understanding. This is consistent with tenets of the organismic perspective, in which humans are assumed to have a natural propensity to seek out optimal challenges as they engage with and assimilate their environments—and when this happens, they tend also to learn at an optimal rate. However, research[21] also shows that this tendency for students to prefer optimal challenges is easily subverted by the introduction of tangible sanctions. . . .

Implications for Reform Proposals That Stress Testing and Sanctioning

With these ideas and findings in mind, let us examine four specific perils which can accompany the testing-and-sanctioning approach to education.

> *Peril #1: Too much focus on tests can lead teachers to adopt a narrowed curriculum, dampening student interest and inhibiting critical thinking.*

When strong emphasis is placed on tests and how student performances "stack up," teachers may narrow their curriculum, teach to the test, or encourage students to focus only on knowing how to get the right answers to test-type questions. One problem with such processes is that students' ability to think broadly may be throttled. In addition, they can stultify intrinsic motivation in the subject and thus forestall the self-directed exploration that is crucial to deeper understanding and mastery.

> *Peril #2: Teacher incentive systems tied to student test scores often cause teachers to become more controlling, thus undermining students' conceptual learning, intrinsic interest in the subject matter, and desire to pursue future education.*

Problems associated with too much focus on tests are magnified when those test results are used by central authorities to generate rewards and punishments for teachers. When teachers' livelihoods are tied to test results, they become less willing to let students explore and experiment with subject materials and may instead become more controlling in their presentations. Furthermore, these teachers readily transmit their own externally based motivation to students, quickly eroding whatever intrinsic subject-matter interests students may have had. For example, Wild, Enzle, and Hawkins showed that musically naive students given a piano lesson reacted very differently if they thought the teacher was motivated by extrinsic concerns rather than intrinsic interest in teaching the lesson. In this study, the teacher was blind to experimental conditions and gave the same lesson to all students. However, students who believed their teacher was intrinsically motivated enjoyed the lesson more, were more interested in further learning, and demonstrated greater exploratory activity during subsequent free play.[22]

> *Peril #3: Student incentive systems tied to test scores can ruin students' intrinsic interest in subject matter and reduce their willingness to challenge themselves.*

Thus far we have discussed how accountability systems may affect teachers. But problems with accountability are worsened when students are given tangible rewards or punishments for their performance. To illustrate, some school districts today punish students who have failing grades by denying them opportunities to participate in extracurricular activities, such as school-sponsored parties or picnics. Such sanctioning systems are likely to cause students to seek the easiest path to better grades rather than to follow their natural (but fragile) propensities to choose optimally challenging tasks.

> *Peril #4: To the extent that accountability systems are seen as a panacea, they can distract us from dealing with the real problems of education.*

More than ever before, students bring problems to the classroom that interfere with their ability to concentrate and learn. Today, many, many American children grow up in poverty, spend their days in miserably funded schools,[23] are surrounded by drugs and violence, receive insufficient attention from parents in dual-career households, and are strongly exposed to the materialistic values and negative role models portrayed in the media. Is it any wonder, then, that they have difficulty with school? Some politicians love to make scapegoats out of teachers and blame them when students do not always succeed in school, but this merely diverts attention from serious social problems those politicians do not want to address. Moreover, those escalating problems mean that the teacher's job today is more difficult than in earlier years. The last thing teachers need is more controlling oversight by politicians and their minions, wielding questionable test scores, focused on narrow domains of academic competence. Instead, the intrinsic motivation that caused teachers to choose this difficult and monetarily unrewarding field in the first place should be nurtured and protected.

Does this mean that teachers will always reject demands for evaluation of their performance? Indeed it does not. Teachers, like other Americans, generally approve of accountability, paying higher wages to persons with outstanding accomplishments, and helping or dismissing those who are incompetent. The problem for teachers, however, is to find legitimate ways to measure their accomplishments in education. Americans set many goals for teaching. Those goals are hard to assess, and teachers who fail to accomplish one or more of them may succeed gloriously in others. Teachers know this: hence, they tend to reject accountability schemes that rely on narrow, simple-minded performance measures. It is possible to imagine an accountability scheme, however, that would assess a wide range of educational goals with sophisticated instruments, and such a scheme might well be embraced by teachers.

In contrast, given the nature of the learning process, accountability schemes that impose sanctions for academic performance on students are almost bound to fail. Learning is best facilitated when students have intrinsic interest in the subject matter, or at least, an identified interest in the task of learning it. But both of these types of motivation are inhibited when student attention is focused on achievement tests and sanctions. Thus, we discover an apparent paradox that applies to student learning. Although maximal student growth may be the goal, if student attention is focused on tests that measure that growth, or on sanctions that reward or punish it, that growth will not be maximized. In contrast, if students are challenged, if their interests in the subject matter are encouraged, if they are given autonomy support, then their intrinsic interests, their motivation for learning, and their test scores will all grow more effectively.

Better Strategies for Reform

The ideas and studies we have reviewed also suggest principles that can be used to guide better reform strategies. For one thing, they suggest that such strategies will be more successful if they are based on trust in students and teachers—if they assume that most students want to learn and most teachers want to teach. Many things can and should be improved in today's classrooms and schools: among them, poor and overcrowded facilities, outdated textbooks, procedures that give too much stress to competition, tracking, lock-step education, and curricula that promote sloth, ignorance, boredom, or prejudice. But these problems are not likely to disappear if we try to force teachers and students to "shape up." Instead, reforms are more likely to succeed if they involve the active and willing participation of teachers and students. This can be done, of course, through encouragement, challenge, and appropriate autonomy-support; that is, through minimizing the salience of external—controls and potential sanctions and emphasizing students' and teachers' rights to be taken seriously, to participate in activities they consider interesting, and to understand the educational importance of other activities in which they have little intrinsic interest. The more such processes occur, the more students and teachers will be encouraged to involve themselves in education, and the greater will be students' growth of knowledge and achievement.

Most teachers know that these goals are important; indeed, many have already received explicit training in how to bring them about. What is needed now is to create a political and administrative climate in which all teachers can be given this knowledge and supported in using it. Or, to return to our opening metaphor, instead of being viewed as assembly-line workers who must be forced to do their jobs, teachers should be given the same types of trust and respect we give to other *professionals*.

Can you imagine calls to impose tough, universal standards for performance, the use of narrow, standardized tests to measure that performance, and sanctions, based on those test scores, upon doctors, physicists, the clergy, or Supreme Court justices? The mind boggles. The reason such proposals would be thought absurd is that we assume that the professional roles of doctors, physicists, and the like are complex, that success in them is hard to measure, and that those who perform them are thoroughly trained, highly motivated, and generally competent to do their jobs. This does not mean, of course, that all such professionals are equally competent, and we count on their professional associations (and the law) to detect, review, and ultimately to cashier those who are truly incompetent. But generally we bestow high status, authority, good salaries, and trust on such professionals—and public school teachers should be given the same grace.

Notes

1. Frederick W. Taylor, *The Principles of Scientific Management* (Westport, CT: Greenwood Press, 1911). See also Raymond Callahan, *Education and the Cult of Efficiency* (New York: Free Press, 1962).

2. Barry Jones, *Sleepers Wake: Technology and the Future of Work* (Melbourne: Oxford University Press, 1982); J. Hirsch, "Fordism and Post-Fordism: The Present Social Crisis and its Consequences," in *Post-Fordism and Social Form,* ed. W. Bonefeld and J. Holloway (Basingstoke, England: Macmillan, 1991), pp. 8–32; and Susan L. Robertson, "Restructuring Teachers' Labor: 'Troubling' Post-Fordisms," in *International Handbook of Teachers and Teaching,* ed. B. J. Biddle, T. L. Good, and I. J. Goodson (Dordrecht, The Netherlands: Kluwer, 1997), pp. 621–70.

3. Kennon M. Sheldon and Tim Kasser, "Coherence and Congruence: Two Aspects of Personality Integration." *Journal of Personality and Social Psychology*, 68 (1995): 531–43.

4. See, among other sources, John Dewey's *Moral Principles in Education* (Boston: Houghton Mifflin, 1909) or *Democracy and Education* (New York: Macmillan, 1916).

5. See Edward L. Deci and Richard M. Ryan, *Intrinsic Motivation and Self-Determination in Human Behavior* (New York: Plenum, 1985); and Edward L. Deci and Richard M. Ryan, "A Motivational Approach to Self: Integration in Personality," in R. Dienstbier, Ed., *Nebraska Symposium on Motivation* (Lincoln, NE: University of Nebraska Press, 1991), pp. 237–88.

6. Kennon M. Sheldon, "Creativity and Self-Determination in Personality," *Creativity Research Journal*, 8 (1995): 61–72.

7. Richard M. Ryan and Jerome Stiller, "The Social Contexts of Internalization: Parent and Teacher Influences on Autonomy, Motivation, and Learning," *Advances in Motivation and Achievement*, 7 (1991): 115–49.

8. John Dewey, *Experience and Education* (New York: Collier, 1938); and Jean Piaget, *Biology and Knowledge* (Chicago: University of Chicago Press, 1971).

9. Russell Ames and Carole Ames, "Motivation and Effective Teaching," in L. Idol & B. F. Hones, Eds., *Educational Values and Cognitive Instruction: Implications for Reform* (Hillsdale, NJ: Lawrence Erlbaum, 1991), pp. 247–71; Carol S. Dweck, "Social Motivation: Goals and Social-Cognitive Processes. A Comment," in J. Juvonen and K. R. Wentzel, Eds., *Social Motivation: Understanding Children's School Adjustment* (New York: Cambridge University Press, 1996), pp. 181–95; and Mark R. Lepper, Sheena Sethi, Dania Dialdin, and Michael Drake, "Intrinsic and Extrinsic Motivation: A Development Perspective" in S. S. Luthar, J. A. Burack, D. Cicchetti, and J. R. Weisz, Eds., *Developmental Psychopathology: Perspectives on Adjustment, Risk, and Disorder* (New York: Cambridge University Press, 1997), pp. 23–50.

10. See Deci & Ryan, "Motivational Approach to Self," for a review of this evidence.

11. Richard deCharms, *Personal Causation: The Internal Affective Determinants of Behavior* (New York: Academic Press, 1968).

12. See Edward L. Deci, Haleh Eghrari, Brian Patrick, and Dean Leone, "Facilitating Internalization: The Self-Determination Theory Perspective," *Journal of Personality*, 62 (1994): 119–42.

13. Christine Chandler and Jim Connell, "Children's Intrinsic, Extrinsic, and Internalized Motivation: A Development Study of Children's Reasons for Liked and Disliked Behavior," *British Journal of Developmental Psychology*, 5 (1987): 357–65.

14. Edward L. Deci, Allan Schwartz, Louise Sheinman, and Richard M. Ryan, "An Instrument to Assess Adults' Orientations Toward Control Versus Autonomy with Children: Reflections on Intrinsic Motivation and Perceived Competence," *Journal of Educational Psychology*, 73 (1981): 642–50.

15. Mark Lepper and David Greene, "Turning Play Into Work: Effects of Adult Surveillance and Extrinsic Rewards on Children's Intrinsic Motivation," *Journal of Personality and Social Psychology*, 31 (1975): 479–86.

16. See Anthony G. Dworkin, *Teacher Burnout in the Public Schools: Structural Causes and Consequences for Children* (Albany: State University of New York Press, 1987); and ibid., "Coping with Reform: The Intermix of Teacher Morale, Teacher Burnout, and Teacher Accountability," in *International Handbook of Teachers and Teaching,* ed. Biddle, Good, and Goodson, pp. 459–98.

17. Edward L. Deci, Nancy H. Spiegel, Richard M. Ryan, Richard Koestner, and M. Christina Kauffman, "The Effects of Performance Standards on Teaching Styles: The Behavior of Controlling Teachers," *Journal of Educational Psychology,* 74 (1982): 852–59.

18. Wendy S. Grolnick and Richard M. Ryan, "Autonomy in Children's Learning: An Experimental and Individual Differences Investigation," *Journal of Personality and Social Psychology,* 52 (1987): 890–898.

19. See Cheryl Flink, Ann K. Boggiano, and Marty Barrett, "Controlling Teaching Strategies: Undermining Children's Self-determination and Performance," *Journal of Personality and Social Psychology,* 42 (1982): 789–97.

20. See Ryan and Stiller, "The Social Contexts of Internalization."

21. Pittman, Emery, and Boggiano, "Intrinsic and Extrinsic Motivational Orientations."

22. See Cameron Wild, Michael Enzle, and Wendy Hawkins, "Effects of Perceived Extrinsic vs. Intrinsic Teacher Motivation on Student Reactions to Skill Acquisition," *Personality and Social Psychology Bulletin,* 1 (1992): 245–51.

23. Bruce J. Biddle, "Foolishness, Dangerous Nonsense, and Real Correlates of State Differences in Achievement," *Phi Delta Kappan,* September 1997, pp. 9–13.

POSTSCRIPT

Will a Push for Standards and Accountability Lead to More Motivated Students?

Sheldon and Biddle offer considerable evidence—most of it from experimental rather than correlational studies—that external rewards or systems of control either decrease students' intrinsic motivation to engage in the controlled activity or leads teachers to alter their behavior in the direction of greater control over the learning process, which in turn limits student motivation. Unfortunately, there are several limitations of the data presented by Sheldon and Biddle that make it impossible to conclude with certainty what effect standards reform will have on student motivation.

Consider two limitations: First, in the research cited by Sheldon and Biddle, the rewards or punishments were grades, prizes, or other relatively minor consequences, and their delivery was contingent on a vague specification of "doing well." Supporters of standards would argue that their plans are very different from the plans embodied in these studies because their plans involve a clearly articulated set of goals associated with far-reaching consequences (e.g., nonpromotion). Second, the studies cited by Sheldon and Biddle were all short-term, involving an assessment of outcomes only a few days or weeks after implementation of the system of external control. It is possible, argue supporters of standards, that the negative effects of an external system of control are transient—a possibility that would require examining student motivation over the course of several semesters or even years.

There are many articles on the issue of standards and accountability. Two papers that focus on the positive elements of standards reform are "Core Knowledge and Standards: A Conversation with E. D. Hirsch, Jr.," by John O'Neill, *Educational Leadership* (March 1999) and "Realizing the Promise of Standards-Based Education," by Mike Schmoker and Robert J. Marzano, *Educational Leadership* (March 1999). Several interesting papers have focused on the establishment of standards in particular content domains, most notably mathematics: "Parrot Math," by Thomas C. O'Brien, *Phi Delta Kappan* (February 1999); "Issues and Options in the Math Wars," by Harold L. Schoen et al., *Phi Delta Kappan* (February 1999); and "A Common Core of Math for All," by Arthur F. Coxford and Christian R. Hirsch, *Educational Leadership* (May 1996). The impact of the push for standards and accountability on multicultural education and the marginalization of students from the nonmajority culture can be found in "Multicultural Education and the Standards Movement: A Report from the Field," by Anita P. Bohn and Christine E. Sleeter, *Phi Delta Kappan* (October 2000).

ISSUE 11

Do Recent Discoveries about the Brain and Its Development Have Implications for Classroom Practice?

YES: **Eric P. Jensen**, from "A Fresh Look at Brain-Based Education," *Phi Delta Kappan* (February, 2008)

NO: **Gerald Coles**, from "Danger in the Classroom: 'Brain Glitch' Research and Learning to Read," *Phi Delta Kappan* (January 2004)

ISSUE SUMMARY

YES: Eric P. Jensen, from the University of California, San Diego and co-founder of the Brain Store and the Learning Brain Expo, argues that recent findings from neuroscience research have important and immediate implications for classroom practices.

NO: Gerald Coles, an educational psychologist who writes regularly on a range of educational issues, considers current claims about the neural bases of reading problems. He concludes that the research is often ambiguous about whether learning problems arise from differences in brain structure or function or from limitations in experience or skill, which in turn affect brain development.

Research in the brain sciences has proceeded at a rapid pace since the 1970s, due in large measure to the advent of some amazing new technologies including positron emission tomography (PET), single photon emission computed tomography (SPECT), magnetic resonance imaging (MRI), functional magnetic imaging (fMRI), and high-density event-related potentials (HD-ERP). These technologies provide high-resolution images of the human brain, yielding information about not only structural characteristics but also about how the brain functions "online" as an individual processes perceptual information, solves complex problems, or makes responses as simple as a button press or as complex as a spoken sentence. Some of these techniques require sedation, exposure to radiation, and injections and are thus of limited utility with young children. Other techniques, however, are noninvasive, typically requiring only that the individual whose brain is being "imaged" sit motionless in a special apparatus while performing the cognitive task being studied, which means that many of these techniques can provide a window into the brains of even very young children.

A few of the findings that have captured the attention of educators (not to mention the news media) in recent years follow:

1. In contrast to what was believed only a few years ago, the structure and function of the human brain is not fixed at birth. It now appears that the brain undergoes dramatic changes in connectedness during infancy. The many neurons (nerve cells) in the baby's brain establish increasing information-exchanging links with each other. The number of connections, or synapses, increases more than 20 times during the first few months of life.
2. The timing of synaptic development varies across different parts of the human brain, which may account in part for the different behavioral capabilities of children at different ages. For example, at 18 to 24 months, a dramatic increase in synaptic density and changes in the metabolic activity of the brain may help to produce the burst in vocabulary learning normally seen at this time.
3. At the same time that synaptic growth is providing the foundation for new skills and capabilities, it is closing off other avenues of learning. For example, there is evidence that early in infancy neurons in the auditory cortex are responsive to a range of speech sounds. As the infant gains exposure to his or her native language, however, neurons become more specialized, responding only to specific, frequently heard sounds, which leaves them "unresponsive" to unfamiliar speech sounds, such as those included in other languages. This seems to occur by 12 months of age.
4. There is evidence that brain regions that are normally responsible for one function can assume other functions depending on the experiences available to the individual. For example, portions of the temporal lobe that are responsive to sound in individuals with normal hearing are sensitive to visual stimuli in congenitally deaf individuals.
5. Chronic traumatic experiences during periods of rapid brain growth can lead to greatly elevated levels of stress hormones, which then flood the brain, altering its structure and function, with serious long-lasting consequences for subsequent learning and behavior.

Educators have enthusiastically embraced findings emerging from work in the brain sciences. After all, our understanding of the brain informs us about learning; doesn't it follow that our understanding of the brain will inform us about teaching as well? In the first of the following selections, Eric P. Jensen argues that current research on brain function does inform educational practice. In the second selection, Gerald Coles argues that research on the brain is often misinterpreted as indicating that learning problems are caused by unusual patterns of brain activation when it is equally plausible that limited experiences or skill actually lead to those patterns of brain activation.

YES

Eric P. Jensen

A Fresh Look at Brain-Based Education

Ten years ago John Bruer, executive administrator of the James S. McDonnell Foundation, began a series of articles critical of brain-based education. They included "Education and the Brain: A Bridge Too Far" (1997), "In Search of . . . Brain-Based Education" (1999), and, most recently, "On the Implications of Neuroscience Research for Science Teaching and Learning: Are There Any?" (2006). Bruer argued that educators should ignore neuroscience and focus on what psychologists and cognitive scientists have already discovered about teaching and learning. His message to educators was "hands off the brain research," and he predicted it would be 25 years before we would see practical classroom applications of the new brain research. Bruer linked brain-based education with tabloid mythology by announcing that, if brain-based education is true, then "the pyramids were built by aliens—to house Elvis."

Because of Bruer's and others' critiques, many educators decided that they were simply not capable of understanding how our brain works. Other educators may have decided that neuroscience has nothing to offer and that the prudent path would be simply to ignore the brain research for now and follow the yellow brick road to No Child Left Behind. Maybe some went so far as to say, "What's the brain got to do with learning?" But brain-based education has withstood the test of time, and an accumulating body of empirical and experiential evidence confirms the validity of the new model.

Many educationally significant, even profound, brain-based discoveries have occurred in recent years, such as that of neurogenesis, the production of new neurons in the human brain. It is highly likely that these discoveries would have been ignored if the education profession hadn't been primed, alerted, and actively monitoring cognitive neuroscience research and contemplating its implications and applications. Here, I wish to discuss how understanding the brain and the complementary research can have practical educational applications. I will make a case that narrowing the discussion to only neurobiology (and excluding other brain-related sciences) diminishes the opportunity for all of us to learn about how we learn and about better ways to teach. In addition, I will show how the synergy of biology, cognitive science, and education can support better education with direct application to schools.

In 1983 a new model was introduced that established connections between brain function and educational practice. In a groundbreaking book,

From *Phi Delta Kappan*, February 2008, pp. 409–413, 414–417. Copyright © 2008 by Eric P. Jensen. Reprinted by permission of Phi Delta Kappan and Eric P. Jensen.

Human Brain, Human Learning, Leslie Hart argued, among other things, that cognitive processes were significantly impaired by classroom threat. While not an earthshaking conclusion, the gauntlet was thrown down, as if to say, "If we ignore how the student brain works, we will risk student success." Many have tied brain function to new models either of thinking or of classroom pedagogy. A field has emerged known as "brain-based" education, and it has now been well over 20 years since this "connect the dots" approach began. In a nutshell, brain-based education says, "Everything we do uses our brain; let's learn more about it and apply that knowledge."

A discussion of this topic could fill books, but the focus here will be on two key issues. First, how can we define the terms, scope, and role of brain research in education? That is, what are the disciplines and relevant issues that should concern educators? These issues are multidisciplinary. Evidence will show that "brain-based" is not a loner's fantasy or narrow-field model; it's a significant educational paradigm of the 21st century. Second, what is the evidence, if any, that brain research can actually help educators do our job better? Is there now credibility to this burgeoning field? What issues have critics raised? Can the brain-based advocates respond to the critics in an empirical way?

Defining Brain-Based Education

Let's start this discussion with a simple but essential premise: the brain is intimately involved in and connected with everything educators and students do at school. Any disconnect is a recipe for frustration and potential disaster. Brain-based education is best understood in three words: engagement, strategies, and principles. Brain-based education is the "engagement of strategies based on principles derived from an understanding of the brain." Notice this definition does *not* say, "based on strategies given to us by neuroscientists." That's not appropriate. Notice it does not say, "based on strategies exclusively from neuroscience and no other discipline." The question is, Are the approaches and strategies based on solid research from brain-related disciplines, or are they based on myths, a well-meaning mentor teacher, or "junk science"? We would expect an educator to be able to support the use of a particular classroom strategy with scientific reasoning or studies.

Each educator ought to be professional enough to say, "Here's *why* I do what I do." I would ask: Is the person actually *engaged in using* what he or she knows, or does he or she simply have knowledge about it without actually using it? Are teachers using strategies based on the science of how our brain works? Brain-based education is about the professionalism of knowing why one strategy is used instead of another. The science is based on what we know about how our brain works. It's the professionalism to be research-based in one's practices. Keep in mind that if you don't know *why* you do what you do, it's less purposeful and less professional. It is probably your collected, refined wisdom. Nothing wrong with that, but some "collected, refined wisdom" has led to some bad teaching, too.

While I have, for years, advocated "brain-based" education, I never have promoted it as the "exclusive" discipline for schools to consider. That's narrow-minded. On the other hand, the brain is involved in everything we do at school. To ignore it would be irresponsible. Thus an appropriate question is, Where exactly is this research coming from?

The Broader Scope of Brain-Based Education

Brain-based education has evolved over the years. Initially it seemed focused on establishing a vocabulary with which to understand the new knowledge. As a result, many of us heard for the first time about axons, dendrites, serotonin, dopamine, the hippocampus, and the amygdala. That was the "first generation" of brain basics, the generation that introduced a working platform for today's generation. There was no harm in doing that, but knowing a few words from a neuroscience textbook certainly doesn't make anyone a better teacher. Times have changed. The brain-based movement has moved on from its infancy of new words and pretty brain scans.

Today's knowledge base comes from a rapidly emerging set of brain-related disciplines. It isn't published in just highly regarded journals such as *Nature*, *Science*, and the *Journal of Neuroscience*. Every people-related discipline takes account of the brain. As an example, psychiatry is now guided by the journal *Biological Psychiatry*, and nutrition is better understood by reading the journal *Nutritional Neuroscience*. Sociology is guided by the journal *Social Neuroscience*. Some critics assert that sociology, physical fitness, psychiatry, nutrition, psychology, and cognitive science are not "brain-based." That's absurd, because if you remove the brain's role from any of those disciplines, there would be no discipline. There is no separation of brain, mind, body, feelings, social contacts, or their respective environments. That assertion is old-school, "turf-based," and outdated. If the research involves the brain in any way, it is "brain-based." The brain is involved in everything we do.

The current model of brain-based education is highly interdisciplinary. Antonio Damasio, the Van Allen Distinguished Professor and head of the department of neurology at the University of Iowa Medical Center and an adjunct professor at the Salk Institute in La Jolla, California, says, "The relation between brain systems and complex cognition and behavior, can only be explained satisfactorily by *a comprehensive blend of theories* and facts related to *all the levels of organization* of the nervous system, from molecules, and cells and circuits, to large-scale systems and physical and social environments. . . . We must beware of explanations that rely on data from one single level, whatever the level may be." Any single discipline, even cognitive neuroscience, should be buttressed by other disciplines. While earlier writings did not reflect it, today we know that brain-based learning cannot be founded on neuroscience; we have learned that it requires a multidisciplinary approach.

The Brain Is Our Common Denominator

Today, many of the school- and learning-related disciplines are looking to the brain for answers. There's no separating the role of the brain and the influence of classroom groupings, lunchroom foods, school architecture, mandated curricula, and state assessments. Each of them affects the brain, and our brain affects each of them. Schools, assessment, environments, and instruction are not bound by one discipline, such as cognitive science, but by multiple disciplines. In short, schools work to the degree that the brains in the schools are working well. When there's a mismatch between the brain and the environment, something at a school will suffer.

Schools present countless opportunities to affect students' brains. Such issues as stress, exercise, nutrition, and social conditions are all relevant, brain-based issues that affect cognition, attention, classroom discipline, attendance, and memory. Our new understanding is that every school day changes the student's brain in some way. Once we make those connections, we can make choices in how we prioritize policies and strategies. Here are some of the powerful connections for educators to make.

1. The human brain can and does grow new neurons. Many survive and become functional. We now know that new neurons are highly correlated with memory, mood, and learning. Of interest to educators is that this process can be regulated by our everyday behaviors. Specifically, it can be enhanced by exercise, lower levels of stress, and good nutrition. Schools can and should influence these variables. This discovery came straight from neuroscientists Gerd Kempermann and Fred Gage.

2. Social conditions influence our brain in ways we didn't know before. The discovery of mirror neurons by Giacomo Rizzolatti and his colleagues at the University of Parma in Italy suggests a vehicle for an imitative reciprocity in our brain. This emerging discipline is explored in *Social Neuroscience,* a new academic journal exploring how social conditions affect the brain. School behaviors are highly social experiences, which become encoded through our sense of reward, acceptance, pain, pleasure, coherence, affinity, and stress. This understanding suggests that we be more active in managing the social environment of students, because students are more affected by it than we thought. It may unlock clues to those with autism, since their mirror neurons are inactive. This discovery suggests that schools should not rely on random social grouping and should work to strengthen prosocial conditions.

3. The ability of the brain to rewire and remap itself by means of neuroplasticity is profound. The new *Journal of Neuroplasticity* explores these and related issues. Schools can influence this process through skill-building, reading, meditation, the arts, career and technical education, and thinking skills that build student success. . . . Without understanding the "rules for how our brain changes," educators can waste time and money, and students will fall through the cracks.

4. Chronic stress is a very real issue at schools for both staff and students. Homeostasis is no longer a guaranteed "set point." The discovery championed by neuroscientist Bruce McEwen is that a revised metabolic state called "allostasis" is an adjusted new baseline for stress that is evident in the brains of those with anxiety and stress disorders. These pathogenic allostatic stress loads are becoming increasingly common and have serious health, learning, and behavior risks. This issue affects

attendance, memory, social skills, and cognition. Acute and chronic stress is explored in *The International Journal of Stress Management, The Journal of Anxiety, The Journal of Traumatic Stress,* and *Stress.*

5. The old-school view was that either environment or genes decided the outcomes for a student. We now know that there's a third option: gene expression. This is the capacity of our genes to respond to chronic or acute environmental input. This new understanding highlights a new vehicle for change in our students. Neuroscientists Bruce Lipton and Ernest Rossi have written about how our everyday behaviors can influence gene expression. New journals called *Gene Expression, Gene Expression Patterns,* and *Nature Genetics* explore the mechanisms for epigenetic (outside of genes) changes. Evidence suggests that gene expression can be regulated by what we do at schools and that this can enhance or harm long-term change prospects.

6. Good nutrition is about far more than avoiding obesity. The journals *Nutritional Neuroscience* and the *European Journal of Clinical Nutrition* explore the effects on our brain of what we eat. The effects on cognition, memory, attention, stress, and even intelligence are now emerging. Schools that pay attention to nutrition and cognition (not just obesity) will probably support better student achievement.

7. The role of the arts in schools continues to come under great scrutiny. Five neuroscience departments and universities (University of Oregon, Harvard University, University of Michigan, Dartmouth College, and Stanford University) currently have projects studying the impact of the arts on the brain. *Arts and Neuroscience* is a new journal that tracks the connections being made by researchers. This is a serious topic for neuroscience, and it should be for educators also. Issues being explored are whether the arts have transfer value and the possibility of developmentally sensitive periods for the arts.

8. The current high-stakes testing environment means some educators are eliminating recess, play, or physical education from the daily agendas. The value of exercise to the brain was highlighted in a recent cover story in *Newsweek.* More important, there are many studies examining this connection in *The Journal of Exercise, Pediatric Exercise Science,* and *The Journal of Exercise Physiology Online.* The weight of the evidence is that exercise is strongly correlated with increased brain mass, better cognition, mood regulation, and new cell production. This information was unknown a generation ago.

9. Stunning strides have been made in the rehabilitation of brain-based disorders, including fetal alcohol syndrome, autism, retardation, strokes, and spinal cord injury. It is now clear that aggressive behavioral therapies, new drugs, and stem cell implantation can be used to influence, regulate, and repair brain-based disorders. *The Journal of Rehabilitation* and *The International Journal of Rehabilitation Research* showcase innovations suggesting that special education students may be able to improve far more than we once thought.

10. The discovery that environments alter our brains is profound. This research goes back decades to the early work of the first trailblazing

biological psychologists: Mark Rosenzweig at the University of California, Berkeley, and Bill Greenough at the University of Illinois, Urbana-Champaign. In fact, a new collaboration has emerged between neuroscientists and architects. "The mission of the Academy of Neuroscience for Architecture" according to the group's website, "is to promote and advance knowledge that links neuroscience research to a growing understanding of human responses to the built environment." This is highly relevant for administrators and policy makers who are responsible for school building designs.

Since our brain is involved in everything we do, the next question is, Is our brain fixed, or is it malleable? Is our brain shaped by experience? An overwhelming body of evidence shows our brain is altered by everyday experiences, such as learning to read, learning vocabulary, studying for tests, or learning to play a musical instrument. Studies confirm the success of software programs that use the rules of brain plasticity to retrain the visual and auditory systems to improve attention, hearing, and reading. Therefore, it stands to reason that altering our experiences will alter our brain. This is a simple but profound syllogism: our brain is involved in all we do, our brain changes from experience, therefore our experiences at school will change our brain in some way. Instead of narrowing the discussion about brain research in education to dendrites and axons, a contemporary discussion would include a wider array of topics. Brain-based education says that we use evidence from all disciplines to enhance the brains of our students. The brain is involved with everything we do at school, and educators who understand take this fact into consideration in the decision-making process.

Brain-Based Education in Action

An essential understanding about brain-based education is that most neuroscientists don't teach and most teachers don't do research. It's unrealistic to expect neuroscientists to reveal which classroom strategies will work best. That's not appropriate for neuroscientists, and most don't do that. Many critics could cite this as a weakness, but it's not. Neuroscience and many related disciplines (e.g., genetics, chemistry, endocrinology) are what we refer to as basic science. The work is done in labs, and the science is more likely to provide general guidelines or to suggest future directions for research. Of all the neuroscience studies published each month, only a small fraction have potential relevance for education.

Clinical and cognitive research are mid-level research domains. In clinical and cognitive studies, humans are more likely (but not always) to be subjects in controlled conditions. Finally, applied research is typically done "in context," such as in a school. Each domain has different advantages and disadvantages. Critics of using neuroscience for educational decision making assert that the leap is too great from basic science to the classroom. I agree with that assertion; education must be multidisciplinary. I never have proposed, and never will, that schools be run solely based on neuroscience. But to ignore the research is equally irresponsible. Let's use a typical example that is "pushed" by the brain-based advocates, such as myself. . . .

Is There Evidence That Brain Research Can Help Educators?

This question is highly relevant for all educators. To repeat our definition, brain-based teaching is the active engagement of practical strategies based on principles derived from brain-related sciences. All teachers use strategies; the difference here is that you're using strategies based on real science, not rumor or mythology. But the strategies ought to be generated by verifiable, established principles. An example of a principle would be "Brains change based on experience." The science tells us how they change in response to experience. For example, we know that behaviorally relevant repetition is a smart strategy for learning skills. We know that intensity and duration matter. Did anyone 20 years ago know the optimal protocols for skill-building to maximize brain change? Yes, some knew them through trial and error. But at issue is not whether any educator has learned a revolutionary new strategy from the brain research. Teachers are highly resourceful and creative; literally thousands of strategies have been tried in the classrooms around the world.

The issue is, Can we make *better*-informed decisions about teaching based on what we have learned about the brain? Brain-based education suggests that we not wait 20 years until each of these correlations is proven beyond any possible doubt. Many theories might never be proven beyond reasonable doubt. It's possible that the sheer quantity of school, home, and genetic factors will render any generalizable principle impossible to prove as 100% accurate. As educators, we must live in the world of "likely" and "unlikely" as opposed to the world of "certainty." . . . The neuroscience merely supports other disciplines, but it's a discipline you can't see with your naked eyes, so it's worth reporting. Brain-based advocates should be pointing out how neuroscience parallels, supports, or leads the related sciences. But neuroscience is not a replacement science. Schools are too complex for that.

The Healthy Role of Critics

Almost 40 years ago, Thomas Kuhn's seminal work, *The Structure of Scientific Revolutions,* described how society responds when there is a significant shift in the prevailing paradigm. Kuhn argued that such a shift is typically met with vehement denial and opposition. Brain-based education has faced all of those reactions, and, a generation later, the paradigm continues to strengthen, not weaken. Over time, as more peer-reviewed research and real-world results accumulate, the novel paradigm gains credibility. The fact is, there will always be critics, regardless of overwhelming, highest-quality evidence. Having critics is a healthy part of society's checks and balances. All paradigm shifts attract critics.

As an example, Harvard's highly respected cognitive scientist Howard Gardner has endured his share of criticism from neuroscientists who were uncomfortable with his brain-based evidence for the theory of multiple intelligences. Yet, while subjected to two decades of criticism, Gardner's work has made and continues to make a profound and positive difference in education worldwide. His ideas are in thousands of schools, and teachers are asking, "How are my students smart?" Some critics were fearful of a new paradigm; others were more territorial, protecting their turf and crying foul at any change in the benchmarks for intelligence. And still others will attack and attack again, offering only negatives. What is unhealthy is when critics resort to sarcasm and sink to linking brain-based education to Elvis, pyramids, and aliens. That displays an embarrassing lack of scholarship and is disrespectful to those who work hard to improve education.

Critics often do have valid criticisms. For example, they mock policies (as they have every right to) that claim that a district is "brain-based" if every kid has a water bottle on his or her desk. No responsible advocate for brain-based education would argue that making water available is based on cutting-edge revelations about the brain. John Bruer argued that "we can only be thankful that members of the medical profession are more careful in applying biological research to their professional practice than some educators are in applying brain research to theirs." This would be humorous except for the fact that, according to a study published in the *Journal of the American Medical Association,* the third leading cause of death in the United States (over 100,000 deaths per year) is medical incompetence and malpractice. Is this the model of research and application that educators should be following? I think not. Give educators some credit. Much better to err on the side of enthusiasm and interdisciplinary research than to be part of the "head in the sand club."

Critics also commonly attempt to marginalize the discussion about brain-based education by using highly selective research (versus that from the prevailing majority of neuroscientists) to dispute scientific points. Examples of artificially "controversial" issues include whether "sensitive developmental periods," "gender differences," or "left-right brain differences" exist or can guide instructional practices. Turning these kinds of mainstream understandings into myths is akin to the current Administration's spin on global warming. For years, conservative Presidents have referred to global warming as the "Global Warming Debate," as if scientists are split 50–50 on the subject. The reality is that there is a nearly universal scientific consensus on both the effects of global warming and who is responsible for it.

The same can be said for the topics mentioned above. There is little controversy over whether sensitive periods, gender differences, or hemispheric specificity exist. There is no controversy over the value of developmentally appropriate instruction or removing gender biases from curriculum and instruction. There is no reputable debate over the significance of hemisphericity, either. Neuroscience giants like Michael Gazzaniga have invested careers exploring this field. Any critic who asserts that there is no significant difference between the instructional implications of our left and right hemispheres should answer the question, If each hemisphere has little functional difference, would you voluntarily undergo a hemispherectomy? That's a ridiculous question and, of course, everyone's answer would be no!

John Bruer says that he is "notorious" for his "skepticism about what neuroscience can currently offer to education." He argues that cognitive psychology, not neuroscience, is the strongest current candidate for a basic science of teaching. I happen to agree with that statement. I do believe that cognitive neuroscience has provided a great deal for educators and will continue to do so. The field has generated countless relevant insights. My own bias is toward psychology because I am currently a Ph.D. student in psychology. But even the term "psychology" is morphing into "cognitive neuroscience" because "psychology" implies a behaviorist orientation and "cognitive neuroscience" suggests a biological underpinning. For me, it's all about the interdisciplinary nature of understanding the brain, the mind, and education.

Having said that, the critics do have one thing right: brain-based education must move from being a "field" to becoming more of a "domain." An academic field is merely an aggregate or collection of forces within that territory. Brain-based education is merely a "field" right now. It is composed of scholars, consultants, publishers, staff developers, neuroscientists, conferences, and school programs. That's far from concise and replicable, yet it is typical for the start of a new movement. For brain-based education to mature, it must become a "domain." Domains have all of the same "players" as "fields," but there's an important distinction. Domains have accumulated a clear set of values, qualities, and even criteria for acceptance and validity. As brain-based education matures, it will become a "domain." From that more credible perspective, it will be easier to say if an instructional or assessment principle is "brain-based" because, right now, we can't say that. Brain-based education has grown past the "terrible twos" and the tween years. The bottom line is that before it can become accepted as a mature adult, it must forge its way out of the tumultuous teens and emerge with an accepted body of core structures that define its identity with more than a pretty picture of a brain scan. That maturing process is well under way.

Validation of Brain-Based Education

Today, as a result of years of work by brain-based educators, educators are a far more informed profession. They are more professional, they look more at research, and they are increasingly more capable of understanding and incorporating new cognitive neuroscience discoveries than they were 10 years ago. More schools of education are incorporating knowledge from the brain sciences than would have done so if we had followed the critics' advice and crawled into an intellectual cave for 25 years. Many forward thinkers have stayed tuned to such sources as Bob Sylwester's monthly column in *Brain Connection,* Scientific Learning's Internet journal that's regularly read by thousands of educators and parents. Sylwester, formerly a professor at the University of Oregon and a widely published authority on brain-based education, has been "connecting the dots" for educators for a decade.

. . . They don't get it; it's all about being interdisciplinary. Another breakthrough is the new face-recognition software for learning social skills called "Let's Face It." It was developed by Jim Tanaka and his research team, who were interested in solutions for autism. It's likely critics will say that the product comes from a long history of human face recognition; ergo, it's not *really* a breakthrough. Other neuroscientists have recently penned "translational" books showing a "science to the classroom" connection. They include the luminary Michael Posner on attention, Sally Shaywitz on dyslexia, and Helen Nevills and Pat Wolfe on reading.

Two major conference organizations, PIRI and the Learning Brain EXPO (the author's company), have produced "science to the classroom" events for 10 years. These biannual events have engaged more than 100 highly reputable, often award-winning, neuroscientists to speak in translational terms to educators. The list of speakers has been a veritable "who's who" in cutting-edge, interdisciplinary neuroscience. This has come about only as a result of the collaboration of educators and scientists linking the research directly to those in the schools. Whether the presenter was a biological psychologist, neuroscientist, or cognitive scientist is irrelevant; they've all spoken on science to the classroom.

How reputable is brain-based education? Harvard University now has both master's and doctoral degrees in it. Every year, Harvard's Mind, Brain, and Education (MBE) program produces about 40 graduates with master's degrees and two to four doctors of education, who go on to interdisciplinary positions in research and practice. "Our mission is to build a movement in which cognitive science and neuroscience are integrated with education so that we train people to make that integration both in research and in practice," says Prof. Kurt Fischer, director of the program. This intersection of biology and cognitive science with pedagogy has become a new focus in education. Interest in the program is high in Canada, Japan, Australia, South Korea, England, South Africa, New Zealand, Argentina, and other countries. There's also a peer-reviewed scientific journal on brain-based education. The journal, which is published quarterly by the reputable Blackwell publishers and the International Mind, Brain, and Education Society (IMBES), features research, conceptual papers, reviews, debates, and dialogue.

Conclusion

Today, 10 years after the mudslinging criticism of brain-based education, it's appropriate to say, "We were right." In fact, because of the efforts of the brain-based community to inform educators, thousands are currently using this knowledge appropriately to enhance education policy and practice. There are degree programs in it, scientific journals, and conferences; and peer-reviewed brain-related research now supports the discipline. There are countless neuroscientists who support the movement, and they demonstrate their support by writing and speaking at educational conferences.

As an author in the brain-based movement, I have reminded educators that they should never say, "Brain research proves . . ." because it does not prove anything. It may, however, suggest or strengthen the value of a particular pathway. What educators should say is, "These studies suggest that XYZ may be true about the brain. Given that insight, it probably makes sense for us, under these conditions, to use the following strategies in schools." This approach, which is a cautionary one, sticks with the truth. When one is careful about making causal claims, the connections are there for those with an open mind.

The science may come from a wide range of disciplines. Brain-based education is not a panacea or magic bullet to solve all of education's problems. Anyone who claims that is misleading people. It is not yet a program, a model, or a package for schools to follow. The discussion of how to improve student learning must widen from axons and dendrites to the bigger picture. That bigger picture is that our brain is involved with everything we do at school. The brain is the most relevant feature to explore, because it affects every strategy, action, behavior, and policy at your school. New journals explore such essential topics as social conditions, exercise, neurogenesis, arts, stress, and nutrition. A school cannot remove arts, career education, and physical education and at the same time claim to be doing what's best for the brains of its students. These are the issues we must be exploring, not whether someone can prove whether a teacher's strategy was used before or after a neuroscience study provided peer-reviewed support for that strategy.

Today, there is still criticism, but the voices are no longer a chorus; they're a diminishing whine. For the critic, it's still "my way or the highway." That's an old, tired theme among critics; the tactic of dismissing another's research by narrowing the discussion to irrelevant issues, such as whether the research is cognitive science, neurobiology, or psychology. They're all about the mind and brain. The real issues that we should be talking about are what environmental, instructional, and social conditions can help us enrich students' lives. To answer that, it's obvious that everything that our brain does is relevant and that's what should now be on the table for discussion. Yes, we are in the infancy of brain research—there's so much more to learn. But dismissing it is not only shortsighted, it's also dead wrong. At this early stage, that would be like calling the Wright Brothers' first flight at Kitty Hawk a failure because it only went a few hundred yards. And let's remember, the Wright Brothers had no credibility either; they were actually bicycle mechanics, not aviators. The future belongs not to the turf protectors, but to those with vision who can grasp interdisciplinary trends as well as the big picture. Nothing is more relevant to educators than the brains of their students, parents, or staff. Brain-based education is here to stay.

Gerald Coles

 **NO**

Danger in the Classroom: "Brain Glitch" Research and Learning to Read

Did you know that recent studies of the brain and reading support the reading instruction mandated in George W. Bush's No Child Left Behind (NCLB) legislation? And did you know that this research also supports the legislation he has proposed to dismantle Head Start's comprehensive approach to preschool education? And were you aware that, thanks to this brain research, we now know how children learn to read and which areas of the brain must first be stocked to promote skilled reading? Did you realize that we now have strong brain-based evidence that the best reading instruction is heavily prescriptive, skills-emphasis, building-blocks teaching that starts with small pieces of written language and proceeds to larger ones—and teachers are fortunate because these features are contained in reading programs like Open Court?

You didn't know all that? Good, because none of it is true, although you would never know that if you just listened to the President, the educators and assorted researchers who support his educational agenda, and the media who repeat their assertions.

Over 25 years ago, when I began appraising theories about faulty brain wiring in beginning readers, my criticism of the research then being conducted was limited to ersatz explanations of so-called brain dysfunctions in children called "learning disabled," "reading disabled," or "dyslexic."[1] Contrary to the assertions made then, the research had never shown that the overwhelming number of these children did not have normal brains. Certainly a portion of poor readers had problems that were the result of exposure to such toxins as lead and cadmium, to food additives, and to other environmental influences. But, I argued, there was no evidence that they accounted for more than a small portion of the large numbers of children given these labels and shunted into special education programs.

At some point, thanks to increased, widespread criticism of these "brain-based" explanations, I had thought a change had started toward more informed, measured interpretations. However, my naive thinking has long been gone. Not only are explanations about "brain glitches," to use the term employed by reading researcher Sally Shaywitz, now being applied more forcefully to "dyslexics," but they have also been reworked to explain how all children learn to

From *Phi Delta Kappan,* January 2004, pp. 344–351 (with omissions). Copyright © 2004 by Phi Delta Kappan. Reprinted by permission of Phi Delta Kappan and Gerald Coles.

read, what single method of instruction must be used to teach them, and why the single method mandated in Bush's Reading First, part of the NCLB legislation, is a wise, scientifically based choice. Thus never have these "brain glitch" explanations been more pervasively intrusive for all beginning readers and their teachers in classrooms across the nation.

In the forefront of the Bush educators who promote claims about brain studies is Reid Lyon, dubbed Bush's "Reading Czar" by the *Wall Street Journal.* Lyon is the chief of a branch of the National Institutes of Child Health and Human Development (NICHD) that has funded much of the reading research used to justify Reading First and comparable instructional mandates at the state level. At least $12 million of these funds have been used for studies on brain activity and reading. When the President introduced legislation to "improve" Head Start by weighting it heavily with building-blocks instruction, he talked about the scientific findings that had informed him and expressed special appreciation to Lyon and like-minded researchers who, the President emphasized, knew what they were talking about because they "studied the brain." "'Reading Czar' Has Talk with Educators" is the headline of a newspaper article describing one of Lyon's many presentations in which he uses "pictures of the brain to illustrate how it functions while a person is reading—or having trouble reading" to promote Reading First instruction in schools around the country.[2]

A new best seller, *Overcoming Dyslexia,* by Sally Shaywitz, who has received considerable NICHD funding for her research, claims to present "the advances in brain science" that inform what "at last we know," which are "the specific steps a child or adult must take to build and then reinforce the neural pathways deep within the brain for skilled reading."[3] Shaywitz served on the panel whose findings, she proudly explains to readers, "are now part of the groundbreaking No Child Left Behind Legislation," and, not surprisingly, she is a reviewer of Reading First grants.[4]

In an interview published last summer, Shaywitz announced, "The good news is that we really understand the steps of how you become a reader and how you become a skilled reader."[5] No wonder the *Time* magazine cover story on dyslexia, which featured the Shaywitz interview, lured readers with the headline "Up to One in Five Kids Might Simply Not Be Wired to Read" and then went on to report that "new researchers know what's wrong—and what to do about it."[6] Similarly, a Florida newspaper headline exclaimed, "Brain Studies May Lead to Reading Revolution."[7]

Given these widely disseminated claims, colleges of education have been bashed for perpetuating the nation's reading crisis by not teaching about brain functioning and the need for building-blocks instruction. "Teachers are rarely if ever taught about how reading gets accommodated in the brain," proclaimed the right-wing Center for Education Reform. "And of course without that knowledge, we'll never be a nation of readers, and the nearly 40% of children who are mainly disadvantaged will never reverse that label."[8]

In this article I will argue that, despite all the unbridled assertions about the wonder of it all, this new "brain glitch" research is theoretically, empirically, and conceptually deficient, as was the deficit-driven work that preceded it by decades and which I reviewed in 1987.[9] More than ever, claims about the research constitute an ideological barrier to a sounder understanding of the connections between brain activity and learning to read. More than ever, this work is a danger in the classroom both because it applies unproven labels to an ever-larger number of children and because it promotes a single kind of instruction that, based on the actual empirical evidence mustered for it, contains no promise for leaving no beginning reader behind. To all of this, add the false and cruel expectations that these claims generate in parents.

To help illustrate my critique, I will use as an example a recent, highly publicized study on reading and brain activity whose co-authors include Reid Lyon, Sally Shaywitz, and several other researchers whose work argues for building-blocks teaching and has been used as evidence for Reading First instruction. (For convenience I call it the Shaywitz/Lyon study.)[10]

Is the Brain "Reading"?

Functional magnetic resonance imagery (fMRI) is a valuable diagnostic and investigative technology that can measure blood flow in the brain and thereby provide information about certain kinds of brain activity when someone is performing a task. However, like every technology used in research, its value and the information it produces are never better than the initial theory and concepts that steer its application. Perhaps the biggest misrepresentation in the "brain glitch" research is that the color scans produced by fMRI provide information about "reading." In fact, they provide no such thing, because the "reading" tasks under study are largely a person's performance on simple sound and sound/symbol (phonics) tasks with words and parts of words, rather than performance in reading as conventionally defined, that is, reading and comprehending sentences and paragraphs. . . .

The puny definition of reading used in this research appears not to concern the investigators, though, because they design their studies on the assumption that these simple tasks involving words and parts of words embrace the core requirements for beginning readers: that is, mastery of phonological awareness (distinguishing and manipulating sounds in words) and sound/symbol relationships. As the Shaywitz/Lyon study explains, there is now "a strong consensus" (that is, a broad unanimity of professional opinion) that phonological awareness is the first building block within the sequence and that reading disability reflects a deficit in this "lower level component" of "the language system."[11] Only after mastering this component can beginning readers effectively continue to master other reading skills.

That's the claim. The reality is that the so-called strong consensus does not exist. I and others have published thorough research reviews that critique—and dismiss—the "lower level component" model and the supposed empirical evidence showing the superior effect of early, direct, and intensive instruction in word sounds on later reading. As I have also argued, this narrow, do-as-you're-told instruction not only pushes aside numerous issues that bear on beginning literacy—such as children's backgrounds, interests, problem-solving approaches, and definitions of "reading"—it also masquerades as a bootstrap policy solution for poor children that takes off the table all other policies required to address the many needs that influence learning success or failure.[12] However, for the advocates of this "strong consensus," especially those linked to the political power pushing these claims, conflicting views are never allowed to ruffle their harmony.

Hence, an experiment, such as those reported in the Shaywitz/Lyon study, can be designed in which subjects do "lower level component" tasks, such as deciding if non-words rhyme ("Do leat and bete rhyme?") or making judgments requiring both phonological and semantic knowledge ("Are corn and rice in the same category?"), and the researchers can claim that the data generated tell us a great deal about "reading," the reading process, and the best kinds of instruction. The conclusions in this work display no awareness of the self-fulfilling prophecy at play when the research focuses solely on "lower level components" decontextualized from a full appraisal of reading, uses no other model of reading and instruction, and then concludes that these components are the initial and key ones in learning to read.

A Real "Brain Glitch"?

Looking more deeply into the research design of the "brain glitch" studies, we find a problem that dyslexia researchers have long encountered but not overcome when organizing an experiment so that data on brain activity can be meaningfully interpreted: the experiment must start by grouping dyslexics separately from other kinds of poor readers. This distinction is required because even in studies using the fMRI, the data are about brain activity associated with the word-level tasks, not about micro brain damage. Therefore, fMRI differences in brain activity among a group of unsorted poor readers would not provide information about the cause and meaning of the various differences in activity.

To solve the problem, these studies and previous ones employing simpler technologies try first to separate from a group of poor readers those whose problems are assumed to have non-neurological causes, such as emotional, familial, social class, and similar "exclusionary" influences, as they have been called. If these poor readers are excluded, researchers have reasoned, the probability is high that the reading problems of those who remain are caused by a "brain glitch." While this might make sense in theory, in practice it has not worked, because researchers have not created evaluation methods and criteria for separating the two groups of poor readers.

Even worse, for decades, researchers have frequently stated that they have used a thorough process of distinguishing between the two groups, but the assertion has rarely been accompanied by evidence. In the Shaywitz/Lyon study, for example, dyslexics were supposedly identified after the researchers had determined that the subjects' reading problems were not caused by emotional problems or "social, cultural, or economic disadvantage." Yet the researchers, so dedicated to obtaining and reporting a surfeit of brain data, offered not a whit of information on this process of elimination. Presumably, readers of the published study were expected to accept without question the assertion that genuine dyslexics had been identified and that these children could then be compared to "nonimpaired" readers (an odd term, since it refers to normal or average readers but is used in the study to underline a priori the assumption that the dyslexics' brains were impaired).

The need to provide evidence of thorough appraisals of the roots of subjects' reading problems is usually obvious to anyone who has actually taught poor readers and, therefore, knows that there can be numerous contextual causes of poor reading in middle-class children that will not be readily apparent. In my extensive work with children, young adults, and adults with severe reading problems, I have found that causes can be uncovered only after spending considerable time *both* evaluating and teaching a student, with the latter especially necessary. Poor teaching—such as using a one-size-fits-all reading program, insufficient individualized instruction, too much phonics, too little phonics—is just one of the many influences that can produce reading problems in a variety of ways, but those problems will not be apparent without thorough analysis of a person's instructional history and current active reading.

Many unusual family circumstances and stresses can impair a child's early reading progress. A parent losing a job, a family moving to another city in the middle of the first grade, overworked parents, grandparents dying around the time a child began school are all examples of problems I have identified. These experiences hinder reading development by distracting and stressing a child, but they are not overt "emotional" problems. Even when a poor reader comes from a family that appears "normal," only an extensive exploration of the family dynamics can determine whether this appearance might cloak problems that have affected a child's beginning reading.

By not providing criteria and evidence that the "dyslexics" are different from other poor readers, the brain research studies use another self-serving, self-fulfilling prophecy: because the fMRI shows differences in brain activity between "dyslexic" and "nonimpaired" readers, the differences in brain activity must be visual demonstrations of impairment and nonimpairment. How do we know the fMRI data reveal impairment? Because one of the groups was initially identified as impaired. How do we know the group was impaired? Because the group was first identified as impaired and the fMRI data corroborated the impairment. No other explanations can explain the dyslexics' different brain activity. Impaired, for sure! No question about it. For more on the logic of this reasoning, let's look at Czechlexia.

What Causes Czechlexia?

The Shaywitz/Lyon study concluded that the "brain activation patterns" provided neurobiological evidence of an "underlying disruption in the neural systems for reading in children with dyslexia and indicate that it is evident at a young age."[13] More specifically, the impaired readers demonstrated "a functional disruption" in the rear area of the brain where visual and sound identification and associations are made during reading. NICHD, which funded the study, summarized the results this way in its press release: "Children who are poor readers appear to have a disruption in the part of their brain involved in reading phonetically."[14]

In the eyes of some, that conclusion does "appear" to be true. But the data could easily suggest other interpretations. Why would anyone assume that the brain activity for two groups who differ in reading abilities would be the same when the groups are engaged in reading-related tasks? Shouldn't the researchers conclude that, unless demonstrated otherwise, a difference in the brain activation between the groups would be caused by the respective reading abilities and not necessarily by a brain impairment? In other words, should not one expect, until demonstrated otherwise, that the brain activity, reading ability, and task performance were simply correlated and that the brain activity did not "cause" the other two? Consider the following experiment. If two groups of normal people were asked to read a Czech text, and if only one group could read Czech, who would expect the brain activation of the two groups to be the same? And who, except those with other agendas, would think that differences in brain activity revealed dysfunctions, not differences, and that the "condition" should be named Czechlexia?

Moreover, as I discussed in *The Learning Mystique,* rather than a brain disruption, many other influences—such as a group's problem-solving approaches, personal meanings, emotions, motivation, and self-confidence—have been shown to affect cognitive outcomes and patterns of brain functioning and could reasonably explain such data. Only deficit-driven interpretations could continue to fail to take any of this into account.

Fixing the "Brain Glitch"

Beyond finding "brain glitches," researchers have reported other good news: building-block skills instruction can remedy the glitch. "An effective reading program" can produce "brain repair," Shaywitz reports. "The brain can be rewired."[15] Elise Temple and her colleagues, who used a skills training program described by the publisher as fitting "with the No Child Left Behind Act," concur. Beginning with the assumption that dyslexia is caused by "a deficit in the neural mechanisms underlying phonological processing," they found that their instructional program ameliorated the "disrupted function in brain regions associated with phonological processing and produce[d] additional compensatory activation in other brain regions."[16] Similarly, an intervention study funded by NICHD reported that a reading program emphasizing skills reversed a brain deficit underlying dyslexia.[17]

Nearly 20 years ago, Leonide Goldstein and I published a study on differences in brain hemisphere activation in adult beginning readers as they were learning to read.[18] We found that these adults, when they were poor readers or nonreaders, did, indeed, demonstrate brain activation that was different from that found among good readers. However, as their reading improved, through the use of a holistic, comprehensive teaching approach over many months, their brain activation changed toward that commonly found in good readers. We interpreted these data as evidence that new knowledge and competencies were linked to concomitant changes in brain structure and functioning, as one would expect *for all kinds of learning.* There was nothing in the data to suggest that these beginning readers started learning to read with anything other than normal brains that were configured as they were at the beginning of the study because the students had not learned to read; no data suggested that the educational intervention we provided somehow repaired or circumvented dysfunctional brain areas.

To restate a central point for appraising these glitch-fixing interventions: although researchers insist that the training programs they use repair or ameliorate brain hardware or glitches, there is no evidence in any of their studies that this rewiring was different from that which is concomitant with the learning that continues throughout our learning lives. Nor does this so-called repair demonstrate that phonological processing is the *initial* key component in learning to read. The subjects apparently lacked this ability and then learned this ability, and their brain processing changed accordingly. Using modern technology to identify and track brain changes related to changes in reading ability is an extraordinary achievement. Using the achievement for ideological ends is not.

Emotionless "Cognition"

Like the assumed "consensus" on building-blocks instruction, "brain glitch" research assumes that cognition—that is, the process that creates images, concepts, and mental operations—is not a construct but an independent reality that actually describes the brain processes associated with reading. Ignored in this assumption is the ever-growing evidence suggesting that thinking is an inseparable interaction of both cognition and emotion (feelings, desires, enthusiasms, antipathies, etc.).

Neurologist Antonio Damasio, for example, rejects the traditional distinction between cognition, thought to be neocortical, and emotions, thought to be subcortical.[19] There are no "higher" and "lower" brain centers, he argues. The neocortex (the "high-level" part of the brain) does not handle reason while the subcortex (the "low-level" part of the brain) handles emotions. Rather, the neural substrates for cognitive responses are associated with neural substrates for emotions: both so-called high and low levels are integrated in thinking processes. Similarly pertinent is the work of neural scientist Joseph LeDoux, who has identified brain pathways connecting sites of emotion, cognition, and memory.[20] These interconnections mean that emotions and cognition are integrated and interactive and that an emotional response can, in terms of pathway activity, precede a cognitive perception and response. Focusing only on cognition when studying the brain and reading ignores the areas of networks whose emotional activation is part of "cognition."

Unfortunately, none of this new perspective on the "continuous and interwoven cognitive-emotional fugue," to use pediatric researcher Michael Lewis' metaphor, has entered the "brain glitch" research.[21] As a result, the question of whether diminished activity in a portion of the brain of someone doing a reading task might be a consequence of an emotional response, in that emotional memories can exert a powerful influence on "thought processes," remains unaddressed. By purging emotions and focusing only on cognition, the "brain glitch" research also purges the alternative: a holistic instructional approach based on the assumption that classrooms are filled with whole children for whom learning is always grounded in the fugue of cognition and affect.

How the Brain Works: Modules?

The interrelationships and interactions missing from the narrow cognitive model of "brain glitch" research lead us to a final concern. A chief premise of this research holds that the brain has specific modules for specialized operations that work in sequence with other modules in learning written language and that foremost of these is at least one module that can process basic sound and sound/symbol skills. This kind of modular model has a certain palpable, visual appeal (not unlike "building-blocks instruction"), but the actual existence of such modules is a theory, not a fact, that has increasingly been questioned. Most likely, the modular model is not one that explains how the brain actually works.

For instance, Merlin Donald, a psychologist who has written extensively on human consciousness, rejects the explanation that modules perform "specialized operations," such as deciphering portions of language. While language areas of the brain, such as those related to aspects of reading, are important in processing particular functions, all are intertwined in extensive networks (a polyphony) of brain areas that are simultaneously and interactively communicating and constructing and reconstructing particular areas within the whole. Yes, the brain has fundamental mechanisms for beginning to learn written language, but it does not begin with a "fixed pattern of connectivity." Instead, the "connectivity pattern is set by experience" with "countless interconnection points, or synapses, which connect neurons to one another in various patterns."[22] In other words, learning and experience create and shape the brain's circuits and how they are used in learning to read; the circuits are not predetermined.

Linguist Philip Lieberman has also criticized modular explanations, calling them "neophrenological theories," that is, theories that "map complex behaviors to localized regions of the brain, on the assumption that a particular part of the brain regulates an aspect of behavior." In these theories, he remarks, the functional organization of the brain is run by "a set of petty bureaucrats each of which controls a behavior." Like Donald, Lieberman proposes that converging behavioral and neurobiological data indicate that human language is composed not of a hierarchical system but of neural networks, including the traditional cortical "language" areas (Broca's and Wernicke's areas), formed through circuits that link populations of neurons in neuroanatomical structures that are distributed throughout the brain. Lieberman stresses, "Although specific operations may be performed in particular parts of the brain, these operations must be integrated into a *network* that regulates an observable aspect of behavior. And so, a particular aspect of behavior usually involves activity in neuroanatomical structures distributed throughout the brain" (emphasis in original).[23]

The view of a "connectivity pattern" that emerges and is activated as children learn to read contrasts with the model of step-by-step progression from module to module. If the former is an accurate model of brain organization and functioning, it suggests that the connectivity pattern should be the focus of research because only by looking at the overall pattern can researchers begin to determine the functioning and interrelationships of any part and the causal, consequential, or interactive function of that part within the entire pattern.

From the perspective of a connectivity pattern model, not only do the brain areas involved in grasping the sound/symbol correspondence *not* have to be primed first before other areas of the pattern can become effectively operable, the creation and functioning of these areas depends on connections within the entire pattern. And because the pattern is not innately fixed, if instruction were to stimulate certain areas more than others, a particular connectivity pattern would emerge. That specific pattern, however, might not necessarily be the sole one required for reading success and might not be superior to other connectivity patterns. Moreover, a more complex connectivity pattern could be created through richer written language learning. None of this is addressed in the "brain glitch" research.

Conclusion

To make research on the brain and reading work, it must be informed by the complexity of reading acquisition, and it must begin to address such questions as: Will alternative teaching approaches configure brain activity in alternative ways? Will children's differing assumptions about what it means to "read" correspond to differing brain activity and organization? How do different aspects of reading, such as comprehension, syntax, and word analysis, interact in certain reading tasks and what kinds of brain activity do the interactions produce? How does the knowledge children bring to literacy learning affect brain activity?

These and similar questions can begin to contribute to a better understanding of the relationship between brain function and reading acquisition, which in turn can help promote ecological approaches that are grounded in an understanding of the unified interrelationships of brain, active child, and learning environment. They can also begin to help identify genuine brain-related reading impairments. Developing this kind of understanding of integrated interrelationships will require that we eschew views that are either "brain based" or conceive of the brain as an extraneous "black box."

Notes

1. Gerald Coles, "The Learning–Disabilities Test Battery: Empirical and Social Issues," *Harvard Educational Review,* August 1978, pp. 313–40.
2. Mary Gail Hare, "'Reading Czar' Has Talk with Educators," *Baltimore Sun,* 17 September 2002.
3. Shaywitz, p. ix.
4. Ibid., p. 175.
5. Christine Gorman, "The New Science of Dyslexia," *Time,* 28 July 2003.

6. Ibid.

7. Robyn Suriano, "Brain Studies May Lead to Reading Revolution," *Orlando Sentinel,* 15 December 2002.

8. Center for Education Reform, "Reading, Riting, and Common Sense," *Monthly Letter,* December 2001, p. 1.

9. Gerald Coles, *The Learning Mystique: A Critical Look at "Learning Disabilities"* (New York: Pantheon, 1987).

10. Bennett Shaywitz, Sally Shaywitz, et al., "Disruption of Posterior Brain Systems of Reading in Children with Developmental Dyslexia," *Biological Psychiatry,* vol. 52, 2002, pp. 101–10. (Hereafter cited as Shaywitz/Lyon.)

11. Shaywitz/Lyon, p. 101.

12. See, for example, Gerald Coles, *Misreading Reading: The Bad Science That Hurts Children* (Portsmouth, N.H.: Heinemann, 2000). Other work that critiques the "consensus" model includes Elaine Garan, "Beyond the Smoke and Mirrors: A Critique of the National Reading Panel Report on Phonics," *Phi Delta Kappan,* March 2001, pp. 500–506; Stephen Krashen, "False Claims About Phonemic Awareness, Phonics, Skills vs. Whole Language, and Recreational Reading," May 2003, . . . and Joanne Yatvin, "Babes in the Woods: The Wanderings of the National Reading Panel," *Phi Delta Kappan,* January 2002, pp. 364–69.

13. Shaywitz/Lyon, p. 101.

14. "Children's Reading Disability Attributed to Brain Impairment," NIH-NICHD Press Release, 2 August 2002. . . .

15. Shaywitz, p. 86.

16. Elise Temple et al., "Neural Deficits in Children with Dyslexia Ameliorated by Behavioral Remediation: Evidence from Functional MRI," *Proceedings of the National Academy of Sciences,* 4 March 2003, p. 2860.

17. Panagiotis Simos et al., "Dyslexia-Specific Brain Activation Profile Becomes Normal Following Successful Remedial Training," *Neurology,* vol. 58, 2002, pp. 1203–13.

18. Gerald Coles and Leonide Goldstein, "Hemispheric EEG Activation and Literacy Development," *International Journal of Clinical Neuropsychology,* vol. 7, 1985, pp. 3–7.

19. Antonio Damasio, *Descartes' Error: Emotion, Reason, and the Human Brain* (New York: Putnam, 1994).

20. Joseph E. LeDoux, *The Emotional Brain: The Mysterious Underpinnings of Emotional Life* (New York: Simon & Schuster, 1996).

21. Michael Lewis et al., "The Cognitive-Emotional Fugue," in Carroll E. Izard, Jerome Kagan, and Robert B. Zajonc, eds., *Emotions, Cognition, and Behavior* (New York: Cambridge University Press, 1984), pp. 264–88.

22. Merlin Donald, *A Mind So Rare: The Evolution of Human Consciousness* (New York: Norton, 2001), pp. 3, 103, 150.

23. Philip Lieberman, *Human Language and Our Reptilian Brain: The Subcortical Bases of Speech, Syntax, and Thought* (Cambridge, Mass.: Harvard University Press, 2000), pp. 2–4.

POSTSCRIPT

Do Recent Discoveries about the Brain and Its Development Have Implications for Classroom Practice?

Any plausible theory of learning must include the assumption that learning involves the brain. Why, then, is there any controversy about the implications of brain research for educational practice? Doesn't any finding about the brain tell us something useful about how to teach? Unfortunately, it is not always possible to move directly from knowledge about the brain to recommendations for educational practice. This is because learning always involves more than the activity of the brain. Learning results from the interaction of the child (and, of course, his or her brain) with the environment.

Consider, for example, the finding that the "spurt" in children's vocabulary seen at 18 to 24 months of age is associated with a rather dramatic increase in the synaptic density and activity of the brain. This finding is important because it suggests that something may "click" in children's brains at this time that increases their preparedness to learn words. But this finding does not by itself tell us very much about what parents and educators should do during this time to assist children. On the one hand, it may be that children are so prepared at this time that they can pick up words effortlessly from just about any sort of interaction and in any environment. On the other hand, what adults do when children are ready to "spurt" may matter a great deal.

Highly recommended for readers interested in learning more about research on brain sciences is a text by Mark H. Johnson, *Developmental Cognitive Neuroscience,* 2d ed. (Blackwell, 2005). It is an up-to-date, comprehensive, and highly readable (although still fairly technical) summary of much of the current wave of research on the brain-behavior relation. For readers who wish to delve into more technical discussions of research and of the methods used in brain research, there is a wonderful collection of papers in the edited volume by G. Reid Lyon and Judith M. Rumsey, *Neuroimaging: A Window to the Neurological Foundations of Learning and Behavior in Children* (Paul H. Brookes, 1996). Highly recommended is a series of articles on educational applications of brain research in the November 1998 and November 2000 issues of *Educational Leadership.* Particularly noteworthy in these series are "The Brain-Compatible Curriculum," by Anne Westwater and Pat Wolfe, *Educational Leadership* (November 2000) and "Unconscious Emotions, Conscious Feelings," by Robert Sylwester, *Educational Leadership* (November 2000). Also highly recommended are a series of articles in *Phi Delta Kappan* that were spurred by the Jensen article reprinted for this issue, including an article by Robert J. Sternberg, "The Answer Depends on the Question: A Reply to Eric Jensen"

(February 2008) and another by Judy Willis, "Building a Bridge from Neuroscience to the Classroom" (February 2008). A book-length treatment of teaching strategies derived from research on neural development and functioning is provided by Eric Jensen in *Teaching with the Brain in Mind* (Association for Supervision and Curriculum Development, 1998). And finally, a recent article on the classroom implications of recent research on neural differences between boys and girls entitled, "With Boys and Girls in Mind," by Michael Guriand and Kathy Stevens, *Educational Leadership* (November 2004), is sure to generate its own controversey.

Internet References . . .

International Reading Association

The International Reading Association (IRA) supports, conducts, and disseminates research on reading processes and instruction. The IRA accomplishes this through conferences and publications. Issues related to whole language and other instructional approaches have been a frequent concern of the organization and its members.

http://www.reading.org

PTO Central

PTO Central is a resource for Parent-Teacher-Organization (PTO) groups. The Web site includes useful documents and links to other sites addressing issues of importance to PTOs, from fundraising to curriculum.

http://www.ptocentral.org

U.S. Department of Education Office of Technology

The Office of Educational Technology assists in developing and implementing policies, research projects, and conferences focused on educational technology. This site includes numerous reports, resources, and recommendation regarding the use of computers and technology in schools.

http://www.ed.gov/about/offices/list/os/technology/index.html

Wisconsin Department of Public Instruction SAGE Program

This site describes one state's attempt at education reform that includes class size reduction as its centerpiece.

http://dpi.wi.gov/sage/

National Education Association

This is the site for an organization whose members include teachers and educational professionals interested in education from preschool to the university level. The site includes many resources, including several on school violence and school safety.

http://www.nea.org/home/16364.htm

American Association of School Administrators

The mission of this association is to promote the development of school leaders. The site includes resources and position papers on a variety of topics, as well as examples of innovative programs.

http://www.aasa.org

Effective Teaching and the Evaluation of Learning

P*edagogical practice is shaped by many factors. The nature of the students being taught and the particular theory of learning adopted by a teacher both help to determine what and how children are taught. But everyday instructional practices are also shaped by other factors. Advances in computer technology, for example, have drastically changed our ability to access information as well as altered the ways we interact with other people. But can and should this technology change how we teach and learn in school? Society has become increasingly violent, and this violence has begun to find its way into our schools with frightening consequences. How should schools react to stem the growing violence within their walls and on their playgrounds? As resources have become more scarce, our classes have become larger—with more students per teacher. Would a move to smaller classes have a benefit? Who should be involved in determining and implementing the curriculum? Should parents have a role? How should we measure the success of our nation's schools? How will we compete with other countries? In this section, we consider the controversies that have arisen as our schools and society have tried to define effective teaching and effective evaluation of learning.*

- Is the Whole Language Approach to Reading Effective?

- Is Greater Parental Involvement at School Always Beneficial?

- Should Schools Embrace Computers and Technology?

- Should Schools Reduce Class Size to Improve Student Outcomes?

- Can a Zero-Tolerance Policy Lead to Safe Schools?

- Should Student Time in School Be Changed?

ISSUE 12

Is the Whole Language Approach to Reading Effective?

YES: Stephen Krashen, from "Defining Whole Language: The Limits of Phonics Instruction and the Efficacy of Whole Language Instruction," *Reading Improvement* (Spring, 2002)

NO: G. Reid Lyon, from "Why Reading Is Not a Natural Process," *Educational Leadership* (March 1998)

ISSUE SUMMARY

YES: Stephen Krashen, a professor emeritus from the University of Southern California, argues that flawed studies and misinterpretations plague research on this topic and that the evidence to date suggests whole language is effective.

NO: G. Reid Lyon, chief of the Child Development and Behavior Branch of the National Institute of Child Health and Human Development (NICHD), at the time of this article, argues that becoming a skilled reader requires explicit, systematic, and direct instruction and practice.

During the late 1980s and into the 1990s there was a change in how reading was taught in U.S. elementary schools—a change that was nothing short of revolutionary. Until that time, instruction in reading emphasized drill-and-practice and "basic skills," particularly those related to learning letter-sound correspondences, or *phonics*. This approach consisted of activities in which students memorized the way particular written symbols, such as c and s, "sounded" in words like *sock, cats,* and *nice*. Students read from basal readers, which emphasized the sound-letter correspondences and rules they were learning: *See Dick run. See Jane run. See Spot run. Run, Spot, run.*

The approach known as *whole language* is very different. With this approach, from kindergarten on, students are engaged in activities that look very much like "real" reading and "real" writing. The whole language approach grew out of the idea that literacy skills are a natural by-product of engaging in *authentic* (i.e., personally meaningful, goal-directed) literacy activities. Proponents of whole language see a parallel between the way in which children learn spoken language and the way in which they learn to read and write.

262

In particular, they argue that children do not learn to speak as the result of explicit instruction. Nor, they argue, do children refrain from participating in real speaking activities (i.e., communication) until they have practiced all the component skills needed to be a fluent speaker. Instead, children learn language naturally and effortlessly by using it to engage in meaningful acts of communication (e.g., to request a desired object or to share joy or distress).

But is the whole language approach effective? Does it lead to the same level of literacy skills as does the more traditional drill-and-practice approach? Critics, who have become more numerous and vocal in recent years, argue that the whole language approach is not effective. States such as California point with frustration to claims that test scores in reading on the National Assessment of Educational Progress (NAEP) have actually declined during the years in which whole language programs have been popular. These critics suggest that children simply are not being given sufficient practice with phonics and, thus, fail to become efficient at decoding (i.e., at translating print into sound). In the long run, they argue, this limits students' ability to recover meaning from written text.

Supporters of whole language counter that many of the successes of the program have been overlooked. They point to gains in reading scores in New Jersey and Ohio, which have implemented whole language instruction on a wide scale. Supporters also argue that many of the failures highlighted by critics actually are due to systemic factors (e.g., inadequate resources) rather than the nature of the instruction delivered. Supporters of whole language also object that the use of standardized tests of reading achievement may not uncover the very real gains in reading and writing made by students experiencing the whole language approach. They argue for replacing standardized tests, which focus on decontextualized applications of low-level skills, with more authentic assessments, which examine the quality of the actual literacy products generated by students (e.g., journals and reports).

In the first of the following selections, Stephen Krashen argues that many studies purporting to show that phonics instruction is superior to whole language instruction are flawed or have been misinterpreted. He argues further that a careful consideration of these studies actually lends support to the greater effectiveness of whole language. In the second selection, G. Reid Lyon argues that *phonemic awareness* (knowledge of the small units of sound that are combined to form words) and the ability to *make meaning* (to link print with previously acquired concepts and experiences) are the keys to successful reading. He also argues that becoming skilled in these areas is not, as whole language advocates contend, a natural process; that is, these skills do not emerge simply as the result of exposure to print and literacy activities. Instead, Lyon contends, these skills depend on explicit, systematic instruction and practice, something that he believes is all too rare in most implementations of the whole language approach.

YES

Stephen Krashen

Defending Whole Language: The Limits of Phonics Instruction and the Efficacy of Whole Language Instruction

The Reading Wars show no signs of stopping. There appear to be two factions: Those who support the Skill-Building hypothesis and those who support the Comprehension Hypothesis. The former claim that literacy is developed from the bottom up; the child learns to read by first learning to read out loud, by learning sound-spelling correspondences. This is done through explicit instruction, practice, and correction. This knowledge is first applied to words. Ultimately, the child uses this ability to read larger texts, as the knowledge of sound-spelling correspondences becomes automatic. According to this view, real reading of interesting texts is helpful only to the extent that it helps children "practice their skills."

The Comprehension Hypothesis claims that we learn to read by understanding message on the page; we "learn to read by reading." Reading pedagogy, according to the Comprehension Hypothesis, focuses on providing students with interesting, comprehensible texts, and the job of the teacher is to help children read these texts, that is, help make them comprehensible. The direct teaching of "skills" is helpful only when it makes texts more comprehensible.

The Comprehension Hypothesis also claims that reading is the source of much of our vocabulary knowledge, writing style, advanced grammatical competence, and spelling. It is also the source of most of our knowledge of phonics.

Whole Language

The term "whole language" does not refer only to providing interesting comprehensible texts and helping children understand less comprehensible texts. It involves instilling a love of literature, problem-solving and critical thinking, collaboration, authenticity, personalized learning, and much more. In terms of the process of literacy development, however, the Comprehension Hypothesis is a central part of whole language.

In this paper I examine some recent research dealing with two fundamental points of contention between the two sides of this debate.

1. The complexity issue: Whole language advocates claim that the rules
   of phonics are complex and have numerous exceptions. For this reason many are unteachable. Skill-building advocates claim that this
   is not the case. For examples, defends giving phonics instruction a
   major role in reading instruction because "more than 90 percent of
   English words are phonetically regular" (p. 70). He does not, however, cite research supporting this claim.
2. The method comparison issue: Skill-Building advocates claim that
   those in phonics-based classes outperform those in whole language
   classes. Whole language advocates argue that when whole language
   is defined correctly, when it includes real reading, students in these
   classes do better on test of reading comprehension, with no difference on skills tests.

The Complexity Argument: Johnson (2001)

Clymer (1963, 1966) investigated 45 phonic generalizations of words in four
basal series and concluded that many did not work very well. This result has
been a central part of the argument against over-teaching phonics. Here are
two well-known examples: The rule "when two vowels go walking the first
does the talking" (when two vowels appear side by side, the long sound of the
first is heard and the second is silent, as in "bead") worked in only 45% of the
cases Clymer examined, and the final e rule (first vowel is long, final e is silent,
as in "cake") worked in only 63% of the cases.

Johnson (2001) re-examined Clymer's conclusions. On reading the title
of her paper ("The utility of phonics generalizations: Let's take another look
at Clymer's conclusions") and the short summary under the title ("English
orthography is not easily reduced to a few rules, but there are some general
recommendations for teaching about vowels that can be helpful."), one gets
the impression that Clymer's results will be contested, and that a new case for
direct phonics instruction will emerge from this article. Johnson promises to
review what she considers neglected studies that followed Clymer, and promises to present a new analysis.

The neglected studies, however, replicate Clymer's results, with only a
few alterations, a conclusion Adams (1990) also arrived at in her discussion of
Clymer's work. And Johnson's new analysis confirms that extensive phonics
teaching is a hopeless endeavor. She provides, in fact, dramatic evidence that
English phonics is extremely complex, which was, in fact, Clymer's point.

Here is an example. As noted above, Clymer concluded that the "two vowels walking" rule applied only 45% of the time. In her re-analysis, Johnson concludes that this rule works well for five two vowel combinations: ay (96.4%),
oa (95%), ee (95.9%), ai (75%) and ay (77%). Of course, one can easily dispute
that 75 or 77% accuracy is enough to justify this conclusion, but more serious is
the fact that the situation is a disaster for the 14 other two-vowel combinations
Johnson presents in her table 2. While four other two-vowel pairs are regular,

none of these meet the criteria of the "walking" rule. Four additional pairs have two possible pronunciations and four more pairs have three possible pronunciations. Finally, another two pairs with two possible pronunciations were considered "very rare." (One of them appears in "fruit," "suit," and "build" and the other in "Asia," "piano," and "official," hardly arcane words.) Very few of these alternative pronunciations follow the "walking rule."

As noted earlier, Clymer concluded that the final e rule worked only 63% of the time. Johnson concludes that for some combinations, it does a bit better (a-o, as in "cake," 77.7%, i-e as in "five," 74.2%, u-e, as in "rule," 76.9%) but it is less efficient for others (for o-e, as in "stove," 58.4%, e-e, as in "these," 16.6%). She concludes that this rule is "surprisingly reliable when restated" (p. 139) and that teachers can teach this rule "with confidence" (p. 138) as long as they encourage a "flexible strategy." This does not seem to be a real step forward: we are trading a simple rule that works 63% of the time for a far more complex rule that is only slightly more efficient.

Johnson's work, in other words, is a strong confirmation of Clymer's: Simple rules don't apply to a large percentage of words. Yes, one can come up with rules that cover more words, but they also have numerous exceptions and are very complex.

Johnson has no clear program for teaching sound-spelling correspondences, other than the suggestion that we also consider rules for higher order units, such as rhymes and "vowel patterns," also, as she points out, numerous and complex.

Buried deep in Johnson's article is the suggestion that some children can acquire phonics generalizations by reading. As noted earlier, Smith (e.g. 1994) has hypothesized that most of our knowledge of phonics is the result of reading and not the cause. Johnson's view differs somewhat from Smith's in that she claims that some children can indeed acquire sound-spelling correspondences by reading, while "need systematic restruction" (p. 141). No evidence is provided for this extremely important claim, a claim that runs counter to current official state and federal government policy that all children must have systematic, intensive phonics instruction.

To support such a claim, one would have to show that there are substantial numbers of children who have learned to read without extensive phonics training (this is easy to find), and also substantial numbers of children who cannot "learn to read by reading," who require extensive phonics instruction. The existence of this second group has never been demonstrated: To do so, one must find large numbers of children who have been read to, who have substantial exposure to comprehensible and interesting texts, and who nevertheless fail to learn to read.

One sees, of course, some children who learn to read less quickly than others do, but this is a statistical necessity in any phenomenon that exhibits any degree of variability. No matter what, we will always have children who fall in the lowest 25% in rate of learning to read. What we very rarely see are those who never learn to read despite the availability of comprehensible and interesting print.

Which phonics generalizations are useful? Which ones really help children understand text? I suggest we ask the real experts: Teachers who have helped children learn to read for many years. A consensus of experienced practitioners will tell us if it is worthwhile to tell children that the a-e combination is pronounced with the long vowel and the final e silent (except when the final syllable is unaccented—then the vowel is pronounced with a short-i sound, as in "palace," or the combination is "are," with words such as "have" and "dance" as exceptions). How many of us who easily and fluently read words with the a-e combination were ever aware of this rule?[1]

The Method Comparison Argument

As noted earlier, each side has claimed victory in method comparison studies. Skill-building advocates claim that children in skills-based classes learn to read better, while whole language advocates claim that whole language is superior, as long as it is defined correctly. I discuss here a recent contribution to this debate.

Jeynes and Littell (2000) reviewed 14 studies and concluded that overall, low SES children do not benefit from whole language instruction, but "there may be some advantages to the whole language approach in its purest form" (p. 21). Of the 14 studies, only four were listed as published in journals or books. Of the ten studies that were listed as unpublished, two, it turned out, were in fact published in the *Reading Research Quarterly*. I was able to locate five others through ERIC, and one other that I believe to be identical to a study on Jeynes and Littell's list. My interpretation of these studies is quite different than Jeynes and Littell's interpretations in most cases.

As usual, the definition of whole language is at issue. Jeynes and Littell classified two studies as "pure" whole language. They satisfied the following criteria: (1) no adapted texts; (2) no whole class, teacher sponsored assignments, (3) "integrated language experiences as opposed to direct instruction in isolated skill sequences" (p. 23). The two studies in this category showed the strongest advantage for whole language. Less "pure" versions of whole language resulted in weaker and negative results.

Jeynes and Littell also classified several "language experience" treatments as whole language, considering language experience to be a "precursor to whole language" (p. 27). The core of language experience consists of students dictating stories to teachers; these stories are transcribed by the teacher and used as reading material.

I object to Jeynes and Littell's definition of whole language. (1) In my view, the issue is not whether texts are adapted or modified but whether they are interesting and comprehensible. (2) There are some instances when a whole class teacher sponsored assignment or activity is appropriate in a whole language class. (3) Some phonics knowledge can help make texts comprehensible. While most whole language proponents prefer to teach phonics in context, I know of no reason why integrated versus isolated teaching of phonics should be part of the core definition of whole language. The real issue is whether texts are comprehensible.

A similar analysis, limited to published studies, appeared in Krashen (1999), examining studies that compared "whole language" and "skills." This analysis focused only on one characteristic: The amount of real reading for meaning done by the children. As noted earlier, comprehensible and interesting reading is not the only characteristic of whole language, but it is at the core of whole language. The conclusion was that children in classes with more real reading tended to do better on tests of reading comprehension, read more, liked reading more, and did just as well as "skills" students on skills tests (reading nonsense words). This analysis included some of the published studies that Jeynes and Littell included.

I present here comments on those studies in Jeynes and Littell I was able to obtain. As in Krashen (1999), I focus primarily on performance on tests of reading comprehension. Reading comprehension is, after all, the goal of reading instruction.

The impact of whole language/language experience was measured by Jeynes and Littell using effect sizes. Effect sizes are usually calculated by subtracting the mean of the comparison group from the mean of the experimental group, then dividing the result by the pooled standard deviation. They are weighted for sample size. Effect sizes can also be computed from other statistics, such as F, t, and r. Following Jeynes and Littell, in this paper, positive effect sizes indicate an advantage for whole language or language experience, and negative effect sizes indicate that comparisons did better.

1. Jeynes and Littell included an unpublished dissertation by J.R. Hoffman, which was not available to me. I did, however, find a study by Carline and Hoffman (1976) with a nearly identical title that was obviously the same study. Although Jeynes and Littell calculated an effect size of −.23 favoring the conventional reading approach over language experience, Carline and Hoffman (1976) concluded that "teachers who use the language experience approach to reading more often . . . showed an increase of 2.9 raw score points more on English reading standardized test scores than those teachers who use it less frequently" (p. 43). Carline and Hoffman reported a correlation of .32 between the amount of language experience used and student gains in English reading, equivalent to an effect size (d) of .64.

2. McCanne (1966) compared the impact of a basal reader approach, an audio-lingual approach, and language experience on Spanish speaking children learning English as a second language. McCanne noted that the language experience approach was not designed for students who are acquiring English as a second language (p. 75). Some modifications in language experience were made in this study; nevertheless, the use of language experience clearly required considerable speaking competence before substantial listening and reading took place, a procedure that violates what is known about language acquisition.

McCanne's results depend on the kind of statistical procedure used. When reading test scores were adjusted for factors such as listening ability in English, measures of cognitive development, SES, measures of teacher competence, and pupil attendance, the basal method was better (d = −.65) . . . based on standard scores. When raw means were used, the language experience students were better (d = .36). . . .

3. Lamb (1972) earned a substantial $-.75$ effect size in Jeynes and Littell, in favor of the comparison group over whole language. Lamb noted however that all five teachers who used the language experience approach had not used it before and participated in monthly training sessions. The entire duration of the study was only four months.

Contrary to Jeynes and Littell's findings, the results were not clearly in favor of the comparisons. Lamb did several different analyses: Analyses of covariance, controlling for IQ scores, teacher experience, and teacher background showed language experience to be superior (for boys, $d = .47$; for girls, $d = .41$) but a one way ANOVA with no control for potential confounding variables found the basal method to be better. . . . Apparently, Jeynes and Littell used only the simple ANOVA results. Note that in McCanne (1976), language experience did better on with raw scores (ANOVA) and worse on adjusted scores (ANCOVA), the opposite pattern. . . . In my summary below I use the adjusted results.

4. Jeynes and Littell included Ewoldt (1976), a comparison of Follow-Through and Non-Follow-Through classes on a story retelling task and reported an effect size of .05 favoring language experience. The Follow-Through Model advocates the language experience approach. A serious problem, however, was that only eight of the Follow-through subjects (out of 36) actually came from classes in which the basic program was language experience. . . . Nine others came from classes that used some language experience as supplemental activities. No information was available about the classes eight of the students participated in, and eight others came from classes that included no language experience. Clearly, this study should not have been included.

5. In Usova and Usova (1993), the number of students in the whole language class was small (m = 8) and the treatment was a combination of a wide variety of activities, emphasizing the combination of art activities with language arts, and also including reading, hearing stories, writing and direct instruction. We are provided with no information whatsoever on the activities of the comparison group, and we have no idea if experimentals and controls differed with respect to the amount of reading done. Neither experimentals nor controls made much progress over the academic year in reading comprehension, experimentals gaining less than one point on a standardized reading test, and controls actually getting slightly worse.

6. Stallings (1975) was awarded a $-.79$ effect size for comparisons over whole language, but it is difficult to determine how Jeynes and Littell arrived at this figure. This study was not a comparison of methods, but sought to determine predictors of achievement in first and third grade classrooms based on one day of observation. Amount of reading done was not one of the predictors considered.

7. Jeynes and Littell included Harris, Serwer and Gold (1966). 1 obtained Harris and Serwer (1966a), which appears to cover exactly the same data. Harris and Serwer (1996b) is a shorter version published in the *Reading Research Quarterly.*

Jeynes and Littell reported an effect size of $-.51$ in favor of comparisons ("skills-centered") over language experience. From Harris and Serwer's table 26, I computed an effect size of $-.18$ in favor of comparisons, based on the Stanford Paragraph Meaning test. What is crucial, however, is that Harris and Serwer report that children in the basal group actually spent more time in reading activities than did the children in language experience. Children in the skills classes spent 56% of the instructional time in reading activities, while children in language experience classes spent only 39.5% of the time on reading activities. It is thus quite likely that the comparison children did more real reading. Thus, both the sign and size of the effect size should be changed for this study. Moreover, Harris and Serwer (1966b) reported positive correlations between the amount of time spent in reading activities and scores on the reading tests. . . .

8. Dahl and Freppon (1994) (also available as Dahl and Freppon, 1995) earned an effect size of .67 in favor of whole language. This figure represents a combination of six different measures of literacy development, including tests of concepts about print, the alphabetic principle, story retelling, and concepts about writing. None were measures of reading comprehension.

A closer look at the results showed that the only significant difference between the whole language and skills children was on a task in which the child pretended to read a picture book without words. The story was rated for the presence of aspects of the written narrative register. I calculated an effect size of 1.79 in favor of whole language for this task.

9. Jeynes and Littell calculated an effect size of .50 for Morrow, O'Connor, and Smith (1990) in favor of whole language. Based only the standardized test used in the study, I calculated an effect size of $d = -.18$ in favor of the skills group over whole language. The test, however, did not contain a measure of reading comprehension. Literature-based students showed more interest in reading: they could name more authors, took more books home to read, reported more reading at home, and named significantly more kinds of reading material. They were also significantly better on an "attempted reading" test, showing more reading-like behaviors.

10. For Morrow (1992), Jeynes and Littell calculated an effect size of 1.24. For the two reading comprehension tests included in the study, I calculated effect sizes of 1.84 and .62, with a mean of 1.23, nearly identical to Jeynes and Littell's results. It is clear that the whole language ("literature based") group read more. Children in the literature based group spent about 3.5 hours per week with basals and about four hours with literature. They were read to daily, engaged in at least three "literacy activities" per week (e.g. retelling and rewriting stories, book sharing, keeping track of what they read), and had at least three sessions per week in a comfortable "literacy center" for 30 minutes at a time, during which time they read, wrote and performed

stories. Comparison students were read to no more than twice a week and focused nearly entirely on the basal and workbook. Free reading was allowed only when children had finished their basal seatwork.

11. Manning, Manning and Long (1989) lasted three years (K to grade 2), and researchers made biweekly visits to classes to "verify the continuity of the two different literacy programs" (p. 5). Both first and second grade whole language students were significantly better in reading comprehension (d = 1.97 in both cases, effect sizes calculated from p values resulting from Mann Whitney U's). Nine out of 11 whole language children could name a favorite author at the end of grade 2. None of the skills taught children could.

The small sample size (n = 11 in each group) is an obvious weakness of this study, but the care for fidelity of treatment and long duration are obvious strengths.

Method Comparisons: Conclusion

Several studies should not have been included in the meta-analysis. In some, it was not at all clear that there was a genuine comparison of whole language/ language experience and basal/skill oriented methods, These include Stallings (1975), which was not a method comparison at all, Ewoldt (1976), in which many "language experience" subjects did not actually have language experience instruction, Usova and Usova (1993), which included a wide variety of activities under "whole language" and had a very small sample size, and McCanne (1966), which used language experience for second language acquirers, which may have been inappropriate because of premature production demands. Applying my criteria of using only tests of reading comprehension eliminates Morrow, O'Connor and Smith (1990) and Dahl and Freppon (1995) as well.

Of the five studies remaining, in three cases I reached conclusions opposite to those of Jeynes and Littell: I have argued that results were inaccurately reported in Carline and Hoffman (1976) and Lamb (1972) and that the direction of the effect size should be reversed in Harris and Serwer (Harris, Serwer and Gold, 1966). If my interpretations are correct, effect sizes for the still-eligible studies should be changed: for Hoffman, from −.23 to +.68; for Lamb, from −.75 to +.44; for Harris and Serwer, from −.51 to .18, for Manning et al., from 1.21 to 1.97. The effect size for Morrow (1992) remains the same.

Only two studies in this set provide clear evidence that one group did more reading than the other, and in both cases those who read more, did better on tests of reading comprehension; Morrow (1992), with an effect size of 1.23, and Harris and Serwer (1966a, 1966b), with an effect size of .18. For other studies in which groups are labeled whole language or language experience, with no clear data on amount read, effect sizes still favor whole language: Carline and Hoffman (1976), with an effect size of .68, Lamb (1972), an effect size of .44, and Manning et al. (1989), with an effect size of 1.97. The average effect size for all five of these studies is +.90 favoring whole language/

language experience. Excluding Manning et al., the study with the largest effect size, the average effect size is +.63. Even if we include McCanne (1966) and exclude Manning et al., the average is +.38 in favor of whole language/ language experience.

Note that this conclusion is not dependent on my policy of limiting measures to tests of reading comprehension. Allowing Morrow, O'Connor and Smith (1990) (d = −.18) and Dahl and Freppon (1995) (d = .67) into the re-analysis does not change the final result very much.

Jeynes and Littell's conclusion was that although "pure" whole language students did well, basal/skill groups were in general a winner over whole language, with a mean effect size of −.65 in favor of the comparison groups. My conclusion is nearly exactly the opposite.

In my view, neither of our results should be taken as definitive. No study considered the amount of real reading done to be a central variable, and only two studies attempted to determine the amount of reading students did. In light of Harris and Serwer's finding (see also Evans and Carr, 1985) that children in skills classes actually spent more time reading than children in language experience, one must be cautious in concluding that children in any language experience or whole language class actually read more than those in traditional classes.

What is clear, however, is that Jeynes and Littell's interpretation of the research is not the only possible one.

Overall Discussion and Conclusion

A detailed reading of Johnson (2001) reveals that Clymer's original conclusions stand: the rules of phonics, at least those reviewed by Johnson, remain enormously complex. A close analysis of the actual studies reviewed by Jeynes and Littell (2000) shows that when tests of reading comprehension are considered, when real reading is considered as the core element of whole language, and when details of studies are examined closely, whole language does very well in method comparison studies. Although the authors conclude otherwise, these studies actually provide evidence for the limits of phonics instruction and the efficacy of whole language.

Note

1. Johnson cites *Becoming a Nation of Readers* (Anderson, Hiebert, Scott, and Wilkinson, 1985) as holding the position that phonics can be reduced to a few simple rules that can easily be taught by the end of grade two. Not quite. Consider this excerpt:

   . . . phonics instruction should aim to teach only the most important and regular of letter-to-sound relationships . . . once the basic relationships have been taught, the best way to get children to refine and extend their knowledge of letter-sound correspondences is through repeated opportunities to read.

If this position is correct, then much phonics instruction is overly subtle and probably unproductive (*Becoming a Nation of Readers,* p. 38).

Weaver (1994) and Goodman (1993) have pointed out that *Becoming a Nation of Readers* sees direct phonics instruction as playing a limited role. In fact, the position presented in the excerpt presented above is not very different from that proposed by Frank Smith (1994): A few straightforward rules of phonics can be taught directly and can be useful in making texts more comprehensible, but most phonics is the result of reading, not the cause.

G. Reid Lyon  **NO**

Why Reading Is Not
a Natural Process

I am frequently asked why the National Institute of Child Health and Human Development (NICHD) conducts and supports research in reading, given that the NICHD is part of the National Institutes of Health, a federal agency that emphasizes basic biomedical science and health-related research. A primary answer is that learning to read is critical to a child's overall well-being. If a youngster does not learn to read in our literacy-driven society, hope for a fulfilling, productive life diminishes. In short, difficulties learning to read are not only an educational problem; they constitute a serious public health concern.

The NICHD has been studying normal reading development and reading difficulties for 35 years. NICHD-supported researchers have studied more than 10,000 children, published more than 2,500 articles, and written more than 50 books that present the results of 10 large-scale longitudinal studies and more than 1,500 smaller scale experimental and cross-sectional studies. Many of the longitudinal research sites initiated studies in the early 1980s with kindergarten children before they began their reading instruction and have studied the children over time. Researchers have studied some children for 15 years, with several sites following the youngsters for at least 5 years. Additional research sites have joined within the past 3 years to investigate the effects of different reading instructional programs with kindergarten and 1st grade children. At most research sites, multidisciplinary research teams study cognitive, linguistic, neurobiological, genetic, and instructional factors related to early reading development and reading difficulties.[1]

Reading Research and Scientific Tradition

The NICHD reading research has centered on three basic questions: (1) How do children learn to read English (and other languages)? What are the critical skills, abilities, environments, and instructional interactions that foster the fluent reading of text? (2) What skill deficits and environmental factors impede reading development? (3) For which children are which instructional approaches most beneficial, at which stages of reading development? Before summarizing findings related to these questions, I would like to explain the NICHD research process.

From *Educational Leadership,* vol. 55, no. 6, March 1998, pp. 14–18. Copyright © 1998 by ASCD. Reprinted by permission. The Association for Supervision and Curriculum Development is a worldwide community of educators advocating sound policies and sharing best practices to achieve the success of each learner. To learn more, visit ASCD at www.ascd.org.

First, the NICHD reading research program is rooted in scientific tradition and the scientific method. The program rests on systematic, longitudinal, field-based investigations, cross-sectional studies, and laboratory-based experiments that are publicly verifiable and replicable. Second, the research integrates quantitative and qualitative methods to increase the richness, impact, and ecological validity of the data. However, using qualitative research methods requires the same scientific rigor employed in quantitative studies. Third, the NICHD reading research program is only one of many programs dedicated to understanding reading development and difficulties. The U.S. Department of Education's Office of Research and Improvement, the Office of Special Education Programs, and the Canadian Research Council have supported many outstanding reading researchers (see Adams 1990 for a research review).

The cumulative work of federally and privately funded researchers illuminates how children develop reading skills, why some children struggle to learn to read, and what can be done to help all readers reach proficiency. Although much remains to be learned, many findings have survived scrutiny, replication, and extension.

The Critical Role of Phonemic Awareness

How do children learn to read English? Reading is the product of decoding and comprehension (Gough et al. 1993). Although this sounds simple, learning to read is much tougher than people think. To learn to decode and read printed English, children must be aware that spoken words are composed of individual sound parts termed phonemes. This is what is meant by *phoneme awareness.*

Phoneme awareness and phonics are not the same. When educators assess phoneme awareness skills, they ask children to demonstrate knowledge of the sound structure of words *without any letters or written words present.* For example, "What word would be left if the /k/ sound were taken away from *cat?*" "What sounds do you hear in the word *big?*" To assess phonics skills, they ask children to link sounds (phonemes) *with letters.* Thus, the development of phonics skills depends on the development of phoneme awareness.

Why is phoneme awareness critical in beginning reading, and why is it difficult for some children? Because to read an alphabetic language like English, children must know that written spellings systematically represent spoken sounds. When youngsters figure this out, either on their own or with direct instruction, they have acquired the alphabetic principle. However, if beginning readers have difficulty perceiving the sounds in spoken words—for example, if they cannot "hear" the /at/ sound in *fat* and *cat* and perceive that the difference lies in the first sound—they will have difficulty decoding or sounding out new words. In turn, developing reading fluency will be difficult, resulting in poor comprehension, limited learning, and little enjoyment.

We are beginning to understand why many children have difficulty developing phoneme awareness. When we speak to one another, the individual sounds (phonemes) within the words are not consciously heard by the listener. Thus, no one ever receives any "natural" practice understanding that words are composed of smaller, abstract sound units.

For example, when one utters the word *bag,* the ear hears only one sound, not three (as in /b/-/a/-/g/). This is because when *bag* is spoken, the /a/ and /g/ phonemes are folded into the initial /b/ sound. Thus, the acoustic information presented to the ears reflects an overlapping bundle of sound, not three discrete sounds. This process ensures rapid, efficient communication. Consider the time it would take to have a conversation if each of the words we uttered were segmented into their underlying sound structure.

However, nature has provided a conundrum here: What is good for the listener is not so good for the beginning reader. Although spoken language is seamless, the beginning reader must detect the seams in speech, unglue the sounds from one another, and learn which sounds (phonemes) go with which letters. We now understand that specific systems in the brain recover sounds from spoken words, and just as in learning any skill, children understand phoneme awareness with different aptitudes and experiences.

Developing Automaticity and Understanding

In the initial stages of reading development, learning phoneme awareness and phonics skills *and* practicing these skills with texts is critical. Children must also acquire fluency and automaticity in decoding and word recognition. Consider that a reader has only so much attention and memory capacity. If beginning readers read the words in a laborious, inefficient manner, they cannot remember what they read, much less relate the ideas to their background knowledge. Thus, the ultimate goal of reading instruction—for children to understand and enjoy what they read—will not be achieved.

Reading research by NICHD and others reveals that "making meaning" requires more than phoneme awareness, phonics, and reading fluency, although these are necessary skills. Good comprehenders link the ideas presented in print to their own experiences. They have also developed the necessary vocabulary to make sense of the content being read. Good comprehenders have a knack for summarizing, predicting, and clarifying what they have read, and many are adept at asking themselves guide questions to enhance understanding.

Linguistic Gymnastics

Programmatic research over the past 35 years *has not* supported the view that reading development reflects a *natural process*—that children learn to read as they learn to speak, through natural exposure to a literate environment. Indeed, researchers have established that certain aspects of learning to read are highly unnatural. Consider the linguistic gymnastics involved in recovering phonemes from speech and applying them to letters and letter patterns. Unlike learning to speak, beginning readers must appreciate consciously what the symbols stand for in the writing system they learn (Liberman 1992).

Unfortunately for beginning readers, written alphabetic symbols are arbitrary and are created differently in different languages to represent spoken language elements that are themselves abstract. If learning to read were natural, there would not exist the substantial number of cultures that have yet to develop a written language, despite having a rich oral language. And, if learning to read unfolds naturally, why does our literate society have so many youngsters and adults who are illiterate?

Despite strong evidence to the contrary, many educators and researchers maintain the perspective that reading is an almost instinctive, natural process. They believe that explicit instruction in phoneme awareness, phonics, structural analysis, and reading comprehension strategies is unnecessary because oral language skills provide the reader with a meaning-based structure for the decoding and recognition of unfamiliar words (Edelsky et al. 1991, Goodman 1996). Scientific research, however, simply does not support the claim that context and authentic text are a proxy for decoding skills. To guess the pronunciation of words from context, the context must predict the words. But content words—the most important words for text comprehension—can be predicted from surrounding context only 10 to 20 percent of the time (Gough et al. 1981). Instead, the choice strategy for beginning readers is to decode letters to sounds in an increasingly complete and accurate manner (Adams 1990, Foorman et al. 1998).

Moreover, the view some whole language advocates hold that skilled readers gloss over the text, sampling only parts of words, and examining several lines of print to decode unfamiliar words, is not consistent with available data. Just and Carpenter (1987), among others, have demonstrated consistently that good readers rarely skip over words, and readers gaze directly at most content words. Indeed, in contrast to conventional wisdom, less-skilled readers depend on context for word-recognition. The word recognition processes of skilled readers are so automatic that they do not need to rely on context (Stanovich et al. 1981). Good readers employ context to aid overall comprehension, but not as in aid in the recognition of unfamiliar words. Whether we like it or not, an alphabetic cipher must be deciphered, and this requires robust decoding skills.

The scientific evidence that refutes the idea that learning to read is a *natural process* is of such magnitude that Stanovich (1994) wrote:

> That direct instruction in alphabetic coding facilitates early reading acquisition is one of the most well established conclusions in all of behavioral science. . . . The idea that learning to read is just like learning to speak is accepted by no responsible linguist, psychologist, or cognitive scientist in the research community (pp. 285–286).

Why Some Children Have Difficulties Learning to Read

Good readers are phonemically aware, understand the alphabetic principle, apply these skills in a rapid and fluent manner, posses strong vocabularies and syntactical and grammatical skills, and relate reading to their own experiences. Difficulties in any of these areas can impede reading development. Further, learning to read begins far before children enter formal schooling. Children who have stimulating literacy experiences from birth onward have an edge in vocabulary development, understanding the goals of reading, and developing an awareness of print and literacy concepts.

Conversely, the children who are most at risk for reading failure enter kindergarten and the elementary grades without these early experiences. Frequently, many poor readers have not consistently engaged in the language play that develops an awareness of sound structure and language patterns. They have limited exposure to bedtime and lap time reading. In short, children raised in poverty, those with limited proficiency in English, those from homes where the parents' reading levels and practices are low, and those with speech, language, and hearing handicaps are at increased risk of reading failure.

However, many children with robust oral language experience, average to above average intelligence, and frequent early interactions with literacy activities also have difficulties learning to read. Why? Programmatic longitudinal research, including research supported by NICHD, clearly indicates that deficits in the development of phoneme awareness skills not only predict difficulties learning to read, but they also have a negative effect on reading acquisition. Whereas phoneme awareness is necessary for adequate reading development, it is not sufficient. Children must also develop phonics concepts and apply these skills fluently in text. Although substantial research supports the importance of phoneme awareness, phonics, and the development of speed and automaticity in reading, we know less about how children develop reading comprehension strategies and semantic and syntactic knowledge. Given that some children with well developed decoding and word-recognition abilities have difficulties understanding what they read, more research in reading comprehension is crucial.

From Research to Practice

Scientific research can inform beginning reading instruction. We know from research that reading is a language-based activity. Reading does not develop naturally, and for many children, specific decoding, word-recognition, and reading comprehension skills must be taught directly and systematically. We have also learned that preschool children benefit significantly from being read to. The evidence suggests strongly that educators can foster reading development by providing kindergarten children with instruction that develops print concepts, familiarity with the purposes of reading and writing, age-appropriate vocabulary and language comprehension skills, and familiarity with the language structure.

Substantial evidence shows that many children in the 1st and 2nd grades and beyond will require explicit instruction to develop the necessary phoneme awareness, phonics, spelling, and reading comprehension skills. But for these children, this will not be sufficient. For youngsters having difficulties learning to read, each of these foundational skills should be taught and integrated into textual reading formats to ensure sufficient levels of fluency, automaticity, and understanding.

Moving Beyond Assumptions

One hopes that scientific research informs beginning reading instruction, but it is not always so. Unfortunately, many teachers and administrators who could benefit from research to guide reading instructional practices do not yet trust the idea that research can inform their teaching. There are many reasons for this lack of faith. As Mary Kennedy (1997) has pointed out, it is difficult for teachers to apply research information when it is of poor quality, lacks authority, is not easily accessible, is communicated in an incomprehensible manner, and is not practical. Moreover, the lack of agreement about reading development and instruction among education leaders does not bode favorably for increasing trust. The burden to produce compelling and practical information lies with reading researchers.

Most great scientific discoveries have come from a willingness and an ability to be wrong. Researchers and teachers could serve our children much better if they had the courage to set aside assumptions when they are not working. What if the assumption that reading is a natural activity, as appealing as it may be, were wrong and not working to help our children read? The fundamental purpose of science is to test our beliefs and intuitions and to tell us where the truth lies. Indeed, the education of our children is too important to be determined by anything but the strongest of objective scientific evidence. Our children deserve nothing less.

Note

1. See Fletcher and Lyon (in press) and Lyon and Moats (1997) for reviews of NICHD reading research findings. Contact the author for a complete set of references of published research from all NICHD reading research sites since 1963.

References

Adams, M. J. (1990). *Beginning to Read: Thinking and Learning about Print.* Cambridge, Mass.: MIT Press.

Edelsky, C., B. Altwerger, and B. Flores. (1991). *Whole Language: What's the Difference?* Portsmouth, N.H.: Heinemann.

Fletcher, J. M. and G. R. Lyon. (in press). *Reading: A Research-Based Approach.* Palo Alto, Calif.: Hoover-Institute.

Foorman, B. R., D. J. Francis, J. M. Fletcher, C. Schatschneider, and P. Mehta. (1998). "The Role of Instruction in Learning to Read: Preventing Reading Failure in At-Risk Children." *Journal of Educational Psychology* 90, 1–15.

Goodman, K. S. (1996). *Ken Goodman on Reading: A Common Sense Look at the Nature of Language and the Science of Reading.* Portsmouth, N.H.: Heinemann.

Gough, P. B., J. A. Alford, and P. Holley-Wilcox. (1981). "Words and Contexts." In *Perception of Print: Reading Research in Experimental Psychology,* edited by O. J. Tzeng and H. Singer. Hillsdale, N.J.: Erlbaum.

Gough, P. B., C. Juel, and P. Griffith. (1992). "Reading, Spelling, and the Ortho-graphic Cipher." In *Reading Acquisition,* edited by P. B. Gough, L. C. Ehri, and R. Trieman. Hillsdale, N.J.: Erlbaum.

Just, C., and P. A. Carpenter. (1980). "A Theory of Reading: From Eye Fixations to Comprehension." *Psychological Review* 87, 329–354.

Kennedy, M. M. (1997). "The Connection Between Research and Practice." *Educational Researcher* 26, 4–12.

Liberman, A. M. (1992). "The Relation of Speech to Reading and Writing." In *Orthography, Phonology, Morphology and Meaning,* edited by R. Frost and L. Katz. Amsterdam: Elsevier Science Publishers B.V.

Lyon, G. R., and L. C. Moats. (1997). "Critical Conceptual and Methodologi-cal Considerations in Reading Intervention Research." *Journal of Learning Disabilities* 30, 578–588.

Stanovich, K. E. (1994). "Romance and Reality." *The Reading Teacher* 47, 280–291.

Stanovich, K. E., R. F. West, and D. J. Freeman (1981). "A Longitudinal Study of Sentence Context Effects in Second Grade Children: Tests of an Interactive-Compensatory Model." *Journal of Experimental Child Psychology* 32, 402–433.

POSTSCRIPT

Is the Whole Language Approach to Reading Effective?

Can empirical research be relied on to determine whether or not whole language is more effective (or at least no less effective) than a basic skills (e.g., phonics) approach to reading instruction? The answer to this question is yes. Unfortunately, however, the current data are not complete enough to allow judgment on whole language to be passed with certainty. Take, for example, the contention of whole language supporters that gains in reading achievement have been observed in many states that have adopted whole language instruction. Although these gains may have been caused by the shift to whole language, it is also possible that the gains had nothing to do with whole language but instead resulted from other factors, such as an increase or redirecting of resources to literacy instruction or a renewed commitment to tackling literacy problems on the part of teachers and administrators. What is needed to provide unequivocal proof that whole language has caused any gains in reading achievement are *experimental* studies, in which students are assigned randomly to various instructional conditions, such as whole language versus phonics/drill-and-practice.

Critics of whole language have been able to bolster their arguments with an impressive array of studies, many of which have, in fact, involved an experimental design. These studies have clearly shown that skilled reading depends on the acquisition and automatization of basic knowledge and skills, including phonics—skills that typically receive little systematic instruction within the context of the whole language approach. Critics also have amassed considerable empirical data demonstrating that many children who have difficulty learning to read (e.g., those with a learning disability) fail precisely because they lack basic knowledge in phonics and other decoding skills.

But does the whole language approach have any advantages over a basic skills approach? Supporters of whole language argue that students who experience a whole language approach will find literacy activities to be inherently more interesting than will children who experience a basic skills approach. Presumably, this difference will lead these students to read and write more, which, in turn, will sharpen their literacy skills over time. Supporters might also argue that the whole language approach assists children in incorporating reading and writing into their other academic pursuits, such as science and social studies, which will lead to greater gains in these latter domains compared to the basic skills approach to literacy. Unfortunately, such assertions have yet to be evaluated fully, largely because most studies in this area, whether correlational or experimental, have included only a narrow set of outcome measures (i.e., measures focused only on reading and writing rather than on other academic domains) or have not charted student progress over a period sufficient to address long-term achievement. Although it is too early to tell, these data may eventually indicate that some combination of whole language and the basic skills approach is most effective in producing the widest gains for the most children.

The controversy surrounding the relative merits of whole language and phonics shows no signs of resolution. Indeed, the report of the National Reading Panel in 2000, which was first used to tout the advantages of phonics, has recently come under fierce attack. A particularly careful, empirically based version of this attack can be found in "Beyond the Smoke and Mirrors: A Critique of the National Reading Report on Phonics," by Elaine Garan, *Phi Delta Kappan* (March 2001). Another interesting critique of the report of the National Reading Panel includes "Readers, Instruction, and the NRP," by G. Pat Wilson, Prisca Martens, Poonam Arya, and Bess Altweger, *Phi Delta Kappan* (November 2004). Readers interested in reading more about whole language should turn to "The Whole Truth about Hole Language—Whoops! I Mean the Hole Truth about Whole Language—Can You Dig It!" by Mimi B. Chenfield, *Early Childhood Education Journal* (vol. 23, no. 3, 1996); "I Didn't Found Whole Language; Whole Language Found Me," by Kenneth S. Goodman, *Education Digest* (October 1993); and "Back to the Basics of Whole Language," by Reggie Routman, *Educational Leadership* (February 1997). Critiques of whole language are numerous and include "Where's the Phonics? Making a Case for Its Direct and Systematic Instruction," by Patrick Groff, *The Reading Teacher* (vol. 52, no. 2, 1998) and "Teaching Decoding," by Louisa C. Moats, *American Educator* (Spring/Summer 1998). The latter article provides an excellent discussion of research on decoding, as well as some concrete pedagogical suggestions. There are also articles in which the authors outline ways in which the whole language and basic skills approaches can be profitably combined: "Every Child a Reader," by Marie Carbo, *American School Board Journal* (February 1997); "Whole Language vs. Phonics: The Great Debate," by Marie Carbo, *Principal* (January 1996); and "Whole-to-Parts Phonics Instruction: Building on What Children Know to Help Them Know More," by Margaret Moustafa and Elba Maldonado-Colon, *The Reading Teacher* (February 1999). For an interesting analysis of the political side of the whole language controversy, see "Politics and the Pendulum: An Alternative Understanding of the Case of Whole Language as Educational Innovation," by Paula Wolfe and Leslie Poynor, *Educational Researcher* (January–February 2001). An interesting pair of articles in the October 2002 issue of *Phi Delta Kappan* address the political debate surrounding reading instruction in California: Richard G. Innis, "There's More Than Mythology to California's Reading Decline," and Stephen Kashen, "Speculation and Conjecture." An eclectic collection of strategies for teaching reading can be found in *Guide to Human Development for Future Educators* by Leonard Abbeduto and Stephen N. Elliott (McGraw-Hill, 1998); *Straight Talk about Reading: How Parents Can Make a Difference during the Early Years* by Susan L. Hall and Louisa C. Moats (Contemporary Books, 1999); and *Best Practices in Literacy Instruction,* edited by Lesley Mandel Morrow et al. (Guilford Press, 2003). Finally, a brief but informative history of the debates around reading instruction is provided by James S. Kim, "Research and the Reading Wars," *Phi Delta Kappan* (January 2008).

ISSUE 13

Is Greater Parental Involvement at School Always Beneficial?

YES: Laura Van Zandt Allen and Eleanor T. Migliore, from "Supporting Students and Parents Through a School-University Partnership," *Middle School Journal* (January 2005)

NO: Rodney T. Ogawa, from "Organizing Parent-Teacher Relations Around the Work of Teaching," *Peabody Journal of Education* (1998)

ISSUE SUMMARY

YES: Laura Van Zandt Allen and Eleanor T. Migliore point to evidence that parental involvement in children's schooling is associated with improvements in children's academic performance and social-emotional development. Van Zandt Allen and Migliore also describe a program to help teachers solicit and use parental input, something the authors argue few teachers are normally prepared to do.

NO: Although Rodney T. Ogawa acknowledges that there is evidence that parental involvement has a positive impact on student outcomes, he questions the assumption that if some parental involvement is good, more must be even better. Ogawa argues, instead, that schools must build "buffers" as well as bridges between themselves and parents.

Parents may be more involved in the schooling of their children today than at any time in the history of public education in the United States. But does parental involvement matter? Does it translate into improvements in children's academic achievement and their increased investment in school? In fact, there is considerable empirical evidence to suggest that parental involvement in schooling does have positive effects. First, it has been found that parent participation in activities at school (e.g., classroom volunteering, attending parent-teacher conferences) is related to student grades, with more parental participation being correlated with higher grades. Second, the extent of parental involvement in school-related activities at home (e.g., assisting with or monitoring homework) is positively correlated with children's scores on standardized achievement tests. It is important to recognize, however, that high levels of parental involvement do not just happen. Instead, they result from the effort and interest not only of parents but also of teachers and school administrators who solicit and provide avenues for parental participation.

Bolstered at least in part by research on the positive effects of parental involvement on children's academic progress, politicians and educational reformers have often made parents the focal point of their plans. Such was the case in Chicago in the late 1980s. Chicago's schools were generally rated as among the most wasteful and least effective in the nation. In an attempt to turn the schools around, massive restructuring of the administrative structure and curriculum were mandated. Schools were decentralized, and parents were placed in charge of their neighborhood schools. Parents could hire and fire staff, including principals. Parents controlled a considerable portion of the budget. Parents even worked with teachers to determine the curriculum and the nature of the instruction that occurred in the classroom. In the 10 years following the decentralization, Chicago schools improved dramatically and that positive trend continues today. Many in the media, politics, and education have given much of the credit for positive change to increased parental involvement.

But is parental involvement always helpful? Is it always a positive force for change? There is often considerable variability among parents in how they wish to deal with controversial issues, such as inclusion of students with special needs in regular classrooms, the effectiveness of whole language instruction, and how to discipline disruptive students. In light of the passionate ways in which parents can express their views on these issues, it is difficult to see how all of them can have a hand in shaping curricular policy. As any principal or administrator will tell you, there are also frequent instances of a parent requesting changes in this or that aspect of the curriculum to better suit his or her child's inclination. Here, too, one wonders if it would be feasible for each and every such parental request to be honored. Can parents be completely shut out of such decisions? On the other hand, should the voices of all parents be heard?

Educators and scholars have also recently begun to question the roles that parents should play in the schooling of their children. Is the involvement of parents always beneficial? In the following selection, Laura Van Zandt Allen and Eleanor T. Migliore enthusiastically support parental involvement, although they do note that often there is considerable work to be done to ensure that parents and school personnel are collaborators rather than adversaries. In the second selection, Rodney T. Ogawa suggests that although schools should build bridges to support parent involvement, schools also need to buffer themselves against unwanted parental influence to ensure that the basic requirements of teaching and learning occur.

YES

Laura Van Zandt Allen
and Eleanor T. Migliore

Supporting Students and Parents Through a School-University Partnership

For many of us, memories of elementary school include not only teachers and classmates but also our parents. A plethora of opportunities existed for their involvement such as homeroom parent, PTO/PTA, Halloween carnivals, Christmas pageants, and monthly "Muffins with Mom" or "Donuts with Dad" gatherings. As we entered middle school, however, the context changed. Multiple teachers, complex subject matter, the importance of peer relationships, and a need for autonomy came to the fore, while the level of parental involvement decreased and, for some, was almost nonexistent by high school.

The evidence is compelling: Parent involvement at school and with schoolwork positively affects a number of student outcomes including achievement, attendance, self-esteem, behavior, and attitudes toward school and learning (Mapp, 1997; National Association of School Psychologists, 1999). Using data from the National Education Longitudinal Study, two reports (Keith, Keith, Quirk, Cohen-Rosenthal, & Franzese, 1996; Singh et al, 1995) found that parental involvement with eighth graders had a significant effect on achievement, especially in math and social studies. In an analysis of 66 studies targeting parent involvement in schooling, Henderson and Berla (1994) concluded that the most accurate predictor of a student's achievement in school is not income or social status, but the extent to which that student's family is able to:

1. Create a home environment that encourages learning
2. Express high (but not unrealistic) expectations for their children's achievement and future careers
3. Become involved in their children's education at school and in the community

Unfortunately, parent involvement declines at the very time young adolescents may need it most (Brough, 1997; Eccles & Harold, 1993; 1996; Epstein & Dauber, 1991). In one study, 39% of parents of children in grades three to five classified themselves as "highly-involved" in their child's school while only 24% of parents with children in grades six to eight did so (U.S. Department of Health and Human Services, 1998). Another report found that three-fourths of parents of eight-, nine-, and ten-year-olds said they were either moderately

From *Middle School Journal*, January 2005, pp. 17–23. Copyright © 2005 by National Middle School Association. Reprinted by permission.

or highly involved with their children's schooling, while by the time children were 16, only half of parents stated this level of involvement (Carnegie Council on Adolescent Development, 1995). Conversely, 72% of students ages 10 to 13 said they would like to talk more with their parents about schoolwork (Nationals Commission on Children, 1991). Given the array of developmental changes occurring during the middle grades years, there is perhaps no more important time for educators to harness the power of parent involvement.

Ironically, preparation on parent involvement has been referred to as one of the "missing elements" in most teacher education programs (Hiatt-Michael, 2001). While the past decade has witnessed an increase in standards addressing families, parents, and community (e.g., National Board for Professional Teaching Standards; National Middle School Association/National Council for the Accreditation of Teacher Education), preservice teachers spend little time studying the experiencing a variety of effective methods for parent involvement (Gray, 2001; Greene & Tichenor; 2001). Studies have found that teacher education prepares future teachers for holding parent conferences but not for initiating and implementing other types of programs such as home-school partnerships, class newsletters, or interactive homework (Epstein, 2001; Hiatt-Michael, 2001). As a result, teachers often enter the profession possessing minimal knowledge and skills for working with parents.

Similar issues are apparent in the education of school psychologists. Viewing the student as part of a system and working with parents and teachers using an ecological paradigm requires a shift in thinking for many in the field who may be more comfortable with a more traditional focus on individual assessments. . . . Although collaborating with teachers and parents is an essential component of the school psychologist's role, nearly 30% of those entering the profession believe that they received "insufficient training . . . in a range of basic teaming skills" (Guest, 2000, p. 243).

The Parent Support Program

To address these issues, educators at Trinity University and Jackson Middle School in San Antonio (North East Independent School District) designed a program to increase parent involvement while providing authentic experiences for preservice teachers and school psychology students. The Parent Support Program (PSP) began with a teacher at Jackson Middle School who realized the need for a structured support program for students and families. The principal also endorsed preventive, proactive collaboratives that kept students out of in-school and off-campus disciplinary settings and buoyed their success in middle school.

The PSP provides free support sessions one evening a week to students and their families with school-related problems during the fall semester. Issues range from using inappropriate language and completing homework on time to developing better communication skills with parents and social adjustment. Support sessions are led by the PSP director (a Jackson teacher with a master's degree in marriage and family counseling) and pairs of school psychology students in Trinity University's graduate school psychology program. Referrals, parent contacts, student background information, and follow-up reports are the responsibility of graduate interns in the Middle Grades Master of Arts in Teaching (MAT) program at Trinity. Together, this school-university collaborative addresses four goals centered around parent involvement at the middle level.

1. The overriding goal of the PSP is to assist parents and teachers in making middle school a positive experience for students.
Brough and Irvin (2001) noted that elementary schools provide concrete roles for parents to play that become less defined as students move into middle school. As a result, parents need leadership and guidance from the school regarding opportunities and expectations for involvement. Epstein and Dauber (1991) found that the strongest and most consistent predictors of parental engagement at school and at home are the specific school programs and teacher practices that encourage and guide parent involvement.

The PSP provides guidance for parents in two ways. First, it identifies a potential problem. While parents may request participation in the PSP, they are more often notified of a recurring problem their child is having at school as a result of a teacher-initiated referral to the program. Young adolescents often share less information with parents as the importance of peer confidences increases; thus, making parents aware of issues that may need to be addressed is key, especially if the issue is not directly related to a specific class or subject (i.e., dress code). Since there are no limiting criteria for participation in the PSP, students who may not qualify for special services have access to a resource often unavailable to the "average" student.

Second, the PSP provides families a means for addressing the problem in a proactive setting. The support sessions help parents and students problem solve; they do not offer counseling. For example, Rachel was referred to the program by a teacher who noticed a discrepancy between her ability and her grades. . . . Rachel, a sixth grade student, lived with her grandmother who often felt overwhelmed with schoolwork dilemmas. The problem was narrowed down to a lack of organization and not turning in homework. Interventions included use of an agenda book for writing down assignments that Rachel and her grandmother went over each evening; setting aside structured homework time daily; checking with teachers each week regarding progress; and suggesting specific homework hints such as reading the assigned questions before the chapter. Breaking the problem down into manageable steps helped Rachel and her grandmother deal with it effectively. . . .

Crystal was referred to the PSP for dress code violations. During the sessions, communication, setting boundaries, and identifying roles surfaced as primary issues between 12-year-old Crystal and her mother. For example, the mother regularly answered questions for her daughter; conversely, Crystal was afraid to voice her true feelings. For the mother, the roles of friend and parent had become entangled resulting in an inability to set limits in many areas. Neither trusted the other, but both genuinely desired to be closer. To address this, the PSP sessions focused on communication and getting to know one another as individuals. This included enacting scenarios, providing specific questions to ask one another, describing the other from one's own perspective, and assigning the pair to spend 30 minutes together each week doing something fun, alternating who chose the activity. As a result, mother and daughter were able to discuss important topics, reach some agreements, and set reasonable limits. Crystal also began dressing more appropriately for school. . . .

Organization, responsibility, communication, boundaries, and roles are issues common to many young adolescents and their parents. Helping families find constructive ways to address these if they become problematic is the key to success at home and at school.

2. Another goal of the PSP is for preservice teachers to experience diverse methods of parent involvement in an authentic context.
Teaching preservice teachers to envision possibilities for home-school connections and then placing them in field experiences that exemplify only traditional methods of parent involvement is counterproductive. To substantively impact students' beliefs and practice, forward-thinking models of parental involvement must be in place, with preservice teachers taking an active role in the implementation and evaluation of the program. Greene and Tichenor (2001) described a four-tiered model for infusing parent involvement curricula in teacher preparation programs. To effect change, such attempts must be intentional, field-based, and move beyond the study of issues into the application of home-school involvement in the field.

Graduate students completing yearlong internships at Jackson Middle School in the Middle Grades MAT program play active and essential roles in the PSP. From day one, interns are instructed to begin mentally gathering potential referrals as they work with students on their team. By week two, interns are given a complete orientation to the program, which includes responsibilities and benefits to their development as teachers. The first step is the collection of two student referrals and the completion of initial phone interviews for each by the beginning of the second six weeks. While interns are enthusiastic about teaching, this requirement is often received with a mixture of hesitation and alarm. "How will I know who needs to be referred?" "School has barely started, and we're already looking for problems?" "I have to call parents? I thought my mentor did that." "I don't know what to say. What if the parent gets upset?" To assist interns with these tasks, specific forms are provided that detail each step of the process including a sample paragraph for introducing the program to parents by phone. Preservice teachers are also reassured that as they journal about their internship experiences, numerous candidates for the PSP will surface and be pointed out by their professor. Referrals, in fact, may come from myriad sources including teams, counselors, administrators, special education teachers, and even parents. By the time referrals are due, interns' attitude toward the process has changed dramatically. One intern wrote, "I made my first parent phone call today. I had been dragging my feet about doing it for days. The student is a painfully bright little boy who is doing poorly and causing behavior problems. He is difficult but completely likable. The conversation with his mother was pleasant. I was telling her nothing she didn't already know. . . . I guess what I'm saying is that it was a thousand times easier than I had expected. I think the PSP sessions will really help this family."

The objectives of this stage are twofold. First, gathering referrals helps interns distinguish between students and issues that respond to standard interventions (i.e., meeting with the student; parent conference) and those that may require additional support from school and home. Next, it forces contact with parents early in the year in a safe, highly structured format.

With referrals and parental consent secured, interns begin work on student case studies. In the fall, this initially involves collecting student background information. To do so, interns learn data collection techniques that help them shadow students for a day, interview teams, talk with counselors, and review records as participant observers (i.e., observation, interviewing, gathering artifacts). Information is then compiled and shared with school psychology students working with specific families prior to the first PSP session. Once sessions begin, interns serve as liaisons between teachers and the PSP, providing critical feedback on student progress. For example, an intern and pair of psychology students may communicate bi-weekly via e-mail to assess the effectiveness of a suggested intervention (e.g., checking agenda book) or meet after school at Jackson prior to scheduled evening sessions.

In January, school psychology students debrief with interns regarding outcomes of the support sessions. Afterwards, interns repeat the same process of data collection used in the fall to assess the potential impact of the PSP for specific students. They also contact parents for feedback on the PSP. Complete case studies are then compiled and shared with the PSP director, school psychology students, and university professors.

The case study addresses two additional objectives. First, it forces interaction and collaboration between teacher interns and school psychologists. Too often, these key stakeholders of student success work in isolation during preservice and inservice experiences. This model requires focused collaboration to ensure no student "falls through the cracks" in the system.

Second, it teaches interns to be proactive. Beginning teachers typically enter the profession full of idealism, only to have this image shattered by the reality of day-to-day teaching. When this occurs, a feeling of powerlessness emerges, and interns shift into survival mode (Kagan, 1992). Working intimately with the PSP provides a way for interns to "do something" about student issues that have yet to be resolved. It is a model for problem solving instead of problem dependence that will, hopefully, set a precedent for the rest of their careers.

3. A third goal of the PSP is to provide school psychology students the experience of working with parents and teachers in a school setting solving real-life problems.

. . . When dealing with a student or family problem, school psychologists are expected to consider the research findings related to the case and determine approaches that would be most effective. Although this is a positive first step, as Sheridan and Gutkin (2000) have pointed out, it is not likely to be sufficient. Indeed, these authors urge school psychologists to focus on learning a process for approaching the problem rather than the specific interventions. Since no two cases are the same, school psychologists must be aware that the research literature studied in class is useful but cannot be transported in its entirety to real-life situations (Phillips, 1999). This expanded scientist-practitioner model involving gathering relevant data, developing hypotheses, generating and implementing intervention plans, and continuing to collect data which then influence new interventions is the approach used by the school psychology students in the PSP (Stoner & Green, 1992). School psychology students are given the opportunity to deal with unique situations that cannot be hypothetically created through textbooks and addressed with "cookbook" solutions. Families arrive with problems needing immediate and flexible approaches. As one school psychology student stated, "Working with our family was different from what you read about in books. You have to go with the flow since they don't present with a perfect sequence of steps." Another commented, "The program gave us the opportunity to enter the student's world, understand family roles and hierarchies, and put theory into practice."

After the briefing by teacher interns, school psychology students meet with families for several hour-long sessions. These collaborative meetings take place in the evening to accommodate busy family schedules. In addition to working with scheduling needs, students learn to meet other individual family preferences (e.g., based on gender, ethnicity, and language). Siblings are welcome, if appropriate, and their presence may add an important dimension while providing helpful information.

To illustrate, Jorge was referred to the PSP because of disrespectful behaviors in several classes. Teachers reported that he did not follow their directions in the classroom and sometimes used profanities. When the PSP director interviewed the parents initially, she noted that they would be more comfortable with Spanish speaking male and female school psychology partners. In addition, Jorge's two siblings also wanted to attend. The PSP was able to meet these requests with positive results.

During the first meeting, students observed that the father was hesitant to set any limits with all three children, while the two boys often ignored their parents' requests for compliance. In addition, both Jorge and his brother spent a great deal of the session competing for attention with their verbalizations or through their physical activities. Their younger sister always sat quite close to either her father or mother. The school psychology students felt that the two boys were jealous of their younger sister who appeared to receive a great deal of attention from both parents. When the father was encouraged to schedule some special after school and weekend time with his sons and establish more appropriate limits with their behaviors, the boys' expressions of anger in the meetings began to lessen. Their language became more appropriate and their physical activity somewhat calmer. All the problems in this case were not resolved, and the parents were still somewhat inconsistent in their limit setting at the end of the sessions; however, the PSP experience was so positive that the family expressed an interest in continuing with a community counselor to which they were referred.

The PSP allows school psychology students to apply or "practice" learning in context. Meeting at the middle school, working with preservice teachers, and problem-solving with families provides essential experience for school psychologists. Perhaps more important, however, is the model of professional collaboration of which they become a part now and, hopefully, in the future.

4. A fourth goal of the PSP is to extend collaboration between the Professional Development School and the university to include family and community.

Professional Development Schools (PDS) address several comprehensive goals. "They bring together university and school-based faculty to share responsibility for the clinical preparation of new teachers, the professional development of experienced faculty, the support of research directed at improving practice, and enhanced student learning" (Levine, 1997, p. 1). Such traditional school-university partnerships center on educational reform and school improvement. Lawson and associates (1995) argued, however, that this is only the beginning and that few partnerships go far enough in regard to making substantive differences in the lives of students. To do so, they advocate school-university-family-community partnerships where the child and family are at the core. In these expanded partnerships, families move from the role of client to that of partner.

> Expanded partnerships cultivate support and empowerment networks for children and families. . . . The agenda that began with school reform is thus expanded to include organizational restructuring, cross-system collaboration, family support, and community development. The intended result is the transformation of the organizations and systems that serve families. (Lawson et al., 1995, 213)

The PSP is a direct effort to include families as partners in their child's middle school experience. The program forces stakeholders to ask new questions, explore different issues, and take bolder risks. It also involves invention, ambiguity, and revision. . . .

Conclusion

The success of the PSP is due to four factors. First, the program was developed to meet an existing need; it was not created from abstract ideas and superimposed on a school setting. While this seems obvious, universities must take care not to project their own agendas on partner schools. Second, all partners were strongly committed to supporting students and families. The PSP director volunteered her time in the evenings; the university provided start-up grant funds for summer program development; professors restructured courses and supervised graduate students; administrators endorsed the school-university-family collaborative; and parents supported the school's efforts to help their children and the learning of beginning teachers and school psychologists. Third, as with any program, the PSP requires extra time and effort. Collaborations among partners resulted in shared responsibilities for program development, implementation, and evaluation. With the sizable demands already placed on educators at all levels, no one group had the necessary resources to establish and sustain this type of program alone. Finally, the program created a "win-win" situation for all stakeholders. Middle school students, parents, teachers, interns, school psychology students, professors, and administrators all benefit in different ways, making the school a true learning community.

Without doubt, the power of parent involvement can be witnessed through the PSP. Hopefully, its impact will provide a model not only for those entering the profession but also for collaborative partnerships between schools, universities, and families.

References

Brough, J. A. (1997). Home-school partnerships: A critical link. In J. L. Irvin (Ed.). *What research says to the middle level practitioner.* Columbus, OH: National Middle School Association.

Brough J. A., & Irvin, J. L. (2001). Parental involvement supports academic improvement among middle schoolers. *Middle School Journal, 32*(5), 56–61.

Carnegie Council on Adolescent Development. (1995). *Great transitions: Preparing adolescents for a new century.* Concluding Report. New York: Carnegie Corporation.

Eccles, J. S., & Harold, R. H. (1993). Parent-school involvement during the early adolescent years. *Teachers College Record, 94*(3), 568–587.

Eccles, J. S., & Harold, R. H. (1996). Family involvement in children's and adolescents' schooling. In A. Booth & J. F. Dunn (Eds.), *Family-school links: How do they affect educational outcomes?* (pp. 3–34). Mahwah, NJ: Lawrence Erlbaum Associates.

Epstein, J. L. (2001). *School, family, and community partnerships: Preparing educators and improving schools.* Boulder, CO: Westview Press.

Epstein, J. L., & Dauber, S. L. (1991). School programs and teacher practices of parent involvement in inner-city elementary and middle schools. *Elementary School Journal, 91*(3), 289–305.

Gray, S. F. (2001). *A compilation of state mandates for home school partnership education in pre-service teacher training programs.* Unpublished manuscript. Culver City, CA: Pepperdine University.

Greene, P. K., & Tichenor, M. S. (2001). Parent involvement strategies in teacher education programs: Applying a four-tier model. *Teacher Education and Practice, 14*(3), 96–118.

Guest, K. E. (2000). Career development of school psychologists. *Journal of School Psychology, 38*(3), 237–257.

Henderson, A., & Berla, N. (Eds.). (1994). *A new generation of evidence: The family is critical to student achievement.* Washington, DC: National Committee for Citizens in Education, Center for Law and Education.

Hiatt-Michael, D. (2001). *Preparing teachers to work with parents.* Washington, DC: ERIC Clearinghouse on Teaching and Teacher Education (ERIC Document Reproduction Service No. 460123).

Kagan, D. (1992). Professional growth among preservice and beginning teachers. *Review of Educational Research, 62,* 129–169.

Keith, T. Z., Keith, P. B., Quirk, K. J., Cohen-Rosenthal, E., Franzese, B. (1996). Effects of parental involvement on achievement for students who attend school in rural America. *Journal of Research in Rural Education, 12*(2), 55–67.

Lawson, H., Flora, R., Lloyd, S., Briar, K., Ziegler, J., &. Kettlewell, J. (1995). Building links with families and communities. In R. Osguthorpe, R. Harris,

M. Harris, & S. Black (Eds.). *Partner schools: Centers for educational renewal* (pp. 205–27). San Francisco: Jossey-Bass Publishers.

Levine, M. (1997). Introduction. In M. Levine &. R. Trachtman (Eds.), *Making professional development schools work: Politics, practice, and policy* (pp. 1–11). New York: Teachers College Press.

Mapp, K (1997). Making the connection between families and schools. *The Harvard Education Letter, 13*(5), 1–3.

National Association of School Psychologists (1999). *Position statement on home-school collaboration: Establishing partnerships to enhance educational outcomes.* Bethesda, MD: Author.

National Commission on Children. (1991). *Speaking of kids: A national survey of children and parents.* Washington, DC: Author.

Phillips, B. N. (1999). Strengthening the links between science and practice: Reading, evaluating, and applying research in school psychology. In C. R. Reynolds &. T. B. Gutkin (Eds.), *The handbook of school psychology* (3rd ed., pp. 56–77). New York: Wiley.

Sheridan, S. M., &. Gutkin, T. B. (2000). The ecology of school psychology: Examining and changing our paradigm for the 21st century. *School Psychology Review, 29*(4), 485–502.

Singh, K., Bickley, P. G., Trivette, P., Keith, T. Z., Keith, P. B., &. Anderson, E. (1995). The effects of four components of parental involvement on eighth-grade student achievement: Structural analysis of NELS:88 data. *School Psychology Review, 24*(2), 299–317.

Stoner, G., &. Green, S. K. (1992). Reconsidering the scientist-practitioner model for school psychology practice. *School Psychology Review, 21*(1), 155–166.

U.S. Department of Health and Human Services, Office of the Assistant Secretary for Planning and Evaluation. (1998). *Trends in the well-being of America's children and youth 1998.* Washington, DC: Author.

Rodney T. Ogawa

 **NO**

Organizing Parent-Teacher Relations Around the Work of Teaching

For as long as most educators can remember, public education in the United States has been undergoing reform. In just the 14 years that have passed since the publication of the highly critical report, *A Nation at Risk* (U.S. Department of Education, 1983), three "waves" of reform are reported to have washed over public schools.

The use of waves as a metaphor for recent educational reform efforts is fitting. After all, from the perspective of most people, waves rise at sea, toss ships and wash ashore, but generally do not significantly disrupt the lives of sailors and seaside dwellers. Like waves, educational reform has originated largely in the external environment of schools, drawn attention and resources, but, in the end, hardly affected the core of the educational enterprise, namely teaching and learning.

The impetus for reform in public education has come largely from the nation's institutional environment, an environment shaped by government and the professions (Ogawa, 1994; Scott, 1987). Political leaders at all levels of government have undertaken administrative initiatives and enacted legislation to set "Goals 2000," to press schools to restructure and, otherwise, to generally improve the nation's public schools. Every leading professional organization—representing teachers, school principals, district superintendents, and others—has forged and advanced an educational reform agenda.

Although successive waves of reform have buffeted schools, they seldom have centered on teaching (Murphy, 1991). On those occasions when reformers have focused directly on teachers, they generally have sought not to capitalize on or facilitate existing practices, but to alter what teachers do (Elmore, 1990). This extends beyond curriculum and pedagogy to include teachers' relationships with administrators, colleagues, and parents.

The second wave of reform, in particular, sought to involve teachers in decision making and to expand their responsibilities to include mentoring novice teachers, developing curriculum and the like, and reaching out to engage parents and the community. Curiously, these efforts to enhance the context and practice of teaching often have not taken teaching, itself, as their starting point. This is nowhere more true than in the campaign to increase parent involvement in schools.

From *Peabody Journal of Education,* vol. 73, no. 1, 1998, pp. 6–13 (references omitted). Copyright © 1998 by Peabody College/Vanderbilt University. Reprinted by permission of Taylor & Francis Informa UK LTD Journals via Copyright Clearance Center.

Parent Involvement:
An Assumption That More Is Always Better

In the search for factors that affect the academic performance of students, educational research has provided few clear-cut answers. One, however, that echoes across a considerable body of research is the family. Families, most notably parents, exert a crucial influence on important student outcomes, including grades and standardized achievement test scores. Consequently, parents, policy makers, and educators have moved to adopt and implement programs aimed at bolstering the involvement of parents in schools, whereas researchers continue to study the relation between parent involvement and student achievement.

Research on family–school relations clearly has made important advances. Researchers, however, typically have adopted a rather narrow view. They tend to approach parent involvement as if it were an unmixed blessing: more always being better. This assumption is apparent in the issues on which researchers have concentrated. For example, Epstein (1995) identified six types of parent involvement, the practices that schools presently employ to encourage each type of involvement, and the challenges posed by each type of involvement. She then redefined each type of involvement with an eye to broadening the scope of parent participation in schools. Her focus is clearly on enhancing and even expanding parent involvement.

It is surprising that the assumption that more parent involvement of all types is always better has gone largely unexamined and unchallenged. After all, this is true of few things in life. Even excessive amounts of oxygen or water can be toxic. Moreover, anyone who has spent much time in schools knows that not all teachers, administrators, or staff members share this view.

The limitations of this view are revealed by a theoretical perspective drawn from organization theory. This perspective suggests that effective organizations create both bridges and buffers between their core technologies and external environments. If teaching is assumed to constitute the core technology of schools, and if parents are assumed to be a crucial and immediate element of the external environment of schools, then schools would be expected to enhance their effectiveness by building bridges to parents under some conditions and buffers against them in others.

Adopting this theoretical orientation provides at least two advantages. First, it treats teaching as the hub around which parent involvement turns. Second, it focuses attention on the organization characteristics of schools, a dimension that is largely ignored by research on family–school relations (Corwin & Wagenaar 1976).

Bridging and Buffering the Core
Technology of Schools

Recently, scholars in the field of educational administration have encouraged the adoption of theoretical perspectives that emphasize the symbolic or interpretive dimension of organizations (Deal & Peterson, 1990; Sergiovanni, 1994).

In embracing perspectives that highlight culture, community, and institution, many scholars have ignored and even criticized perspectives that emphasize organizations' technical cores as the bases for developing structure. However, pronouncements of the technical perspective's demise may be premature, because it continues to shed conceptual light on important educational issues.

Briefly, the technical perspective contends that organizations develop formal structures to enhance the effectiveness and efficiency of core technologies, especially where technologies are relatively routinized. This includes developing structures to manage organizations' relations with the technical dimension of their external environment (Aldrich, 1979; Thompson, 1967). Organizations manage their relations with the technical environment in two basic ways: They bridge between their core technologies and the environment and they buffer their core technologies from the environment.

Organizations bridge when they depend on their environments for resources to fuel their core technologies (Scott, 1992; Thompson, 1967). Three conditions increase the dependency of organizations on their environments. First, organizations are more dependent when resources are scarce. Second, organizations are more dependent when resources are concentrated, or available from a limited number of sources. Third, organizations are more dependent when the sources of inputs are coordinated.

When confronted by these conditions, typically in some combination, organizations employ several bridging strategies to manage relations with sources of inputs. They include bargaining, contracting, and co-opting.

Organizations buffer to protect their core technologies from uncertainty that the environment can introduce (Thompson, 1967). Uncertainty undermines the rationality and thus the effectiveness and efficiency of core technologies by compromising the certitude and uniformity with which organizations yield products. Environmental uncertainty can result from several conditions, including heterogeneity and instability (Scott, 1992). To manage uncertainty, organizations develop many buffering strategies, including simply blocking or limiting access and coding. Coding involves the classification of inputs prior to their introduction to the technical core.

What Does the Research Say?

Is there evidence that this framework applies to schools? Do schools face the environmental conditions that lead organizations to build bridges and buffers? If so, do schools employ bridging and buffering strategies? The answer to all of these questions is a tentative "yes." Research indicates that the conditions of interdependence and uncertainty exist in schools' environments and that schools employ both bridging and buffering strategies in response. However, the evidence is indirect because researchers have not explicitly focused on bridging and buffering in school organizations.

The Core Technology of Schools

Previous studies, although not guided by the theoretical framework outlined in this [selection], have produced findings that are consistent with many of the framework's elements. Since Cohen, March, and Olsen (1972) coined the concept of *organized anarchy,* it has become axiomatic among scholars of educational administration that school organizations do not have clear technologies.

However, research suggests that school organizations do possess a core technology that is characterized by a degree of routineness, or certainty. For example, Rowan, Raudenbush, and Cheong (1993) reported that some teachers perceive their work to be fairly routinized.

Two related studies conducted nearly 2 decades apart offer a broader sense of how teachers view their work. Lortie's (1975) groundbreaking study in which "teachers describe their world" (p. ix) and Cohn and Kottkamp's (1993) partial replication reveal that social interaction lies at the very center of teaching. Lortie noted that teachers emphasize the interpersonal dimension over interest in subject matter. Cohn and Kottkamp reported that teachers identify three general categories of skills that members of their profession must possess to be successful. The first includes skills that teachers employ to develop basic and direct relations with students. The second involves skills that teachers use to organize students, individually or in groups, for instruction. The third consists of skills to engage students in the subject matter being taught or in the instructional process itself (Ogawa, 1996).

Research suggests, then, that teaching is characterized by a measure of routineness, or clarity. Moreover, there is evidence that such clarity lies in teaching's social technology. Thus, schools would be expected to employ bridges and buffers to manage relations between the social technology of teaching and the external environment, including the parents of students.

The Use of Bridging Strategies

The findings of research on parent involvement in schools reflect the use of bridging strategies by schools to manage relations with parents. It is clear that schools confront conditions that give rise to the use of bridging. Schools are dependent on parents to provide resources that affect the academic performance of students. For example, research indicates that parent involvement in school activities is associated with grades received by students in school; other research demonstrates that parent involvement in education-related activities at home is a predictor of students' performance on standardized achievement tests (Schneider & Coleman, 1993).

Given this dependency, we would expect to find that schools regularly construct bridges to parents. In fact, research documents the use of several types of bridging strategies by educators (Becker & Epstein, 1982; Epstein, 1990, 1995). In some cases, these strategies take the form of organized programs in districts and schools that seek to enhance communications between schools and families, involve parents on school-based management councils, provide parent effectiveness workshops, and dispense health and social services. However, in many instances individual teachers employ bridging strategies to encourage parents to read to their children, discuss school with their children, monitor their children's completion of homework assignments, and engage in education-related activities (e.g., visiting the local public library).

The Use of Buffering Strategies

Research on family–school relations does not directly address whether or how schools buffer their core technology from uncertainties that parents may introduce. However, research on a variety of other educational topics is a bit more instructive. Research suggests that families are, indeed, a source of uncertainty for school organizations. The uncertainly takes two general forms. First, there is the uncertainty that can be introduced when parents directly interfere with the professional discretion of teachers and principals. Studies suggest that well-educated, middle-class parents are sometimes perceived by educational professionals as intruding into their domain by insisting on or questioning particular practices or programs (Chavkin & Williams, 1987; Davies, 1987; Epstein & Becker, 1982). Second, families can present schools with uncertainties in the form of both heterogeneity and instability. For example, research documents the increasing ethnic and linguistic diversity of families served by schools in many sections of the United States (Coleman, 1987). Other studies record the high mobility rates of families served by many of the nation's schools and the changing composition of families (Hoffer & Coleman, 1990). Faced with increasing uncertainty, schools would be expected to buffer their core technology.

Although research has not focused on the use of buffering strategies, some evidence exists. For example, research consistently demonstrates that teachers expect principals to shield them from undue parental influence and that principals do perform this function. We are all familiar with the sign placed on the front of every public school, directing all visitors, including parents, to check in at the school office. Moreover, a large body of research documents the use of grouping strategies by schools and teachers, which bear a striking resemblance to coding as an approach to buffering. Although such groupings are usually and arguably based on student ability or interest, they also reflect differences in family background. For example, research shows that, beginning as early as kindergarten, teachers place students in groups that correspond closely to the students' socioeconomic backgrounds (Rist, 1970). Research also demonstrates that educational tracks correlate with social class and that curriculum content varies across tracks, and, thus across class (Oakes, 1985). In addition, programs that provide students with breakfast and health care and their families with social services are aimed at buffering schools from conditions that can undermine their efforts to instruct students by minimizing uncertainties posed by such hinders as poor health and dysfunctional family situations.

Conclusions

Existing research documents that school organizations, indeed, confront environmental conditions to which bridging and buffering are appropriate responses. Moreover, it reveals that school organizations implement programs and individual educators employ practices that correspond to bridging and buffering. Thus, research seems to demonstrate that the dominant conceptualization of family–school relations, which treats parent involvement as an unmixed blessing, is conceptually blind to half of the picture.

The theoretical perspective advanced in this [selection] holds the promise of extending the study of parent involvement by providing a more balanced and, thus, complete view. The proposed approach would build on existing research, which highlights positive forms of parent involvement by adding research that examines the ways in which schools buffer their core technology from disruptive forms of parent involvement. Ultimately, the framework leads to considering how a combination, or balance, of bridging and buffering contributes to the effectiveness of school organizations and, hence to the academic performance of students.

However, the research cited is merely suggestive, not confirmatory. The evidence is largely indirect; that is, it arose from studies that were not intended to examine bridging and buffering in school organizations. As a consequence, the research did not address several potentially important issues. For instance, research has neither done the basic work of describing strategies that school organizations use to buffer uncertainties introduced by parents, nor has it addressed the issue noted in the previous paragraph: assessing the impact of various combinations of buffering and bridging on the instructional effectiveness of schools.

More complex conceptual issues also remain. For example, existing evidence on the use of bridging and buffering by educators suggests that the theoretical framework does not adequately depict the structure of these practices in school organizations. Theory emphasizes the role of managers in controlling the relations between organizations and environments. However, research on schools suggests that administrators alone do not bridge and buffer. Rather, teachers, staff members, as well as principals buffer and bridge through both formal and informal means, some of which are not reflected in existing theoretical treatments.

The theoretical framework also does not adequately explain relations between bridging and buffering. The examples cited in this [selection] suggest that the line distinguishing bridging from buffering may not be all that clear. For example, increasing numbers of schools are working with public health and social service agencies to provide assistance to families of students. The bridging and buffering involved in these programs is complex and occurs at several levels. The schools must bridge with the agencies on which they must depend for services that they, themselves, do not provide. They must also build bridges to parents in order to gain their participation. However, all of this is done in order to buffer schools from uncertainties that can be introduced by parents who do not provide their children with adequate health care or stable home environments. These and other issues await the attention of scholars. Although the applicability of the concepts of bridging and buffering has not been established empirically, they can bring attention to previously unacknowledged theoretical and empirical issues, which is promising in and of itself.

POSTSCRIPT

Is Greater Parental Involvement at School Always Beneficial?

Can we answer this question with empirical data? The answer is yes, but a cautious yes. One reason for caution is that it is likely that the only way to collect such empirical data would be within the context of a correlational study, which is often associated with some ambiguity regarding its findings. Consider the case of the Chicago public schools, which we described in the introduction to this issue. At first glance, the interpretation seems clear: the Chicago schools were decentralized so that parents had greater involvement, and then student achievement improved. The cause of the improvement must be increased parental involvement. What else could it be? In fact, a more careful analysis brings to light several other, equally plausible, explanations for the improvement in student achievement. Perhaps the increased scrutiny in the media brought about increased effort by teachers and principals, either because of fear for their jobs or because they were reinvigorated by the knowledge that the city cared about education. Or perhaps the changes in curriculum and disciplinary practices were responsible, changes that could have been implemented without increased parental involvement. Or maybe the schools received increased financial resources for direct instruction because the administrative budget was trimmed. Any or all of these factors could have been involved in producing the gains in student achievement in addition to, or even instead of, increased parental involvement.

Caution is also in order because the answer to the question ultimately may be dictated as much by a political or ideological agenda as by empirical evidence regarding the effects of parental involvement. That is, parental involvement in children's schooling may be viewed by some people to be a parent's right or even a parent's obligation. From this point of view, the question of whether parental involvement leads to higher achievement or other tangible outcomes for students is not important. What is important, it could be argued, is that schools must create multiple routes by which parents can have input into their children's education.

Readers interested in the various ways in which schools could involve, or have involved, parents in their children's schooling will find the following articles useful: "School-Family-Community Partnerships: Caring for the Children We Share," by J. L. Epstein, *Phi Delta Kappan* (1995); "Parental Involvement in the Reform of Mathematics Education," by Dominic Peressini, *The Mathematics Teacher* (September 1997); "Parental Involvement Supports Academic Improvement among Middle Schoolers," by J. A. Brough and J. L. Irvin, *Middle School Journal* (2001); "Parent Involvement Strategies in Teacher

Education Programs: Applying a Four-Tier Model," by P. K. Greener and M. S. Tichenor, *Teacher Education and Practice* (2001); and "A Transition Program Based on Identified Student and Parent Concerns," by Angela Koppang, *Middle School Journal* (September 2004). See also *The Parent Project: A Workshop Approach to Parent Involvement* (Stenhouse Publishing, 1994).

ISSUE 14

Should Schools Embrace Computers and Technology?

YES: Marcia C. Linn and James D. Slotta, from "WISE Science," *Educational Leadership* (October 2000)

NO: Lowell W. Monke, from "The Overdominance of Computers," *Educational Leadership* (December 2005/January 2006)

ISSUE SUMMARY

YES: Marcia C. Linn, a professor of cognition and development, and James D. Slotta, director of the Web-based Integrated Science Environment (WISE) project library at the University of California, Berkeley, present an overview of the WISE project, which is designed to teach science and technological literacy through Web-based activities. They contend that this project will make teachers more effective and increase their flexibility in the classroom.

NO: Lowell W. Monke, an assistant professor at Wittenberg University, argues that schools have been too uncritical in their adoption of computers and related technologies. Moreover, he suggests that younger students might not be "ready" for such technology and that the premature introduction of the technology might interfere with their ability to acquire important academic, social, and ethical foundation.

Computers and related technologies have become intertwined with every facet of our daily lives. They can be found in nearly every place of business, from Wall Street to the neighborhood auto shop. In the United States desktop computers can be found in millions of homes.

Computers are also becoming increasingly commonplace in schools. More than 6 million computers were in U.S. schools by the mid-1990s, and this number is likely to continue growing as government support for technology increases. Not only are computers increasing in number in schools, but so are the educational devices they power and the educational functions they perform. Educational devices include CD-ROMs, digital cameras, laser disc players, overhead projector panels, and scanners. Educational functions include computer-assisted instruction, word processing, desktop publishing, e-mail, Internet searching, and distance education. Many of these devices and functions have been organized into networked systems for presenting the entire curriculum in a subject area to students across multiple classrooms and schools.

Many educators and policymakers have embraced computer-based technologies. In large measure, this is because these technologies appear to be consistent with constructivist theory, which now holds sway among many educational researchers and practitioners. According to this theory, we construct new knowledge when the results of our physical and mental actions on the world challenge our current ways of knowing. This implies that schooling should provide students with opportunities to act on the material to be mastered and to "figure things out for themselves," rather than transmit ready-made knowledge to them through an all-knowing teacher. Moreover, because different students will come to the material to be learned with different "ways of knowing," they may require different experiences and different amounts of time to achieve mastery. Computer-based instruction is appealing because students are actively involved in the learning process, they can work at their own pace, and presumably they can receive lessons that are well suited to their current ways of knowing.

Critics, however, argue that much of the interest in these technologies reflects a rather naive desire to use whatever is new with little attention to its appropriateness for the educational goal in question. As a result, critics argue, sophisticated technologies are often put to rather trivial uses, uses for which other, less-expensive approaches are available. Perhaps more important, critics suggest that there may be features of the current technologies that are antithetical to the goals that most educators hope to achieve. For instance, they suggest that activities such as surfing the Internet may encourage a superficial, unsystematic approach to studying rather than one that is focused, goal-directed, and self-reflective. Others argue that the technology makes learning an individual, isolated activity rather than the cultural activity that they believe best facilitates learning. Finally, some critics raise the possibility that because computer-mediated instruction depends critically on a student's ability to monitor his or her own progress, such technology may increase the gap between the more- and the less-capable students; that is, highly motivated students with good self-monitoring skills will flourish, whereas those who are less motivated or less self-reflective will flounder without the benefit of a human teacher to support them.

In the first of the following selections, Marcia C. Linn and James D. Slotta describe their Web-based library of science projects, each of which is designed to be adaptable to the needs and interests of teachers and students from elementary school to high school. Linn and Slotta argue that the projects facilitate debate among students and make technology available to all students. In the second selection, Lowell W. Monke argues that students need to acquire various foundational skills before they are able to use computers in effective and socially responsible ways. He argues further that introducing computers too early actually interferes with the development of important academic, cognitive, social, and moral reasoning skills.

YES

Marcia C. Linn and
James D. Slotta

WISE Science

How can we bridge the barrier between research innovations and their adoption in science classrooms? Too often, educational research demonstrates exciting learning gains for local students but never reaches schools outside the initial research partnership.

A partnership of classroom teachers, technologists, natural scientists, and pedagogical researchers has designed a flexible learning environment that makes teachers more effective in their classrooms and enables them to respond creatively to state standards, prior student experiences, time commitments, and available resources. New groups of teachers and schools can bridge the gap between educational research and classroom practice by using the Web-based Integrated Science Environment (WISE) project library.

Partnerships supported by the National Science Foundation and others have created a library of WISE projects. These partners have designed pilot projects, observed their use in science classrooms, and refined the projects on the basis of their observations. WISE projects can be improved by teachers, tailored to their course topics, and connected to local conditions and to state and national standards.

Schools and individual teachers can join WISE by going to the Web site (http://wise.berkeley.edu) and selecting activities for their classes from the project library. Classes—using only a Web browser and an Internet connection—can register to use WISE at school or at home. A video of teachers using WISE and a book called *Computers, Teachers, Peers* (Linn & Hsi, 2000) are also available.

The Design Framework

The WISE learning environment implements design principles to promote lifelong science learning along with language and technology literacy (Linn & Hsi, 2000). These principles reflect the scaffolded knowledge integration framework, as well as cognitive apprenticeship (Collins, Brown, & Holum, 1991), intentional learning (Scardamalia & Bereiter, 1991), and the traditions of constructivist psychology. The design framework—developed from 15 years of classroom research—helps students connect, refine, and revisit all their science ideas rather than isolate and forget the science that they have studied in school. We organize the design framework around four design strategies.

Make science accessible.   WISE design partnerships seek an appropriate level of analysis for the scientific content of a project so that students can restructure, rethink, compare, critique, and develop more cohesive ideas. The WISE curriculum uses scientific models that students can easily grasp and connects these models to personally relevant problems. The WISE learning environment represents the scientific inquiry process through an inquiry map, which leads students though inquiry steps, providing cognitive and procedural guidance along the way.

Make thinking visible.   WISE partnerships make scientific arguments more visible by carefully designing interactive simulations, model-building environments, and argument-representation tools. WISE projects use embedded assessments to make student thinking visible and to engage students as designers (diSessa, 2000).

Help students learn from one another.   WISE projects use collaborative tools— such as online discussions, peer review, and debate—to help students take advantage of classmates' ideas. Online tools enable all students to participate in the deliberations of science, allowing equitable access to the discourse and rhetoric of science (Hoadley & Linn, in press; Hsi, 1997).

Foster lifelong learning.   To help students become lifelong science learners, students critique Web sites, design arguments, or debate science controversies, such as the reasons for the observed decline in amphibian populations. Students reflect on scientific materials including Web sites (Davis & Linn, in press).

Design Studies

WISE classroom research combines the features of Japanese lesson studies (Lewis & Tsuchida, 1997; Linn, Tsuchida, Lewis, & Songer, 2000) and design experiments (Brown, 1992; Collins, 1999; diSessa, 2000) in what we call *design studies* (Linn, in press). The effectiveness of a curriculum project can increase by as much as 400 percent using this approach (Linn & Hsi, 2000).

In our customization research, teachers have made WISE curriculum projects locally relevant to students in diverse geographical or demographic areas, have made projects more successful on the basis of classroom trials, and have tailored instruction to personal practices.

Houses in the Desert

In the Houses in the Desert project, students collaborate with a partner in designing a house that is comfortable for living in the desert. The project, created by physical-science experts, teachers, and educational researchers, is targeted to the middle school level. Students create a preliminary design and then critique several Internet sites advocating varied energy-efficient house designs. Next, they analyze alternate materials for designing walls, roofs, and windows, and they specialize in one housing component. Students revise their preliminary designs, perform a heat-flow analysis, and submit their design for peer review.

After reviewing peer comments, they finalize and publish their desert-house designs on a secure class Website. In the course of this project, students gain science and language literacy by critiquing Web sites, collaborating in design, and contributing to peer review. They gain technology literacy by searching for relevant materials on the Web and using design tools.

To make thinking visible, the project uses animated representations of heat flow through building materials, such as wood or glass, which enables students to distinguish insulators and conductors. The project also illustrates the interaction between air and ground temperature during day and night in the desert. To make the science accessible, the project connects to real-life experiences; for example, students use the heat-flow model to compare designs for picnic coolers and to discuss how to keep a drink cold in their lunch box. To promote lifelong learning, the project helps students critique Web sites, formulate critical questions, and develop arguments to support design decisions. Finally, to help students learn from one another, the project orchestrates peer review of designs, helping students develop a set of shared criteria for evaluating house designs.

To help teachers make the project relevant to their students, the partners included a Web site where students could compare climate data in a desert to the climate in any specified location, including their own school. Students reflect on how their climate is different from that of the desert. Teachers also add Web sites that feature local house designs—for example, students in some classes explored a solar house in Maine—making the project more relevant and engaging.

Plants in Space

In the Plants in Space project, students construct a small hydroponic garden in their classroom, analyze factors responsible for plant growth (such as light, water, and soil), compare the growth of earth plants and Wisconsin Fast Plants (referred to as NASA space plants), and analyze what factors are important for plant growth in a space-station environment. NASA scientists, research biologists, teachers, educational researchers, and technology specialists designed the project. Web-based materials bring the space station to life and raise questions that are relevant to elementary students: Can we grow plants without dirt?

To make science accessible, students explore a personally relevant problem and investigate their ideas about plant growth. Students asked, Do plants eat dirt? To help make thinking visible, students represent plant growth through online graphing. To promote lifelong learning, students reflect on the Web evidence, record observations about the plants in their own minigardens, and report on their recommendations. To help students learn from one another and from experts, the project includes online discussions with NASA scientists about the challenges of growing plants in space.

Teachers can customize the hints, prompts, discussions, and even the focus of the project—for example, they can choose whether to emphasize plant growth factors or conditions aboard the space station. After first using the Plants in Space project, one 5th grade teacher added Internet materials about photosynthesis, enhanced online discussions about light and energy, and revised the hints and prompts. The students using the second version developed a more coherent understanding of plant growth as a result (Williams, 2000).

Cycles of Malaria

In the Cycles of Malaria project, students debate three different perspectives on how to control malaria worldwide: developing an effective pesticide that targets the anopheles mosquito; developing a vaccine against the disease; and creating social programs that reduce exposure to mosquitoes, such as distributing mosquito nets or having community cleanups. Students explore evidence related to each control method and debate alternate approaches. The project is targeted at upper-middle and high school biology students and has been customized by advanced-placement biology teachers.

To make thinking visible, the project includes animations and videos of the mosquito and parasite life cycles, as well as maps showing the worldwide incidence of malaria. To make the project accessible to students, teachers draw connections to diseases in North America, such as HIV or sickle-cell anemia. The project promotes lifelong learning by helping students understand scientific viewpoints, evaluation of evidence, and policy trade-offs. To learn from others, students participate in asynchronous electronic discussions with peers and engage in class debates.

Cycles of Malaria has been customized by teachers working in a wide range of grade levels and topic areas and with diverse teaching approaches. These teachers added activities and varied their patterns of interaction with students. Middle school biology teachers included field trips to local ponds or puddles to collect mosquito larvae. Another teacher added a short story about the struggles of the family of Kofi, a young African villager with malaria. Norwegian teachers connected the material to international policies for DDT use. A high school chemistry teacher focused on the chemical compounds within the DDT pesticide and how they affect the environment.

To determine whether WISE is robust enough to support these diverse customizations while retaining the instructional framework, we contrasted the adaptations of Cycles of Malaria by three different teachers in a middle school that has implemented WISE in every science class. We found that teachers varied greatly in the frequency and duration of their interactions with students during the project. One teacher spent considerable time talking in depth with each student group, visiting groups once, at most, during a class period. Another teacher interacted for very short periods of time but visited each group several times.

Although WISE strives to enable teachers to interact deeply with their students, we were gratified that WISE accommodated even these major differences in teaching practice. Students were challenged to reflect and make connections to rich problem contexts. For example, in the post-assessment for the Cycles of Malaria project, teachers measured the improvement in students' understanding of disease vectors, vaccines, life cycles, and medical research. Students connected applications to personally relevant situations (such as traveling to a foreign country) and transferred ideas to novel situations (such as advising a small country on a pending law to clean up standing water around all rural villages). Students in all three classes showed identical, substantial learning gains. The assessments were sensitive to teaching styles as well. For example, students who had longer interactions with their teacher gave more coherent answers to complex questions. This research helps us understand how diverse teaching approaches influence outcomes and how curriculum designs can meet the needs of diverse teachers.

Three Literacies

WISE promotes lifelong learning by addressing three mutually reinforcing literacies: technology, science, and language.

Technology literacy.   We base our definition of technology literacy on the National Academy of Sciences report on what everyone should know about information technology (Snyder et al., 1999). The WISE curriculum interweaves technology with science instruction, targeting three complementary aspects of technology literacy. First, students learn to use technology in complex, sustained problem solving—identifying unanticipated consequences, searching for relevant information, communicating, collaborating, and critiquing. Second, students learn contemporary skills, such as using e-mail, the Internet, word processing, and spreadsheets. Third, students learn the concepts of technology, such as modeling, simulations, and the societal impacts of technology.

WISE helps students develop technology literacy in school instead of relying on inequitable home access (American Association of University Women, 2000). More students are developing fluency with information technology at home. They join chat rooms, play networked versions of games, do homework on word processors, and use graphics and drawing tools. These experiences prepare many students to use technology in the classroom, but they also divide students along economic lines.

WISE remedies these inequalities by incorporating technologies for tomorrow's workforce in the classroom. In many schools, students come with a good understanding of digital media, only to find that their teachers employ an old-fashioned, low-tech presentation of science and other topics. Schools often relegate computers to a lab space where they are used for "skills training" or extracurricular project work rather than for universal technology literacy. This disconnect between technology in the home and technology in the classroom contributes to the increasing sense of irrelevance and disinterest that students feel about science instruction.

Science literacy. Science literacy requires reconsidering scientific ideas and seeking a more coherent understanding of them. To respond to rapid increases in science knowledge, frequent job changes, and consequential policy debates, citizens must constantly update their science knowledge. Nutritional decisions (Is butter or margarine more healthy?), environmental decisions (Should I choose paper or plastic?), and political or economic issues require citizens to revisit their ideas as well as critique contradictory, persuasive messages in the popular press and on the Internet. Schools can no longer cover all the science topics that students will use in their lives, so we must motivate students to continue to learn. WISE projects connect to relevant issues—such as space exploration, environmental stewardship, and wilderness survival—to set students on a path toward lifelong learning.

Language literacy. Lifelong science learning depends on a critical reading of science material, effective communication about science issues, and clear writing about science topics (Heath, 1983). In WISE, students communicate about scientific topics, evaluate scientific texts, ask questions about science policies, participate in debates about contemporary controversies, and create and critique arguments.

WISE Conclusions

Students need opportunities to independently explore complex problems, to flounder, to learn from their peers, to reflect on their experiences, and to become responsible stewards of their own learning. This linked, coherent learning only arises when science instruction presents students with theories and principles that they can connect to personal experiences, interests, and past instruction.

The process of thinking about science, reorganizing ideas, incorporating new information, and remaining skeptical of evidence is both difficult and exhilarating. If we convert the science curriculum to a lifelong learning enterprise, we can capture that exhilaration. This approach can amplify the rewards that teachers feel when they teach students about science and can also increase the opportunities for researchers to make science instruction effective and successful.

References

American Association of University Women (AAUW). (2000). *Tech-savvy: Educating girls in the new computer age.* Washington, DC: Author.

Brown, A. L (1992). Design experiments: Theoretical and methodological challenges in creating complex interventions in classroom settings. *Journal of the Learning Sciences, 2*(2), 141–178.

Collins, A. (1999). Design issues of learning environments. In *Psychological and educational foundations of technology-based education.* New York: Springer-Verlag.

Collins, A., Brown, J. S., & Holum, A. (1991). Cognitive apprenticeship: Making thinking visible. *American Educator, 15*(3), 6–11, 38–39.

Davis, E. K, & Linn, M. C. (in press). Scaffolding students' knowledge integration: Prompts for reflection in KIE. *International Journal of Science Education, Special Issue, 22*(8), 819–837.

diSessa, A. A. (2000). *Changing minds: Computers, learning, and literacy.* Cambridge, MA: MIT Press.

Heath, S. B. (1983). *Ways with words: Language, life, and work in communities and classrooms.* New York: Cambridge University Press.

Hoadley, C., & Linn, M. C. (in press). Teaching science through on-line peer discussions: Speak Easy in the knowledge integration environment. *International Journal of Science Education,* Special Issue, *22*(8), 839–857.

Hsi, S. (1997). *Facilitating knowledge integration in science through electronic discussion: The multimedia forum kiosk.* Unpublished doctoral dissertation, University of California, Berkeley.

Lewis, C., & Tsuchida, I. (1997). Planned educational change in Japan: The case of elementary science instruction. *Journal of Educational Policy, 12*(5), 303–331.

Linn, M. C. (in press). Designing the knowledge integration environment: The partnership inquiry process. *International Journal of Science Education,* Special Issue, *22*(8), 781–796.

Linn, M. C., & Hsi, S. (2000). *Computers, teachers, peers: Science learning partners.* Mahwah, NJ: Lawrence Erlbaum Associates.

Linn, M. C., Tsuchida, I., Lewis, C., & Songer, N. B. (2000). Beyond fourth grade science: Why do U.S. and Japanese students diverge? *Educational Researcher, 29*(3) 4–14.

Scardamalia, M., & Bereiter, C. (1991). Higher levels of agency for children in knowledge building: A challenge for the design of new knowledge media. *Journal of the Learning Sciences 1*(1), 37–68.

Snyder, L., Aho, A. V., Linn, M. C., Packer, A., Tucker, A., Ullinan, J., & Van Dam, (1999). Be FIT! Being fluent with information technology. Washington, DC: National Academy Press.

Williams, L. M. (2000). *Exploring how a web-based integrated science environment and hands-on science can promote knowledge integration.* Paper presented at the annual meeting of the American Education Research Association, New Orleans, LA.

Lowell W. Monke

NO

The Overdominance of Computers

The debate churns on over the effectiveness of computers as learning tools. Although there is a growing disillusionment with the promise of computers to revolutionize education, their position in schools is protected by the fear that without them students will not be prepared for the demands of a high-tech 21st century. This fallback argument ultimately trumps every criticism of educational computing, but it is rarely examined closely.

Let's start by accepting the premise of the argument: Schools need to prepare young people for a high-tech society. Does it automatically follow that children of all ages should use high-tech tools? Most people assume that it does, and that's the end of the argument. But we don't prepare children for an automobile-dependent society by finding ways for 10-year-olds to drive cars, or prepare people to use alcohol responsibly by teaching them how to drink when they are 6. My point is that preparation does not necessarily warrant early participation. Indeed, preparing young people quite often involves strengthening their inner resources—like self-discipline, moral judgment, and empathy— before giving them the opportunity to participate.

Great Power and Poor Preparation

The more powerful the tools—and computers are powerful—the more life experience and inner strength students must have to handle that power wisely. On the day my Advanced Computer Technology classroom got wired to the Internet, it struck me that I was about to give my high school students great power to harm a lot of people, and all at a safe distance. They could inflict emotional pain with a few keystrokes and never have to witness the tears shed. They could destroy hours of work accomplished by others who were not their enemies—just poorly protected network users whose files provided convenient bull's-eyes for youth flexing newfound technical muscles.

I also realized that it would take years to instill the ethical discipline needed to say no to flexing that technical power. Young people entering my course needed more firsthand experiences guided by adults. They needed more chances to directly connect their own actions with the consequences of those actions, and to reflect on the outcomes, before they started using tools that could trigger serious consequences on the other side of the world.

Students need more than just moral preparation. They also need authentic experiences. As more students grow up spending much of their time in environments dominated by computers, TV, and video games, their diminished experience with real, concrete things prevents them from developing a rich understanding of what they study on computers. The computer is a purely symbolic environment; users are always working with abstract representations of things, never with the things themselves. In a few months my students could learn to build complex relational databases and slick multimedia presentations. But unless they also had a deep knowledge of the physical world and community relationships, they would be unable to infuse depth and meaning into the information they were depicting and discussing.

Do Computers Help Achievement?

Educational technology researchers, who tend to suffer from a severe inability to see the forest for the trees, typically ignore the impact that saturating society with computers and other screen environments is having on children. University of Munich economists Thomas Fuchs and Ludger Woessmann recently examined data from a study of 174,000 15-year-olds in 31 nations who took the Programme for International Student Assessment tests. They found, after controlling for other possible influences, that the more access students had to computers in school and at home, the lower their overall test scores were (2004). The authors suggest that rather than inherently motivating young people or helping them learn, computers more likely distract them from their studies. But there may be other problems behind this phenomenon that point to inherent contradictions in the use of educational technology.

For example, although we know that computer programs can help small children learn to read, we also know that face-to-face interaction is one of the most important ingredients in reading readiness (Dodici, Draper, & Peterson, 2003). As a result of increased time spent with computers, video games, and TV, the current generation of elementary students will experience an estimated 30 percent fewer face-to-face encounters than the previous generation (Hammel, 1999). Thus, teachers may be employing the very devices for remediating reading problems that helped cause the problems in the first place.

The issue is not just balancing computer time with other activities in schools. Both inside and outside school, children's lives are dominated by technology. Nearly everything a child does today—from chatting with friends to listening to music to playing games—tends to involve the use of technologies that distance children from direct contact with the living world. If the task of schools is to produce men and women who live responsible, fulfilling lives—not just human cogs for the high-tech machinery of commerce—then we should not be intensifying children's high-tech existence but compensating for it. Indeed, as advanced technology increasingly draws us toward a mechanical way of thinking and acting, it becomes crucial that schools help students develop their distinctly human capacities. What we need from schools is not balance in using high technology, but an effort to balance children's machine-dominated lives.

To prepare children to challenge the cold logic of the spreadsheet-generated bottom line, we need to teach them to value what that spreadsheet cannot factor in: commitment, loyalty, and tradition. To prepare them to find meaning in the abstract text and images encountered through screens, we need to first engage them in physical realities that screen images can only symbolize. To fit students to live in an environment filled with human-made products, we need to first help them know and respect what cannot be manufactured: the natural, the living, the wild. To prepare students to live well-grounded lives in a world of constant technological change, we need to concentrate their early education on things that endure.

The Cost of Failing to Compensate

Anyone who has spent time in schools knows that what is keeping today's youth from succeeding academically has nothing to do with a lack of technical skills or access to computers. Rather, it is the lack of qualities like hope, compassion, trust, respect, a sense of belonging, moral judgment, stability, community support, parental care, and teacher competence and enthusiasm that keeps so many students imprisoned in ignorance.

Ironically, what students will most need to meet the serious demands of the 21st century is the wisdom that grows out of these inner human capacities and that is developed by community involvement. If the 20th century taught us anything at all, it should have been that technology can be a very mixed blessing. Children entering elementary schools today will eventually have to wrestle with the mess that their elders have left them because of our own lack of wisdom about technology's downside: global warming, increasingly lethal weapons, nuclear waste, overdependence on automobiles, overuse of pesticides and antibiotics, and the general despoiling of our planet. They will also have to take on ethical conundrums posed by advanced technology, such as what to do about cloning, which decisions are off-limits to artificial intelligence devices, and whether or not parents should be allowed to "enhance" the genetic makeup of their offspring (only the wealthy need apply).

Those decisions should not be left to technicians in labs, CEOs in boardrooms, or politicians in debt to those who stand to profit from the technology. Our children should be at the decision tables as adults, and we want them to be able to stand apart from high technology and soberly judge its benefits and detriments to the entire human race.

How can young people develop the wisdom to judge high technology if they are told from the moment they enter school, implicitly if not explicitly, that they need high-tech tools to learn, to communicate, to think? Having been indoctrinated early with the message that their capacity to deal with the world depends not on their own internal resources but on their use of powerful external machines, how can students even imagine a world in which human beings impose limits on technological development or use?

Where to Go from Here

Keep to Essentials in the Early Years

So how, specifically, should educators make decisions and policies about the appropriateness of digital technologies for students of different ages?

One approach to tackling this dilemma comes from the Alliance for Childhood. During the last eight years, the Alliance (whose board of directors I serve on) has engaged educators, children's health professionals, researchers, and technology experts in developing guidelines for structuring a healthy learning environment for children, and has developed a list of essential conditions. Educators should ask themselves to what extent heavy use of computers and the Internet provides children in the lower grades with these essential school experiences:

- Close, loving relationships with responsible adults.
- Outdoor activity, nature exploration, gardening, and other encounters with nature.
- Time for unstructured play as part of the core curriculum.
- Music, drama, puppetry, dance, painting, and the other arts, both as separate classes and as a catalyst to bring other academic subjects to life.
- Hands-on lessons, handicrafts, and other physically engaging activities that provide effective first lessons for young children in the sciences, mathematics, and technology.
- Conversation with important adults, as well as poetry, storytelling, and hearing books read aloud.

This vision places a high priority on a child's direct encounters with the world and with other living beings, but it does not reject technology. On the contrary, tools are an important pan of the vision. But at the elementary level, the tools should be simple, putting less distance between the student and the world and calling forth the student's own internal resources.

Schools must also be patient with children's development. It would strike anyone as silly to give the smallest student in a 2nd grade class a scooter so that the child could get around the track as fast as the other kids his or her age. But our society shows decreasing willingness to wait for the natural emergence of students' varying mental and emotional capacities. We label students quickly and display an almost pathological eagerness to apply external technical fixes (including medications) to students who often simply aren't ready for the abstract, academic, and sedentary environment of today's early elementary classrooms. Our tendency to turn to external tools to help children cope with demands that are out of line with their tactile and physically energetic nature reflects the impact that decades of placing faith in technical solutions has had on how we treat children.

Study Technology in Depth after Elementary School

After children have had years to engage in direct, firsthand experiences, and as their abstract thinking capacities emerge more fully, it makes sense to gradually introduce computers and other complex, symbolic environments. Computer hardware and software should also become the focus of classroom investigation. A student in a technological society surrounded by black boxes whose fundamental principles he or she does not understand is as functionally illiterate as a student in a world filled with books that he or she can't read. The only thing worse would be to make technology "invisible," preventing children from even being aware of their ignorance.

By high school, digital technologies should take a prominent place in students' studies, both as tools of learning and as tools to learn about. During the last two years of high school, teachers should spend considerable time outfitting students with the high-tech skills they will need when they graduate. This "just-in-time" approach to teaching technical skills is far more efficient—instructionally and financially—than continually retraining younger students in technical skills soon to be obsolete. In addition, students at all education levels should consciously examine technology's role in human affairs.

I am not suggesting that we indiscriminately throw computers out of classrooms. But I do believe it's time to rethink the past decision to indiscriminately throw them in. The result of that rethinking would be, I hope, some much-needed technological modesty, both in school and eventually in society in general. By compensating for the dominance of technology in students' everyday lives, schools might help restore the balance we need to create a more humane society.

The irony of postmodern education is that preparing children for a high-tech future requires us to focus our attention more than ever before on the task of understanding what it means to be human, to be alive, to be part of both social and biological communities—a quest for which technology is increasingly becoming not the solution but the problem.

References

Dodici, B. J., Draper, D. C., & Peterson, C. A. (2003). Early parent-child interactions and early literacy development. *Topics in Early Childhood Special Education, 23*(3), 124–136.

Fuchs, T., & Woessmann, L. (2004, November). *Computers and student learning: Bivariate and multivariate evidence on the availability and use of computers at home and at school.* CESifo Working Paper Series (#1321). . . .

Hammel, S. (1999, Nov. 29). Generation of loners? Living their lives online. *U.S. News and World Report*, p. 79.

POSTSCRIPT

Should Schools Embrace Computers and Technology?

Can we rely on empirical research to decide whether computers and related information technologies are superior to other instructional methods? The answer is a cautious yes. In principle, it should be possible, for example, to compare a computer-based approach to teaching American history to a more traditional, teacher-centered approach. Of course, the curricula covered by the two approaches would have to be identical so that any observed differences in student achievement could be attributed to the instructional approach rather than to the curriculum. The results of such a study should be interpreted cautiously, however, for at least six reasons. First, results obtained from a study based on teaching American history might not match results obtained for a study on teaching algebra, language arts, physics, etc. Perhaps American history lends itself more (or less) readily to computer-based instruction than other subjects do. A second consideration is the age or grade level of the students participating in the study. Although the computer-based approach might be highly effective in teaching high school-level American history, it might not be the best option for teaching an elementary school version of this same subject. Third, this study would not be a test of computer technology in general but rather of one particular software package, hardware configuration, and set of activities. Fourth, there would remain the question of whether or not any advantages found for the computer-based approach really have anything at all to do with technology. It is possible, for example, that benefits associated with a computer-based approach derived from the fact that the students were actively involved with the material to be learned rather than passively listening to the teacher present the information. Fifth, how would researchers know they had observed students for a sufficient length of time to know the full effects of computer-based approach to instruction? Finally, even if there were benefits of the computer-based approach in terms of more rapid or increased mastery of the content taught, it is possible that there could also be negative "side effects." For example, interpersonal skills or a sense of community might be diminished. Measuring such side effects and evaluating their importance might be difficult and might require reliance on value judgments rather than empirical data.

Comprehensive reviews of research on the impact of computers on academic achievement and cognitive development can be found in "Technology's Promises and Dangers in a Psychological and Educational Context," by Gavriel Salomon, *Theory into Practice* (vol. 37, no. 1, 1998), and "Educational Psychology and Technology: A Matter of Reciprocal Relations," by Gavriel Salomon and Tamar Almog, *Teachers College Record* (Winter 1998). Also see

"The I-Generation—From Toddlers to Teenagers: A Conversation with Jane M. Healy," by Carol Tell, *Educational Leadership* (October 2000); "Mad Rushes into the Future: The Overselling of Educational Technology," by Douglas Noble, *Educational Leadership* (November 1996); and "Generation of Loners? Living Their Lives Online," by S. Hammel, *U.S. News and World Report* (November 1999). For examples of educational programs based on computer technologies, see "Attacking Literacy with Technology in an Urban Setting," by Michael R. Blasewitz and Rosemarye T. Taylor, *Middle School Journal* (January 1999); "From Compliance to Commitment: Technology as a Catalyst for Communities of Learning," by Mary Burns, *Phi Delta Kappan* (December 2002); and "Integrating Technologies Throughout Our Schools," by Richard L. Schwab and Lin J. Foa, *Phi Delta Kappan* (April 2001). For a book-length critique of technology in the schools, see *Oversold and Underused: Computers in the Classroom* by Larry Cuban (Harvard University Press, 2001).

ISSUE 15

Should Schools Decrease Class Size to Improve Student Outcomes?

YES: Bruce J. Biddle and David C. Berliner, from "Small Class Size and Its Effects," *Educational Leadership* (February 2002)

NO: Kirk A. Johnson, from "The Downside to Small Class Policies," *Educational Leadership* (February 2002)

ISSUE SUMMARY

YES: Bruce J. Biddle, a professor emeritus of psychology and sociology at the University of Missouri, Columbia and David C. Berliner, a regent's professor of psychology in education at Arizona State University, argue that the gains from smaller classes in the primary grades benefit all types of students, and, importantly, that the gains are greatest for students traditionally disadvantaged in educational access and opportunity.

NO: Kirk A. Johnson, a senior policy analyst in the Center for Data Analysis, Heritage Foundation, argues that although the notion of reducing class size is popular among politicians, it is a costly initiative. He argues that the research suggests that in terms of raising achievement, reducing class size does not guarantee success.

Among the most common visual metaphors for public education in the United States is the one-room school house. Children of all ages and abilities were taught as a single class in one room under one roof. In a largely agrarian society, the arrangement was one of necessity. Following the arrival of the Industrial Revolution, rapid urbanization, and population growth, compulsory education emerged, in part, to supply an educated labor force. School enrollments increased and children were stratified into graded classrooms by chronological age.

Concerns about class size in relation to student outcomes appear as early as the 1920s and for the next four decades informal and opinion-based reviews seemed to support the generally held view that class size was unrelated to academic outcome. Then, a series of research method innovations led to quantitative reviews of the available research literature suggesting the opposite;

student outcome and class size appeared to be related. At the same time, dramatic sociopolitical changes were occurring with respect to civil rights and equal access to educational opportunities. Schools changed again with further diversity and increasing enrollment. Open education became a prominent perspective with issues related to student grouping and classroom arrangement practices receiving further scrutiny.

The argument concerning class size continues unresolved in contemporary education. There are many stakeholders with often conflicting points of view that involve rhetoric as much as research and values as much as facts. In general, proponents maintain on logical and empirical grounds that smaller class size makes sense because of increased opportunities for student-teacher interaction and therefore learning, reduced problem behavior because of a smaller student-teacher ratio, and overall improved classroom climate. Opponents, however, contend that there is little solid evidence supporting these claims, that reducing class size is a costly venture, and that student outcomes are better served by increasing the quality, not the quantity of teachers. The issue is never far from a political platform and in the late 1990s through the early part of the twenty-first century class size reduction moved through the legislative process and became a provision of the Elementary and Secondary Education Act (ESEA).

The debate surrounding class size and student achievement is illustrated in the following selections. In the first selection, Bruce Biddle and David Berliner argue that the current best evidence, based on well-conceived and controlled educational research studies, provides an increasingly strong platform from which to make several conclusions with respect to class size and educational outcomes, notably, that early grade experience matters with greater gains associated with longer exposure to smaller classes. And, although all types of students benefit from smaller class sizes, the greatest gains are reported for historically disadvantaged groups of school children. They go on to explore policy implications of why, given the strength of the research findings, there are not more effective reform efforts underway in most primary schools in the United States. In the second section, Kirk Johnson argues, however, the evidence is less than compelling that small class size is essential for positive academic outcomes and further, that the cost associated with reducing class size may be too high a price pay. The real difference maker Johnson implies is not more teachers but better teachers.

YES

**Bruce J. Biddle and
David C. Berliner**

Small Class Size and Its Effects

Studies of the impact of class size on student achievement may be more plentiful than for any other issue in education. Although one might expect this huge research effort to yield clear answers about the effects of class size, sharp disagreements about these studies' findings have persisted.

Advocacy groups take opposite stances. The American Federation of Teachers, for example, asserts that

> taken together, these studies . . . provide compelling evidence that reducing class size, particularly for younger children, will have a positive effect on student achievement. (Murphy & Rosenberg, 1998, p. 3)

The Heritage Foundation, by contrast, claims that "there's no evidence that smaller class sizes alone lead to higher student achievement" (Rees & Johnson, 2000).

Reviewers of class size studies also disagree. One study contends that "large reductions in school class size promise learning benefits of a magnitude commonly believed not within the power of educators to achieve" (Glass, Cahen, Smith, & Filby, 1982, p. 50), whereas another claims that "the . . . evidence does not offer much reason to expect a systematic effect from overall class size reduction policies" (Hanushek, 1999, p. 158).

That the American Federation of Teachers and the Heritage Foundation sponsor conflicting judgments is easy to understand. But why have reviewers come to such divergent views about the research on class size, and what does the evidence really say?

Early Small Field Experiments

To answer these questions, we must look at several research traditions, beginning with early experiments on class size. Experiments have always been a popular research technique because investigators can assign their subjects randomly to different conditions and then compare the results of those conditions—and this human intervention can appear to provide information about causes and effects. Experiments on class size, however, are nearly always done in field settings—schools—where uncontrolled events can undermine the research and affect results.

Small experimental studies on the effects of class size began to appear in the 1920s, and scores of them emerged subsequently. In the 1960s, informal reviews of these efforts generally concluded that differences in class size generated little to no effect. By the late 1970s, however, a more sophisticated research method, meta-analysis, had been invented, which facilitated the statistical assembly of results from small-but-similar studies to estimate effects for the studies' populations. Reviewers quickly applied meta-analysis to results from early experiments in class size (Glass & Smith, 1979; Educational Research Service, 1980; Glass et al., 1982; Hedges & Stock, 1983) and eventually emerged with a consensus that short-term exposure to small classes generates—usually minor—gains in student achievement and that those gains are greater in the early grades, in classrooms with fewer than 20 students, and for students from groups that are traditionally disadvantaged in education.

Most of these early class size experiments, however, had involved small samples, short-term exposures to small classes, only one measure of student success, and a single education context (such as one school or school district). Poor designs had also made results of some studies questionable. Researchers needed to use different strategies to ascertain the effects of long-term exposure to small classes and to assess whether the advantages of early exposure to small classes would generalize to other successes and be sustainable.

Surveys

Survey research has provided evidence on the effects of class size by analyzing naturally occurring differences in schools and classrooms and by asking whether these differences are associated with student outcomes.

Well-designed surveys can offer evidence about the impact of variables that experiments cannot manipulate—such as gender, minority status, and childhood poverty—but survey research cannot easily establish relationships between causes and effects. For example, if a survey examines a sample of schools where average class size varies and discovers that those schools with smaller classes also have higher levels of student achievement, has the survey ascertained that class size generated achievement? Hardly. Those schools with smaller classes might also have had more qualified teachers, better equipment, more up-to-date curriculums, newer school buildings, more students from affluent homes, or a more supportive community environment—factors that may also have helped generate higher levels of achievement. To use survey data to make the case for a causal relation between class size and student outcomes, then, researchers must use statistical processes that control for the competing effects of other variables.

Serious surveys of education achievement in the United States began in the 1960s with the famous Coleman report (Coleman et al., 1966). Written by authors with impressive reputations and released with great fanfare, this massive, federally funded study involved a national sample and took on many issues then facing education. Today, most people remember the report for its startling claim that student achievement is almost totally influenced by the students' families and peers and not by the characteristics of their schools.

This claim was widely accepted—indeed, was greeted with dismay by educators and endorsed with enthusiasm by fiscal conservatives—despite flaws in the report's methods that were noted by thoughtful critics.

Since then, researchers have conducted surveys to establish whether differences in school funding or in the reforms that funds can buy—such as small class sizes—are associated with desired education outcomes. Most of these surveys, usually designed by economists, have involved questionable design features and small samples that did not represent the wide range of U.S. schools, classrooms, or students.

In the 1980s, economist Eric Hanushek began to review these flawed studies and to discuss their supposed implications. Hanushek, committed to the notion that public schools are ineffective and should be replaced by a marketplace of competing private schools, concluded that differences in public school funding are not associated with education outcomes (see Hanushek, 1986, and various publications since).

Other analysts have challenged Hanushek's methods and conclusions on several grounds. Larry Hedges and Rob Greenwald, for example, have pointed out that Hanushek merely counts the number of effects that he believes are statistically significant, but because most of the studies that he reviewed had small samples, he has, of course, found few statistically significant effects. When researchers combine those effects in meta-analyses, however, they find that differences in school funding and the benefits that funds can buy—such as small classes—do, indeed, have an impact (see Hedges, Laine, & Greenwald, 1994, and other publications since).

Other commentators have noted that Hanushek's reviews include many studies that used inappropriate samples or did not employ controls for other school characteristics whose effects might be confused with those of class size. In addition, most of the studies did not examine class size directly but looked instead at student-teacher ratio—that is, the number of students divided by the number of "teachers" reported for a school or school district. Such an approach ignores the actual allocation of students and teachers to classrooms and includes as "teachers" such persons as administrators, nurses, counselors, coaches, specialty teachers, and other professionals who rarely appear in classrooms. Such a ratio does not tell us the number of students actually taught by teachers in classrooms.

Hanushek has not responded well to such criticisms; rather, he has found reasons to quarrel with the details and to continue publishing reviews claiming that small classes have few to no effects. These efforts have allied Hanushek with political conservatives who have extolled his conclusions, complimented his efforts, and asked him to testify in various forums where class size issues are debated. Because of these responses and activities, it is no longer possible to give credence to Hanushek's judgments about class size.

Fortunately, a few well-designed, large-scale surveys have investigated class size directly (see, for example, Elliott, 1998; Ferguson, 1991; Ferguson & Ladd, 1996; Wenglinsky, 1997). These studies concluded that long-term exposure to small classes in the early grades can be associated with student achievement; that the extra gains that such exposure generates may be substantial;

and that such gains may not appear with exposure to small classes in the upper grades or at the secondary school levels.

Trial Programs and Large Field Experiments

Other types of small class research have addressed some of the shortcomings of early experiments and surveys. In the 1980s, state legislatures in the United States began political debates about the effects of small class size, and some states began trial programs or large-scale field experiments.

Indiana's Project Prime Time

In 1981, the Indiana legislature allocated $300,000 for a two-year study on the effects of reducing class size for the early grades in 24 randomly selected public schools. But initial results were so impressive that the state allocated funds to reduce class sizes in the 1st grade for all Indiana schools in 1984–85 and for K–3 by 1987–88, with an average of 18 students for each teacher.

Because of the statewide design of the initiative, it was impossible to compare results for small classes with a comparable group of larger classes. Some schools in the state had small classes before Project Prime Time began, however, so researchers compared samples of 2nd grade achievement records from six school districts that had reduced class size with three that had not. They found substantially larger gains in reading and mathematics achievement for students in small classes (McGivern, Gilman, & Tillitski, 1989).

These results seemed promising, but critics soon pounced on the design of the Project Prime Time study, decrying the fact that students had not been assigned to experimental and control groups on a random basis; pointing out that other changes in state school policy had also been adopted during the project; and suggesting that the state's teachers were motivated to make certain that small classes achieved better results because they knew how the trial program's results were supposed to come out. Indiana students probably did benefit from the project, but a persuasive case for small classes had not yet been made. A better experiment was needed.

Tennessee's Project STAR

Such an experiment shortly appeared in Tennessee's Project STAR (Student/ Teacher Achievement Ratio), arguably the largest and best-designed field experiment ever undertaken in education (Finn & Achilles, 1990; Finn, Gerber, Achilles, & Boyd-Zaharias, 2001; Folger, 1989; Grissmer, 1999; Krueger, 1999, 2000; Krueger & Whitmore, 2001; Mosteller, 1995; Nye, Hedges, & Konstantopoulos, 1999).

In the mid-1980s, the Tennessee legislature funded a four-year study to compare the achievement of early-grade students assigned randomly to one of three conditions: *standard classes* (with one certificated teacher and more than 20 students); *supplemented classes* (with one teacher and a full-time, noncertificated teacher's aide); and *small classes* (with one teacher and about 15 students). The study began with students entering kindergarten in 1985 and called for each student to attend the same type of class for four years. To control variables, the study asked each participating school to sponsor all three types of classes and to assign students and teachers randomly to each type. Participating teachers received no prior training for the type of class they were to teach.

The project invited all the state's primary schools to be in the study, but each participating school had to agree to remain in the program for four years; to have the class *rooms* needed for the project; and to have at least 57 kindergarten students so that all three types of classes could be set up. Participating schools received no additional support other than funds to hire additional teachers and aides. These constraints meant that troubled schools and those that disapproved of the study—and schools that were too small, crowded, or underfunded—would not participate in the STAR program, so the sample for the first year involved "only" 79 schools, 328 classrooms, and about 6,300 students. Those schools came from all corners of the state, however, and represented urban, inner-city, suburban, and rural school districts. The sample population included majority students, a sizable number of African American students, and students receiving free school lunches.

At the beginning of each year of the study, the sample population changed somewhat. Some participating students had moved away, been required to repeat kindergarten, or left the study because of poor health. Other families moved into the districts served by STAR schools, however, and their children filled the vacant seats. Also, because attending kindergarten was not then mandatory in Tennessee, some new students entered the STAR program in the 1st grade.

In addition, some parents tried to move their children from one type of STAR class to another, but administrators allowed only a few students to move from a standard class to a supplemented class or vice versa. By the end of the study, then, some students had been exposed to a STAR class for four years, but others had spent a shorter time in such classes. These shifts might have biased STAR results, but Alan Krueger's careful analysis (1999) concluded that such bias was minimal.

Near the end of each year, STAR students took the Stanford Achievement Test battery and received separate scores for reading, word-study skills, and mathematics. Results from these tests were similar for students who were in the standard and supplemented classes, indicating that the presence of untrained aides in supplemented classes did *not* contribute to improving student achievement. Results for small classes were sharply different, however, with long-term exposure to small classes generating substantially higher levels of achievement and with gains becoming greater the longer that students were in small classes.

. . . STAR investigators found that the students in small classes were 0.5 months ahead of the other students by the end of kindergarten, 1.9 months ahead at the end of 1st grade, 5.6 months ahead in 2nd grade, and 7.1 months ahead by the end of 3rd grade. The achievement advantages were smaller, although still impressive, for students who were only exposed to one, two, or three years of small classes. STAR investigators found similar (although not identical) results for word-study skills and mathematics.

Small-class advantages appeared for all types of students participating in the study. The gains were similar for boys and girls, but they were greater for impoverished students, African American students, and students from inner-city schools—groups that are traditionally disadvantaged in education.

These initial STAR findings were impressive, but would students who had been exposed to small classes in the early grades retain their extra gains when they entered standard size classes in 4th grade? To answer this question, the Tennessee legislature authorized a second study to examine STAR student outcomes during subsequent years of schooling.

At the end of each year, until they were in the 12th grade in 1997–1998, these students took the Comprehensive Tests of Basic Skills and received scores in reading, mathematics, science, and social science. The results showed that average students who had attended small classes were months ahead of those from standard classes for each topic assessed at each grade level. . . .

Students who had attended small classes also enjoyed other advantages in the upper grades. They earned better grades on average, and fewer dropped out or had to repeat a year. And when they reached high school, more small class students opted to learn foreign languages, study advanced-level courses, and take the ACT and SAT college entrance examinations. More graduated from high school and were in the top 25 percent of their classes. Moreover, initial published results suggest that these upper-grade effects were again larger for students who are traditionally disadvantaged in education.

. . . Instruction in small classes during the early grades had eliminated more than half of the traditional disadvantages that African American students have displayed in participation rates in the ACT and SAT testing programs.

Taken together, findings from the STAR project have been impressive, but they are not necessarily definitive. The STAR student sample did not quite match the U.S. population, for example, because very few Hispanic, Native American, and immigrant (non-English-speaking) families were living in Tennessee in the middle-1980s. Also, news about the greater achievement gains of small classes leaked out early during the STAR project, and one wonders how this may have affected participating teachers and why parents whose children were in other types of classes did not then demand that their children be reassigned to small classes. Finally, the STAR schools had volunteered to participate, suggesting that the teachers and principals in those schools may have had strong interests in trying innovative ideas. Questions such as these should not cause us to reject the findings from the STAR project, but we should keep in mind that this was a single study and that, as always, other evidence is needed to increase certainty about class size effects.

Wisconsin's SAGE Program

Findings from Project STAR have prompted class size reduction efforts in other states. One type of effort focuses on increasing the number of small, early-grade classes in schools in disadvantaged neighborhoods. STAR investigators supervised such a program in Tennessee in 1989, reducing K–3 class sizes in 17 school districts where the average family income was low. The results of this and similar projects in North Carolina, Michigan, Nevada, and New York have confirmed that students from small classes generate higher achievement scores when compared with their previous performance and with those of students in other schools. Most of these projects, however, have been small in scope.

A much larger project focused on the needs of disadvantaged students is Wisconsin's Student Achievement Guarantee in Education (SAGE) Program (Molnar et al., 1999, 2000; Zahorik, 1999). Led by Alex Molnar, this program began as a five-year pilot project for K–3 classes in school districts where at least 50 percent of students were living below the poverty level. The program invited all schools in these districts to apply for the program, but it was able to fund only a few of these schools, and no additional schools were to be added during the pilot project. Schools received an additional \$2,000 for each low-income student enrolled in SAGE classrooms. All school districts that applied were allowed to enter the program, and 30 schools in 21 districts began the program at the K–1 grade levels in 1996, with 2nd grade added in 1997 and 3rd grade in 1998.

The SAGE program's major intervention was to reduce the average K–3 class size to 15 students for each teacher. To assess outcomes of the program, researchers compared results from small class SAGE schools with results from standard class size schools in the same districts having similar K–3 enrollments, racial compositions, average family incomes, and prior records of achievement in reading. Findings so far have indicated larger gains for students from small classes—in achievement scores for language arts, reading, and mathematics—that are roughly comparable to those from Project STAR. In addition, as with Project STAR, African American students have made relatively larger gains.

Like project STAR, the SAGE program studied schools that had volunteered for the program and provided them with sufficient funds to hire additional teachers. The SAGE program, however, involved more Hispanic, Asian, and Native American students than had the STAR project.

After the announcement of findings from the initial effort, the Wisconsin legislature extended the SAGE program to other primary schools in the state. Therefore, what began as a small trial project has now blossomed into a statewide program that makes small classes in the early grades available for schools serving needy students.

The California Class Size Reduction Program

In 1996, California began a class size reduction program that has been far more controversial than such programs elsewhere. In earlier years, California had experienced many social problems, and major measures of achievement ranked California schools last in the United States. That year, however, a fiscal windfall became available, and then-governor Pete Wilson announced that primary schools would receive \$650 annually for each student (an amount later increased to \$800) if they would agree to reduce class sizes in the early grades from the statewide average of more than 28 students to not more than 20 students in each class (Hymon, 1997; Korostoff, 1998; Stecher, Bohrnstedt, Kirst, McRobbie, & Williams, 2001).

Several problems quickly surfaced. First, the California definition of a small class was larger than the size recommended in other studies. In fact, the size of small classes in California matched the size of standard classes in some other states. On the other hand, some California schools had been coping with 30–40 students in each classroom in the early grades, so a reduction to 20 students constituted an improvement.

The second problem was that the program's per-student funding was inadequate. Contrast the SAGE program's additional $2,000 for each student with the $650 or $800 offered by California. Nevertheless, the lure of additional funding proved seductive, and most California school districts applied to participate. This inadequate funding imposed serious consequences on poorer school districts, which had to abolish other needed activities to afford hiring teachers for smaller classes. In effect, then, the program created rather than solved problems for underfunded school districts.

In addition, when the California program began, many of its primary schools were overcrowded, and the state was suffering from a shortage of well-trained, certificated teachers. To cope with the lack of space, some schools created spaces for smaller classes by cannibalizing other needed facilities such as special education quarters, child care centers, music and art rooms, computer laboratories, libraries, gymnasiums, or teachers' lounges. Other schools had to tap into their operating budgets to buy portable classrooms, resulting in delays in paying for badly needed curricular materials or repairs for deteriorating school buildings. And to staff their smaller classes, many schools had to hire teachers without certification or prior training.

So far, results from the California program have been only modest. Informal evidence suggests that most students, parents, and teachers are pleased with their schools' smaller classes. And comparisons between the measured achievements of 3rd grade students from districts that did and did not participate in the early phases of the program have indicated minor advantages for California's smaller classes. These effects, however, have been smaller than those reported for the STAR and SAGE programs.

In many ways, the California initiative has provided a near-textbook case of how a state should *not* reduce class size. After failing to conduct a trial program, California adopted an inadequate definition of class size, committed insufficient funds to the initiative, and ignored serious problems of overcrowding and teacher shortages. This example should remind us that small classes are not a panacea for education. To be effective, programs for reducing class size need careful planning and consideration of the needs and strengths of existing school systems.

What We Now Know about Small Classes

What should we conclude about the effects of small classes? Although the results of individual studies are always questionable, a host of different studies suggest several conclusions.

- When planned thoughtfully and funded adequately, small classes in the early grades generate substantial gains for students, and those extra gains are greater the longer students are exposed to those classes.

- Extra gains from small classes in the early grades are larger when the class has fewer than 20 students.
- Extra gains from small classes in the early grades occur in a variety of academic disciplines and for both traditional measures of student achievement and other indicators of student success.
- Students whose classes are small in the early grades retain their gains in standard size classrooms and in the upper grades, middle school, and high school.
- All types of students gain from small classes in the early grades, but gains are greater for students who have traditionally been disadvantaged in education.
- Initial results indicate that students who have traditionally been disadvantaged in education carry greater small-class, early-grade gains forward into the upper grades and beyond.
- The extra gains associated with small classes in the early grades seem to apply equally to boys and girls.
- Evidence for the possible advantages of small classes in the upper grades and high school is inconclusive.

Tentative Theories

Why should reducing class size have such impressive effects in the early grades? Theories about this phenomenon have fallen largely into two camps.

Most theorists focus on the teacher, reasoning that small classes work their magic because the small class context improves interactions between the teacher and individual students. In the early grades, students first learn the rules of standard classroom culture and form ideas about whether they can cope with education. Many students have difficulty with these tasks, and interactions with a teacher on a one-to-one basis—a process more likely to take place when the class is small—help the students cope. In addition, teachers in small classes have higher morale, which enables them to provide a more supportive environment for initial student learning. Learning how to cope well with school is crucial to success in education, and those students who solve this task when young will thereafter carry broad advantages—more effective habits and positive self-concepts—that serve them well in later years of education and work.

The need to master this task confronts all students, but doing so is often a more daunting challenge for students who come from impoverished homes, ethnic groups that have suffered from discrimination or are unfamiliar with U.S. classroom culture, or urban communities where home and community problems interfere with education. Thus, students from such backgrounds have traditionally had more difficulty coping with classroom education, and they are more likely to be helped by a reduction in class size.

This theory also helps explain why reductions in class size in the upper grades may not generate significant advantages. Older students normally have learned to cope with standard classrooms and have developed either effective or ineffective attitudes concerning academic subjects—and these attitudes are not likely to change just because of a reduction in class size.

The theory also suggests a caution. Students are likely to learn more and develop better attitudes toward education if they are exposed to well-trained and enthusiastic teachers, appropriate and challenging curriculums, and physical environments in their classrooms and schools that support learning. If conditions such as these are not also present, then reducing class size in the early grades will presumably have little impact. Thus, when planning programs for reducing class size, we should also think about the professional development of the teachers who will participate in them and the educational and physical contexts in which those programs will be placed.

A second group of theories designed to account for class size effects focuses on the classroom environment and student conduct rather than on the teacher. We know that discipline and classroom management problems interfere with subject-matter instruction. Theories in this group argue that these problems are less evident in small classes and that students in small classes are more likely to be engaged in learning. Moreover, teacher stress is reduced in small classes, so teachers in the small class context can provide more support for student learning. Studies have also found that small instructional groups can provide an environment for learning that is quite different from that of the large classroom. Small instructional groups can create supportive contexts where learning is less competitive and students are encouraged to form supportive relationships with one another.

Theories such as these suggest that the small class environment is structurally different from that of the large class. Less time is spent on management and more time is spent on instruction, students participate at higher levels, teachers are able to provide more support for learning, and students have more positive relationships. Such processes should lead both to greater subject-matter learning and to more positive attitudes about education among students, with more substantial effects in the early grades and for those groups that are traditionally disadvantaged in education.

These two theories are not mutually exclusive. On the contrary, both may provide partial insights into what happens in small classes and why small class environments help so many students. Collecting other types of evidence to assess such theories directly would be useful, particularly observational studies that compare the details of interaction in early-grade classes of various sizes and surveys of the attitudes and self-concepts of students who have been exposed to classes of different sizes. Unfortunately, good studies of these effects have been hard to find.

Policy Implications and Actions

Given the strength of findings from research on small classes, why haven't those findings provoked more reform efforts? Although many state legislatures have debated or begun reform initiatives related to class size, most primary schools in the United States today do not operate under policies that mandate small classes for early grades. Why not?

This lack of attention has several causes, among them ignorance about the issue, confusion about the results of class size research and ineffective dissemination of those results, prejudices against poor and minority students, the politicizing of debates about class size effects and their implications, and practical problems associated with adopting small classes.

Recent debates about class size have become quite partisan in the United States, with Democrats generally favoring class size reductions and Republicans remaining hostile to them. Responding to President Bill Clinton's 1998 State of the Union address, the U.S. Congress set up a modest program, aimed at urban school districts with high concentrations of poverty, which provided funds for hiring additional teachers during the 1999 and 2000 fiscal years. This program enabled some districts to reduce class sizes in the early grades, and informal results from those cities indicated gains in student achievement.

Republicans have been lukewarm about extending this program—some apparently believing that it is ineffective or is merely a scheme to enhance the coffers of teachers' unions—and have welcomed President George W. Bush's call for an alternative federal program focused on high-stakes achievement tests and using results from those tests to apply sanctions to schools if they do not perform adequately.

The major problems standing in the way of reducing class sizes, however, are often practical ones. In many cases, cutting class sizes means hiring more teachers. With the looming shortage of qualified teachers, recruiting more teachers may be even more difficult than finding the funds to pay their salaries. Further, many schools would have to find or create extra rooms to house the additional classes created by small class programs, which would require either modifying school buildings or acquiring temporary classroom structures.

In many cases, meeting such needs would mean increasing the size of public school budgets, a step abhorred by fiscal conservatives and those who are critical of public education. The latter have argued that other reforms would cost less and be more effective than reducing class sizes. In response to such claims, various studies have estimated the costs of class size reduction programs or compared their estimated costs with those of other proposed reforms. Unfortunately, studies of this type must make questionable assumptions, so the results of their efforts have not been persuasive.

Nevertheless, reducing the size of classes for students in the early grades often requires additional funds. All students would reap sizable education benefits and long-lasting advantages, however, and students from educationally disadvantaged groups would benefit even more. Indeed, if we are to judge by available evidence, no other education reform has yet been studied that would provide such striking benefits. Debates about reducing class sizes, then, are disputes about values. If citizens are truly committed to providing a quality public education and a level playing field for all students regardless of background, they will find the funds needed to reduce class size.

References

Coleman, J. S., Campbell, E. Q., Hobson, C. J., McPartland, J., Mood, A. M., Weinfeld, F. D., & York, R. L. (1966). *Equality of educational opportunity.* Washington, DC: U.S. Government Printing Office.

Educational Research Service. (1980, December). Class size research: A critique of recent meta-analyses. *Phi Delta Kappan, 70,* 239–241.

Elliott, M. (1998). School finance and opportunities to learn: Does money well spent enhance students' achievement? *Sociology of Education, 71,* 223–245.

Ferguson, R. F. (1991). Paying for public education: New evidence on how and why money matters. *Harvard Journal on Legislation, 28,* 465–498.

Ferguson, R. F., & Ladd, H. F. (1996). How and why money matters: An analysis of Alabama schools. In H. F. Ladd (Ed.), *Holding schools accountable: Performance-based reform in education* (pp. 256–298). Washington, DC: Brookings Institution.

Finn, J. D., & Achilles, C. M. (1990). Answers and questions about class size: A statewide experiment. *American Educational Research Journal, 27*(3), 557–577.

Finn, J. D., Gerber, S. B., Achilles, C. M., & Boyd-Zaharias, J. (2001). The enduring effects of small classes. *Teachers College Record, 103*(1), 145–183.

Folger, J. (Ed.). (1989). Project STAR and class size policy. *Peabody Journal of Education* (Special Issue), *67*(1).

Glass, G. V., Cahen, L. S., Smith, M. L., & Filby, N. N. (1982). *School class size: Research and policy.* Beverly Hills, CA: Sage.

Glass, G. V., & Smith, M. L. (1979). Meta-analysis of research on class size and achievement. *Educational Evaluation and Policy Analysis, 1,* 2–16.

Grissmer, D. (Ed.). (1999). Class size: Issues and new findings. *Educational Evaluation and Policy Analysis* (Special Issue), *21*(2).

Hanushek, E. A. (1986). The economics of schooling: Production and efficiency in public schools. *Journal of Economic Literature, 24,* 1141–1177.

Hanushek, E. A. (1999). Some findings from an independent investigation of the Tennessee STAR experiment and from other investigations of class size effects. *Education Evaluation & Policy Analysis, 21*(2), 143–163.

Hedges, L. V., Laine, R. D., & Greenwald, R. (1994). Does money matter? A meta-analysis of studies of the effects of differential school inputs on student outcomes. *Educational Researcher, 23*(3), 5–14.

Hedges, L. V., & Stock, W. (1983). The effects of class size: An examination of rival hypotheses. *American Educational Research Journal, 20,* 63–85.

Hymon, S. (1997, July 7). A lesson in classroom size reduction: Administrators nationwide can learn from California's classroom size reduction plan and how districts implemented it. *School Planning & Management, 36*(7), 18–23, 26.

Korostoff, M. (1998). Tackling California's class size reduction policy initiative: An up close and personal account of how teachers and learners responded. *International Journal of Educational Research, 29,* 797–807.

Krueger, A. B. (1999). Experimental estimates of education production functions. *The Quarterly Journal of Economics, 114*(2), 497–532.

Krueger, A. B. (2000). Economic considerations and class size. Princeton University, Industrial Relations Section, Working Paper #447.

Krueger, A. B., & Whitmore, D. M. (2001). The effect of attending a small class in the early grades on college-test taking and middle school test results: Evidence from Project STAR. *Economic Journal, 111,* 1–28.

McGivern, J., Gilman, D., & Tillitski, C. (1989). A meta-analysis of the relation between class size and achievement. *The Elementary School Journal, 90*(1), 47–56.

Molnar, A., Smith, P., Zahorik, J., Palmer, A., Halbach, A., & Ehrle, K. (1999). Evaluating the SAGE program: A pilot program in targeted pupil-teacher reduction in Wisconsin. *Educational Evaluation and Policy Analysis, 21,* 165–177.

Molnar, A., Smith, P., Zahorik, J., Palmer, A., Halbach, A., & Ehrle, K. (2000). Wisconsin's student achievement guarantee in education (SAGE) class size reduction program: Achievement effects, teaching, and classroom implications. In M. C. Wang & J. D. Finn (Eds.), *How small classes help teachers do their best* (pp. 227–277). Philadelphia: Temple University, Center for Research in Human Development and Education.

Mosteller, F. (1995). The Tennessee study of class size in the early school grades. *The Future of Children, 5*(2), 113–127.

Murphy, D., & Rosenberg, B. (1998, June). Recent research shows major benefits of small class size. *Educational Issues Policy Brief 3.* Washington, DC: American Federation of Teachers.

Nye, B., Hedges, L. V., & Konstantopoulos, S. (1999). The long-term effects of small classes: A five-year follow-up of the Tennessee class size experiment. *Educational Evaluation and Policy Analysis, 21,* 127–142.

Rees, N. S., & Johnson, K. (2000, May 30). A lesson in smaller class sizes. *Heritage Views 2000 . . .*

Stecher, B., Bohrnstedt, G., Kirst, M., McRobbie, J., & Williams, T. (2001). Class-size reduction in California: A story of hope, promise, and unintended consequences. *Phi Delta Kappan, 82,* 670–674.

Wenglinsky, H. (1997). How money matters: The effect of school district spending on academic achievement. *Sociology of Education, 70,* 221–237.

Zahorik, J. (1999). Reducing class size leads to individualized instruction. *Educational Leadership, 57*(1), 50–53.

Kirk A. Johnson  **NO**

The Downside to Small Class Policies

From the attention and financial support given to class size reduction by politicians and the public, one might assume that research has shown small class size to be essential to positive academic outcomes. In fiscal year 2000, the U.S. Congress allocated $1.3 billion for the class size reduction provision of the Elementary and Secondary Education Act (ESEA). During the Clinton administration, class size received a great deal of attention through proposals to pump large sums of money into efforts to increase the number of teachers in public elementary schools, thereby decreasing the ratio of students to teachers (The White House, 2000).

Proponents of class size reduction claim that small classes result in fewer discipline problems and allow teachers more time for instruction and individual attention and more flexibility in instructional strategies (Halbach, Ehrle, Zahorik, & Molnar, 2001).

Do small classes make a difference in the academic achievement of elementary school students? Are class size reduction programs uniformly positive, or does a downside exist to hiring and placing more teachers in U.S. public schools?

The California Experience

In 1995, California enacted one of the broadest-reaching laws for ensuring small classes in the early grades. Strong bipartisan approval of the class size reduction measure in the California legislature reflected broad support among constituents for reducing class sizes. The program has been wildly popular over its short lifetime, but it has faced substantial obstacles to success.

California's class size reduction program has suffered from a lack of qualified teachers to fill classrooms. More or less simultaneously, nearly all elementary schools in the state demanded more teachers, and some schools—typically suburban—attracted far more teaching applicants than did those in the inner city.

A consortium of researchers from RAND, the American Institutes for Research (AIR), Policy Analysis for California Education (PACE), EdSource, and WestEd analyzed the effects of California's class size reduction initiative and outlined two basic problems. First, K–3 classes that remained large were

From *Educational Leadership,* February 2002, pp. 27–29. Copyright © 2002 by ASCD. Reprinted by permission. The Association for Supervision and Curriculum Development is a worldwide community of educators advocating sound policies and sharing best practices to achieve the success of each learner. To learn more, visit ASCD at www.ascd.org.

"concentrated in districts serving high percentages of minority, low-income, or English learner (EL) students" (Stecher & Bohrnstedt, 2000, p. x). Second,

> the average qualifications (that is, education, credentials, and experience) of California teachers declined during the past three years for all grade levels, but the declines were worst in elementary schools. . . . Schools serving low-income, minority, or EL students continued to have fewer well-qualified teachers than did other schools. (p. x)

Do Students Learn More in Small Classes?

Clearly, if billions of dollars are to be spent on reducing class size, tangible evidence should exist that students benefit academically from such initiatives. As yet, evidence of the efficacy of class size reduction is mixed at best.

One of the most frequently cited reports on class size is Mosteller's (1995) analysis of the Project STAR study of elementary school students in Tennessee. Mosteller found a significant difference in achievement between students in classes of 13–17 students per teacher and those in classes of 22–25.

University of Rochester economist Eric Hanushek, however, questioned Mosteller's results, noting that "the bulk of evidence . . . points to no systematic effects of class size reductions within the relevant policy range" (1999, p. 144). In other words, no serious policy change on a large scale could decrease class size enough to make a difference.

The current class size reduction debate often ignores the fact that class sizes have been dropping slowly but steadily in the United States over the course of many years. In 1970, U.S. public schools averaged 22.3 students per teacher; by the late 1990s, however, they averaged about 17 students per teacher—a result of a combination of demographic trends and conscious policy decisions to lower pupil-teacher ratios (U.S. Census Bureau, 1999).

Local and programmatic changes in class size can be illustrative, but does research indicate that, on a national level, students in small classes experience academic achievement gains superior to those of their peers in large classes?

The National Assessment of Educational Progress

The most useful database for analyzing whether small classes lead to better academic achievement is the National Assessment of Educational Progress (NAEP). First administered in 1969, the NAEP measures the academic achievement of 4th, 8th, and 12th graders in a variety of fields, including reading, writing, mathematics, science, geography, civics, and the arts. Students take the math and reading tests alternately every two years. For example, students were assessed in reading in 1998; they were tested in math in 1996 and 2000.

The NAEP is actually two tests: a nationally administered test and a state-administered test. More than 40 states participate in the separate state samples used to gauge achievement within those jurisdictions.

In addition to test scores in the subject area, the NAEP includes an assortment of background information on the students taking the exam, their main subject-area teacher, and their school administrator. Background information includes students' television viewing habits, students' computer usage at home and at school, teacher tenure and certification, family socioeconomic status, basic demographics, and school characteristics. By including this information in their assessment of the NAEP data, researchers can gain insight into the factors that might explain differences in NAEP scores found among students.

Results from the Center for Data Analysis

A study from the Center for Data Analysis at the Heritage Foundation examined the 1998 NAEP national reading data to determine whether students in small classes achieve better than students in large classes (Johnson, 2000). Researchers assessed students' academic achievement in reading by analyzing assessment scores as well as six factors from the background information collected by the NAEP: class size, race and ethnicity, parents' education attainment, the availability of reading materials in the home, free or reduced-price lunch participation, and gender.

Class size. The amount of time that a teacher can spend with each student appears to be important in the learning process. To address class size, the Center for Data Analysis study compared students in small classes (those with 20 or fewer students per teacher) with students in large classes (at least 31 students per teacher).

Race and ethnicity. Because significant differences exist in academic achievement among ethnic groups, the variables of race and ethnicity were included in the analysis.

Parents' education. Research indicates that the education attainment of a child's parents is a good predictor of that child's academic achievement. Because the education level of one parent is often highly correlated with that of the other parent, only a single variable was included in the analysis.

The availability of reading materials in the home. The presence of books, magazines, encyclopedias, and newspapers generally indicates a dedication to learning in the household. Researchers have determined that these reading materials are important aspects of the home environment (Coleman, Hoffer, & Kilgore, 1982). Essentially, the presence of such reading materials in the home is correlated with higher student achievement. The analysis thus included a variable controlling for the number of these four types of reading materials found at home.

Free and reduced-price lunch participation. Income is often a key predictor of academic achievement because low-income families seldom have the resources to purchase extra study materials or tutorial classes that may help their children perform better in school. Although the NAEP does not collect data on household income, it does collect data on participation in the free and reduced-price school lunch program.

Gender. Although data on male-female achievement gaps are inconsistent, empirical research suggests that girls tend to perform better in reading and writing subjects, whereas boys perform better in more analytical subjects such as math and science.

After controlling for all these factors, researchers found that the difference in reading achievement on the 1998 NAEP reading assessment between students in small classes and students in large classes were statistically insignificant. That is, across the United Sates, students in small classes did no better on average than those in large classes, assuming otherwise identical circumstances.

Such results should give policymakers pause and provoke them to consider whether the rush to hire more teachers is worth the cost and is in the best interest of students. In terms of raising achievement, reducing class size does not guarantee success.

When Irwin Kurz became the principal of Public School 161 in Brooklyn, New York, well over a decade ago, the schools' test scores ranked in the bottom 25th percentile of schools in Brooklyn's 17th District. Today, P.S. 161 ranks as the best school in the district and 40th of 674 elementary schools in New York City, even though a majority of its students are poor. The pupil-teacher ratio at P.S. 161 is 35 to 1, but the teachers make neither class size, nor poverty, nor anything else an excuse for poor performance. As Kurz likes to say, "better to have one good teacher than two crummy teachers any day."

References

Coleman, J., Hoffer, T., & Kilgore, S. (1982). *High school achievement.* New York: BasicBooks.

Halbach, A., Ehrle, K., Zahorik, J., & Molnar, A. (2001, March). Class size reduction: From promise to practice. *Educational Leadership, 58*(6), 32–35.

Hanushek, E. (1999). Some findings from an independent investigation of the Tennessee STAR experiment and from other investigations of class size effects. *Educational Evaluation & Policy Analysis, 21*(2), 143–164.

Johnson, K. (2000, June 9). *Do small classes influence academic achievement? What the National Assessment of Educational Progress shows* (CDA Report No. 00-07). Washington, DC: Heritage Foundation.

Mosteller, F. (1995). The Tennessee study of class size in the early school grades. *The Future of Children, 5*(2), 113–127.

Stecher, B., & Bohrnstedt, G. (Eds.). (2000). *Class size reduction in California: The 1998–99 evaluation findings.* Sacramento: California Department of Education.

U.S. Census Bureau. (1999). *Statistical abstract of the United States.* Washington, DC: Government Printing Office.

The White House (2000, May 4). President Clinton highlights education reform agenda with roundtable on what works [Press release].

POSTSCRIPT

Should Schools Decrease Class Size to Improve Student Outcomes?

Critics of class size reduction contend that there should be tangible evidence of large benefits associated with reduced numbers. The standard should be high, the argument goes, because the financial costs underlying reducing class size are high. Even if there is some evidence that some students benefit, the majority of the evidence is mixed and policymakers should be reluctant to take up such measures in the absence of clear and compelling data. Johnson, for example, cites economic analyses arguing against large-scale policy change because the gains are either negligible or modest at best. In sum, the critics against reducing class size are not convinced that the evidence base unequivocally supports policy initiatives centered on reducing class size.

But what of those students that benefit? Proponents argue that the current best evidence from well-designed studies does provide convincing and sufficient evidence that there are gains, they occur early, and they are sustainable as a function of length of exposure. In other words, the earlier and longer a student experiences a small class size, the more pronounced the effects on later academic success. Moreover, these gains appear greatest for traditionally disenfranchised student groups. As Biddle and Berliner point out, research studies addressing the issue of class size and student achievement may be among the most abundant in all of educational research and yet there remain no coordinated policies based on consensual agreement. They summarize several likely causes for this, including different perspectives of what is at issue, confusion concerning research results and their interpretation, poorly disseminated findings, political agenda, and practical realities confronting local decision making, to name a few. Perhaps the research agenda needs to continue forward with an even more refined eye toward exploring in greater detail the circumstances under which class size reduction is and is not beneficial and for which students. Presumably, as the evidence accrues from studies in which the design is agreed upon by both sides of the argument, there will be less room for disagreement about what the findings mean.

Readers interested in the original articles from the Tennessee STAR study should read "Answers and Questions about Class Size: A Statewide Experiment," by J. D. Finn and C. M. Achilles, *American Educational Research Journal* (vol. 27, 1990), and "Project STAR and Class Size Policy," by J. Folger, *Peabody Journal of Education* (Special Issue, vol. 67, 1989). But, to see an alternative account of the findings, see "Some Findings from an Independent Investigation of the Tennessee STAR Experiment and from Other Investigations of Class Size Effects," by E. A. Hanushek, *Education Evaluation & Policy Analysis* (vol. 21,

1999). To learn more about the economics of achievement, see "How Money Matters: The Effects of School District Spending on Academic Achievement," by H. Wenglinsky, *Sociology of Education* (vol. 70, 1997). For a historical account of many of the issues behind the contemporary viewpoints, review *Equality of Educational Opportunity* by J. S. Coleman, E. Q. Campbell, C. J. Hobson, J. McPartland, A. M. Mood, F. D. Weinfeld, and R. L. York (Washington, DC: U.S. Government Printing Office, 1966).

ISSUE 16

Can a Zero-Tolerance Policy Lead to Safe Schools?

YES: Albert Shanker, from "Restoring the Connection Between Behavior and Consequences," *Vital Speeches of the Day* (May 15, 1995)

NO: Alfie Kohn, from "Safety from the Inside Out: Rethinking Traditional Approaches," *Educational Horizons* (Fall 2004)

ISSUE SUMMARY

YES: The late Albert Shanker, long-time president of the American Federation of Teachers (AFT), advocates a policy of zero tolerance for violence and other disruptive behavior in school. He argues that such a policy is necessary because disruptive and violent behavior denies equal access to educational opportunities for the nonoffending students in a class or school.

NO: Alfie Kohn, a writer and commentator on issues related to children, parenting, and schools, argues that not only are zero-tolerance polices ineffective, they are also harmful—creating fear rather than a sense of security and trust and replacing programs that are effective in treating the root causes of youth violence.

As violence has become more commonplace in society, many people— particularly parents—have taken solace in the assumption that at least the children are safe at school. This seemed guaranteed by the fact that schools are populated only by teachers, who always have the best interests of the children at heart, and students, who, because of their tender ages, are all but incapable of acts of violence or criminality. Unfortunately, this sentimental image of school as a safe haven has been shattered—repeatedly—in recent years. The turn of the century brought horrific scenes of death and destruction in schools in Arkansas, Colorado, Kentucky, California, and Virginia, all of which were perpetrated by young people, some as young as 10 years old. For teachers and other school personnel, these acts of brutality are only extreme examples of a larger problem. It has become all too commonplace for students to bring weapons to school, to get into fist fights, to sexually harass classmates, and to use or sell illegal drugs. Less dramatic, although perhaps no less disruptive of teaching and learning in the classroom, are the unruly students who curse, act out, threaten, or simply refuse to follow basic rules of classroom decorum and conduct. In short, neither safety nor unfettered access to educational opportunities are guaranteed for students in U.S. schools today, and the causes are the students themselves—at least some of them.

Schools have implemented a variety of strategies to deal with problem students. Some strategies involve providing counseling, therapy, or special educational services. Other strategies focus on controlling the more serious problem behaviors by instituting various security measures, such as police officers patrolling the corridors, metal detectors at school entrances, locker searches for drugs and weapons, and random urine testing for illegal drug use. Critics have questioned the effectiveness—and the ethics and legality—of nearly all of these strategies.

Arguably, however, the most controversial of all of these strategies has been the so-called *zero-tolerance* policies. These policies generally specify a list of "unacceptable" behaviors and a set of explicit consequences for students found to be engaging in such behaviors. Invariably, more serious behaviors (e.g., bringing a weapon to school) or repeat offenses (e.g., being disciplined for frequent fighting) earn a suspension or even expulsion. The cornerstone of this policy is the idea that consequences are immediate and applied without regard for extenuating circumstances. Supporters argue that zero tolerance not only removes problem students, thereby increasing the safety and access to instruction for the remaining students, but that it also acts as a deterrent, making students think twice before violating the school's behavior code. Critics of zero tolerance, however, have characterized it as an ineffective overreaction to a real but exaggerated problem.

In the first of the following selections, Albert Shanker argues that a zero-tolerance policy is necessary because disruptive and violent behavior denies equal access to educational opportunities for nonoffending students. Moreover, he condemns programs that devote special attention to the offenders (e.g., programs targeting self-esteem) as ineffective, as diverting resources from the education of deserving students, and as perhaps reinforcing the offending behavior. In the second selection, Alfie Kohn begins by pointing out that violence involving youth is actually more common outside of schools than within them, which suggests the need for a broad-based strategy reaching beyond the school to prevent such violence. He also argues that zero-tolerance policies are destructive in that they are applied inequitably across races and economic classes, reinforce the notion that power and force are the answers to one's problems, and destroy the trust between students and teachers that is needed for learning. Kohn also argues for programs that move beyond a focus on behaviors to understand what motivates those behaviors.

YES

Albert Shanker

Restoring the Connection Between Behavior and Consequences

I can't think of a more important topic. . . . [T]here have been and will be a number of conferences on this issue. I can assure you, all of the other conferences resemble each other, and this one will be very different. It will have a very different point of view.

We have had, over the last decade or more, a national debate on the issue of school quality. And there is a national consensus that we need to do a lot better. We are probably doing better than we used to, but we're not doing as well as other industrial countries. And in order to do well, we are going to have to do some of the things that those other countries are doing, such as develop high standards, assessments related to those standards, and a system of consequences so that teachers and youngsters and parents know that school counts. School makes a difference, whether it's getting a job or getting into a college or getting into a training program.

We're well on the way. It's going to take time, but we're on the way to bringing about the improvement that we need. But you can have a wonderful curriculum and terrific assessments and you can state that there are consequences out there but none of this is going to do much good in terms of providing youngsters with an education if we don't meet certain basic obvious conditions. And those conditions are simply that you have to have schools that are safe and classrooms where there is sufficient order so that the curriculum means something. Without that, all of this stuff is nonsense. You can deliver a terrific curriculum, but if youngsters are throwing things, cursing and yelling and punching each other, then the curriculum doesn't mean anything in that classroom. The agenda is quite different.

And so we have a very interesting phenomenon. We have members of Congress and governors and state legislators talking about choice and vouchers and charter schools, and you know what the big incentive is for those issues. Parents are not really pushing for these things, except in conditions where their children seem to be unsafe or in conditions where they can't learn. And then they say, well, look, if you can't straighten things out here, then give me a chance to take my youngster somewhere else. And so we're about to put in place a ridiculous situation. We're going to create a system of choice and vouchers, so that 98 percent of the kids who behave can go someplace and be safe. And we're going to leave the two percent who are violent and disruptive to take over the schools. Now, isn't it ridiculous to move 98 percent of the kids, when all you have to do is move two or three percent of them and the other 98 percent would be absolutely fine?

Now this is a problem which has a number of aspects and I want to talk about them. First, there is, of course, the problem of extreme danger, where we are dealing with violence or guns or drugs within the school. And, as we look to the schools, what we find is that the schools seem to be unable to handle this. We had headlines here in DC . . . saying that the mayor and school officials say they don't know what else to do. In other words, they've done everything that they can, and the guns, and the knives, and the drugs are still there. So, it just happens that they have actually said it, but that is, in fact, how many school administrators and school boards across the country behave. They treat violence as a fact of life, that's what society is like, and they just go through a couple of ritual efforts to try to show that they're doing something. But, basically they give up.

What we have is what amounts to a very high level of tolerance of this type of activity. Now, of course, the violence and the guns and the drugs have to be distinguished from another type of activity. This other type isn't deadly in the sense that you are going to read tomorrow morning that some youngster was stabbed or shot. And that's the whole question of just plain out-and-out disruption: the youngster who is constantly yelling, cursing, jumping, fighting, doing all sorts of things, so that most of the time the other students in the class and the teacher is devoted, not to the academic mission of the schools, but to figuring out how to contain this individual. And in this area, we have an even higher tolerance than we do in the area of violence, where occasionally youngsters are suspended or removed for periods of time. . . .

Last year when Congress was debating the Goals 2000 education program, there were an awful lot of people who said, you know, in addition to having different kinds of content standards—what you should learn—and performance standards—how good is good enough—you ought to have opportunity-to-learn standards. It's not fair to hold kids to these standards unless they've had certain advantages. It's not fair, if one kid has had early childhood education and one hasn't, to hold them to the same standard. It's not fair, if at this school they don't have any textbooks or the textbooks are 15 years old, and in that school they have the most modern books. It's not fair, if in this school they've got computers, and in that school kids have never seen a computer.

Well, I submit to you that if you want to talk about opportunity-to-learn standards, there are a lot of kids who've made it without the most up-to-date textbooks. It's better if you have them. There are a lot of kids who've made it without early childhood education. It's a lot better if you've got it, and we're for that. Throughout history, people have learned without computers, but it's better if you've got them. But nobody has ever learned if they were in a classroom with one or two kids who took up 90 percent of the time through disruption, violence, or threats of violence. You deprive children of an opportunity to learn if you do not first provide an orderly situation within the classroom and within the school. That comes ahead of all of these other things.

Now, I said that this conference was going to be different from every conference that I've been to and every conference that I've read about. I have a report here that was sent to me by John Cole [President of the Texas Federation of Teachers], who went to The Scholastic Annual Summit on Youth Violence on October 17 [1994]. I'm not going to read the whole thing, but I'll just read enough that you get the flavor of what these other conferences are like:

"So start with the concept that the real victims of violence are those unfortunate individuals who have been led into lives of crime by the failure of society to provide them with hope for a meaningful life. Following that logic, one must conclude that society has not done enough for these children and that we must find ways to salvage their lives. Schools must work patiently with these individuals offering them different avenues out of this situation. As an institution charged with responsibility for education, schools must have programs to identify those who are embarking on a life of crime and violence and lift them out of the snares into which they have fallen. Society, meanwhile, should be more forgiving of the sins of these poor creatures, who through no real fault of their own are the victims of racism and economic injustice.

"Again and again and again, panelists pointed out that the young people we are talking about, to paraphrase Rodney Danger-field, 'don't get no respect.' The experts assured us that young people take up weapons, commit acts of violence, and abuse drugs because this enables them to obtain respect from their peers. I found myself thinking that we aid and abet this behavior when we bend over backwards to accommodate those young people who have bought into this philosophy. By lavishing attention on them, we may even encourage a spread of that behavior. Many of these programs are well meaning but counterproductive.

"I don't want to condemn this conference as a waste of time. Obviously, we do need programs to work with these young people, and we should try to salvage as many as we can. However, we must somehow come to grips with the idea that individuals have responsibility for their own actions. If we assume that society is to blame for all of the problems these young people have, may we then assume that society must develop solutions that take care of these young people's problems? We take away from each individual the responsibility for his or her own life. Once the individual assumes that he or she has lost control of his own destiny, that individual has no difficulty in justifying any act because he or she feels no responsibility for the consequences."

Now with that philosophy, the idea is not that we want to be punitive or nasty, but essentially schools must teach not only English and mathematics and reading and writing and history, but also teach that there are ways of behaving in society that are unacceptable. And when we sit back and tolerate certain types of behavior, we are teaching youngsters that certain types of behavior are acceptable, which eventually will end up with their being in jail or in poverty for the rest of their lives. We are not doing our jobs as teachers.

And the system is not doing its job, if we send youngsters the message that this is tolerable behavior within society. . . .

All we ask of our schools is that they behave in the same way that a caring and intelligent parent would behave with respect to their own children. I doubt very much, if you had a youngster who was a fire bug or a youngster who used weapons, whether you would say, well, I owe it to this youngster to trust him with my other children to show him that I'm not separating him out or treating him differently. Or I'm going to raise his self-esteem by allowing him to do these things. All of these nutty things that we talk about in school, we would not do. So the starting point of this conference, which is different from all of the others, is that I hope that you people join with me in a sense of outrage that we have a system that is willing to sacrifice the overwhelming majority of children for a handful. And not do any good for that handful either. And we need to start with that outrage, because without that we're not going to change this system.

That outrage is there among parents. That outrage was partly expressed in the recent election as people's anger at the way government was working. Why can't government do things in some sort of common sense way? And this is one of the issues that's out there. Now, what are some of the things that enter into this? Well, part of it is that some people think of schools as sort of custodial institutions. Where are we going to put the kids? Put them here. Or they think the school's job is mostly socialization. Eventually troubled kids will grow up or grow out of this, and they're better off with other youngsters than they are separated. Of course, people who take that point of view are totally ignoring the fact that the central role of schools, the one that we will be held accountable for, is student academic achievement. We know the test scores are bad. And we know that our students are not learning as much as youngsters in other countries. So we can't just say we know we are way behind, but, boy, are we good custodians. Look at how socialized these youngsters are.

People are paying for education and they want youngsters who are going to be able to be employed and get decent jobs. We want youngsters who are going to be as well off or in better shape than we are, just as most of us are with respect to our parents and grandparents. And the academic function is the one that's neglected. The academic function is the one that's destroyed in this notion that our job is mainly custodial.

So our central position is that we have to be tough on these issues, and we have to be tough because basically we are defending the right of children to an education. And those who insist on allowing violence and disruptive behavior in the school are destroying the right to an education for the overwhelming majority of youngsters within our schools.

Two years ago or three years ago, I was in Texas at a convention of the Texas Federation of Teachers. I didn't know this was going to happen, but either just before I got there or while I was there, there was a press conference on a position the convention adopted, and they used the phrase "zero tolerance." They said that with respect to certain types of dangerous activities in schools, there would be zero tolerance. These things are not acceptable and there are going to be consequences. There might be suspension, there might be expulsion, or there might be something else, but nevertheless, consequences will be clear. Well, that got picked up by radio, television, legislators. I was listening to a governor the other night at the National Governors Association, who stood up and came out for zero tolerance. It is a phrase which has caught on and is sweeping the country.

I hope it is one that all of you will bring back to your communities and your states, that there are certain types of activities that we will not tolerate. We will not teach youngsters bad lessons, and we're going to start very early. When a youngster does something that is terribly wrong, and all of the other youngsters are sure that something is going to happen to him because he did something wrong, we had better make sure that we fulfill the expectations of all those other youngsters that something's going to happen. And they're all going to say, "Thank God, I didn't do a terrible thing like that or I would be out there, and something would be happening to me." That is the beginning of a sense of doing something right, as against doing wrong.

And we have to deal with this notion that society is responsible, social conditions are responsible. The AFT does not take second place to anybody in fighting for decent conditions for adults and for youngsters and for minorities and for groups that have been oppressed. We're not in a state of denial; we're not saying that things have been wonderful. But when your kids come home and say "I'm doing these terrible things because of these conditions," if you're a good parent, you'll say, "That's no excuse." You are going to do things right, because you don't want your youngster to end up as a criminal or in some sort of horrible position. . . .

Now what should schools do? Schools should have codes of conduct. These codes can be developed through collective bargaining or they can be mandated in legislation. I don't think it would be a bad idea to have state legislation that every school system needs to have a code of discipline that is very clear, not a fuzzy sort of thing, something that says these things are not to be done and if this happens, these are the consequences. A very clear connection between behavior and consequences. And it might even say that, if there is a legitimate complaint from a group of parents or a group of teachers or a group of students that clearly shows the school district doesn't have such a code or isn't enforcing it, there would be some sort of financial penalty against the district for failing to provide a decent education by allowing this type of violence and disruption to continue.

Taxpayers are sending money into the district so that the kids can have an education, and if that district then destroys the education by allowing one or two youngsters to wipe out all of the effects that money is supposed to produce, what the hell is the point of sending the money? If you allow these youngsters to so disrupt that education, you might as well save the money. So there's a reason for states to do this. And, by the way, I think that you'll find a receptive audience, because the notion of individuals taking responsibility for their actions is one of the things fueling the political anger in this country—that we have a lot of laws which help people to become irresponsible or encourage them not to take responsibility for their own actions.

Now, enforcement is very important. For every crime, so to speak, there ought to be a punishment. I don't like very much judgment to be used, because once you allow judgment to be used, punishments will be more severe for some kids than for others and you will get unfairness. You will get prejudice. The way to make sure that this is done fairly and is not done in a prejudiced way is to say, look, we don't care if you're white or Hispanic or African-American or whether you're a recent immigrant or this or that, for this infraction, this is what happens. We don't have a different sanction depending upon whether we like you a little more or a little less. That's how fairness would be ensured, and I think it's very important that we insist on that. . . .

One of the big problems is school administrators. School administrators are concerned that, if there are a large number of reports of disruptions and violence in their schools, their reputations will suffer. They like to say they have none of those problems in their schools. Now, how do you prove that you have none of these problems in your school? Very simple. Just tell the teachers that if they report it, it's because they are ineffective teachers. If you tell that to one or two teachers, you will certainly have a school that has very little disruption or violence reported. You may have plenty of disruption and violence. So, in many places we have this gag rule. It's not written, but it's very well understood.

As a teacher, I myself faced this. Each time I reported something like this, I was told that if I knew how to motivate the students properly, this wouldn't happen. It's pretty universal. It wasn't just one district or just my principal. It's almost all of them. Therefore, I think that we ought to seek laws that require a full and honest reporting of incidents of violence and extreme disruption. And that would mean that, if an administrator goes around telling you to shut up or threatening you so that you're not free to report, I think that there ought to be penalties. Unless we know the extent of this problem, we're never going to deal with it adequately.

Of course, parents know what the extent of it is. What is the number one problem? It's the problem of violence and order in the schools. They know it. The second big problem and obstacle we face is, what's going to happen if you put the kid out on the streets? It reminds me of a big campaign in New York City to get crime off the streets, and pretty soon they were very successful. They had lots of policemen on the streets, and they drove the criminals away. The criminals went into the subways. Then they had a campaign about crime in the subways, and they drove them back up into the streets. So the business community, parents, and others will say, you can't just throw a kid out and put them on the streets. That's no good. But you could place some conditions on it. To return to school, students would have to bring with them a parent or some other grown-up or relative responsible for them. There is a list of ways in which we might handle it. But we can't say that we're going to wait until we build new schools, or build new classrooms, or have new facilities. The first thing you do is separate out the youngster who is a danger to the other youngsters.

Now, let me give an example. And I think it's one that's pretty close. We know that, when we arrest adults who have committed crimes and we jail them, jail will most likely not help those who are jailed. I don't think it does, and I don't think most people do. However, most of us are pretty glad when someone who has committed a pretty bad crime is jailed. Not because it's going to do that person any good, but because that person won't be around to do the same thing for the next ten or fifteen years. And for the separation of youngsters who are destroying the education of others, the justification is the same. I'm not sure that we can devise programs that will reach those youngsters that will help them. We should try. But our first obligation is to never destroy the education of the twenty or twenty-five or thirty because you have an obligation to one. Especially when there's no evidence that you're doing anything for that one by keeping him there.

Now, another big obstacle is legal problems. These are expensive and time consuming. If a youngster gets a lawyer and goes to court, the principal or some other figure of authority from the school, usually has to go to court. They might sit a whole day and by the end of the first day, they decide not to hear it. And they come a second day, and maybe it's held over again. It might take three or four days for each youngster. So if you've got a decent-sized school, even if you're dealing with only two or three percent of the youngsters, you could spend your full time in court, instead of being in school. Well, I wouldn't want to do that if I were the principal of the school. And then what does the court do when you're all finished? The court says, well, we don't have any better place to put him, so send him right back. So, that's why a lot of teachers wouldn't report it, because nothing happens anyway. You go through all of this, you spend all of that time and money, and when you're all finished, you're right back where you started. So we need to change what happens with respect to the court, and we have two ideas that we're going to explore that have not been done before.

One of the things we need to do is see whether we can get parents, teachers, and even perhaps high school students to intervene in these cases and say, we want to come before the judge to present evidence about what the consequences are for the other children. When you go to court now, you have the lawyer for the board of education, the lawyer for the youngster, and the youngster. And the youngster, well, he's just a kid and his lawyer says, "This poor child has all of these problems," and the judge is looking down at this poor youngster. You know who is not there? The other 25 youngsters to say, this guy beats me up every day. If I do my homework, I get beat up on the way to school because he doesn't want me to do my homework. So instead of first having this one child standing there saying, "Poor me, let me back in school, they have kicked me out, they have done terrible things to me," you also have some of the victims there saying, "Hey, what about us?" You'll get a much fairer consideration if the judge is able to look at both sides, instead of just hearing the bureaucrat from the board of education. None of these board of education lawyers that I've met talk about the other students. They talk about the right of the board of education under the law to do thus, and so what you have is a humane judge who's thinking of the bureaucrat talking about the rights of the board of education as against the child. I think we need to balance that.

Now, there's a second thing we are going to explore. We are all familiar with the fact that most of our labor contracts have a provision for grievance procedures. And part of that grievance procedure is arbitration. Now, you can take an arbitration award to court and try to appeal it, but it's very, very difficult to get a court to overthrow an arbitrator's award. Why? Because the court says, look, you had your day, you went to the arbitrator and you presented all your arguments, the other side presented all their arguments. In order for me to look into that arbitration and turn it over, you're going to have to prove to me that something in this arbitration was so terrible that we have to prove that the arbitrator was absolutely partial or that he broke the law. You've got to prove something outrageous. Otherwise, the judge is going to say, "You've had your day in court."

Now, why can't school districts establish a fair, inexpensive, due-process arbitration procedure for youngsters who are violent or disruptive? So that when the youngster goes to court, they can say, "Hey, we've had this procedure. We've had witnesses on both sides, and here was the determination. And, really, you shouldn't get into this stuff unless you can show that these people are terribly prejudiced or totally incompetent or something else." In other words, we don't have to use the court.We could create a separate school judicial system that had expertise and knowledge about what the impact is on students and teachers and the whole system of these kinds of decisions. Arbitration is a much cheaper, much faster system, especially if you have an expedited arbitration system. There is a system in the American Arbitration Association of expedited arbitration that says how many briefs you're allowed to write and how much time each side can take, and all of that. So we have a legal team and we're going to explore the notion of getting this stuff out of the courts and creating a system that is inexpensive and fair to the youngster and fair to the other youngsters in the school.

Now, let me point out that a lot of the tolerance for bad behavior is about to change, because we are about to have stakes attached to student academic outcomes. In other words, in the near future, we are going to have a situation where, if you don't make it up to this point, then you can't be admitted into college. Or if you don't make it here, then you will not get certified for a certain type of employment. But in Chapter I schools, this is going to start very soon. There is a provision in the new Chapter One, now called Title I, and very soon, if Title I schools do not show a substantial progress for students, the school's going to be punished. And one of the punishments is reconstitution of the school. The school will be closed down, teachers will go elsewhere, students will go elsewhere, and the school will open up with a new student body, slowly rebuild. That's one of the punishments. There are other punishments as well. So if you've got a bunch of these disruptive youngsters that prevent you from teaching and the other students from learning, it won't be like yesterday, where nobody seems to care, the kids are all going to get promoted anyway and they can all go to college, because there are no standards. There are no stakes.

Now, for the first time, there will be stakes. The teachers will know. The parents will know, hey, this school's going to close. I'm going to have to find a way of getting my kid to some other school because of the lack of learning that comes from this disruption. Teachers are going to say, hey, I'm not going to have my job in this school a couple of years from now because they're going to shut it down. I don't know what the rules are, what happens to these teachers, whether other schools have to take them or not. But we are entering a period where there will be consequences and parents and teachers are going to be a lot more concerned about achievement.

Now, one of the other issues that has stood in the way of doing something here is a very difficult one to talk about in our society, and that's the issue of race. And whenever the topic of suspension or expulsion comes up, there's always the question of race. Cincinnati is a good example. The union there negotiated a good discipline code as part of a desegregation suit. And the question was raised, "Well, is there a disparate impact, with more minority kids being suspended than others?" And who are the teachers who are suspending them? Do you have more white teachers suspending African-American kids?

Our position on that is very clear. In any given school, you may have more white kids with infractions or you may have more African-American kids, or you may have more Hispanic kids. We don't know. I don't think anybody knows. But we handle that by saying, "Whatever your crime is and whoever you are, you're going to get exactly the same punishment." If we do that, I'm sure that the number who will be punished will end up being very, very small. Because, as a young kid, if you see that there is a consequence, you will change your behavior. . . .

Now we have another very big problem, and we're going to try to deal with this in legislation. Under legislation that deals with disabled youngsters, we have two different standards. Namely, if a youngster in this class is not disabled and commits an infraction, you can do whatever is in that discipline code for that youngster. But if the youngster is disabled and is in that same class (for instance, the youngster might have a speech defect), you can't suspend that youngster while all of the proceedings are going on because that's a change in placement. It might take you a year-and-a-half in court, and meanwhile that youngster who is engaged in some threatening or dangerous behavior has to stay there. This makes no sense. We have a lot of support in the Congress on this, and we think we have a good chance of changing this. . . .

Well, that's the whole picture. And to return to the theme at the beginning, we have a cry for choice, a cry for vouchers, a cry for charters. It's not really a cry for these things. People really want their own schools, and they want their kids to go to those schools, and they want those schools to be safe and orderly for their youngsters.

It is insane to set up a system where we move 98 percent of our kids away from the two percent who are dangerous, instead of moving the two percent away from the 98 percent who are OK. We need to have discipline codes, we need to have a new legal system, we need to have one standard for all students. We need to have a system where we don't have to wait for a year or a year-and-a-half after a student has perpetrated some terrible and atrocious crime before that student is removed for the safety of the other students. How are we going to do this? We are going to do this, first of all, by talking to our colleagues within the schools. Our polls show that the overwhelming majority accepts these views.

The support of African-American parents for the removal of violent youngsters and disruptive students is higher than any other group within our society. Now very often when youngsters are removed, it's because some parents' group or some committee starts shouting and making noise, and the school system can't resist that. Now I think that it's time for us to turn to business groups, it's time for us to turn to parents' groups. When youngsters commit such acts, and when they've had a fair due-process within the system, we need to have a system of public support, just as we have in the community when someone commits a terrible crime. People say, send that person to jail, don't send him back to us. We need to have a lot of decent people within our communities, when you have youngsters who are destroying the education of all the others, who will stand up and say, "Look, we don't want to punish this kid, but for the sake of our children, you're going to have to keep that one away, until that one is ready to come back and live in a decent way in society with all of the other youngsters."

I'm sure that if we take this back to our communities, and if we work on it, the appeal will be obvious. It's common sense. And we will save our schools and we will do something which will give us the basis for providing a decent education for all of our children.

Alfie Kohn  **NO**

Safety from the Inside Out: Rethinking Traditional Approaches

For many people, the idea of safety in an educational context brings to mind the problem of school violence, and specifically the string of shootings at schools across the country in recent years. Let's begin, then, by noting that the coverage of those events has obscured several important facts:

- The real horror is that young people die, not where they die. To be sure, there's something deeply unsettling about the juxtaposition of the words "violence" and "schools." But keep in mind that the vast majority of young homicide victims are killed at home, on the streets, or somewhere else other than school. During one three-year period in the 1990s, for example, about eighty homicides took place on school grounds—while more than 8,000 children were killed elsewhere. This is important to keep in mind, both so that we recognize the full extent of the problem and so we don't exaggerate how dangerous schools really are.
- There is a tendency, upon hearing about stunning cases of school violence, to infer that adolescents are Public Enemy No. 1. But Mike Males, a sociologist, urges us to focus our attention on the "far more common phenomenon of adults killing kids." He points out that Americans blame teenagers too easily, and usually inaccurately, for what's wrong with our society.[1]
- When school violence does occur, low-income students of color are disproportionately likely to be the victims, Columbine and other notorious school-shooting incidents notwithstanding. If that fact is surprising, it may be because of the media's tacit assumption that any problem—crime, drugs, violence—is more newsworthy when white people in the suburbs are affected.

Yet another series of mistaken assumptions comes into play when educators and policymakers try to respond to violence—or to their fear of it. Questionable beliefs often lead to wrongheaded policies.

First, we Americans love to imagine that *technical fixes* will take care of complicated problems. (Remember the V-chip, which was supposed to be the solution to children's exposure to violent television programming?) Some people still cling to the hope that schools can be made safer if we just install enough surveillance cameras and metal detectors. In reality, though, it's simply not feasible to guard every doorway or monitor every screen. The number of cameras at one Washington, D.C., high school was recently doubled, from thirty-two to sixty-four, but the principal admitted that it's hard to keep guns "on the outside of the school unless we become armed camps, and I don't think anyone wants to send their child to an armed camp." His comments were reported in a newspaper article that was aptly headlined "Trust, Not Cameras, Called Best Prevention."[2]

Pedro Noguera, who teaches at New York University, put it this way: "Design and staffing of schools are driven by security concerns, but no thought is given to how these designs and atmospheres make students and [teachers] feel. If we use prisons as our models for safe schools—well, prisons are not safe places, right? Safety comes from human relations. I'd say we'd do much better to invest in counselors than armed guards."[3]

Second, when we do focus on the human element of violence prevention, we often assume that students just need to be taught the appropriate *skills*.[4] This model is so simple and familiar to us that we don't even think of it as a model at all. It seems a matter of common sense that if children don't pay attention to what someone else is saying, they would benefit from some remedial listening skills. If they fail to lend a hand to someone in distress, they need to hone their helping skills. If they're reluctant to stand up for themselves, they're candidates for assertiveness training. Thus, by analogy, if violence keeps breaking out, all we need to do is teach students the skills of conflict resolution.

Unfortunately, skills are not enough. Most kids already know how to listen, how to help, and how to assert themselves. The question is why they sometimes lack the *disposition* to act in these ways. It's much the same with efforts to raise academic achievement: a skills-based approach has its limits if we ignore the question of how interested students are in what they're being taught. Such efforts may even do more harm than good if an emphasis on teaching basic skills makes school downright unappealing. The same goes for literacy in particular: consider how many children know how to read, but don't. In short, what matters is not only whether people can learn, or act, in a particular way, but whether they have the inclination to do so.

Why, then, do we spend so much time teaching skills? For one thing, this implies that it's the students who need fixing. If something more complicated than a lack of know-how is involved, we might have to question our own practices and premises, which can be uncomfortable. Moreover, a focus on skills allows us to ignore the structural elements of a classroom (or school or family). If students hurt one another, it's easier for us to try to deal with each individual's actions than it is to ask which elements of the system might have contributed to the problem.

A skills-based approach is also compatible with behaviorism, whose influence over our schools—and, indeed, over all of American society—is difficult to overstate. Behaviorism dismisses anything that can't be reduced to a discrete set of observable and measurable behaviors. This dogma lies behind segmented instructional techniques, as well as many of the most popular approaches to character education, classroom management, and our practices with students who have special needs.

When we're preoccupied with behaviors, we're less likely to dig deep in order to understand the reasons, values, and motives that give rise to those behaviors. We end up embracing superficial responses, such as trying to improve the climate of a school by forcing students to dress alike. (Among other limitations of such a policy, our assumption seems to be that we can reduce aggression by borrowing an idea from the military.) But any time we talk about changing students' "behaviors," we run the risk of ignoring the students who are doing the behaving. We lose the human beings behind the actions. Thus, we may come to see students as computers that can be reprogrammed, or pets that can be retrained, or empty receptacles that can be refilled—all dangerously misleading metaphors. We offer behavioral instruction in more appropriate ways to express anger, but the violence continues because we haven't gotten anywhere near where the problem is.

⚬⟨⚬⟩⚬

It often doesn't work, then, to employ technical fixes or to teach skills. But there's a third response that isn't merely ineffective—it's actively counterproductive. I have in mind the policies that follow from assuming we can stamp out violence—or create safety—by *coercive means.* In her book *A Peaceable School,* Vicky Dill remarked that while it can be bad to have no plan for dealing with school violence, "it can be much worse to have a simplistic, authoritarian policy."[5]

A reliance on old-fashioned discipline, with threats of punishments for offenders, not only distracts us from dealing with the real causes of aggression, but in effect *models* bullying and power for students. Many school officials fail to understand that fact and end up throwing fuel on the fire by responding to signs of student distress with ever-harsher measures. Consistent with the tendency to ignore the structural causes of problems, they seem to think sheer force will make the bad stuff go away; if students are made to suffer for doing something wrong, they will see the error of their ways. When that proves ineffective, it's assumed that *more* punishment—along with tighter regulations and less trust—will do the trick.[6]

The shootings at Columbine provoked a general panic in which hundreds of students across the country were arrested, while "countless others were suspended or expelled for words or deeds perceived as menacing."[7] The fear here is understandable: administrators wondered whether their districts, too, might be incubating killers. But we need to understand the difference between *overreaction,* such as closing down a school to search for bombs after a student makes an offhand joke, and *destructive reactions,* such as coercive policies.

A particularly egregious example of the latter is the so-called "zero tolerance" approach, which is based on the premise that harsh punishment works better if it's meted out indiscriminately—indeed, in robotic fashion. It took a few years before this strategy began to attract critical attention in the media.[8] Research, meanwhile, has been accumulating to confirm that it makes no sense at all. One study discovered that students in schools with such a policy "actually report feeling less safe . . . than do students in schools with more moderate policies."[9] That subjective impression is supported by objective evidence: another analysis showed that "even after schools with zero tolerance policies had implemented them for more than four years, those schools were still less safe than schools without such policies."[10] Moreover, zero tolerance doesn't affect everyone equally: African-American and Latino students are more likely than their white counterparts to be targeted by this sort of punitive discipline.[11] As a society, we seem to have a lot more tolerance for the misbehavior of white children.

The finding that schools become less safe as a result of adopting zero-tolerance policies will sound paradoxical only to those readers who believe that threats and punishment can create safety. In reality, safety is put at risk by such an approach. A safe school environment is one where students are able to really know and trust—and be known and trusted by—adults.[12] Those bonds, however, are ruptured by a system that's about doing things *to* students who act inappropriately rather than working *with* them to solve problems. "The first casualty" of zero-tolerance policies "is the central, critical relationship between teacher and student, a relationship that is now being damaged or broken in favor of tough-sounding, impersonal, uniform procedures."[13]

Zero tolerance is bad enough, but the situation becomes even worse when the punishments in question are so harsh that students are turned into criminals. Across the country, the *New York Times* reported in early 2004, schools "are increasingly sending students into the juvenile justice systems for the sort of adolescent misbehavior that used to be handled by school administrators."[14] Apart from the devastating effects that turning children over to the police can have on their lives, the school's climate is curdled because administrators send the message that a student who does something wrong may be taken away in handcuffs and, in effect, exiled from the community. Here we see the *reductio ad absurdum* of trying to improve schools by relying on threats and fear.

There are many explanations for this deeply disturbing trend, including the loss of school-based mental health services due to budget cuts. But Mark Soler of the Youth Law Center, a public interest group that protects at-risk children, observes that these days "zero tolerance is fed less by fear of crime and more by high-stakes testing. Principals want to get rid of kids they perceive as trouble" because doing so may improve their school's overall test results.[15] School safety is at risk, that is, not merely because some educators wrongly believe that stricter or more consistent application of punitive discipline will help, but because of the pressure to raise test scores.

What's more, that same pressure, which leads some people to regard students in trouble as disposable commodities, also has the effect of squeezing out efforts to help them avoid getting into trouble in the first place. Programs to promote conflict resolution and to address bullying and other sorts of violence are being eliminated because educators are themselves being bullied into focusing on standardized test results to the exclusion of everything else.

Scott Poland, a school psychologist and expert in crisis intervention, writes: "School principals have told me that they would like to devote curriculum time to topics such as managing anger, violence prevention and learning to get along with others regardless of race and ethnicity, but . . . [they are] under tremendous pressure to raise academic scores on the state accountability test."[16]

Thus, argues Margaret McKenna, the president of Lesley University, "Some of the most important lessons of Columbine have been all but forgotten—left behind, so to speak, in no small measure because of . . . the No Child Left Behind Act. The law's narrow focus on yearly improvement in test scores has [made schools] . . . even less conducive to teachers' knowing their students well." To drive home the point that our priorities have become skewed, she observes that "the test scores at Columbine High were among the highest in Colorado."[17]

                            ✿

Even in cases where a student's actions pose a significant risk to the safety of others, an educator's first response should not be "Have we used sufficient force to stamp out this threat?" but "What have we done to address the underlying issues here? How can we transform our schools into places that meet students' needs so there is less chance that someone will be moved to lash out in fury?"

Here's another way to look at it: we need to stop talking primarily about creating peaceful schools, which is not a particularly ambitious or meaningful goal. Schools, after all, are completely peaceful at 3 a.m. Similarly, a classroom full of docile, unquestioning students may be peaceful, even if they aren't learning much of value, don't care much about one another, and would rather be someplace else. What we need to work for is the creation of schools that are *peaceable*—that is, committed to the value of peace and to helping students feel safe, in all senses of that word.[18]

Physical safety, the most obvious kind, has understandably been the priority, particularly where it seems to be in short supply. But intellectual and emotional safety matter, too—in their own right and also because they're related to physical safety. Bullying and other violent acts are less likely to happen in a school that feels like a caring community, a place where children experience a sense of connection to one another and to adults, a place where they come to think in the plural and feel a sense of belonging. That's the polar opposite of a school where kids are picked on for being different or uncool, to the point that they fear entering certain hallways or sections of the cafeteria. Caring school communities don't let that happen: they regard any evidence of nasty cliques or hurtful exclusion as serious problems to be addressed. They do everything possible so that no one fears being laughed at, picked on, or humiliated.

These efforts take place in individual classrooms and also as a matter of school policy. Proactive efforts to build community and resolve conflicts are important, but so too must educators focus on what gets in the way of safety and community. Thus, teachers not only hold class meetings on a regular basis so that students can participate in making decisions; they also use these meetings to address troubling things that may be going on. One teacher spoke up after a math lesson, for example, to talk with her students about

> something I *don't* like and I *don't* want to hear because it makes me feel bad, and if it makes me feel bad it probably makes someone else in here feel bad. It's these two words. (She writes "That's easy" on the chalkboard and draws a circle around the phrase.) . . . When I am struggling and trying so hard, [hearing that phrase] makes me feel kind of dumb or stupid. Because I am thinking, gosh, if it's so easy why am I having so much trouble with it? . . . And what's one of our rules in here? It's to be considerate of others and their feelings.[19]

Such an intervention may be motivated not only by a general commitment to ensuring that students don't feel bad, but also by a desire to promote high-quality learning. There are intellectual costs when students don't feel safe to take risks. A classroom where kids worry that their questions will be thought silly is a classroom where unself-conscious engagement with ideas is less likely to take place. (Of course, students often are unwilling to ask questions or acknowledge that they're struggling for fear of the reaction from the teacher, not just from their classmates.)

On a schoolwide level, intellectual and emotional safety require that students are freed from being rated and ranked, freed from public pressure to show how smart they are—or even worse, how much smarter they are than everyone else. Awards assemblies and honor rolls are very effective ways to destroy the sense of safety that supports a willingness to learn. Some schools that pride themselves on their commitment to high standards and achievement have created a climate that really isn't about learning at all—let alone about caring. Such places are more about results than about kids. Their students often feel as though they're in a pressure cooker, where some must fail in order that others can succeed. The message students get is that other people are potential obstacles to their own success.[20]

There is much more to be said, of course, about how and why to build community, to meet kids' needs, to create a culture of safety and caring.[21] The benefits of doing so are most pronounced in schools that have more low-income students,[22] yet such schools are often distinguished instead by punitive discipline and a climate of control. However, schools in affluent areas may also feel unsafe in various ways. Columbine High School was reportedly a place where bullying was common and a sharply stratified social structure was allowed to flourish, one in which athletes were deified. (Some of these sports stars taunted other students mercilessly "while school authorities looked the other way."[23]) In some suburban schools, the curriculum is chock full of rigorous advanced placement courses and the parking lot glitters with pricey SUVs, but one doesn't have to look hard to find students who are starving themselves, cutting themselves, or medicating themselves, as well as students who are taking out their frustrations on those who sit lower on the social food chain.

Even in a school free of weapons, children may feel unsafe and unhappy. And that's reason enough to rethink our assumptions, redesign our policies, and redouble our commitment to creating a different kind of educational culture.

Notes

1. Mike Males, "Who's Really Killing Our Schoolkids?" *Los Angeles Times*, May 31, 1999. Also see other writings by Males, including his book *The Scapegoat Generation: America's War on Adolescents* (Monroe, Maine: Common Courage Press, 1996).

2. The article, by Debbi Wilgoren, appeared in the *Washington Post* on February 3, 2004: A-7.

3. Pedro A. Noguera, "School Safety Lessons Learned: Urban Districts Report Progress," *Education Week*, May 30, 2001: 15.

4. This section is adapted from my article "The Limits of Teaching Skills," *Reaching Today's Youth*, Summer 1997, . . .

5. Vicky Schreiber Dill, *A Peaceable School: Creating a Culture of Non-Violence* (Bloomington, Ind.: Phi Delta Kappa, 1997), 24. Also see Irwin A. Hyman and Pamela A. Snook, *Dangerous Schools* (San Francisco: Jossey-Bass, 1999), an excerpt from which appeared in the March 2000 issue of *Phi Delta Kappan*.

6. This section is adapted from my article "Constant Frustration and Occasional Violence: The Legacy of American High Schools," *American School Board Journal*, September 1999. . . . For more on the counterproductive effects of—and some alternatives to—punitive "consequences" and rewards, see my book *Beyond Discipline: From Compliance to Community* (Alexandria, Va.: Association for Supervision and Curriculum Development, 1996).

7. Caroline Hendrie, "In Schools, a Sigh of Relief as Tense Spring Draws to a Close," *Education Week*, June 23, 1999.

8. For example, see Dirk Johnson, "Schools' New Watchword: Zero Tolerance," New York Times, December 1, 1999; and Jesse Katz, "Taking Zero Tolerance to the Limit," *Los Angeles Times*, March 1, 1998.

9. This quotation is from Robert Blum of the University of Minnesota. The study, to which he contributed, was published in the *Journal of School Health* and summarized in Darcia Harris Bowman, "School 'Connectedness' Makes for Healthier Students, Study Suggests," *Education Week*, April 24, 2002: 16.

10. John H. Holloway, "The Dilemma of Zero Tolerance," *Educational Leadership*, December 2001/January 2002:84. The analysis summarized here was published by the National Center for Education Statistics in 1998. Also see an excellent review of the effects of such policies in Russ Skiba and Reece Peterson, "The Dark Side of Zero Tolerance: Can Punishment Lead to Safe Schools?" *Phi Delta Kappan*, January 1999: 372–76, 381–82.

11. A report by a civil rights group called The Advancement Project, based on an analysis of federal statistics, was described in Kenneth J. Cooper, "Group Finds Racial Disparity in Schools 'Zero Tolerance,'" *Washington Post*, June 15, 2000.

12. For example, see Deborah Meier, *In Schools We Trust* (Boston: Beacon Press, 2002).

13. William Ayers and Bernadine Dohrn, "Have We Gone Overboard with Zero Tolerance?" *Chicago Tribune*, November 21, 1999.

14. Sara Rimer, "Unruly Students Facing Arrest, Not Detention," *New York Times,* January 4, 2004: A-1.

15. That explanation also makes sense to Augustina Reyes of the University of Houston: "If teachers are told, 'Your [test] scores go down, you lose your job: all of a sudden your values shift very quickly. Teachers think, 'With bad kids in my class, I'll have lower achievement on my tests, so I'll use discretion and remove that kid.'" Both Reyes and Soler are quoted in Annette Fuentes, "Discipline and Punish," *The Nation,* December 15, 2003: 17–20.

16. "The Non-Hardware Side of School Safety," *NASP* [National Association of School Psychologists] *Communique* 28:6 (March 2000). Poland made the same point while testifying at a congressional hearing on school violence in March 1999—a month before the shootings at Columbine.

17. Margaret A. McKenna, "Lessons Left Behind," *Washington Post,* April 20, 2004: A-19.

18. The distinction between peaceful and peaceable was popularized by Bill Kreidler, who worked with Educators for Social Responsibility and wrote several books about conflict resolution. He died in 2000 at the unripe age of forty-eight.

19. Paul Cobb, Erna Yackel, and Terry Wood, "Young Children's Emotional Acts While Engaged in Mathematical Problem Solving." In *Affect and Mathematical Problem Solving: A New Perspective,* ed. D. B. McLeod and V. M. Adams (New York: Springer-Verlag, 1989), 130–31.

20. Our culture's uncritical acceptance of the ideology of competition is such that even people who acknowledge the damaging effects of an "excessive" emphasis on winning may continue to assert that competition *per se* is inevitable or productive. If this assertion is typically unaccompanied by evidence, that's probably because the available data support exactly the opposite position—namely, that a win/lose arrangement tends to hold us back from doing our best work and from optimal learning. I've reviewed some of that evidence in *No Contest: The Case Against Competition* (Boston: Houghton Mifflin, 1986).

21. See my article "Caring Kids: The Role of the Schools," *Phi Delta Kappan,* March 1991: 496–506 (available at <www.alfiekohn.org/teaching/cktrots.htm>); and chapter 7 ("The Classroom as Community") of *Beyond Discipline,* op. cit. Many other writers, of course, have also addressed this question.

22. Victor Battistich, Daniel Solomon, Dong-il Kim, Marilyn Watson, and Eric Schaps, "Schools as Communities, Poverty Levels of Student Populations, and Students' Attitudes, Motives, and Performance: A Multilevel Analysis," *American Education Research Journal* 32 (1995): 627–58.

23. Lorraine Adams and Dale Russakoff, "Dissecting Columbine's Cult of the Athlete," *Washington Post,* June12, 1999: A-1.

POSTSCRIPT

Can a Zero-Tolerance Policy Lead to Safe Schools?

Currently, there are few data available to allow us to evaluate whether or not a zero-tolerance policy leads to safer schools. What do we need to do to find such data? Ideally, we would like to rely on data from experimental studies of a sufficient number of schools, some implementing a zero-tolerance policy and others not. Experimental rather than correlational data would be preferred because the random assignment of schools to conditions that would be entailed by an experiment would ensure that the schools with and without a zero-tolerance policy were similar on important variables, such as the racial, ethnic, and socioeconomic make-up of the student body. Unfortunately, correlational studies often involve comparisons of very different types of schools; for example, zero-tolerance programs are more likely to be implemented in urban schools than rural schools, in schools serving poorer neighborhoods than affluent neighborhoods, etc. It really is not sufficient simply to compare what happens at a school before and after the implementation of a zero-tolerance policy. Often such programs are implemented after a highly publicized incident (e.g., a shooting). As a result, before and after differences *may* be due to the zero-tolerance policy *or* to increased parental awareness of the need to monitor their children, to increased caution on the part of students about being caught, to a greater police presence in and near the school, or even to a change of demographics in the schools (e.g., with more affluent parents opting to send their children to private schools).

But with what should a zero-tolerance policy be compared? Should schools with such a policy be compared to schools with no program of any kind for dealing with violence and unruly behavior? Probably not. It is not particularly compelling to conclude that zero tolerance is better than doing nothing. Instead, it would be more reasonable to compare the effectiveness of a zero-tolerance policy with another, very different type of program for dealing with unacceptable behavior. Reasonable candidates would include programs that focus on keeping offending students in school and improving their behavior through counseling, self-esteem enhancement, and the like, as well as programs that focus on improving school climate and the conflict resolution skills of all students. As Shanker points out, it is these programs that are seen as the approach of choice by many educators, so it is important to know which of the two options—zero tolerance or offender-focused intervention—is more effective.

On what variables or dimensions should we compare these programs to determine their relative effectiveness? What should we expect to change as a result of these programs? Certainly, we would want data on the rates of violence and other deviations from acceptable behavior. However, we might also want information about what happens to the students who offend. Are they "saved" by the policy, or do they engage in other problem behaviors? Do they drop out of school? Do they go on to commit more serious crimes out of school? Answers to these questions are relevant because if a school program can decrease all sorts of unacceptable behaviors, including criminal behaviors, it has to be considered a success for the society as a whole. In addition, we might also want to learn about the impact of the various programs on *nonoffending* students. Recall Shanker's statement that the zero-tolerance policy is motivated, in part, by the contention that disruptive students prevent their classmates from gaining full access to a high-quality education. This suggests that a successful program should lead to increases in the amount of actual instructional time that nonoffending students receive and, perhaps, to increases in their achievement. If zero tolerance does not lead to improvements for nonoffending students, is it really worth implementing in light of the ethical problems accompanying it?

There are many articles on both sides of the zero-tolerance issue, as well as many articles on alternatives to zero tolerance. Highly recommended articles on these alternatives are "Setting Limits in the Classroom," by Robert J. Mackenzie, *American Educator* (Fall 1997); "Making Violence Unacceptable," by Carole Remboldt, *Educational Leadership* (September 1998); "Waging Peace in Our Schools: Beginning with the Children," by Linda Lantieri, *Phi Delta Kappan* (January 1995); "Zero Tolerance for Zero Tolerance," by Richard L. Curwin and Allen N. Mendler, *Phi Delta Kappan* (October 1999); "Creating Peaceful Classrooms: Judicious Discipline and Class Meetings," by Mary Anne Raywid and Libby Oshiyama, *Phi Delta Kappan* (February 2000); and "Feeling Scared," by Thomas J. Cottle, *Educational Horizons* (Fall 2004). An interesting comparison of several popular violence prevention programs is provided in "Evaluating the Effectiveness of School-Based Violence Prevention: Developmental Approaches," by Christopher Henrich, Joshua Brown, and J. Lawrence Aber, *Social Policy Report* (vol. 13, no. 3, 1999), published by the Society for Research in Child Development. Finally, a brief discussion of some of the evidence on the effectiveness of zero-tolerance policies can be found in "The Dilemma of Zero Tolerance," by John H. Holloway, *Educational Leadership* (December 2001/ January 2002).

ISSUE 17

Should Student Time in School Be Changed?

YES: Elena Rocha, from "Choosing More Time for Students: The What, Why, and How of Expanded Learning," *Center for American Progress* (August 2007)

NO: Larry Cuban, from "The Perennial Reform: Fixing School Time," *Phi Delta Kappan* (December 2008)

ISSUE SUMMARY

YES: Elena Rocha, a scholar at the Center for American Progress and education consultant, uses multiple case examples and argues that the expansion of school learning time is necessary for meaningful school reform and improving student outcomes.

NO: Larry Cuban, a professor emeritus of education at Stanford University, provides a brief history of school reform efforts related to school time and argues that the call for expanding learning time in the form of lengthening the school day or year is not new and has little evidence supporting its effectiveness.

Classic (e.g., *A Nation at Risk*) and contemporary (e.g., *Prisoners of Time*) critiques of the U.S. public education system all recommend reform. And the reform recommended almost always requires changing school time—increasing the time a student spends in school daily, weekly, or annually. The history of debate over the issue parallels the history of U.S. public education itself reflecting various points along a timeline representing the evolution of the purposes of American public education. The current circumstances surrounding time in school have historical antecedents, often forgotten, that may have little obvious contemporary relevance. Indeed, this is a primary premise in the current arguments to change school time. Once practices become established, however, they can easily become part of the system's structure. In the less distant past, for example, strong forces and voices ranging from the tourist industry to teacher unions to parents—usually, demographically, upper middle class and above—have, in fact, argued for maintaining the status quo, that is, the long summer break for reasons related to revenue, respite, and recreation, respectively.

What, then, are the contemporary arguments behind changing school time? One argument centers on the problem of summer learning loss. Here the issue is whether the extended summer break is detrimental to academic outcomes because material learned in the prior year is not retained and consequently has to be 're-taught' at the beginning of the following school year. This issue is related also to the achievement gap between poor inner city urban student/school performance and affluent suburban student/school performance. The evidence, albeit limited, suggests that summer learning loss is more pronounced in the former. Another argument comes from comparative education in which student and school outcomes from other leading industrialized nations are compared with U.S. student and school outcomes and, in almost all cases, are shown to be superior. Because almost all other industrialized nations require either longer school days or longer school years or both, time in school is considered a primary culprit in the gap between U.S. student and school performance outcomes and the rest of the industrialized world. The problem has taken a strong hold in political (state and federal) and business sectors so much so that the purpose of public education is equated with producing a competitive workforce (but see Larry Cuban's comment on this). Taken together, these two issues represent essential elements in much of contemporary school reform efforts. Indeed, it is argued that changing school time is essential for meaningful reform.

Given the above issue and arguments, what do we know about changing or expanding school time? What kinds of models are there? There are at least three general approaches. The first is simply extending the school day. The next is extending the school year. Different still is a year-round school year. Year round education (YRE) can take one of two primary forms—single- and multi-track calendars. As you might guess, each of these different approaches has different pros and cons or costs and benefits (for a good review, see S. P. Johnson & T. E. Spradlin's *Education Policy Brief* mentioned below as well as E. Silva's *On the Clock: Rethinking the Way Schools Use Time* [Washington, DC: Education Sector, 2007]). By extending the school day and particularly the year it is argued that the United States will be brought in line with the rest of the industrialized world. There are significant costs associated with doing so, however, with no guarantee that it will produce the intended effect (a highly skilled competitive labor force). In the YRE models, the existing school days (approximately 180) are redistributed throughout the calendar year providing more continuous learning with the traditional long summer vacation broken up in shorter, more frequent breaks throughout the school year. In this approach, part of the argument is that a more balanced calendar can offset the learning loss associated with long summer breaks. There are additional arguments associated with some YRE models that are based more on administrative issues and the effective use of limited space. It is expensive to have a facility sitting vacant for 1/4 of the calendar year, and YRE provides a more efficient use of space. Regardless of the model or approach adopted, common to all is the goal of changing time in school to improve outcomes.

In the following selections, Elena Rocha suggests that major school reform could and should start with altering the length of the school day and year. Alternatively, Larry Cuban concludes that major reform efforts based on extending school time are not likely to be successful for a myriad of reasons related to the multiple purposes of U.S. public education and that very little research supports such changes.

YES

Elena Rocha

Choosing More Time for Students: The What, Why, and How of Expanded Learning

Setting the Stage

A crescendo of support from education researchers, analysts, reform advocates, and lawmakers about the need for additional learning time for our nation's under-performing students may well result in the coming months in meaningful reform. In fact, U.S. Secretary of Education Margaret Spellings believes that the expansion of learning time will be the next major push in school reform. The reason: our nation's public school students need to meet the demands and challenges of the 21st century but they simply cannot in public school systems that remain much the same as they were 50 years ago. The shift in educational rigor that globalization has ushered in is pushing policymakers to embrace systemic change in public education, with particular focus on closing achievement gaps between disadvantaged students and their peers.

In rethinking what it will take for our public schools to better serve students who are academically behind, wisdom tell us that a comprehensive approach that encompasses numerous options will provide the best opportunity to support student learning. The expansion of learning time can serve as one effective vehicle to modernize our schools because it allows teachers, principals, community organizations and leaders, and parents to build multiple curriculums to best educate our children to succeed in the 21st century. Expanded learning time turns dissatisfaction with the limitations of the current six-hour, 180-day school year into a proactive strategy that will create a new school structure for children.

Making more and better use of learning time by lengthening the school day, week, or year doesn't just change what happens between the hours of 3 p.m. and 5 p.m. Expanding learning time changes what happens from 8 a.m. and 5 p.m. and often encompasses additional days in the school calendar throughout the year to accelerate student learning and development. In short, expanding time for learning will revolutionize the way we teach our children.

To navigate through this forthcoming and thorough-going school reform effort, this paper will define what expanded learning time means, highlight what model programs look like when used effectively, and address how to successfully implement such reform efforts. As will become clear, expanded learning time is all about using time in ways that greatly benefit our students.

Choosing More Time for Students

What Is Expanded Learning Time?

Expanded learning time is a school-wide improvement strategy to boost student academic performance, close achievement gaps, and expand enrichment opportunities. The policy definition we prefer is the lengthening of the school day, school week or school year for all students in a given school. The purpose: to focus on core academics *and* enrichment activities to enhance student success. Such an increase in academic learning time requires an engaging, rigorous curricula as well as activities that expand the opportunities typically available to students. Because expanded learning time initiatives have the potential to result in substantial student achievement gains and other positive outcomes, it is widely considered an important strategy for low-performing, high-poverty schools.

At the core of expanded learning time is a critical and fundamental principle that cannot be overlooked—the complete redesign of the school's educational program. Successful implementation of expanded learning initiatives occur in tandem with other reform strategies and practices that take place through the redesign process. Without conjoining expanded learning time with the redesign principle, more time risks being "more of the same" and a promising school improvement strategy becomes a band-aid.

Expanded learning time schools formally incorporate the after-school hours into the official school day or add days to the official school calendar. These schools align rigorous academic and enrichment content with curriculum standards and student needs, are typically led by regular teachers and paraprofessionals, and frequently partner with successful community-based or other local organizations to provide enrichment opportunities and support.

Over the years, expanded or extended learning opportunities have been described as encompassing an array of activities, including before- and after-school programming, tutoring or summer programming, early childhood education, supplemental educational services, distance learning, and school-based or school-connected cultural and recreational activities. In addition, study hall, homework clubs, advanced coursework opportunities, and block scheduling or double periods have commonly been considered expanded learning time activities.

While such programs and activities extend learning time or use earmarked periods of time in new or non-traditional ways, they differ in format and content from expanded learning time initiatives that redesign a school's entire educational program.

Education advocates, researchers, and academics are currently assessing how much time is necessary to bring under-performing students to proficiency and put them on the path to long-term success. Although the debate continues, current thinking is that schools need to expand learning time by a minimum of 30 percent. The Center for American Progress, together with Massachusetts 2020, an educational nonprofit institution, is promoting the expansion of learning time for high-poverty, low-performing schools by no less than the equivalent of two hours per day, or 360 hours per year, to the districts' standard school schedule. This is roughly the equivalent of 30 percent more time. Other efforts, such as the Knowledge Is Power Program nationwide network of charter schools, are expanding learning time by as much as 62 percent.

Why Expanded Learning Time?

Expanded learning time is just one strategy with the potential to boost student achievement—but a promising one. It considers time a resource and capitalizes on the best uses of learning time while expanding it. This approach provides schools with added flexibility to exercise innovation in a very deliberate manner. Time, as a strategy, can be conceptualized in multiple ways. Four constructs of additional time are presented below.

Time as an Enabler

The expansion of learning time allows schools to do what is being asked of them—to help all students meet proficiency goals and prepare them for life after high school. Expanded learning provides more time and in-depth learning opportunities for students in the areas of math, science, literacy, and other core subjects to support academic excellence. More time also enables schools to expand the curriculum and integrate or maintain important enrichment activities in the school day and year, avoiding the crowding out of engaging programming such as art, music, sports, and drama. Together, greater attention to academics and enrichment can help to produce 21st century knowledge workers with technology, communication, problem-solving, critical thinking, and team-building skills—all skills necessary for life-long success in a global society.

Time as a Catalyst

Lengthening the school day, school week and/or school year for any significant amount of time requires leaders to rethink school reform in a way that is not incremental. Redesigning a school's structure to integrate additional learning time requires innovation and retooling from the ground up. It demands thoughtful consideration of all aspects of school-wide improvement such as curriculum development, teacher training and collaboration, and budgeting, as well as the technical components of large-scale reform such as transportation, program evaluation, and teacher contract negotiations. This school-improvement strategy allows community, school, and district leaders to put incrementalism aside in favor of comprehensive reform.

Time as a Unifier

Transforming the components of school redesign into a successful strategy necessitates the meaningful involvement of parents, teachers, and communities at-large throughout planning and implementation. Because expanded learning time is not an incremental strategy, outreach and inclusion of these actors in decision-making and design are central to the effort's success. As with most successful school reform initiatives, empowering and giving ownership to parents, teachers, and other valuable community members pays off. The process of expanding learning time therefore serves to unite these actors, giving them a role in the fundamental changes of their schools.

Time as a Preference

Student and school needs vary from community to community. Because there is no single reform strategy to improve student or school performance, multiple options must be available to families. Schools that expand learning time can broaden the choice options available. Presenting families with educational options for their children empowers them to choose the type of educational experiences and settings they feel will best meet the needs of their children. Although not a strategy for all students and schools, expanded learning time can be successful in many locations, such as larger school districts that may have greater capacity or access to other choice options.

How Has Time Historically Been Used?

The pursuit of challenging, extensive learning opportunities for students today is not unlike the ways in which privileged children have historically excelled. Boarding schools, study abroad, and the most rigorous academic and college preparation programs made different use of learning time, often by expanding it.

Today, many students are seeking additional opportunities to increase their academic growth and chances for success; they are taking advantage of extra academic opportunities during the traditional and non-traditional school hours. In doing so, these students use academic resources, particularly time, in different ways.

An increasingly common phenomenon is advanced students enrolling in summer school, after-school, intersession programs, and virtual learning courses to get a leg up on their academic progress. To hone their academic skills and increase their chances for acceptance into college, for example, students are attending summer classes to meet basic high school course requirements in order to take Advanced Placement or International Baccalaureate courses during the school year. Once considered prime time for remediation, these non-traditional learning blocks are becoming pre-requisites for high achievers.

These strategies, which have worked for so many privileged and academically advanced students, should not just be considered options for the elite. The lessons learned from alternative, innovative learning strategies that make more and better use of time are ripe for study and replication, particularly for struggling students and continually low-performing schools and districts, many of which lack access to expanded learning opportunities.

What Are the Benefits of More Time?

Initiatives that expanded learning time have facilitated school and classroom innovation to enhance teaching and learning. Through the expansion of learning time, teachers, for example, can provide students with more one-on-one instruction, teach in longer blocks to emphasize subject content, help students develop portfolios of their work, or utilize hands-on learning activities such as science labs and projects to help facilitate learning through application. The presence of more in-school time coupled with new and effective instructional strategies can have great impact on student performance. Incorporating additional time into the school experience also helps to address the individual needs of students by providing them with extra supports such as working with specialists and by encouraging participation in engaging activities of interest.

But the benefits of expanded learning time reach beyond improvements in student academic performance, their personal development, and preparation for adulthood. Expanding time also serves teachers well by providing them with more time to engage in high-quality professional development, participate in support activities such as mentoring, plan and work collaboratively with others, and analyze data to improve instruction and student achievement. Providing substantial quality professional development opportunities for teachers results in higher quality education for students.

Schools, too, gain from the expansion of learning time by allowing community-based partnerships to play a critical role in the implementation and strengthening of educational curriculum. Community-based partnerships not only offer enrichment programming for students but also carve time out of the academic calendar for teachers to participate in training and planning activities. For instance, if there are seven learning periods in the school day, one of them may be led by a community partner such as the Boys & Girls Club or a community college. Or a local organization or institution such as a hospital or museum may teach a monthly class at their facility, providing students with an enriched learning opportunity outside of the school walls. These partner-led classes, in turn, free up teachers to participate in professional development or common planning activities while other skilled adults are working with students.

Beyond school boundaries, employers and post-secondary educational institutions also recognize the influence that additional learning time can have on workplace and college readiness. Both are looking for individuals with solid academic preparation as well as critical thinking and problem-solving skills. The business community in particular has been very vocal about their increasing need for 21st century knowledge workers. They caution that without significant school reform, businesses will be challenged even more than they are today to find skilled workers.

Parents and communities are also enthusiastic about the expansion of learning time and the ability for schools to focus on core academic content while engaging students in enrichment activities both inside and outside of schools. A longer school day or year provides children with a safe, supervised, and rich environment for a greater number of hours while parents are working.

While some efforts to expand learning time have been met with a degree of parental opposition, the Massachusetts experience reveals three important lessons. First, the more parents know about the benefits of additional learning time, the more in favor they are of the strategy. Second, lower-income parents who want their children to have the same academic and enrichment experiences as their more affluent peers are particularly in support of more learning time. And lastly, opposition to expanded learning time tends to come from a vocal minority of mostly middle-income parents who are able to provide individually tailored opportunities for their children like music lessons, horseback riding, or drama lessons.

Even students themselves seem to be open-minded to a longer school day, week, or year. Schools that have implemented greater learning time into the school calendar recognize that there is an adjustment period for students. School leaders, however, are finding that students, particularly those in elementary school, quickly adjust. An engaging curriculum and enrichment activities that interest students help to overcome the challenges in transitioning to additional learning time. When successful, reengaged students are more likely to stay in school and graduate.

What Role Does Research Play in Supporting Expanded Learning Time?

Admittedly, there is not a large body of research supporting the expansion of learning time. However, the concept of expanding learning time draws on decades of research on time and learning and whether and how time impacts student outcomes. This research, begun in 1963 with the work of educational psychologist John Carroll, concludes that instructional time is a determinant of academic outcomes and students achieve maximal learning when time spent learning matches time needed to learn. Additional research that contributes to the movement to expand learning time focuses on enrichment opportunities such as after-school programs. This research finds that participation in non-core academic activities raises engagement and academic outcomes.

The modern conceptualization of time and learning is captured by what is known as the Academic Learning Time, or ALT, model. Developed out of research conducted by David Berliner and Charles Fisher of Arizona State University, this model goes beyond the basic construct of time in an academic setting to address how time should be used in such a setting. In other words, academic learning time considers the quantity and quality of learning time, the level of student engagement, and measures of success or outcomes.

Further research on time and learning reveals that children lose some of what they've learned during the summer months in what is known as summer learning loss or the "summer slide." For many low-income children who lack engaging and enriching experiences during their time off, they can lose as much as two months of learning.

While much academic and scientific research exists on time and learning, brain development and cognitive abilities, and enrichment, it has yet to be directly linked to the concept of expanded learning time in school—although researchers and advocates are in the midst of developing a research agenda and design to directly study the impact of a longer school day, week, or year on academic achievement.

As the result of this lack of direct research, proponents of expanded learning time tend to rely on evidence from the schools and districts that have successfully implemented more time into the school calendar. The discussion below addresses the evidence and highlights four model expanded learning time programs.

Over the years, research has shown that poor and minority children tend to begin school at an academic deficit compared to their higher-income and white peers. Research also documents that students who start school behind academically are likely to stay behind. The reality is that too many disadvantaged children lack high-quality educational experiences and access to engaging, enriching programs during traditional school time, the after-school hours, and summer months, and consequently never catch up.

Unfortunately, too many schools have responded to this challenge by narrowing the curriculum in order to place greater emphasis on core subjects such as reading and math. Cognitive researchers, however, caution that this does greater harm than good by removing students from learning experiences that can actually help them gain broader knowledge and context to better understand what they are learning. Additional learning time used well can make school for these students about catching up and accelerating.

Are There Model Expanded Learning Time Programs?

The success of extended learning time is evident in a number of model programs. Several charter and public schools have implemented expanded learning time initiatives over a number of years, as have educational management organizations like New York-based Edison Schools that operate numerous schools for local school districts. Charter schools, however, appear to be the leading force in the movement to increase learning time and expand educational opportunities—perhaps because they have greater flexibility than public schools to develop and implement new programs. The Center for Education Reform conducted a national survey in 2005 of charter schools and found that 57 percent of respondents expand learning time: 13 percent expand the school day and year, 24 percent expand the school day, and 20 percent expand the school year.

But public schools are also embracing expanded learning time. School-based efforts to increase learning time have recently started to dot the country in growing numbers. Because these efforts are new, data may not yet reveal improvements in student achievement or result in schools making adequate yearly progress as required by the 2002 federal No Child Left Behind Act. Nonetheless, these schools should be carefully supported and their impact on student and school success documented.

Additional evidence of the growing popularity of expanded learning initiatives comes from media reports. Investigation of chronically low- or under-performing schools that are now showing signs of improvement often reveal the use of more learning time. For example, according to the Council of Great City Schools, the membership organization for leaders of the nation's largest school districts, several high-performing urban schools have implemented extended time programs and are seeing positive results. . . .

One of the most high-profile efforts is taking place in the state of Massachusetts. In 2005, it became the first state to undertake a state-wide effort to implement expanded learning time in multiple schools. Made possible by the appropriation of new state dollars, this effort is currently in place in 10 schools in five districts, with continued funds to grow the number of schools to 19 beginning in Fall 2007 (additional schools are also in the planning pipeline). New York City and school districts in Florida, California, and Pennsylvania have successfully implemented expanded learning time initiatives as well. Several other model programs in both schools and districts across the country that serve a variety of students will be profiled in an upcoming report by the Center for American Progress.

Although the search for schools that have successfully implemented greater learning time into the school calendar beyond the well-known KIPP Academies or Massachusetts school efforts, for example, is intensive, the practice of expanding time in schools is likely more widely used than known. In fact, there are several model expanded learning time programs, four of which are presented here.

Miami-Dade County Public Schools, School Improvement Zone

In 2004, Miami-Dade County Public Schools Superintendent Rudy Crew created the School Improvement Zone to help many of the district's most under-performing schools. He sought to improve student and school performance and remedy the low performance feeder patterns between primary and secondary schools in the district. To do so, he established criteria to identify the schools for inclusion in the School Improvement Zone. Selected schools had at least a three-year history of low performance, were high-poverty schools, were part of the district's low performance feeder patterns, and had strong school leadership.

The School Improvement Zone includes 39 schools: 20 elementary, 11 middle, and 8 high schools. Partial implementation of the Zone began with the 2004–2005 school year, with full-scale implementation the following year. Enrolling more than 43,000 students, the Zone's schools serve a student population that is 66 percent African American, 30 percent Hispanic, 78 percent low-income, and 17 percent English-language learners.

Schools in the School Improvement Zone expand the school day by one hour and lengthen the school year by two weeks. With a focus on literacy, the School Improvement Zone aims to enhance student comprehension and critical thinking skills while also focusing on mathematics. In addition, the School Improvement Zone emphasizes character development and enables students to participate in enrichment classes in what is known as the Academic Improvement Period.

Professional development is a major component of the School Improvement Zone and is offered to all teachers and staff. Professional development teams help to: guide reading, math and science instruction; analyze student-level data; provide content area support; and help teachers build learning communities. Teachers in the Zone are compensated for their extra time, receiving a 20 percent increase in pay.

While there have been gains in academic achievement, they are larger in elementary schools than middle and high schools. When the School Improvement Zone first began, there were nine schools ranked "F" and no schools ranked "A" under the Florida school grading system. Now there are three "F" schools and two "A" schools. Results also show other positive outcomes, such as increased attendance, decreased suspensions, increased parental involvement, and school improvement.

Fairfax County Public Schools

In 1997, Daniel Domenech became Superintendent of Fairfax County Public Schools in Northern Virginia. One of the first things he did in his new capacity was to identify the county's lowest performing schools and develop a strategy to turn them around. A significant part of the strategy for the 20 elementary schools identified was to expand learning time and focus on literacy.

Fairfax County Public Schools did so by first instituting full-day kindergarten and making Monday a full school day for all grades (originally they were half days to allow for teacher professional development). Making Monday a full instructional day did not interrupt professional development as the Superintendent worked professional training and development opportunities into the expanded school calendar.

Domenech then implemented an optional year-round school calendar that ran from August to the end of June to combat summer learning loss. To move to this schedule, the school community had to show overwhelming support of the idea through a parent vote. Those who did not support a modified school calendar had the choice to opt out, although very few did so. The year-round schedule allows for nine weeks in school followed by three weeks off. During these intersession breaks, additional learning opportunities are available to students on a voluntary basis.

Participation in intersession programs is approximately 70 percent. Currently, there are five Fairfax County Public Schools with a year-round calendar.

With the clear purpose of closing achievement gaps and improving school performance, Domenech sought to increase learning time across the whole school year. To do so, he had to make tough financial decisions and reallocate money to internally finance the expansion of learning time. Teachers in the schools with a modified calendar receive a 7.5 percent salary increase to compensate them for the additional 15 percent of time worked. Domenech's efforts to assist the district's low-performing schools continue today and have resulted in academic achievement gains over the years.

An Achievable Dream Academy

An Achievable Dream Academy in Newport News, Virginia, is a unique kindergarten through eighth grade public school that has successfully implemented expanded learning time and closed the academic achievement gaps with schools with more advantaged students. The school, created 12 years ago, grew out of an after-school tennis and tutoring program for local students. Well supported, it soon became an expanded learning school for the community's most underserved students. The school was developed through a partnership with the school district and the city of Newport News. It operates under the guidelines of the school district but is given additional fexibility that is traditionally afforded to charter schools.

Led by Director Richard Coleman, Sr., An Achievable Dream is a year-round school with four nine-week sessions followed by three weeks of break. Learning opportunities are available to students during the intersession breaks, two of which are mandatory. Students are tested during the nine-week session and the data is used to help teachers identify student's areas of need. These needs are then addressed during the intersessions.

In addition to a modified school calendar, the schedule expands the school day to eight and half hours. Half-day Saturday classes are available for students in the lowest quartile. The school currently enrolls almost 1,000 children. Ninety-nine percent of the students are African American, 96 percent qualify for free and reduced price lunch, and 75 percent are from single-parent homes.

Achievable Dream's mission is to promote social, academic, and moral education, known as S.A.M.E. To fulfill this mission, the school focuses on academic excellence and character development such as etiquette, conflict resolution, and healthy living. All students participate in tennis, in keeping with the history and tradition of the school. Students are taught reading and writing in 90-minute learning blocks that incorporate science and social studies. Students also participate in enrichment activities such as art, music, physical education, and computers and technology.

The school's program has received wide support from parents who understand the benefit of more time on student achievement. Parents are required to sign a contract to demonstrate their commitment and support of the school's S.A.M.E. mission. The school has also benefited from minimal teacher turnover. To be sure that teachers understand the demands of working in an expanded learning time school, the school's leaders clearly define what will be expected of them. To support the needs of these teachers, the school provides professional development and compensation for the additional time worked.

Achievable Dream expands learning time in a significant way. To do so, it receives funding from the city to compensate teachers for the expanded time, as well as funds from local businesses, grants from the U.S. Departments of Education and Justice, and money from fundraisers. But the school's efforts have paid off. Achievable Dream has successfully closed the achievement gap, exceeded federal and state annual yearly progress requirements, and has been a model for two additional area elementary schools that have recently transitioned to an expanded day school.

Amistad Academy and Achievement First Schools

Amistad Academy is a public charter school serving students in New Haven, Connecticut in the fifth through eighth grades. Founded in 1999, Amistad Academy is a college preparatory school that lengthens the school day by one and one-half hours to focus on mathematics and English language arts. The school has a mandatory 15-day summer academy to focus on core academics, and offers before and after-school programming and tutoring. Encore!, Amistad's after-school enrichment program, provides students with daily instruction in theater, karate, dance, and web design, for example. The program has been so successful that it has inspired other efforts such as that of Gompers Charter Middle School in San Diego, CA.

Amistad's student population, which is selected through a lottery system, is about 64 percent low income, 63 percent African American, 35 percent Hispanic and 2 percent Caucasian. During the school's initial years, leaders were focused on closing the learning gap, securing high quality teachers, and creating a supportive learning environment for students. These efforts paid off as the school saw its students make signifcant academic gains. Amistad students routinely score higher on state and national reading, writing, and math tests than many of their peers in wealthier school districts. In fact, Amistad has succeeded in closing the achievement gap of its students.

Amistad's success led to the creation and launch of Achievement First, a non-profit organization dedicated to sharing Amistad's secrets with other low-performing schools. Today, there are nine Achievement First schools in New Haven and Brooklyn, New York, serving students from kindergarten to 12th grade. Achievement First schools focus on both academics and character development. The core curriculum includes a daily three-hour reading block, additional time for math and writing each day, physical education or music, and history or science daily.

Teachers at Achievement First schools are assessed every six weeks and use the results to inform instruction. They also receive 13 days of professional development and work in collaboration with other teachers to provide strong learning opportunities to students. Teachers, parents, and students of Achievement First schools are required to sign a contract demonstrating their commitment to learning and student support.

What Have We Learned?

Clearly, school and district approaches to expanded learning time can vary in focus, structure, and content, among other things. Because expanded learning time is a choice and efforts to implement it are designed to meet the needs of specifc students in particular schools, multiple strategies to expand learning time should be embraced. Although there is no single expanded learning time model, there are similarities among efforts.

Successful expanded learning time initiatives share a set of fundamental principles. In-depth analysis of new and existing initiatives and consultation with the individuals that led such initiatives identifes five key characteristics or pillars of success.

Bold leadership

Visionary leadership is the foundation of any reform effort. To implement successful expanded learning strategies, school, district, and community leaders must be fully committed to moving in a new direction and fearless in taking a stand on the need for substantial change. Expanding learning time is a demanding strategy that requires careful planning before implementation. Leaders must therefore engage intensively in program design and clearly articulate the goals and expectations of the strategy. They must build and maintain the political will and support necessary for such change and as such serve as liaisons to all stakeholders. Engaging in continuous and meaningful public outreach is a critical component of leadership and necessary to support successful implementation.

Cases in point:

- Daniel Domenech, former Superintendent of Fairfax County Public Schools, created a Plan for Excellence in 1998.

    Part of the plan outlined a strategy to improve the district's lowest-performing schools by expanding learning time. Understanding that principal leadership was necessary to successfully implement more time on task, he developed support among school leaders. He then made the tough decisions that enabled him to financially support the expansion of learning time in 20 of the district's schools. His perseverance led to structural changes that still exist today to combat learning gaps.
- The founders of Amistad Academy visited successful schools around the nation to learn their secrets in order to apply them to a school improvement strategy to close achievement gaps. These visionary leaders then created Achievement First, a non-profit organization, to replicate the Academy in other low-performing schools in Connecticut and New York.

Teacher Participation and Leadership

Highly effective teachers delivering a rigorous curriculum in the classrooms of schools with extra time are a fundamental element of this strategy's success. Teachers in schools with more time should want to be there, be highly motivated, be dedicated to the school's mission and goals, and be well-trained. Teachers are leaders in the classroom and at school; they must be highly invested in student learning and school success. Because teacher support is critical to school success, they must play a vital role in the redesign process and reach consensus with school leaders about the vision for school improvement.

Cases in point:

- An Achievable Dream Academy places great importance on teacher-student relationships and the need for teachers to understand the needs of their students. As such, the school plays a proactive role in conveying to teachers and potential teachers what is required of them to work in a year-round, expanded learning time school. During the interview and hiring process, administrators determine a teacher's passion for their work, gauge their understanding of the challenges they will have to undertake, and make sure that teachers understand what it takes to make and keep a high-performing school successful.

- The Massachusetts effort to expand learning time refects the various ways in which teacher contracts can be constructed to support the needs of teachers in schools with expanded learning time. One school that extends the day by two hours requires all teachers to teach for the first of these two hours. The second hour is optional because community partners are brought in to lead activities. In a second school, teachers received a 30 percent increase in their salaries and were offered the option to transfer out of the school if they didn't want to extend their work day. A third school allowed existing teachers to opt out, but required new teachers or incoming teachers to teach for the additional time.

Use of Data

The use of data in expanded learning time efforts serves multiple functions. In the beginning, student-level data must be analyzed to inform leaders about the academic needs of students in the school. Doing so will demonstrate that schools and districts understand the needs of their students and are therefore designing a strategy of interventions around those students' needs. Assessment, portfolio, and other types of student performance data can also be used to influence student instruction and teaching methods, track academic growth over time, and connect students to teachers. Collecting and maintaining student, teacher, and school-level data also serves as educational research and development; it can provide researchers and education advocates with valuable information on the effect of systemic reform by linking educational strategies and inputs to student outcomes.

Case in point:

- Miami-Dade County Public Schools relied on school-level data to assess which schools were the lowest-performing and contributing to a low performance feeder pattern between elementary, middle and high schools. Based on this data, 39 schools were selected for inclusion in the School Improvement Zone: 20 elementary schools, 11 junior highs, and eight high schools. After three years of implementation, the Zone continues to use student- and school-level data to guide its intervention efforts and document its impact.

Community Support and Partnerships

Successful school reform efforts are those embraced by most stakeholders especially parents. Visionary leaders, and schools themselves, can't achieve reform on their own efforts alone. To sustain viable expanded learning time initiatives, they need broad-based community support and long-term commitment from partners. Actively involving communities in the design of the expanded school calendar will pay off with great dividends. Strategies that establish a balance between community outreach and involvement and the technical dimensions of program design are typically the most successful.

Case in point:

- Massachusetts 2020, the leading organization in the promotion of the state's effort to expand learning time, invested two years in the planning of this effort. In doing so, they conducted surveys to gauge public sentiment and support for education reform and the expanded learning time strategy, and embarked on a public education campaign aimed at parents and other members of the community. They also worked closely with teachers and the teacher unions—early on—and invested great care in helping to negotiate teacher contracts, when an objective voice was needed. In addition, the organization played a key role in securing community-based partners to work with schools that expanded their learning time.

Focused, Aligned Use of Time That Engages Students

At their core, schools that expand learning time must be focused and purposeful about how they do it. This focus begins with intentional choices about how to use time in ways that align with the school's goals and curriculum. Schools that expand learning time do not simply add enrichment courses such as art, music, or drama. Instead, they choose to offer courses that align academic content with enrichment programming and connect to student needs and interests. How these schools use expanded learning time must also align with state standards and appropriately relate to a state's school improvement plan. Such careful creation of a school's curriculum and use of learning time, and its fexibility to develop appropriately tailored interventions that will have lasting value for each student, is what makes expanded learning time a promising strategy that is far from "more of the same." Some expanded learning time schools have chosen to focus on being college preparatory institutions, while others focus on technology and science or communication and the arts.

Case in point:

- Miami's School Improvement Zone emphasizes literacy and enhancing student comprehension and critical thinking. The early elementary grades therefore focus on reading and writing skills. Later elementary and middle school grades participate in a Transition Academy, which expands the literacy focus and combines it with graduation and career preparation, character development, and study skills. Students in the later grades also participate in one-on-one tutoring if needed.

In addition to these fve pillars, successful expanded learning time initiatives also create a strong school culture to foster student learning. Development of the school's culture occurs organically through the redesign process which induces consideration by leaders of every aspect of schooling including the school's mission and goals—two primary components of institutional culture. As such, expanded learning initiatives are intentionally driven and applied. Successful initiatives provide students with a structured and supportive atmosphere to nurture learning. Such initiatives relate and connect to student needs and interests, are engaging and of high quality, include structured student and adult interactions, and maintain high expectations for student learning. Another component impacting school culture is parental engagement or involvement. Many schools with increased time ask parents to volunteer or sign contracts committing them to participate in their child's education through various activities like nightly reading logs.

As schools and districts explore the expansion of learning time, these five components should be thoughtfully considered and carefully incorporated into both planning and implementation efforts. Each one of them, however, involves more than just a slogan and brief defnition.

Conclusion

More and better use of learning time benefits *all* children, especially those who are academically behind and too often from low-income and minority families. Without comprehensive, school-wide reform, the challenge of getting under-performing students to grade level and beyond—while maintaining a rich, full curriculum—will remain difficult. Putting these students on a path to success will require nothing less than the best—the best teachers, the best principals, the best curriculum, the most time, the best supports, and the social security that accompanies a positive, strong learning environment. Well-implemented expanded learning time initiatives can provide all students in a school with the time, instruction, and structures necessary to achieve academic success and other positive outcomes.

Larry Cuban  **NO**

The Perennial Reform: Fixing School Time

*E*ducation critics often call for longer school days and years. But there is little research to support such demands and several reasons why little will change.

In the past quarter century, reformers have repeatedly urged schools to fix their use of time, even though it is a solution that is least connected to what happens in classrooms or what Americans want from public schools. Since *A Nation at Risk* in 1983, *Prisoners of Time* in 1994, and the latest blue-ribbon recommendations in *Tough Choices, Tough Times* in 2007, both how much time and how well students spend it in school has been criticized no end.

Business and civil leaders have been critical because they see U.S. students stuck in the middle ranks on international tests. These leaders believe that the longer school year in Asia and Europe is linked to those foreign students scoring far higher than U.S. students on those tests.

Employers criticize the amount of time students spend in school because they wonder whether the limited days and hours spent in classes are sufficient to produce the skills that employees need to work in a globally competitive economy. Employers also wonder whether our comparatively short school year will teach the essential workplace behaviors of punctuality, regular attendance, meeting deadlines, and following rules.

Parents criticize school schedules because they want schools to be open when they go to work in the morning and to remain open until they pick up their children before dinner.

Professors criticize policy makers for allotting so little time for teachers to gain new knowledge and skills during the school day. Other researchers want both policy makers and practitioners to distinguish between requiring more time in school and *academic learning time*, academic jargon for those hours and minutes where teachers engage students in learning content and skills or, in more jargon, time on task.

Finally, cyberschool champions criticize school schedules because they think it's quaint to have students sitting at desks in a building with hundreds of other students for 180 days when a revolution in communication devices allows children to learn the formal curriculum in many places, not just in school buildings. Distance learning advocates, joined by those who see cyberschools as the future, want children and youths to spend hardly any time in K–12 schools.

From *Phi Delta Kappan,* December 2008, pp. 240–250. Copyright © 2008 by Phi Delta Kappan. Reprinted by permission of Phi Delta Kappan and Larry Cuban.

Time Options

Presidential commissions, parents, academics, and employers have proposed the same solutions, again and again, for fixing the time students spend in school: Add more days to the annual school calendar. Change to year-round schools. Add instructional time to the daily schedule. Extend the school day.

What has happened to each proposal in the past quarter century?

Longer School Year.   Recommendations for a longer school year (from 180 to 220 days) came from *A Nation at Risk* (1983) and *Prisoners of Time* (1994) plus scores of other commissions and experts. In 2008, a foundation-funded report, *A Stagnant Nation: Why American Students Are Still at Risk*, found that the 180-day school year was intact across the nation and only Massachusetts had started a pilot program to help districts lengthen the school year. The same report gave a grade of F to states for failing to significantly expand student learning time.

Year-Round Schools.   Ending the summer break is another way to maximize student time in school. There is a homespun myth, treated as fact, that the annual school calendar, with three months off for both teachers and students, is based on the rhythm of 19th-century farm life, which dictated when school was in session. Thus, planting and harvesting chores accounted for long summer breaks, an artifact of agrarian America. Not so.

Actually, summer vacations grew out of early 20th-century urban middle-class parents (and later lobbyists for camps and the tourist industry) pressing school boards to release children to be with their families for four to eight weeks or more. By the 1960s, however, policy maker and parent concerns about students losing ground academically during the vacation months—in academic language, "summer loss"—gained support for year-round schooling. Cost savings also attracted those who saw facilities being used 12 months a year rather than being shuttered during the summer.

Nonetheless, although year-round schools were established as early as 1906 in Gary, Indiana, calendar innovations have had a hard time entering most schools. Districts with year-round schools still work within the 180-day year but distribute the time more evenly (e.g., 45 days in session, 15 days off) rather than having a long break between June and September. As of 2006, nearly 3,000 of the nation's 90,000 public schools enrolled more than 2.1 million students on a year-round calendar. That's less than 5% of all students attending public schools, and almost half of the year-round schools are in California. In most cases, school boards adopted year-round schools because increased enrollments led to crowded facilities, most often in minority and poor communities—not concerns over "summer loss."

Adding Instructional Time to the School Day.   Many researchers and reformers have pointed out that the 6 and 1/2-hour school day has so many interruptions, so many distractions that teachers have less than five hours of genuine instruction time. Advocates for more instructional time have tried to stretch the actual amount of instructional time available to teachers to a seven-hour day (or 5 and 1/2 hours of time for time-on-task learning) or have tried to redistribute the existing secondary school schedule into 90-minute blocks rather than the traditional 50-minute periods. Since *A Nation at Risk*, this recommendation for more instructional time has resulted only in an anemic 10 more minutes per day when elementary school students study core academic subjects.

Block scheduling in public secondary schools (60- to 90-minute periods for a subject that meets different days of the week) was started in the 1960s to promote instructional innovations. Various modified schedules have spread slowly, except in a few states where block schedules multiplied rapidly. In the past decade, an explosion of interest in small high schools has led many traditional urban comprehensive high schools of 1,500 or more students to convert to smaller high schools of 300 to 400 students, sometimes with all of those smaller schools housed within the original large building, sometimes as separate schools located elsewhere in the district. In many of these small high schools, modified schedules with instructional periods of an hour or more have found a friendly home. Block schedules rearrange existing allotted time for instruction; they do not add instructional time to the school day.

Extended School Day.   In the past half century, as the economy has changed and families increasingly have both (or single) parents working, schools have been pressed to take on childcare responsibilities, such as tutoring and homework supervision before and after school. Many elementary schools open at 7 a.m. for parents to drop off children and have after-school programs that close at 6 p.m. PDK/Gallup polls since the early 1980s show increased support for these before- and after-school programs. Instead of the familiar half-day program for 5-year-olds, all-day kindergartens (and prekindergartens for 4-year-olds) have spread swiftly in the past two decades, especially in low-income neighborhoods. Innovative urban schools, such as the for-profit Edison Inc. and KIPP (Knowledge Is Power Program), run longer school days. The latter routinely opens at 7:30 a.m. and closes at 5 p.m. and also schedules biweekly Saturday classes and three weeks of school during the summer.

If reformers want a success story in fixing school time, they can look to extending the school day, although it's arguable how many of those changes occurred because of reformers' arguments and actions and how many from economic and social changes in family structure and the desire to chase a higher standard of living.

Cybereducation.   And what about those public school haters and cheerleading technological enthusiasts who see fixing time in school as a wasted effort when online schooling and distance learning can replace formal schooling? In the 1960s and 1970s, Ivan Illich and other school critics called for dismantling public schools and ending formal schooling. They argued that schools squelched natural learning, confused school-based education with learning, and turned children into obedient students and adults rather than curious and independent lifelong learners. Communication and instructional technologies were in their infancy then, and thinkers such as Illich had few alternatives to offer families who opted out.

Much of that ire directed at formal public schooling still exists, but now technology has made it possible for students to learn outside school buildings. Sharing common ground in this debate are deeply religious families who want to avoid secular influences in schools, highly educated parents who fear the stifling effects of school rules and text-bound instruction, and rural parents who simply want their children to have access to knowledge unavailable in their local schools. These advocates seek home schooling, distance learning, and cyber schools.

Slight increases in home schooling may occur—say from 1.1 million in 2003 to 2 to 3 million by the end of the decade, with the slight uptick in numbers due to both the availability of technology and a broader menu of choices for parents. Still, this represents less than 3% of public school students. Even though cheerleaders for distance learning have predicted wholesale changes in conventional site-based schools for decades, such changes will occur at the periphery, not the center, because most parents will continue to send their children to public schools.

Even the most enthusiastic advocates for cyberschools and distance education recognize that replacing public schools is, at best, unlikely. The foreseeable future will still have 50 million children and youths crossing the schoolhouse door each weekday morning.

3 Reasons

Reformers have spent decades trotting out the same recipes for fixing the time problem in school. For all the hoopla and all of the endorsements from highly influential business and political elites, their mighty efforts have produced minuscule results. Why is that?

Cost is the usual suspect. Covering additional teacher salaries and other expenses runs high. Minnesota provides one example: shifting from 175 to 200 days of instruction cost districts an estimated $750 million a year, a large but not insurmountable price to pay. But costs for extending the school day for instruction and childcare are far less onerous.

Even more attractive than adding days to the calendar, however, is the claim that switching to a year-round school will *save* dollars. So, while there are costs involved in lengthening the school calendar, cost is not the tipping point in explaining why so few proposals to fix school time are successful.

I offer two other reasons why fixing school time is so hard. Research showing achievement gains due to more time in school are sparse; the few studies most often displayed are contested. Late 20th-century policy makers seriously underestimated the powerful tug that conservative, noneconomic goals (e.g., citizenship, character formation) have on parents, taxpayers, and voters. When they argued that America needed to add time to the school calendar in order to better prepare workers for global competition, they were out of step with the American public's desires for schools.

Skimpy Research

In the past quarter century of tinkering with the school calendar, cultural changes, political decisions, or strong parental concerns trumped research every time. Moreover, the longitudinal and rigorous research on time in school was—and is—skimpy. The studies that exist are challenged repeatedly for being weakly designed. For example, analysts examining research on year-round schools have reported that most of the studies have serious design flaws and, at best, show slight positive gains in student achievement—except for students from low-income families, for whom gains were sturdier. As one report concluded: "[N]o truly trustworthy studies have been done on modified school calendars that can serve as the basis for sound policy decisions." Policy talk about year-round schools has easily outstripped results.

Proving that time in school is the crucial variable in raising academic achievement is difficult because so many other variables must be considered —the local context itself, available resources, teacher quality, administrative leadership, socioeconomic and cultural background of students and their families, and what is taught. But the lack of careful research has seldom stopped reform-driven decision makers from pursuing their agendas.

Conflicting School Goals

If the evidence suggests that, at best, a longer school year or day or restructured schedules do not seem to make the key difference in student achievement, then I need to ask: What problem are reformers trying to solve by adding more school time?

The short answer is that for the past quarter century—*A Nation at Risk* (1983) is a suitable marker—policy elites have redefined a national economic problem into an educational problem. Since the late 1970s, influential civic, business, and media leaders have sold Americans the story that lousy schools are the reason why inflation surged, unemployment remained high, incomes seldom rose, and cheaper and better foreign products flooded U.S. stores. Public schools have failed to produce a strong, post-industrial labor force, thus leading to a weaker, less competitive U.S. economy. U.S. policy elites have used lagging scores on international tests as telling evidence that schools graduate less knowledgeable, less skilled high school graduates—especially those from minority and poor schools who will be heavily represented in the mid-21st century workforce—than competitor nations with lower-paid workforces who produce high-quality products.

Microsoft founder Bill Gates made the same point about U.S. high schools.

> In district after district across the country, wealthy white kids are taught Algebra II, while low-income minority kids are taught how to balance a checkbook. This is an economic disaster. In the international competition to have the best supply of workers who can communicate clearly, analyze information, and solve complex problems, the United States is

falling behind. We have one of the highest high school dropout rates in the industrialized world.

And here, in a nutshell, is the second reason why those highly touted reforms aimed at lengthening the school year and instructional day have disappointed policy makers. By blaming schools, contemporary civic and business elites have reduced the multiple goals Americans expect of their public schools to a single one: prepare youths to work in a globally competitive economy. This has been a mistake because Americans historically have expected more from their public schools. Let me explore the geography of this error.

For nearly three decades, influential groups have called for higher academic standards, accountability for student outcomes, more homework, more testing, and, of course, more time in school. Many of their recommendations have been adopted. By 2008, U.S. schools had a federally driven system of state-designed standards anchored in increased testing, results-driven accountability, and demands for students to spend more time in school. After all, reformers reasoned, the students of foreign competitors were attending school more days in the year and longer hours each day, even on weekends, and their test scores ranked them higher than the U.S.

Even though this simplistic causal reasoning has been questioned many times by researchers who examined education and work performance in Japan, Korea, Singapore, Germany, and other nations, "common sense" observations by powerful elites swept away such questions. So the U.S.'s declining global economic competitiveness had been spun into a time-in-school problem.

But convincing evidence drawn from research that more time in school would lead to a stronger economy, less inequalities in family income, and that elusive edge in global competitiveness—much less a higher rank in international tests—remains missing in action.

The Public's Goals for Education

Business and civic elites have succeeded at least twice in the past century in making the growth of a strong economy the primary aim of U.S. schools, but other goals have had an enormous and enduring impact on schooling, both in the past and now. These goals embrace core American values that have been like second-hand Roses, shabby and discarded clothes hidden in the back of the closet and occasionally trotted out for show during graduation. Yet since the origins of tax-supported public schools in the early 19th century, these goals have been built into the very structures of schools so much so that, looking back from 2008, we hardly notice them.

Time-based reforms have had trouble entering schools because other goals have had—and continue to have—clout with parents and taxpayers. Opinion polls, for example, display again and again what parents, voters, and taxpayers want schools to achieve. One recent poll identified the public's goals for public schools. The top five were to:

- Prepare people to become responsible citizens;
- Help people become economically sufficient;
- Ensure a basic level of quality among schools;
- Promote cultural unity among all Americans;
- Improve social conditions for people.

Tied for sixth and seventh were goals to:

- Enhance people's happiness and enrich their lives; and
- Dispel inequities in education among certain schools and certain groups.

To reach those goals, a democratic society expects schools to produce adults who are engaged in their communities, enlightened employers, and hard-working employees who have acquired and practiced particular values that sustain its way of life. Dominant American social, political, and economic values pervade family, school, workplace, and community: Act independently, accept personal responsibility for actions, work hard and complete a job well, and be fair, that is, willing to be judged by standards applied to others as long as the standards are applied equitably.

These norms show up in school rules and classroom practices in every school. School is the one institutional agent between the family, the work-place, and voting booth or jury room responsible for instilling those norms in children's behavior. School is the agent for turning 4-year-olds into respect-ful students engaged in their communities, a goal that the public perceives as more significant than preparing children and youths for college and the labor market. In elite decision makers' eagerness to link schools to a growing economy, they either overlooked the powerful daily practices of schooling or neglected to consider seriously these other goals. In doing so, they erred. The consequences of that error in judgment can be seen in the fleeting attention that policy recommendations for adding more time in school received before being shelved.

Teaching in a Democracy

Public schools were established before industrialization, and they expanded rapidly as factories and mills spread. Those times appear foreign to readers today. For example, in the late 19th century, calling public schools "factory-like" was not an epithet hurled at educators or supporters of public schools as it has been in the U.S. since the 1960s. In fact, describing a public school as an assembly-line factory or a productive cotton mill was considered a com-pliment to forward-looking educators who sought to make schools modern through greater efficiency in teaching and learning by copying the successes of wealthy industrialists. Progressive reformers praised schools for being like industrial plants in creating large, efficient, age-graded schools that standard-ized curriculum while absorbing millions of urban migrants and foreign immi-grants. As a leading progressive put it:

Our schools are, in a sense, factories in which the raw products (children) are to be shaped and fashioned into products to meet the various demands of life. . . . It is the business of the school to build its pupils to the specifications [of manufacturers].

Progressive reformers saw mills, factories, and corporations as models for transforming the inefficient one-room schoolhouse in which students of different ages received fitful, incomplete instruction from one teacher into the far more efficient graded school where each teacher taught students a standardized curriculum each year. First established in Boston in 1848 and spreading swiftly in urban districts, the graded school became the dominant way of organizing a school by 1900. By the 1920s, schools exemplified the height of industrial efficiency because each building had separate classrooms with their own teachers. The principal and teachers expected children of the same age to cover the same content and learn skills by the end of the school year and perform satisfactorily on tests in order to be promoted to the next grade.

Superintendents saw the age-graded school as a modern version of schooling well adapted to an emerging corporate-dominated industrial society where punctuality, dependability, and obedience were prized behaviors. As a St. Louis superintendent said in 1871:

The first requisite of the school is Order: each pupil must be taught first and foremost to conform his behavior to a general standard. . . . The pupil must have his lessons ready at the appointed time, must rise at the tap of the bell, move to the line, return; in short, go through all of the evolutions with equal precision.

Recognition and fame went to educators who achieved such order in their schools.

But the farm-driven seasonal nature of rural one-room schoolhouses was incompatible with the explosive growth of cities and an emerging industrial society. In the early 20th century, progressive reformers championed compulsory attendance laws while extending the abbreviated rural-driven short hours and days into a longer school day and year. Reformers wanted to increase the school's influence over children's attitudes and behavior, especially in cities where wave after wave of European immigrants settled. Seeking higher productivity in organization, teaching, and learning at the least cost, reformers broadened the school's mission by providing medical, social, recreational, and psychological services at schools. These progressive reformers believed schools should teach society's norms to both children and their families and also educate the whole child so that the entire government, economy, and society would change for the better. So, when reformers spoke about "factory-like schools" a century ago, they wanted educators to copy models of success; they were not scolding them. That changed, however, by the late 20th century.

As the U.S. shifted from a manufacturing-based economy to a post-industrial information-based economy, few policy makers reckoned with this history of schooling. Few influential decision makers view schools as agents of *both* stability and change. Few educational opinion makers recognize that the conservative public still expects schools to instill in children dominant American norms of being independent and being held accountable for one's actions, doing work well and efficiently, and treating others equitably to ensure that when students graduate they will practice these values as adults. And, yes, the public still expects schools to strengthen the economy by ensuring that graduates have the necessary skills to be productive employees in an ever-changing, highly competitive, and increasingly global workplace. But that is just one of many competing expectations for schools.

Thus far, I have focused mostly on how policy makers and reform-minded civic and business elites have not only defined economic problems as educational ones that can be fixed by more time spent in schools but also neglected the powerful hold that socialization goals have on parents' and taxpayers' expectations. Now, I want to switch from the world of reform-driven policy makers and elites to teachers and students because each group views school time differently from their respective perch. Teacher and student perspectives on time in school have little influence in policy makers' decision making. Although the daily actions of teachers and students don't influence policy makers, they do matter in explaining why reformers have had such paltry results in trying to fix school time.

Differing Views of Time in School

For civic and business leaders, media executives, school boards, superintendents, mayors, state legislators, governors, U.S. representatives, and the President (what I call "policy elites"), electoral and budget cycles become the timeframe within which they think and act. Every year, budgets must be prepared and, every two or four years, officials run for office and voters decide who should represent them and whether they should support bond referenda and tax levies. Because appointed and elected policy makers are influential with the media, they need to assure the public during campaigns that slogans and stump speeches were more than talk. Sometimes, words do become action when elected decision makers, for example, convert a comprehensive high school into a cluster of small high schools, initiate 1:1 laptop programs, and extend the school day. This is the world of policy makers.

The primary tools policy makers use to adopt and implement decisions, however, are limited and blunt—closer to a hammer than a scalpel. They use exhortation, press conferences, political bargaining, incentives, and sanctions to formulate and adopt decisions. (Note, however, that policy makers rarely implement decisions; administrators and practitioners put policies into practice.) Policy makers want broad social, political, economic, and organizational goals adopted as policies, and then they want to move educators, through encouragement, incentives, and penalties, to implement those policies in schools and classrooms that they seldom, if ever, enter.

The world of teachers differs from that of policy makers. For teachers, the time-driven budget and electoral cycles that shape policy matter little for their classrooms, except when such policies carry consequences for how and what teachers should teach, such as accountability measures that assume teachers and students are slackers and need to work harder. In these instances, teachers become classroom gatekeepers in deciding how much of a policy they will put into practice and under what conditions.

What matters most to teachers are student responses to daily lessons, weekly tests, monthly units, and the connections they build over time in classrooms, corridors, during lunch, and before and after school. Those personal connections become the compost of learning. Those connections account for former students pointing to particular teachers who made a difference in their lives. Teacher tools, unlike policy maker tools, are unconnected to organizational power or media influence. Teachers use their personalities, knowledge, experience, and skills in building relationships with groups of students and providing individual help. Teachers believe there is never enough time in the daily schedule to finish a lesson, explain a point, or listen to a student. Administrative intrusions gobble up valuable instructional time that could go to students. In class, then, both teachers and students are clock watchers, albeit for different reasons.

Students view time differently as well. For a fraction of students from middle- and low-income families turned off by school requirements and expectations, spending time in classrooms listening to teachers, answering questions, and doing homework is torture; the hands of the clock seldom move fast enough for them. The notion of extending the school day and school year for them—or continuing on to college and four more years of reading texts and sitting in classrooms—is not a reform to be implemented but a punishment to be endured. Such students look for creative shortcuts to skip classes, exit the school as early as they can, and find jobs or enter the military once they graduate. Most students, however, march from class to class until they hear "Pomp and Circumstance." But a high school diploma, graduates have come to realize, is not enough in the 21st-century labor market.

College for Everyone

In the name of equity and being responsive to employers' needs, most urban districts have converted particular comprehensive high schools into clusters of small college-prep academies where low-income minority students take Advanced Placement courses, write research papers, and compete to get into colleges and universities. Here, then, is the quiet, unheralded, and unforeseen victory of reformers bent on fixing time in school. They have succeeded unintentionally in stretching K–12 into preK–16 public schooling, not just for middle- and upper-middle class students, but for everyone.

As it has been for decades for most suburban middle- and upper-middle class white and minority families, now it has become a fact, an indisputable truth converted into a sacred mission for upwardly mobile poor families: A high school diploma and a bachelor's degree are passports to high-paying jobs and the American Dream. For families who already expect their sons and daughters to attend competitive colleges, stress begins early. Getting into the best preschools and elementary and secondary schools and investing in an array of activities to build attractive résumés for college admission officers to evaluate become primary tasks. For such families and children, there is never enough time for homework, Advanced Placement courses, music, soccer, drama, dance, and assorted after-school activities. For high-achieving, stressed-out students already expecting at least four more years of school after high school gradua-tion, reform proposals urging a longer school year and an extended day often strike an unpleasant note. Angst and fretfulness become familiar clothes to don every morning as students grind out 4s and 5s on Advanced Placement exams, play sports, and compile just the right record that will get them into just the right school. For decades, pressure on students to use every minute of school to prepare for college has been strongest in middle- and upper-middle-class suburbs. What has changed in the past few decades is the spread of the belief that everyone, including low-income minority students, should go to college.

To summarize, for decades, policy elites have disregarded teacher and student perspectives on time in school. Especially now when all students are expected to enter college, children, youths, and teachers experience time in school differently than policy makers who seek a longer school day and school year. Such varied perceptions about time are heavily influenced by the socialization goals of schooling, age-graded structures, socioeconomic status of families, and historical experience. And policy makers often ignore these per-ceptions and reveal their tone-deafness and myopia in persistently trying to fix time in schools. Policy elites need to parse fully this variation in perceptions because extended time in school remains a high priority to reform-driven pol-icy makers and civic and business leaders anxious about U.S. performance on international tests and fearful of falling behind in global economic competi-tiveness. The crude policy solutions of more days in the year and longer school days do not even begin to touch the deeper truth that what has to improve is the quality of "academic learning time." If policy makers could open their ears and eyes to student and teacher perceptions of time, they would learn that the secular Holy Grail is decreasing interruption of instruction, encouraging richer intellectual and personal connections between teachers and students, and increasing classroom time for ambitious teaching and active, engaged learning. So far, no such luck.

Conclusion

These three reasons—cost, lackluster research, and the importance of conser-vative social goals to U.S. taxpayers and voters—explain why proposals to fix time in U.S. schools have failed to take hold. Policy elites know research stud-ies proving the worth of year-round schools or lengthened school days are in short supply. Even if an occasional study supported the change, the school year is unlikely to go much beyond 180 days. Policy elites know school goals go far beyond simply preparing graduates for college and for employability in a knowledge-based economy. And policy elites know they must show courage in their pursuit of improving failing U.S. schools by forcing students to go to school just as long as their peers in India, China, Japan, and Korea. That courage shows up symbolically, playing well in the media and in proposals to fix time in schools, but it seldom alters calendars.

While cost is a factor, it is the stability of schooling structures and the importance of socializing the young into the values of the immediate community and larger society that have defeated policy-driven efforts to alter time in school over the past quarter century. Like the larger public, I am unconvinced that requiring students and teachers to spend more time in school each day and every year will be better for them. How that time is spent in learning before, during, and after school is far more important than decision makers counting the minutes, hours, and days students spend each year getting schooled. That being said, I have little doubt that state and federal blue-ribbon commissions will continue to make proposals about lengthening time in school. Those proposals will make headlines, but they will not result in serious, sustained attention to what really matters—improving the quality of the time that teachers and students spend with one another in and out of classrooms.

POSTSCRIPT

Should Student Time in School Be Changed?

Based on the two readings, it's clear that the issue of changing school time is a core component of educational reform. Thus, there are policy perspectives but also practice perspectives that are relevant. One way of reading the selections is to see Rocha's paper as a call for what ought to be or could be, whereas Cuban's paper reflects what is. If the real overlying issue is education or school reform, than from that it follows that changing the school year is a part—but only one part—of a large school improvement strategy. To see changing school time as a "silver bullet" that will solve a set of interconnected problems in contemporary U.S. public education is misguided at best and naïve (neither piece suggested this, per se). As reform strategies go, steps can be taken (incrementalism) or a system can be overhauled (comprehensive). From both the selections, it is clear that there is more needed at a policy level than simply deciding to change time in school; there are community-level cultural issues, there are practice-level teacher implementation issues, and so on. As one moving part among many, any significant changes in school time have to be integrated with the needs and preferences of a number of stakeholders (students, parents, educators, politicians).

In this era of evidence-based practice (EBP), it should be second nature to ask what is the evidence supporting any policy decision with such a direct effect on practice. And, if there is evidence, how good is it? The majority of the evidence reviewed in Rocha's paper was either anecdotal and/or based on cases (a specific school/district) in which the reform effort had been adopted. This kind of evidence provides "proof of principle" but by itself is not necessarily confirmatory. One general problem with anecdotal or case-based evidence is that it is easy to include positive instances supporting a position and overlook negative instances contrary to a position. On the issue of changing school time, for example, it might be noted that the state of California—which has the largest number of YRE programs—will phase out almost all of their year-round schools by 2012 (for additional reading on California's "Concept 6," see B. M. Allen, *The Williams vs. California Settlement: The first year of implementation* [San Diego, CA: ACLU Foundation of Southern California, 2005]). Positive and negative cases notwithstanding, the body of research evidence directly related to changing some aspect of school time is disappointingly small, with few well designed and executed research studies. This state of affairs leads to conclusions like that found in a review by H. Cooper and colleagues (mentioned later) that not enough dependable studies have been completed on which to base an informed policy decision for changing the school calendar. Part of the issue, however, as mentioned earlier, may be that if changing school time is really only one part of a larger school reform effort, then evaluating calendar change in isolation from changing other components of the system is more than likely going to lead to mixed, modest, or no effects.

Finally, the notion of increasing time in school is treated, implicitly in most cases, as a synonym for the expansion of learning time. It is fair to wonder, then, what exactly is learning time? And, does a longer school day or year equal increased learning time? It turns out, as you might expect, that adding time and adding time learning are not necessarily synonymous (see, for example, K. R. Stanley and colleagues, "The Daily Schedule: A Look at the Relationship Between Time and Academic Achievement," in the *Education Policy Brief* from the Center for Evaluation and Education Policy, vol. 5, Summer 2007). In one study examining student outcomes as a function on changing the daily schedule or calendar (longer blocks), J. McCreary and C. Hausman found very small effects and concluded that there was limited evidence about the relationship between structural change and student outcomes (ERIC Document ED457590, 2001). Consistent with the notion mentioned earlier, it seems likely that it would be a mistake, based on the available evidence, to expect that changing school time would produce pronounced effects without simultaneously addressing professional development so that teachers can capitalize on the additional time. H. Pennington, in *Expanding Learning Time in High Schools* (Center for American Progress, 2006), reaches the same conclusion and provides ample examples and models related to the component parts that must change *simultaneously* for meaningful school reform—and changing school time is just one. It would seem, then, that there is a clear and important distinction between adding time to the school day or year and adding learning to the day or year (allocated school time, allocated class time, instructional time, and adding learning to the day are related but different concepts [see E. Silva's report referenced later]). Any informed discussion about expanding school time must recognize this distinction from the outset if there is to be a meaningful discussion and debate about the issue.

For those interested in further reading on school time, the following are recommended. First, to contextualize the issue in the larger push for school reform, there is the report from the National Commission on Excellence in Education, *A Nation at Risk* (Washington, DC: U.S. Government Printing Office, 1983) and from the National Education Commission on Time and Learning, *Prisoners of Time* (Washington, DC: U.S. Government Printing Office, 1994). Among many selections related to the history of public education in the United States and school time, there is T. D. Rakoff's *School Time* (Montreal, Quebec, Canada: American Educational Research Association, 1999) as well as David B Tyack's *The One Best System: A History of American Urban Education* (Cambridge: Harvard University Press, 1974). For a comprehensive peer-reviewed article summarizing the outcomes of specific studies empirically examining the effects of manipulating time, see H. Cooper, J. C. Valentine, K. Chariton, and A. Melson "The Effect of Modified School Calendars on Student Achievement and on School and Community Attitudes," published in *Review of Educational Research* (vol. 73, 2003). For a specific example of a study examining school time, there is B. J. McMillen's report on "A Statewide Evaluation of Academic Achievement in Year Round Schools" in *The Journal of Educational Research* (vol. 95, 2001). S. P. Johnson and T. E. Spradlin provide a very informative overview of several aspects of the school time issue in their education policy brief on *Alternatives to the Traditional School Year* (Center for Evaluation and Education Policy, vol. 5, Spring 2007). The most recent comprehensive "think-tank" review of the school time issue can be found from Education Sector and E. Silva's *On the Clock: Rethinking the Way Schools Use Time* (Washington, DC: 2007).

Although not directly addressed in either of the two selections for this section, there is a related issue concerning early school start time and adolescent health and development issues specific to sleep. M. Hansen, I. Jannsen, A. Schiff, P. Zee, and M. Dubocvich report on "The Impact of School Daily Schedule on Adolescent Sleep" in the journal *Pediatrics* (vol. 115, 2005). Similarly, G. Mitru, D. L. Millrood, and J. H. Mateika published "The Impact of Sleep on Learning and Behavior in Adolescents" in *Teachers College Record* (vol. 104, 2002). Finally, there are numerous Web resources related to the issue, including the National Association of Year-Round Education (NAYRE: http://www.nayre .org), Education Sector (http://educationsector.org), and the Center for American Progress (http://www.americanprogress.org).

Contributors to This Volume

EDITORS

LEONARD ABBEDUTO, a developmental psychologist, is the Charles J. Anderson professor of educational psychology at the University of Wisconsin–Madison. He is also associate director for behavioral sciences and director of the University Center on Excellence in Developmental Disabilities at the Waisman Center at the university. He has authored more than 100 articles, chapters, and reviews, and he has written or edited three other books, including *Guide to Human Development for Future Educators,* with Stephen N. Elliott (McGraw-Hill, 1998), which is a text designed to demonstrate how research and theory in developmental psychology can be applied in the classroom. Professor Abbeduto is well known for his research on language development, families, and developmental disabilities, which has been supported by numerous grants from the National Institutes of Health. He is currently the editor of the *American Journal of Intellectual and Developmental Disabilities.* For more than a decade, he has directed an NIH-funded program designed to train future researchers interested in the behavioral aspects of developmental disabilities. In 1996, he was recognized with the Emil A. Steiger Award for distinguished teaching at the University of Wisconsin–Madison. In 2008, he received the Distinguished Faculty Achievement Award from the School of Education at the University. Professor Abbeduto earned his Ph.D. from the University of Illinois at Chicago in 1982. He has two sons, Jackson and Mack. He credits his sons with teaching him about the importance of the controversies in educational psychology for the lives of America's children.

FRANK SYMONS is an associate professor in the Department of Educational Psychology and coordinator of the special education programs in the College of Education and Human Development at the University of Minnesota. His work for the past decade has focused on the assessment and treatment of severe behavior disorders in vulnerable populations. He has been principal investigator (PI) or co-PI on five NIH-funded studies in these areas continuously since receiving his Ph.D. from Peabody College at Vanderbilt University. Most recently, he has been involved in randomized clinical trials supported by the Institute for Education Sciences (IES) for improving outcomes for elementary school-aged children already identified for or at-risk of being identified for special education services for emotional or behavioral disorders. He has published over 40 peer-reviewed research articles in a wide range of scientific periodicals, ten chapters, and three coedited books related to substantive and methodological issues in behavioral research and developmental disabilities. His work was recognized by the University of Minnesota through an endowed McKnight Land-Grant Professorship award as well as through a National Institutes of Health Career Development Award.

AUTHORS

LAURA VAN ZANDT ALLEN is on the faculty in the department of education at Trinity University in San Antonio, Texas. She is the author of many articles on the middle school curriculum and the education of adolescents.

ALEXANDRA BEATTY is affiliated with Character Education Partnership in Washington, DC.

DAVID C. BERLINER is regent's professor of psychology in education, College of Education, Arizona Statue University, Tempe, Arizona. He is coauthor, along with Dr. Biddle, of *The Manufactured Crisis: Myths, Fraud, and the Attack on America's Public Schools* (New York: Addison-Wesley-Longman 1995). Additional books by Dr. Berliner include *Educational Psychology* (6th edition) (with N. L. Gage) and *The Handbook of Educational Psychology* (edited with R. L. Calfee). He has served as president of the American Educational Research Association and of the Educational Psychology Division of the American Psychological Association. Berliner is a fellow of the Center for Advanced Study in the Behavioral Sciences and a member of the National Academy of Education.

BRUCE J. BIDDLE is professor emeritus of psychology and of sociology at the University of Missouri, Columbia, Missouri. He is coauthor, along with Dr. Berliner, of *The Manufactured Crisis: Myths, Fraud, and the Attack on America's Public Schools* (New York: Addison-Wesley-Longman 1995). His research interests include examining the relations between social theory, research, and social policy impact. This work has produced several papers, a handbook chapter, and an edited book concerned with social research impact in education.

MICHELE BRIGHAM is a high school special education teacher in Virginia.

CAROL CORBETT BURRIS is the principal of South Side High School in Rockville Centre, New York. She has written articles for *Education Week, Phi Delta Kappan,* and other periodicals.

GERALD COLES is an educational psychologist who writes regularly on a range of educational issues, especially issues related to the teaching of reading.

LARRY CUBAN is professor emeritus of education at Stanford University. His research focuses on the teaching of social studies, the history of school reform, curriculum and instruction, and leadership. Prior to becoming a professor, Cuban spent 14 years teaching high school social studies in big city schools, directed a teacher education program that prepared returning Peace Corps volunteers to teach in urban schools, and served as a superintendent. Trained as a historian, he received a Ph.D. from Stanford University.

EILEEN DACHNOWICZ is a teacher of English in Cranford High School. She is an activist in implementing programs that accent interdisciplinary studies, equity education, writing across the curriculum and public engagement.

TASHAWNA K. DUNCAN is a licensed psychologist, a licensed school psychologist, and a nationally certified school psychologist with more than 10 years of experience working with children, adolescents, and families in clinical and educational settings. She holds master's degrees in elementary education and school psychology from the University of Florida, where she received her doctoral training.

ANTHONY GARY DWORKIN is a professor of sociology and a cofounder of the Sociology of Education Research Group (SERG) at the University of Houston, and editor of *The New Inequality* at SUNY Press. He has published on teacher burnout and student dropout, minority-majority relations, and the impact of accountability systems on student achievement.

SARA EFRON is on the faculty at National-Louis University.

NANCY FREY is an associate professor of literacy in the School of Teacher Education at San Diego State University, San Diego, California. Her research interests are in literacy, assessment, and school improvement in the City Heights Educational Collaborative.

HOWARD GARDNER is John H. and Elisabeth A. Hobbs Professor of Cognition and Education at the Harvard Graduate School of Education. He is also senior director of Harvard Project Zero. Dr. Gardner is the originator of the theory of multiple intelligences.

MICHAEL F. GIANGRECO is a professor in the Department of Education and Center on Disability and Community Inclusion at the University of Vermont. His scholarly work is focused on strategies for inclusion of students with disabilities in general education classrooms.

E. D. HIRSCH, JR., is a professor at the University of Virginia, Charlottesville, and president and founder of the Core Knowledge Foundation. He is the author or coauthor of numerous publications, including *The Schools We Need: And Why We Don't Have Them* (Doubleday, 1999) and, with John Holdren, *What Your First Grader Needs to Know: Fundamentals of a Good First-Grade Education,* rev. ed. (Dell, 1998).

ERIC P. JENSEN is from the University of California, San Diego, and cofounder of the Brain Store and the Learning Brain Expo.

KIRK A. JOHNSON is senior policy analyst in the Center for Data Analysis, Heritage Foundation, Washington, DC. He focuses on estimating the outcome of policies that affect low-income Americans. To that end, he focuses on welfare program participation issues, employment-labor policy, marriage, family, and education. His statistical models help answer the "what if" questions in welfare policy analysis. His analysis and commentary has been featured in numerous media sources, including the *Los Angeles Times, Investor's Business Daily, Forbes, Chicago Tribune, Washington Post, Miami Herald, Detroit Free Press,* and the Fox News Channel, among others. Dr. Johnson holds a Ph.D. in public policy from George Mason University.

PAMELA BOLOTIN JOSEPH is a faculty member at Antioch University.

JAMES M. KAUFFMAN is professor emeritus of education at the University of Virginia at Charlottesville. His interests include emotional and behavioral disorders and learning disabilities.

KRISTEN N. KEMPLE is an associate professor in the School of Teaching and Learning at the University of Florida. She has taught young children in a wide variety of early childhood programs, including Head Start, a parent cooperative, and a teen parenting center. She holds a Ph.D. from the University of Texas at Austin.

PERRY D. KLEIN is on the faculty at the University of Western Ontario.

ALFIE KOHN is a writer and commentator on issues related to children, parenting, and schools, with 11 books and many articles to his credit.

MINDY KORNHABER is an associate professor of education at the Pennsylvania State University. Previously, she was an educational researcher at Harvard University for more than a decade. Her interests are in educational policy and theory.

STEPHEN KRASHEN is a professor emeritus from the University of Southern California.

MARCIA C. LINN is a professor of cognition and development at the University of California, Berkeley. She earned her Ph.D. in educational psychology from Stanford University in 1970. Her publications include *Computers, Teachers, Peers: Science Learning Partners,* coauthored with Sherry Hsi (Lawrence Erlbaum, 1999).

JON LORENCE is an associate professor of sociology and a cofounder of the Sociology of Education Research Group (SERG) at the University of Houston. His interests include the impact of grade retention on student academic achievement, determinants of teacher effectiveness, the evaluation of educational programs, and test measurement.

G. REID LYON is chief of the Child Development and Behavior Branch of the National Institute of Child Health and Human Development, National Institutes of Health and Human Services, in Bethesda, Maryland. He is coeditor, with Judith M. Rumsey, of *Neuroimaging: A Window to the Neurological Foundations of Learning and Behavior in Children* (Paul H. Brookes, 1996).

MAUREEN A. MANNING is a school psychologist in the Maryland public schools.

WILLIAM J. MATHIS is superintendent of Rutland Southeast Supervisory Union, a school district in Vermont.

KATHLEEN McGEE is a special education teacher at the high school level.

ELEANOR T. MIGLIORE is an associate professor in the department of education and director of school psychology at Trinity University.

LOWELL W. MONKE is an assistant professor of education at Wittenberg University who writes frequently on educational technology. He was a teacher in the K–12 system in this country and abroad before earning his Ph.D.

SEANA MORAN was a graduate student at Harvard University when she wrote the selection in this volume. She is currently a postdoctoral fellow with the Youth Purpose Project in the Center on Adolescence at Stanford University.

SARAH COTTON NELSON was director of grants and research at the Dallas Women's Foundations in 2004, which is an organization designed to support community programs focused on creating opportunities for women and girls.

RODNEY T. OGAWA is a professor in the School of Education at the University of California, Santa Cruz. Dr. Ogawa is well known for his research on the organization of schools and the connections between schools and communities.

LAUREN B. RESNICK is director of the Learning Research and Development Center and a professor of psychology at the University of Pittsburgh. Her many publications include *Discourse, Tools, and Reasoning: Essays on Situated Cognition* (Springer-Verlag, 1998), coedited with Clotilde Pontecorvo and Roger Saljo.

ELENA ROCHA is an education consultant with an expertise in expanded learning time, the education of English language learners and bilingual education, early childhood education, standards-based education, and the education of low-income and minority students. Prior to becoming a consultant, Rocha was a Senior Education Analyst at the Center for American Progress. She holds a master's degree in public service and administration from Texas A&M University and a bachelor's degree in cultural anthropology and Mexican-American studies from the University of Arizona.

JO SANDERS is a gender equity consultant and director of the Center for Gender Equity Studies. Her articles have appeared in numerous educational periodicals, including published articles on gender equity in *Educational Leadership* and *Phi Delta Kappan.*

MERLE J. SCHWARTZ is affiliated with Character Education Partnership in Washington, DC.

ALBERT SHANKER (1928–1997) was president of the American Federation of Teachers in Washington, D.C., an organization that works with teachers and other educational employees at the state and local levels in organizing, collective bargaining, research, educational issues, and public relations. A leader in the educational reform movement, he was recognized as the first labor leader elected to the National Academy of Education. He was the author of the Sunday *New York Times* column "Where We Stand."

KENNON M. SHELDON is an assistant professor in the Department of Psychology at the University of Missouri–Columbia.

JAMES D. SLOTTA is the research cognitive science director of the Web-based Integrated Science Environment (WISE) project library in the Graduate

School of Education at the University of California, Berkeley. He also codirected the Knowledge Integration Environment (KIE) project at the university. His current research focuses on the design of inquiry activities, online community supports, and teacher professional development approaches. He earned his Ph.D. in psychology from the University of Pittsburgh in 1996.

TINA M. SMITH is an assistant professor in the Department of Educational Psychology at the University of Florida. Her research interests include temperament and behavioral adjustment of high-risk preschoolers, development of children with prenatal exposure to drugs and alcohol, and school psychology. She holds a Ph.D. from the University of North Carolina, Chapel Hill.

FRANCES R. SPIELHAGEN was a postdoctoral research fellow at the Center for Gifted Education at the College of William and Mary, when she wrote the selection in this volume. She is currently is an assistant professor of education at Mount Saint Mary College.

ROBERT SYLWESTER is an emeritus professor of education at the University of Oregon. His research focuses on the educational implications of new developments in science and technology, and he is the author of *A Biological Brain in a Cultural Classroom: Applying Biological Research to Classroom Management* (Corwin Press, 2000) and *Emotion and Attention: How Our Brain Determines What's Important* (Zephyr Press, 1998).

KEVIN G. WELNER is an associate professor of education at the University of Colorado at Boulder. He has written extensively about educational policy and legislative issues that affect education. He is the author of *Legal Rights, Local Wrongs: When Community Control Collides with Educational Equity* (SUNY Press, 2001).

MARK WINDSCHITL is an assistant professor of curriculum and instruction in the College of Education at the University of Washington in Seattle, Washington. He is coauthor of *Cultures of Curriculum* (Lawrence Erlbaum, 1999).

CHARLES H. WOLFGANG is a professor of early childhood education at Florida State University. His research interests include cognitive process, discipline models, early childhood education, and teacher education. He holds a Ph.D. from the University of Pittsburgh.